The Essential Guide to Flash CS4 with ActionScript

Paul Milbourne, Chris Kaplan, and
Michael Oliver with Serge Jespers

friendsof

DESIGNER TO DESIGNER™

an Apress® company

The Essential Guide to Flash CS4 with ActionScript

ISBN-13 (pbk): 978-1-4302-1811-1

ISBN-13 (electronic): 978-1-4302-1812-8

Printed and bound in the United States of America 9 8 7 6 5 4 3 2 1

Trademarked names may appear in this book. Rather than use a trademark symbol with every occurrence of a trademarked name, we use the names only in an editorial fashion and to the benefit of the trademark owner, with no intention of infringement of the trademark.

Distributed to the book trade worldwide by Springer-Verlag New York, Inc., 233 Spring Street, 6th Floor, New York, NY 10013. Phone 1-800-SPRINGER, fax 201-348-4505, e-mail orders-ny@springer-sbm.com, or visit www.springeronline.com.

For information on translations, please contact Apress directly at 2855 Telegraph Avenue, Suite 600, Berkeley, CA 94705. Phone 510-549-5930, fax 510-549-5939, e-mail info@apress.com, or visit www.apress.com.

Apress and friends of ED books may be purchased in bulk for academic, corporate, or promotional use. eBook versions and licenses are also available for most titles. For more information, reference our Special Bulk Sales–eBook Licensing web page at http://www.apress.com/info/bulksales.

The information in this book is distributed on an "as is" basis, without warranty. Although every precaution has been taken in the preparation of this work, neither the author(s) nor Apress shall have any liability to any person or entity with respect to any loss or damage caused or alleged to be caused directly or indirectly by the information contained in this work.

The source code for this book is freely available to readers at www.friendsofed.com in the Downloads section.

Credits

Lead Editor Clay Andres	**Production Editor** Laura Esterman
Technical Reviewer Kunal Mittal	**Compositor** Molly Sharp
Editorial Board Clay Andres, Steve Anglin, Mark Beckner, Ewan Buckingham, Tony Campbell, Gary Cornell, Jonathan Gennick, Michelle Lowman, Matthew Moodie, Duncan Parkes, Jeffrey Pepper, Frank Pohlmann, Ben Renow-Clarke, Dominic Shakeshaft, Matt Wade, Tom Welsh	**Proofreader** Martha Whitt **Indexer** Carol Burbo
Project Manager Denise Santoro Lincoln	**Artist** April Milne
Copy Editor Ami Knox	**Interior and Cover Designer** Kurt Krames
Associate Production Director Kari Brooks-Copony	**Manufacturing Director** Tom Debolski

To Katie and Sara, for celebrating everything and never letting me forget what is truly important in life. To Lindsey, for making sure that life was taken care of during this journey.
—*Chris*

To Erica, the love of my life and still the kissin'est in the world, thanks for your consummate patience. I'm guessing you'll be calling the shots for a while!
—*Paul*

To my colleagues and staff at Corent Technology, without whom I simply could not have done it.
—*Mike "Ollie" Oliver*

CONTENTS AT A GLANCE

CONTENTS

PART THREE: ACTIONSCRIPT

Chapter 8: The Programming Primer: A Flash Designer's
Intro to ActionScript 3.0

xiii

FOREWORD

When I started fooling around with Flash, back in the late 1990s, I remember being blown away by sites like Eye4U, GaboCorp, and NRG. What they did with Flash was absolutely revolutionary and never seen before on the Web, and wouldn't have been possible with traditional web technologies. When I start reminiscing about those days, I always think back to the early conferences. I remember going to the first Flash Forward in San Francisco. I wonder if anyone remembers getting a free copy of Dreamweaver or a free copy of GoLive. I'm sure I'm not the only one who went home with both, right? A few months later, I went to the first Flash Forward conference in New York. Anyone who was there must remember that Adobe party with the live performance of Run DMC, right? I also remember the Adobe keynote with a couple of guys in suits. I wonder if they still work at Adobe. Sigh, those were the days. Who would have thought back then that Adobe would one day buy Macromedia? The Flash community was certainly a little skeptical about that merge, but I'm sure everyone will now agree that it has made the Flash Platform even stronger.

Flash has definitely changed the way we think about the Web, and it continues to do so with every new release. The Flash Player has become a trusted household name and a synonym for interactive and engaging web experiences. With Flash Player installs being upgraded faster and faster, it literally only takes a few months before reaching critical mass. This almost immediately gives designers and developers the ability to use the new features introduced in a new version of the Flash Player.

The way we interact with web content isn't the only thing that changed. The content you find on the Web also significantly changed throughout the years. It's not just about animations and video anymore. More and more applications find their way to the Web. Rich Internet Applications are pretty common these days. RIAs combine the best of the Web with the power of desktop applications. With that shift in mind, Adobe added the Adobe Integrated Runtime (AIR) to the Flash Platform. Flash designers and developers can now use their existing skills to build applications that run on the desktop and are not restricted by the browser sandbox.

With every new release, I am always amazed when I see what people do with Flash, and I am very curious to see where all this leads to in the future. Flash has become incredibly powerful, and the new features in Flash CS4 and Flash Player 10 will raise the bar once more. *The Essential Guide to Flash CS4 with ActionScript* will give you an excellent overview on how to use these new features. You'll deploy your work targeted at Flash Player 10 or the AIR runtime in no time. Flash on!

Serge Jespers
Platform evangelist
Adobe Systems

ABOUT THE AUTHORS

 **Chris Kaplan** is a multimedia consultant for Mosaic Learning, located in Greenbelt, Maryland. An award-winning multimedia developer, Chris has been working in Flash for over 10 years on teams contributing to interactive experiences for the U.S. Mint, UNICEF, Ameriquest, the Bill of Rights Institute, and many others. As an audio engineer and composer, he has worked on productions for *National Geographic*, *TLC*, *America's Most Wanted*, and in 2005, with Two Animators! LLP (www.twoanimators.com), he was a finalist for Best Cartoon at the Flash Forward Film Festival for his work on *The Poochinos—Dog Mafia*. Chris has been streaming live video over the Internet for over 10 years as a webcast engineer for events with Vice President Al Gore, Cisco Systems, the Peace Corps, Buzz Aldrin, and the Office of Head Start. Chris brings considerable experience in combining live webcasting, video production, and postproduction disciplines with creating multimedia experiences. He currently lives with his wife, Lindsey, and two daughters in Maryland.

 **Paul Milbourne** is an Adobe Certified Expert and Instructor for Flash. He has been a Flash platform consultant in the Washington-Baltimore metropolitan area for the better part of a decade. His journey has allowed him to work with such clients as the Washington Redskins, Baltimore Ravens, Democratic National Committee, and many others. For the most part, Paul has made a handsome career cleaning up after other developers. This experience has exposed him to most aspects of Flash development through a multitude of industries.

His true passion is the advancement of the Flash community in that area. Paul is the principal and founding member of the Baltimore-Washington Adobe Flash User Group, which now boasts more than 300 members. His vision is to unite that community in a collaborative effort, both informationally and vocationally.

Paul currently studies computer science and art at the University of Maryland. And, though he was a professional chef in a former life, he is not responsible for any of the food references in this book!

Michael Oliver is chief technology officer of Corent Technology. He has 38+ years of experience in the industry with Sun Microsystems, Sperry Corp, SAIC, OpenText, and several Internet startups in roles from salesperson to CTO and almost everything in between. He is an Apache Software Foundation committer and a published author, and has been active in promoting standards such as WfMC, IETF, and others.

ABOUT THE TECHNICAL REVIEWER

 **Kunal Mittal** serves as an executive director of technology at Sony Pictures Entertainment where he is responsible for the SOA and Identity Management programs. He provides a centralized engineering service to different lines of business and consults on the Content Management, Collaboration, and Mobile strategies.

Kunal is an entrepreneur who helps startups define their technology strategy, product roadmap, and development plans. With strong relations with several development partners worldwide, he is able to help startups and even large companies build appropriate development partnerships. He generally works in an advisor or consulting CTO capacity and serves actively in the project management and technical architect functions.

Kunal has authored and edited several books and articles on J2EE, WebLogic, and SOA. He holds a master's degree in software engineering and is an instrument-rated private pilot.

ACKNOWLEDGMENTS

First and foremost, to Lindsey, who has been my link to reality through this amazing experience. Her support has not only seen me through this project, but all of the projects prior that led to me being able to contribute to this book in the first place. Thank you.

To Mom and Dad, thank you for the tools. They are not perfect, but they are mine because you cared enough to make sure I had them. They have made all the difference in my life.

To Sherry for always cheering for me.

To Greg Kaplan (www.rootsolutions.com) and Tamara Yee (www.yeezersinteractive.com) for constantly raising the bar and then patiently helping me reach it.

This book would not be a book without the talent and hard work of the editorial and production teams at Apress. It has been truly amazing to watch our primitive manuscripts evolve through developmental edits and technical review that, when combined together with the production layout process, produced what you would most certainly call a book when you flip through it. A big thank you to all who have worked so hard with us on this book to bring it to its current form.

To the Flash team at Adobe for continuing the evolution of this tool. Without their ingenuity and openness with the Flash development community, we would have little to write about.

To every author of every Flash book and online tutorial I've ever read. Without them, finding my way through Flash would be much like eating a soup sandwich. A special nod to Colin Moock, who single-handedly cracked open the guts of ActionScript, poured them into a book, and pointed at all the parts in a way that made sense to me.

To Tom and Joe Costantini of Two Animators! LLP (www.twoanimators.com) for pushing my limits and inspiring me, and who, together with Steven Karp of Karptoons (www.karptoons. com), lent me insight into their approach to character animation in Flash.

To Woody Scally and everyone at Mosaic Learning (www.mosaiclearning.com) for allowing me the luxury of a full-time job and the flexibility I needed to complete this book.

Finally, to Paul for inviting me to join him in writing this book. Thank you.

Chris

ACKNOWLEDGMENTS

To Clay for giving us the opportunity to write this book and his incomparable grace. What an amazing person to have met.

To Denise, the lady who shares my love of the kitchen—I can only say thank you, I'm sorry, and I hope you still have all your hair. If we are ever on the same coast, I owe you a meal!

To Valerie—I appreciate your work very much. I don't know how I would have kept my sanity without you. Thanks for seeing me to port.

To Ollie for hanging in there! Your insights and encouragement were always helpful.

To Kunal and Serge for picking up the slack and plugging the holes.

To Ami, Laura, and everyone thereafter—Wow! You guys have definitely cornered the market on spit and polish. Thanks for all your hard work.

To all the fish that died during the writing of this book—sorry fellas, better luck next time!

To Chris—you had better watch whose hand you shake in the parking lot, they may steal 6 months of your life. Thanks for being a stand-up guy and really going to bat late in the game. I will never figure out when you sleep, but I am thankful for how much you gave up.

Paul

I would like to thank Paul Milbourne for having me on this fine book and to all the staff at Apress who put up with my constant delays. It is amazing how patient they have been. I would also like to acknowledge my wife and my coworkers and business partners for giving me the time and support to do it.

Ollie

PREFACE

There are more pantomimists on the planet than Flash developers—this book intends to do something about it!

What you need to know about this book is that it was written for beginning to intermediate users of Flash. That being said, we made a concerted effort to write examples that included an entire process using best practices within a *real-world context* as much as possible in order to present them in a way that would be most useful in day-to-day work, not in a petri dish.

Having been a beginner in Flash for more than 10 years now, I (Chris) thought that I might be able to help introduce this technology with an approach that not only demonstrates *how* to do something, but also explains *why* it works when you do it that way.

The parts of this book are organized into clear disciplines and should serve you well as a focused reference that includes solutions and explanations of common work tasks facing the Flash developer and designer alike, as well as a thorough introduction to the new features of Flash CS4 including IK and the new Motion Editor.

Flash has evolved in so many ways to be so many things. It has been a daunting task to attempt to explore and demonstrate the many uses of this tool in a single book. We sincerely hope that you can use this book from your first introduction to Flash through to some fairly advanced applications of the concepts within. Now take it—and go kick some pantomimist butt!

Layout conventions

To keep this book as clear and easy to follow as possible, the following text conventions are used throughout.

Important words or concepts are normally highlighted on the first appearance in **bold type**.

Code is presented in fixed-width font.

New or changed code is normally presented in **bold fixed-width font**.

Menu commands are written in the form Menu ➤ Submenu ➤ Submenu.

Where we want to draw your attention to something, we've highlighted it like this:

> *Ahem, don't say we didn't warn you.*

Sometimes code won't fit on a single line in a book. Where this happens, we use an arrow like this: ➡.

```
This is a very, very long section of code that should be written all on ➡
the same line without a break.
```

PART ONE
BASICS

 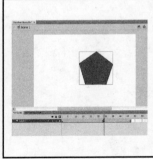 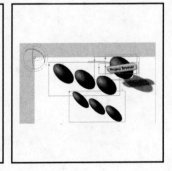

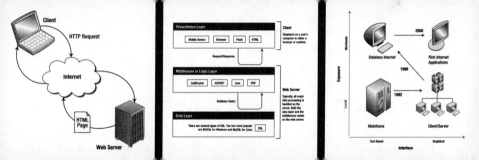

For designers and developers, there has never been a better time to become involved in the Flash culture. Flash has firmly cemented its status as one of the most versatile pieces of commercial software ever written. And, nearly 20 years after its creation, Flash continues to redefine the way interactive material is delivered. What began as a tablet drawing program has enjoyed continuous development and innovation, thanks to feedback from virtually every corner of new media development.

With the release of Flash CS4, Flash takes its next step into the explosive world of mass extendibility and open source development. A recent increase in the number of external solutions offered in the form of plug-ins and third-party APIs is unparalleled compared to those for previous versions of Flash. Users now enjoy integrated support for many external environments, such as kuler and PixelBender.

Finally, the persistent rise in the number of high-caliber programmers using Flash continues to motivate the evolution of ActionScript, Flash's native scripting language, toward a full-fledged, standards-compliant, object-oriented programming language.

Animators, coders, designers, oh my . . .

We realize there are people coming to Flash from different backgrounds, with different needs. Some of us might use Flash for design, lacking only a touch of ActionScript to finish the job. Others may be programming an interface and need to gain a relatively quick understanding of the various graphics and animation elements Flash has to offer. Flash has become such a powerful, versatile tool that presenting this book to "all people" for "all purposes" is a daunting challenge at best. Nonetheless, it is our goal to write a book that helps people understand this powerful tool and to see how it can be used. This release brings improvements to workflows and tool sets for animators, coders, and designers alike.

If you are a programmer migrating from another language, you can use this book as your transition into the world of Flash. You can easily take your familiarity with another language and apply those principles to ActionScript.

Simply stated, because Flash is so versatile with so many practical applications in so many industries, this book will serve as an excellent starting point for anyone looking to start learning and applying Flash to their specific needs.

What is this thing called Flash?

If you have had no prior exposure to using Flash, you may be wondering what Flash is, exactly. For most people, Flash is the software that is used to make "super cool" web sites. It has traditionally been used to add a level of pizzazz to the Web either through sophisticated animation or highly dynamic page elements like buttons.

As a piece of software, however, Flash is somewhat of an enigma. As you will learn in the rest of this chapter, and eventually the rest of this book, Flash is somewhat of a Frankenstein's monster. It is certainly true that Flash was originally intended to bring animation to the Internet. However, as Flash becomes older, it acquires a greater scope of functionality and purpose.

People now use Flash to any end that requires an interactive solution. Not only is Flash used for enhancing web sites, it can also be used for the creation of presentations, casual games, kiosks, e-learning courseware, and much more. Flash also has the ability to be deployed via the Internet, DVDs, CDs, or local networks. The possibilities are really endless. Because Flash is so adaptable to the needs of the users, it will continue to evolve to meet any requirement the industry places on it.

How did we get here?

Our story begins in the late 1600s, when Sir Isaac Newton wrote a letter to the then-head of the Royal Society, Robert Hooke. You may be wondering how Isaac Newton is relevant to becoming a Flash developer. Well, he isn't—at least, not directly.

You see, Newton had an appreciation for the foundation of his accomplishments. In his correspondence, Newton wrote, "If I have seen further, it is by standing on the shoulders of giants." Now, consider for a moment that Sir Isaac Newton had one of the most influential minds of the last thousand years. His accomplishments in theology, astronomy, optics, mathematics, and chemistry were all revolutionary for his time—and much of his work was in new territory. But what he confided to Robert Hooke is a profoundly humble insight.

Whatever his personal accomplishments, Sir Isaac Newton never failed to recognize and incorporate the hard work of those who laid the foundation before him. He also believed that until a person had sufficient mastery over the fundamental principles of a subject, they had very little business in the realm of discovery.

So, if you're an eager beaver and you want to jump right into Flash, we would suggest you skip directly to Chapter 2.

However, if you are a person who values the completeness that comes with a well-rounded education, we invite you to take a few minutes and learn the peculiar origins of Flash: how it went from a simple vector drawing program to what is now an entire industry. This history is as important to understanding why Flash works the way it does in day-to-day use as it is to gaining insight into how it may evolve in the future.

Creating Flash: SmartSketch

The story of Jonathan Gay and the origins of Flash is a rather interesting one. Having started his professional programming career in high school, Gay achieved more success before graduating college than most current programmers achieve in a lifetime.

As a high school student in the early 1980s, Gay first flexed his programming prowess on the Apple II computer. It was in this environment that Gay took his first steps into the world of graphics editing software. Though his first program didn't sell a million copies, it did attract the attention of soon-to-be-colleague Charlie Jackson.

Gay first met Jackson at a local Macintosh user group that Jackson organized. At the time, Jackson was interested in starting a software firm aimed at the development of Macintosh-based software titles. Though he did have the necessary capital and hardware resources, Jackson required a relatively inexpensive solution to his development needs. Since Gay was a proven programmer but still a high school student, he had the necessary skills and financial flexibility to accommodate Jackson's requirements. Gay began to work for Silicon Beach Software, Jackson's newly formed software firm, while still a senior in high school.

Gay spent his college years writing gaming titles for Silicon Beach. Some of his more notable titles, such as Airborne, Dark Castle, and Return to Dark Castle, won awards and were critically acclaimed. It was during this period that Gay began to develop his interest in rapid and responsive interactive programs. Because of his exposure to animation and interactivity, Gay credits this time as the original inspiration for what would become Flash.

Still in college, Gay returned to graphics development software with his work on Superpaint 2. Superpaint was a ground-breaking program that combined the editability of both vector illustration and raster-based graphics (bitmaps). In this respect, Superpaint was well ahead of its time: the combination of vector and bitmap-based technologies was not effectively realized as an industry standard until the release of Adobe Photoshop 6 in 2000—more than a decade later. (In fact, today's leaders in the production of graphic editing software, like Adobe, still maintain independent environments for the editing of bitmaps and vector drawings.)

In the early 1990s, Gay graduated from college and began full-time work on a pen computing program known as IntelliDraw. Soon after, Silicon Beach Software was acquired by the Aldus Corporation, and IntelliDraw was first released. It was at this time that Gay realized the forthcoming success of the pen computing market. By working as a developer on IntelliDraw, Gay became aware of the how he could revolutionize the user's experience with pen-styled computing. He approached Charlie Jackson with his ideas and suggested that they form a software company devoted to developing cutting-edge, pen-based computing.

In 1993, Gay and Jackson started FutureWave Software. Along with programmer Robert Tatsumi, FutureWave began development on SmartSketch, an innovative pen-based drawing program to run on GO Corporation's PenPoint operating system. Unfortunately for the FutureWave team, PenPoint was discontinued shortly after the release of SmartSketch. This obviously left SmartSketch without a viable platform for deployment. Faced with some tough choices, FutureWave decided to write versions of SmartSketch for both the Macintosh and Windows systems. With existing industry-standard drawing programs already in place for those systems, FutureWave faced stiff competition. It was at this point that the true essence of Flash was born.

Flash's greatness is driven by both innovative vision and an abundance of user feedback. While attending SIGGRAPH in 1995, the creators of SmartSketch received a considerable number of requests for their tool to offer animation functionality. It was also around this time that the emergence of the World Wide Web was beginning to take hold. At this point, the Web was still stateless, and the only way to offer more complex interaction was through Java Applets. Gay knew that this added functionality would ultimately be the key to giving SmartSketch its needed diversification, uniqueness, and edge. This enhanced version of SmartSketch, called FutureSplash Animator, was released in 1996, offering full Netscape

1

support (via plug-in) and an integrated time line for frame-based animations. The combined features of this new software made it possible to quickly and easily deploy vector-based animation to the Web.

It didn't take long for FutureSplash to make its mark on the world of design. When the Microsoft and Disney corporations harnessed its potential for their respective web sites, FutureSplash won the respect of more established and substantially larger software development companies. Because of this exposure, FutureWave was approached by Macromedia. Excited at the prospect of financial stability, FutureWave agreed to be purchased and assimilated by Macromedia.

Thus, in 1996 Macromedia Flash was born. With the release of Dreamweaver in 1997, Flash helped Macromedia successfully redefine itself as the premiere company for the development of web authoring tools. Jonathan Gay remained with Macromedia (and Flash) until its eventual purchase by the Adobe Corporation in 2005. For more than a decade, Gay championed the innovation, direction, and vision of the Flash Platform. This vision is ultimately given much of the credit for moving Flash and the web industry in the direction of the Rich Internet Application (RIA).

It has been over 20 years since Gay first began writing graphics editing programs. In that time, the Flash Player has become one of the most widely distributed pieces of software in the history of computing.

The world today—addicted to change

Before we go any further, it's important to understand the way technologies propagate through popular culture. For example, at the time of this book's writing, the world is entering the social networking and collective intelligence era of web application development. This is not to say that web-based social networking is a new technology—it isn't by any stretch of the imagination. It simply means that, for the next several months, social networking will be the focus of what most companies try to achieve for their respective businesses.

Companies specializing in social networking have been around for years (for example, MySpace and Facebook). However, now that the gold has been discovered, the rush will be on to harness as much of this potential as the market will bear. Subsequently, dozens of lesser-know companies will offer their interpretations of what effective social networking should be.

By the time you read this, social networking will be as relevant to the future of web technologies as the phrase, "You've got mail." Not that it will be obsolete; it will simply be so commonplace and expected that it will no longer be the driving force of our industry.

Please do not misconstrue the previous statements: the fact that this is happening does not mean that the web technologies industry is fickle. Rather, it reveals how quickly web technology evolves. Per Moore's Law, every major aspect of computer hardware doubles about every two years. This holds true for storage, speed, transistor count, and the halving of chip size and cost. In just over a decade the average household Internet connection speed has also gone from 56 kilobytes per second to around 16 megabytes per second. This increase in speed is about 300 percent over 10 years. Though this growth is not actually explained through Moore's Law, but rather Nielsen's Law, there is no doubt that the two are related. It should then come as no big surprise that because hardware cost and capability is advancing so rapidly, new doors are opened everyday for what this hardware is used for.

As a professional in the realm of new media, you will need to possess some degree of discernment when you hear the buzzwords that typically plague our industry. The truth of the matter is that most of these terms are associated with some kind of significant revelation that has occurred in the landscape. Unfortunately, many of them are completely misunderstood and are seldom defined in a commonly acceptable manner.

Therefore, rather than have you, the reader, become lost in the thickets of what would be the endless definitions of the terms "RIA" and "Web 2.0," we will go ahead and break this down . . . according to Flash.

Rich Internet Applications

What then is an RIA? **Rich Internet Application** refers to the process of web pages moving away from a stateless Internet. We understand that this definition probably needs some elaboration. But in terms of clarity, this is probably the most concise and direct definition of what the term "Rich Internet Application" means.

Functionally, however, Rich Internet Applications are commonly referred to as web applications that behave more like desktop applications, the primary difference being that a trip to the server is no longer required for a web page to process information. In fact a majority of the processing can and is handled by the human-computer interface itself.

Flash was instrumental in this movement because it was both capable of changing states and possessed a native programming language capable of manipulating user information. And, because it was popular and lightweight, it instantly became the platform of choice for deploying Rich Internet Applications.

To gain a better understanding of how important this was to the web industry and why Flash was such a tremendous component, we will take a look at the limitations of the early Internet and what it took to break the stateless barrier.

The stateless Internet

The first thing that needs to be understood is the concept of a stateless Internet. "Stateless" simply means that early web pages did not have "state," or they lacked the ability to change. If a page wanted to update or change its information, it would have to request a new page from the server. Subsequently, all major functionality would have to be performed on the server.

The term "client-server" was then adopted from post-mainframe computing to describe the type of interaction that was occurring on the Internet. As demonstrated in Figure 1-1, if the web page, or **client**, wanted a change to occur, it would need to request new information via an HTTP request. In order for this process to be completed, the request would need to traverse the Internet and make contact with a **web server**. The server would then need to process the applicable request and return the response to the client machine in the form of a new HTML page. This is also referred to as a **refresh**.

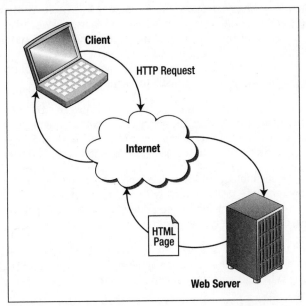

Figure 1-1. The request-response round trip that occurs when a web page is requested

Because of their inability to perform any functional processing of their own, web pages were often referred to as **thin clients**. The term "client" is typically used to refer to the part of an application that allows a human to interface with its data.

Unfortunately, the web-based client-server model suffered because potentially significant errors could occur from multiple points of failure. At any given point of this exchange, the request or response could be dropped, and the process would not be complete. One example you are sure to remember is the old web shopping cart checkout that failed to process orders, leaving users wondering if they had just made a purchase or not!

Three-tiered application model

Now that you have firm grasp on the concept of the stateless Internet, it would be advantageous to take a moment to look at the important components of a typical web application. As a new developer begins to become involved with the world of web technologies, it can certainly take a lot of mental work to gain a solid footing: "Should I use ASP or PHP? Will I benefit from using Ajax? Should I use a combination of multiple technologies?" For someone first starting out, the abundance of choices can be overwhelming. The reality of this situation is that, for the most part, web programming languages all behave in essentially the same manner. And, they are definitely responsible for governing the same tasks.

When building web applications, or any application for that matter, a developer needs to focus on three main components, or layers:

Database or data layer   Data represents anything that is going to be stored for future use. This can be the storing of states, similar to the way Microsoft Word has the ability to remember where and how you have arranged your toolbars. Likewise, data layers can also be used for the storing of user or product information needed to run an online store. Though the complete list of users, products, comments, reviews, and all the details that are associated with running Amazon.com are significantly more convoluted than how you have arranged the toolbars in Word, it is still the same basic principle.

Please keep in mind that though this is an extremely loose explanation of the data layer, it is important for any application to have the ability to remember. Therefore, if users return to Amazon.com, all of their credit card information is ready to go when they get there. Imagine how annoying it would be to have to reenter this information over and over again.

The most popular technology for the development of web application databases is Structured Query Language (SQL). Several types or brands of SQL exist, but for the scope of this discussion it is sufficient for you to understand that web applications need databases. And these databases are typically written using some form of SQL.

Middleware or logic layer   The term "middleware," as it applies to web technologies, is commonly used to refer to the part of an application that connects the data to the presentation (or client) layer. It gets this name because it operates between or in the middle of the other two layers.

The two most commonly used languages for handling this functionality are PHP and ASP.NET. Though quite a few other options exist, most web developers are divided into these two camps. In fact, if you were to try and register for standard web hosting, it is more than likely that you would be asked the question, "Windows or Linux?" This is really the same as asking you if you wanted to have the server configured to run ASP (Windows) or PHP (Linux).

More recently, the world has also become familiar with Asynchronous JavaScript and XML (Ajax). Though not really a language by definition, Ajax is a collection of congruent technologies that effectively use the JavaScript language to access databases directly. Most users will be familiar with Ajax through the use of standard Google applications like Gmail and Google Docs.

One of the other main points of understanding for middleware technologies is that not only can they communicate with the presentation layer, but they also have the ability to be the presentation layer. For example, the "X" in Ajax stands for XML. And for sake of discussion, HTML is a type of XML. Therefore, because HTML is the primary and most basic element for web presentation, Ajax is more or less an intermingling of the presentation layer and the middleware. ASP is also an XML-based language. ColdFusion is another XML-based technology. Though they, like Ajax, have intermingled processing capabilities, the basic language is markup. Subsequently, you could attest that most technologies used for middleware could effectively handle the presentation layer as well.

Presentation layer   The presentation layer, also referred to as the client, is where the interaction between the human user and the computer takes place. In the case of the Internet, it is the web page. Traditionally, HTML has been the primary language for rendering web pages. And, if you are viewing web content through a browser, Flash or otherwise, HTML is required.

1

HTML is a descendant of Generalized Markup Language (GML), which was developed almost 50 years ago by IBM. The purpose of GML was to give meaningful labels to content for the purposes of structure and formatting. This process is similar to the writing of a book, in which the author only needs to appropriately label a chapter heading as a header, and the publishing company takes care of the rest. The publisher will effectively be able to apply the appropriate font size and typeface simply by the author's having labeled certain text as a header. This is essentially how markup languages work. Tags are used to label certain areas of a document, or certain blocks of text, and the browser knows how to format these areas based on style guidelines. Therefore, all languages with the letters "ML" (short for markup language) on the end are going to be concerned with giving structured meaning to otherwise structureless content.

The intended purpose of HTML was to do exactly that. Initially the Internet was to be used for the connecting of communication, documentation, and information. It was never intended that the Internet be what is, quite literally, another dimension of existence. So originally, HTML was created to "format documents" for viewing over the Internet.

The diagram shown in Figure 1-2 illustrates how these three layers communicate between one another. The presentation layer is, again, where users interact with an application either through mobile device, web browser, or browserless application (like iTunes). Therefore this information, once accessed, exists on a user's computer. When displaying information in a browser, HTML is required. This is also the layer where Flash content exists. For basic web applications, this layer communicates with a server using the response-request method.

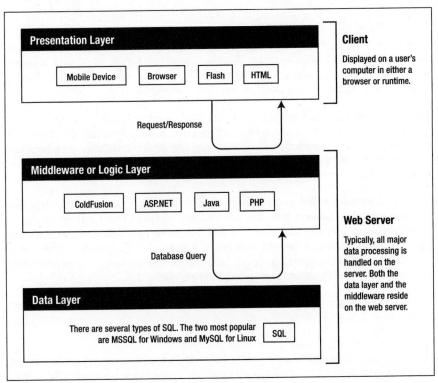

Figure 1-2. A diagram of the three-tiered application model

The middleware or logic layer serves as the liaison between the presentation layer and the data layer. This layer exists on the web server and can access information in a database through a database query. Traditionally, all major functionality was handled by the logic layer. As mentioned previously, though several other solutions such as Java and ColdFusion exist, the two most common languages used for logical processing are ASP.NET and PHP. And, though many people can list the pros and cons of either language, the primary reason to choose one over the other only has to do with which language a developer feels more comfortable with.

Finally, the data layer is a database that also resides on the web server. And just to review, most modern databases are handled by a language called SQL. Like the solutions with the middleware, there are several types of SQL to choose from. The two most common types coincide with the two most popular choices for middleware technology. If you are a developer who is more comfortable with ASP.NET, you will use MSSQL as your brand of SQL. This also has to do with having your web server configured to run Windows. If you are a PHP developer, you will more than likely be communicating with MySQL on a Linux-based web server.

> We should point out that these are traditional configurations. It is possible to have PHP communicate with MSSQL and have ASP.NET communicate with MySQL. Most web developers and web hosting companies will operate in accordance with the traditional approach.

Natural evolution of thin clients

As the natural evolution of the Internet occurred, the demand for client-side functionality became more and more apparent. At this time developers could use Java Applets, JavaScript, and VBScript to add greater flexibility. There were, however, still significant limitations to what could be done programmatically over the Internet.

Though greater client-side functionality was rising, the Internet was still stateless. And, in order for an information change of any kind to take place, new information would need to be sent from the server. A web page couldn't even add 2 plus 2 without refreshing the page. It was within this void that Flash ultimately met a need and found its place in the driver's seat of where the Web is going next.

By now you should have at least a basic working understanding of how web applications function. You should be familiar with the fact that applications need a memory (data), a place for humans to interact (client), and a way for these two layers to communicate (middleware). You should also be well aware of the significant limitations to the client-server model as we have discussed it. Finally, you should also be familiar with how all of these components came together to present a stateless Internet.

With this understanding, we will now take a look at true development of the Rich Internet Application. In all actuality, the only thing that differentiated an RIA from everything else on the stateless Internet was the evolution of the client.

Up to now, you have only been introduced to the client (presentation layer) as just that, a client. It would now be appropriate for us to describe clients, as we have defined them, as

thin clients. The term "thin client" simply refers to a human-computer interface (client) that is dependent on a centralized server to handle all of its processing. It is incapable of processing any significant data on its own. We use the term "thin" to suggest a degree of flimsiness; the client does not have the ability to stand on its own.

The evolution of the Internet is not unlike the evolution of the personal computer. This is no doubt why terms like "client" have been derived from traditional computing to describe web-based ideas. Figure 1-3 demonstrates the parallels between these two evolutions and shows how they are related in the linear advance of computing.

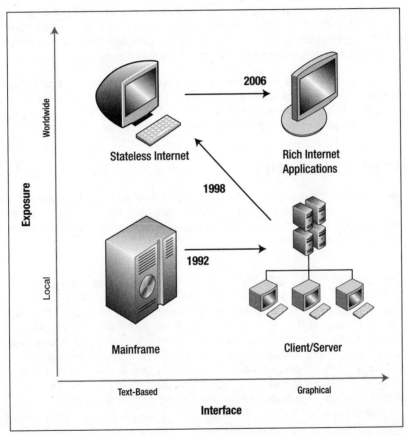

Figure 1-3. The evolution of computing ranging from mainframe computing to the birth of RIAs

Back in the days of mainframe computing, all files and applications for a business resided on a central processing unit, or mainframe. If employees needed to access particulars, they would have to log in through a terminal. Terminals, as you may have guessed, were also referred to as clients.

As Bill Gates and Steve Jobs began to duke it out over global domination, the world was gifted with the personal computer. The beauty of the personal computer was that each unit had its own central processing capability. Therefore, each unit had the ability to effectively manage all of its own data and processing. Additionally, the human-computer interface began to adopt a graphics metaphor with operating systems like Windows and Mac OS.

Because of these advancements, it became necessary for the industry to differentiate between the types of clients that were being used. Subsequently, in light of the fact that personal computers now had the ability to store and process their own information, they were affectionately given the labels of **fat client** or **thin client**. Similarly, as mentioned earlier, their predecessors were officially given the label of thin client.

This change also brought some significant differences in the way clients interacted with data. Because they could now handle most of their own processing, the only thing that needed to be stored centrally was the data. This new relationship between client terminals and data servers was eloquently referred to as the client-server model.

As the world moved into the Internet era, computing took a step backward. Though the Internet was actually made functional by the client-server model, it was more accurately performing like the mainframe model. The clients had returned to text-based representations that were dependent on a centralized source for all data and processing.

The rise of ActionScript

Enter Flash! Around the end of 2003, Macromedia released its seventh installment of the Flash development environment, Flash MX 2004. What made this release of Flash so special was the presence of ActionScript 2.0. This was significant because it gave Flash its first real object-oriented capabilities.

> *Object-oriented programming* is a style of programming that uses objects to organize the functionality of an application. It has been debated whether or not ActionScript 2.0 was an object-oriented programming language. We have read many articles that have stated emphatically that it is not. The reality is that ActionScript 2.0 is no less an object-oriented language than a three-year-old child is a human. Admittedly some significant elements of object-oriented languages were not present. However, the basis of the language was the formation, manipulation, and instantiation of objects. Therefore, ActionScript 2.0 was certainly an object-oriented language. It just lacked the punch of some of its predecessors.

It was around this time that the phrase "Rich Internet Application" began to surface into the mainstream. As stated before, the thing that defines the Rich Internet Application as such is the evolution of the client. Much like the change that occurred when the first thin clients evolved into personal computers, Flash now possessed the tools to grant web pages the ability to process all significant functionality at the presentation layer.

Further, it was already being used for complex, web-based animations. Therefore, Flash was able to effectively break down the barriers of the stateless Internet. Users could now be introduced to rich interactive and engaging experiences that were capable of dazzling aesthetically and process all major functionality on the client. Users could now go to their favorite web store, shop, add and subtract items from the cart, enter their personal information, and check out without ever making a request to the server.

It was during this period (between Flash MX 2004 and Flash 8) that the development of Flash as a platform began to emerge.

Flash Platform, open source, and Web 2.0

Now, the ability of Flash to break the barriers of statelessness was only one part of the total equation. One of the greatest advantages to Flash as a technology is described in the phrase "Flash Player ubiquity." The word "ubiquity," by definition, means omnipresence, and that is basically what we have. The Flash Player is the most widely distributed piece of software in the history of computing. At present, an estimated 864 million PCs worldwide are running the Flash Player. This number approximately represents 99 percent of Internet-enabled personal computers.

When these statistics are bridged with the technological advancements that were being made by Flash development, it certainly becomes quite evident why and how Flash began to move itself into the pole position of Internet technologies. In addition, the continual upgrades to the Flash Player itself helped to deliver content that was not only engaging and highly interactive, but also in file sizes that were more economical for Internet delivery.

The Flash Platform

Because of the many culminating factors surrounding Flash as a web solution, Macromedia (later Adobe) began to develop what became known as the Flash Platform. The **Flash Platform** is essentially a series of related technologies all built around or upon the Flash development framework. These technologies included Flash, Flex, Breeze, and later Apollo (now AIR) for browserless applications. The architecture for the Flash Platform effectively outlined integration with most popular web technologies including PHP, .NET, Java, and SQL. In essence, this offered Flash as the complete solution for any web-based client in any situation including enterprise-level applications and web-based conferencing.

Web 2.0 means what you want it to

Web 2.0, like Rich Internet Applications, is the defining of an evolution of web-based technology. Web 2.0, however, is considerably more difficult to define. If you were to begin doing research on Web 2.0 by means of the Internet, you would more than likely find dozens of articles written on the topic. Unfortunately, most of those articles would give you completely conflicting definitions of what Web 2.0 means.

How is this possible? Well, as stated earlier, our industry is plagued with buzzwords used to promote self-understanding and competitive intelligence. In the case of Web 2.0, we have seen this phenomenon explode to astronomical proportions. In fact, some definitions are even unclear as to whether Web 2.0 is a technical advancement or an advancement of aesthetics. We can assure you it has nothing to do with aesthetics.

Web 2.0 is essentially the Internet catching up to traditional computing. Remember, we spoke earlier of the Internet being a step backward in the world of computing. We are all well aware that we can perform significantly more advanced processes from our desktop computers than through the Internet. But as sure as I (Paul) am typing this, one of my coauthors is 20 miles away making simultaneous edits and adjustments to this document.

The difficulty in diagnosis comes when we think of this evolutionary process in tandem with what is already occurring on desktop computers. Many applications, such as Skype or iTunes, are in fact desktop applications that communicate over the Internet. The diagnosis becomes even more difficult when we consider applications like eBay Desktop, a program that gives users the full functionality of eBay from the convenience of their desktop. Applications like this are built on the Flash Platform using the browserless AIR environment. They are essentially desktop applications using Flash technology—or, more accurately, web applications being run on a desktop.

Web 2.0 basically began its realization with the advent of the Rich Internet Application, which found its mainstream exposure through the Flash Platform. Fueled by the now widespread availability of broadband Internet, it is now coming into full bloom with the explosion of social networks, massively multiuser environments, and ever enhanced means of online collaboration.

In much the same fashion that personal computers stopped relying on a central processing source and actually started being data sources, the Internet is beginning to see the same kind of evolution. Users now have the ability to add value and contribute to the bigger picture. They are no longer restricted to simply request-response type interaction.

Flash remains at the forefront of the Web 2.0 movement. Because of its incredible rate of distribution and the power of the rapidly evolving ActionScript programming language, Flash continues to redefine the landscape of web-based computing. Further, an arsenal of third-party APIs have accelerated the way new technologies are being integrated with Flash. Much like a snowball rolling down a mountain, the more Flash advances, the more people want to advance it. And the more people want to advance it, the more it advances.

The open source Flash explosion

The most wonderful thing to happen to Flash in the past couple years is the development of an open source programming community. With the release of ActionScript 2.0, and more recently ActionScript 3.0, Flash has had the benefit of attracting a more sophisticated community of software architects and engineers. And, as you learned earlier, Flash has always benefited from its community. With this new insurgence of programmers, the Flash community was widely introduced to proper programming practices and theory. As a side effect, users began to see the arrival of many third-party APIs and development libraries.

The open source Flash community is now responsible for creating several animation engines like Fuse and Tweener; APE, the ActionScript physics engine; a number of 3D environments including the popular Papervision 3D; Red5, an open source Flash server; and many others. It is even possible to use Flash to write games that can be played on the

Nintendo Wii. In fact, this movement has gained so much momentum that entire books have been devoted to the use of open source technologies in Flash, such as *The Essential Guide to Open Source Flash Development* by Aral Balkan et al. (friends of ED, 2008).

Summary

Now that you have been formally introduced to Flash, its capabilities, where it came from, and where it is going, you are more than likely chomping at the bit to get started with learning Flash and ActionScript. Well, we won't hold you back any longer. We will simply offer one final gem of understanding for those just beginning the journey. The Flash world is immense! For many of the chapters in this book, it is possible to find several other books on only that topic, and have a career in only that facet of the Flash world. Some people make a good living off simply keeping tabs on what is going on in the Flash world. So find out what kind of Flash user you are, don't get overwhelmed, and above all other things have fun!

We covered the following points in this chapter:

- What Flash is and what it is used for
- The three-tiered application model
  - Data
  - Middleware
  - Presentation
- Why Flash was instrumental in breaking the stateless barrier

CHAPTER 2
THE NEW INTERFACE OF FLASH CS4

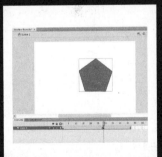

If you've ever watched the TV show *Iron Chef*, you might wonder how those chefs manage to create such amazing food so quickly. Obviously they are masters in their craft, and all of the experience and training that goes into becoming a master is important. But at the foundation of that training is an understanding so complete of all the tools at their disposal that knowing what tool to use for a task is second nature. Even though some pretty amazing things come out of experimenting or "happy accidents," your day-to-day success depends on knowing what your tools do and how to use them.

Beyond the tool set is the kitchen itself, which has a place for storing food, a place for preparing food to cook, a place for cooking food, and even a place to keep recipes or other information about what the chefs need to make. And then there are the spices and . . . well we could go on and on, but you get the idea, and since we're not writing a cookbook here, we'll spare you the complete analogy. Suffice it to say that Flash works like a kitchen in many ways, and the better you know your tools and workspace, the happier you will find yourself while making your next masterpiece with the "mystery ingredient"—the customer.

If you're coming to Flash CS4 from an older version of Flash, you should feel at home right away. A few notable additions/changes include the Motion Editor, which we'll cover in detail in Chapter 6, a slightly new approach to the Property inspector, and a handful of new tools.

Continue on with this chapter to get acquainted with the new interface of Flash CS4.

Welcome Screen

The first thing you will see when you launch Flash CS4 is the Welcome Screen (see Figure 2-1). The Welcome Screen allows you to open recent documents, create new documents, or create new documents from a template. This page also has useful links to tutorials and other product information and resources including Adobe Exchange, where you can find hundreds of extensions built for Flash by the developer community. You can create content for the Web, mobile devices, and even the desktop using Flash. The Welcome Screen provides you with a number of options under Create New to help you get started.

The Welcome Screen opens by default when you launch Flash and will reopen after closing all open documents. You can turn off the Welcome Screen by selecting the Don't show again check box at the lower left of the page. Alternatively, you can turn it back on by opening the Preferences dialog (select Edit ➤ Preferences or press Ctrl+U in Windows, or select Flash ➤ Preferences or press Cmd+U in OS X) and under the General category setting the On launch drop-down to Welcome Screen.

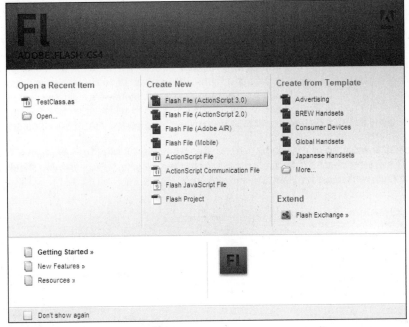

Figure 2-1. The Welcome Screen of Flash CS4

Choosing Flash File (Action Script 2.0) creates a new Flash file that targets Flash Player 10 using ActionScript 2.0. Using ActionScript 2.0 will give you the flexibility of publishing content that is backward-compatible with older versions of the Flash Player (back to Flash Player 6).

Selecting Flash Player 6 as your target player will now automatically optimize content for Flash Player 6 r65 (new in CS4).

Choosing Flash File (Action Script 3.0) creates a new Flash file that targets Flash Player 10. Content that uses ActionScript 3.0 will be compatible only with Flash Player 9 and higher. Using ActionScript 3.0 not only brings with it a tool set geared toward object-oriented programming similar to other important languages, but also changes the behavior of the interface in some ways, which we'll note throughout the book.

Choosing Flash File (Mobile) will launch Adobe Device Central, a handy utility made to help you create content that targets the various versions of the Flash Lite player based on your target device(s). Flash Lite is a runtime that uses a simplified set of ActionScript. Device Central also includes a Flash Lite emulator. Nice!

Choosing Flash File (Adobe AIR) lets you create content for the desktop. AIR, which stands for Adobe Integrated Runtime, allows you to leverage your existing Flash and other web technology chops to create desktop applications that are first-class citizens on the user's computer.

The Flash CS4 interface is nearly identical between operating systems

Changes to the Flash CS4 authoring environment have made the interface behavior and appearance consistent across operating systems. The addition of an application window paradigm has allowed the grouping of panels and document window(s) together on the Mac, and conversely made floating document windows possible in Windows. In fact the interface looks nearly identical between operating systems until you open a modal settings dialog.

That was a whole lot of everything in general and nothing specific. So if you haven't done so already, select Flash File (ActionScript 3.0) from the Welcome Screen, and you should see the default workspace for Flash CS4 shown here in Figure 2-2.

Figure 2-2. The default workspace of Flash CS4

Working with panels and windows

Within the application window the Flash CS4 interface is made up of one or more document windows and several panels. Here we'll explore the other various types of interface elements, how to interact with and modify them in general, the basic operation of each, and finally how to customize and arrange them to best suit your needs.

Understanding panels (color-coded panel parts—three shades of gray)

Panels have three distinct areas that make up the header or bar that runs across the top: the group header (dark gray), panel header (medium gray), and panel tab (light gray), as shown in see Figure 2-3. The exception to this is the document window, which we'll talk about in the section "The document window" later in this chapter.

Figure 2-3.
The panel tab, panel header, and panel group header

Panel tab

Clicking the panel tab gives focus to that panel, bringing it in front of any floating panels or to the front of a panel group so that you can interact with it. (Floating panels will always appear in front of panels that are docked to the application window.) Dragging the panel tab allows you to move that panel in the workspace, arrange it within a panel group, add it to or remove it from a panel group, or dock that panel to a docking point in the workspace.

Panel header

The panel header affects all the panels in a panel group as one. Clicking the panel header will vertically collapse/expand the panel and any other panels in a group, but only after bringing that panel or panel group into focus. Dragging the panel header allows you to move that panel or panel group in the workspace, add it to or remove it from another panel or panel group, or dock that panel or panel group to a docking point in the workspace. At the upper-right corner of all panels (except for the Tools panel) is the panel menu. This menu will have options related to the content of the panel. We discuss these in more detail throughout the book.

> *Save yourself a few clicks (and master the workspace) by thinking about whether or not the panel you are reaching for is open already. If it is open, click the tab, or you'll waste a click reopening it. If it's closed, reach for the panel header bar—this will give the panel focus, bring it to the front, and expand it, all in one click. It may sound like a silly thing to consider, but these little things make working in Flash faster and more enjoyable.*

Panel group header

Figure 2-4.
A panel group
collapsed to icons

The panel group header affects every panel group stacked under it. Clicking the panel group header (dark gray) will reduce the panels down to icons. This collapsed-to-icons view is a super-efficient use of space and reduces a sprawling expanse of panels into a compact collection of buttons. As the name implies, you can group panels together in a way that makes sense to you and the way you work. (Figure 2-4 shows a panel group collapsed to icons.) When you click a panel button while collapsed to icons, the panel group that that panel belongs to pops out. Giving focus to any other part of the interface outside of that panel or its panel group will collapse the group automatically. (Horizontally stacked panels or panel groups collapsed to icons do not close automatically.) The panel header appears as two rows of dots above the panel buttons (which function as panel tabs).

Docking, grouping, stacking, and floating

We have mentioned panel groups, docking, and floating a few times, and you may be wondering exactly what these terms mean. See Figure 2-5 for examples of each.

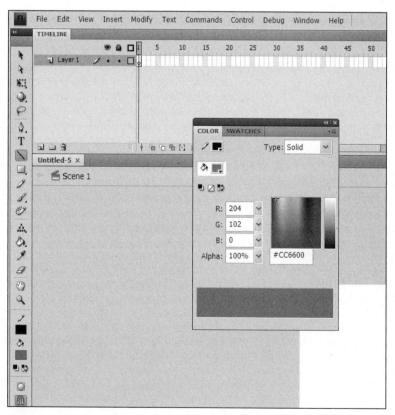

Figure 2-5. Panels in groups, floating and docked

Docking is attaching a panel or panel group to the inside bounds of the application window. This behavior has changed on the Mac from Flash CS3. Instead of an application window, you could dock panels and groups to the bounds of the desktop. This is not an option in Flash CS4 on Macs, although you can still do this on PCs. A side note: you can expand the Tools panel to any width (very cool!).

To see how docking works, drag the timeline away from the panel group it is in. You'll see the entire panel becomes translucent as you drag it. Dragging it close to the side of the application window will cause a light blue line and a translucent gray bar to appear (see Figure 2-6). Releasing the panel here will "dock" it to the application window.

Grouping is basically stacking panels on top of one another (like a deck of cards)—each accessible by tabs running across the top of the panel group. To see how grouping works, drag a panel tab into another panel or panel group. You will see a light blue line around the outside of the panel or panel group you are about to join. In Figure 2-7 we are dragging the Info panel from the bottom group up to the group with the Color and Swatches panels. You can drag panel groups into other panel groups as well by dragging the panel group header instead of a single panel tab.

Figure 2-6.
The Tools panel
as it is about to
be docked to the
application window

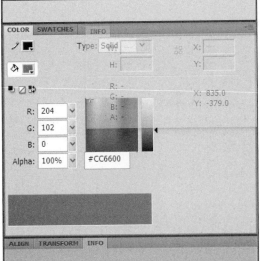

Figure 2-7. The Info panel
being grouped with the
Color and Swatches panels

Stacking is basically docking panel groups to other panel groups. You can stack vertically and horizontally. Using these features is a great way to organize your workspace. Study Figures 2-7 and 2-8 to see the visual cues used in grouping and stacking. To stack a panel or panel group, grab the panel tab or panel group header and drag it below, above, or in between another panel group or groups. You will see a single light blue line appear where your new panel or group will appear in the stack.

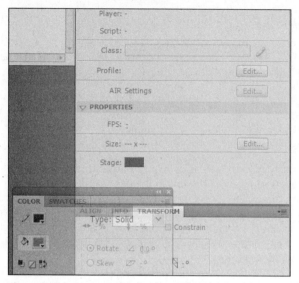

Figure 2-8. A panel group being inserted above another panel group in a stack

Stacking horizontally will always align the new group to the top of the stack.

By default a panel will open with the same position and the same dimensions it had when it was closed. It will also open any other panels it was grouped with and any other groups that its group was stacked on. This is sometimes convenient, sometimes annoying—read the section "Customizing the interface with workspaces" later in this chapter for more on how to make it work for you.

The Property inspector—one panel to rule them all

The Property inspector is a context-sensitive panel for modifying the properties of whatever object has focus. As you change focus, say from the workspace to a frame on the timeline to symbols on stage or to some of the tools in the Tools panel, the content of the Property inspector changes to suit what you have selected. We'll cover specific settings and what they do as we go through the book.

Changing numeric property values (new behavior!)

You may be noticing that the numeric values in various panels are underlined with a dotted line. This is known as **hot text**. Where older versions of Flash had pop-up slider bars and input fields for entering property values, CS4 does away with the sliders and adds mouse control (see Figure 2-9).

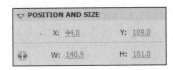

Figure 2-9.
New numeric value input areas with dotted underlines indicating hot text

Hovering over one of these and then scrolling your mouse wheel will increment the value up or down by 1. If you scroll while holding the Shift key, it will increment up or down by 10. Finally, if you hold down the Ctrl (Cmd) key while scrolling, it will increment up or down by .1. How convenient is that?! If you don't have a scroll wheel, you can click and drag using the same modifiers with the same result. And of course, single-clicking any of these will allow you to input values via the keyboard but also allow you to continue to adjust using the scroll functions described previously, the difference being that you will not see the changes until you apply them by clicking away or pressing the Enter key.

The document window

As you can probably guess from the name, the document window reflects the output of your work. Tangible characteristics like dimensions and frame rate as well as background color are determined in the Property inspector (which we'll explore shortly) when the document window has focus. The document window contains your stage and work area. Closing it will close the file. You may have more than one document window open at a time. Opening an existing file or creating a new one will open a new document window and group it with the currently active document window, even if it is not docked to the application window. You can then separate it by dragging it away from the group.

Understanding the document window

Like panels, document windows can be grouped—but only with other document windows. Also, they cannot be collapsed. And they can only dock with the application window. Figure 2-10 shows a document window. In the upper-left corner is the **window tab**, and as you can see we have open the infamous document Untitled-1. Under the window tab is a bar called the **edit bar**. You can turn this on and off by selecting Window ➤ Toolbars ➤ Edit bar from the application menu. On it is a breadcrumb of sorts that shows you what symbol and timeline your stage belongs to and its hierarchical relationship to the stage.

Figure 2-10. A single document window

On the right-hand side of the edit bar are three controls. Left to right they are the Edit Scene, Edit Symbol, and Stage Magnification selectors. Clicking the Edit Scene button will open a drop-down menu of available scenes to edit. Selecting one will change the stage and timeline to reflect the scene you selected in the same state you left it in, including playhead position and selected items, if any.

Clicking the Edit Symbol button will open a drop-down menu of every symbol in your library while keeping folder hierarchy intact using the operating system's style of submenus. (See next section for discussion on the Stage Magnification selector.)

Controlling the document window

So now that you have an understanding of what the document window is and where it fits into the Flash CS4 interface, you are probably wondering what you can actually do with it. Beyond its showing you the stage, what can you do to determine *how* it shows that to you?

Stage view options

In addition to view percentage, you have a handful of rules-based ways to look at the stage.

The Stage Magnification drop-down offers six preset levels of magnification, but you can dial in any percentage you want between 8 percent and 2000 percent. There are also descriptive options as well, including Fit in Window, Show Frame, and Show All.

- Fit in Window: This setting does exactly what it says. It sizes the stage to fill the visible area of the document window (see Figure 2-11). This also removes the vertical and horizontal scrollbars. (If the document window is floating, this will fill the document window, obscured or not, and resizing it will not bring it to the front.)

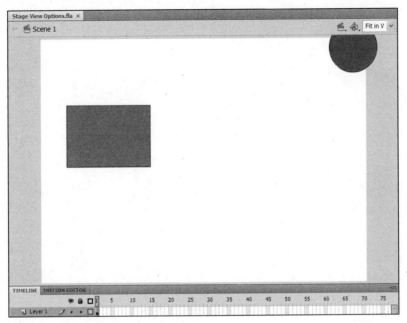

Figure 2-11.
Our stage after selecting
Fit in Window

- Show Frame: This setting will either zoom in or out to show you all of the contents
  of the stage (see Figure 2-12).

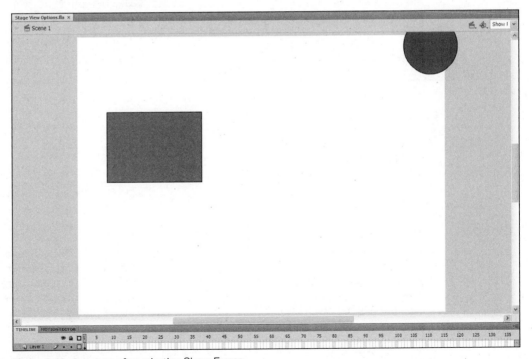

Figure 2-12. Our stage after selecting Show Frame

■ Show All: This setting will zoom in or out as far as it needs to and reposition the stage in order to show you all of the symbols currently on the stage and pasteboard (see Figure 2-13).

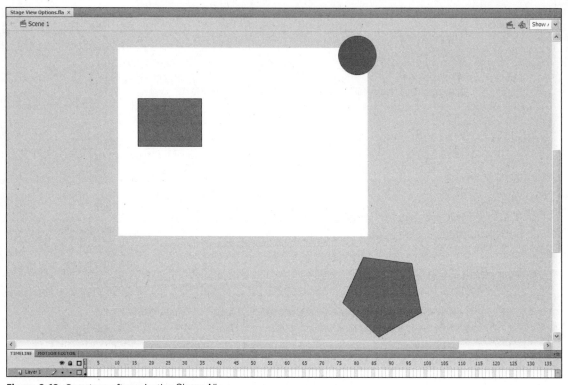

Figure 2-13. Our stage after selecting Show All

Tools for using the interface

While many of the tools are used for creating and modifying objects in some way, a couple of tools deal specifically with manipulating the workspace itself—the Hand tool and the Zoom tool.

Hand tool

Use the Hand tool to move the stage within the document window. This comes in quite handy while zoomed in. To access the Hand tool without "putting down" your current tool, press the spacebar. When you see the hand, feel free to drag. To resume using your selected tool, simply release the spacebar. This technique might seem a little awkward at first, but it becomes a huge time-saver after just a little practice.

Double-clicking the Hand *tool in the* Tools *panel will set the document zoom setting to* Show Frame. *(For a description of* Show Frame *see "Stage view options" earlier in this chapter.*

Zoom tool (Z is for bones, silly rabbit!)

To zoom in or out of the workspace, use the Zoom tool. Select the Zoom tool (or magnifying glass) from the Tools panel by pressing M. In previous versions of Flash, you could also press Z for the Zoom tool; however, CS4 assigns the Z shortcut to the Bone tool by default. You can change this default behavior. Read "Customizing keyboard shortcuts" later in this chapter to find out how.

Clicking the document window with the Zoom tool selected will zoom to two times the current magnification (at 150 percent, a click magnifies to 300 percent, the next click magnifies to 600 percent, etc.). Holding the Option key while clicking with the Zoom tool will zoom out by half, or "pull out," the current magnification (at 600 percent, a click decreases the view to 300 percent, the next click decreases the view to 150 percent, etc.).

You can also drag around an area on the stage, and Flash will zoom to show only that area.

Double-clicking the Zoom tool will return the stage to 100 percent.

Rulers, guides, and snapping

Although Flash has fantastic auto-align and snapping options that go beyond rulers and guides, the document window also includes rulers and guides to help you position items on the stage when there may not be anything else to align with or snap to. Ruler and guide options remain under the View menu.

Select View ➤ Rulers to toggle the rulers off and on. Rulers must be on in order to create guides but not to view or move them.

To create a guide, drag from a ruler toward the stage. As you drag you will see a line appear. When you release the mouse, this will become a guide. While you can have any tool active to make guides, you must use the Selection tool to change their position or remove them individually.

To move a guide, make sure you have the Selection tool active. When you hover over a guide with the Selection tool, an arrow with a line will appear next to it indicating that you can click and drag the guide to move it. To remove the guide, drag it onto the ruler.

To edit guides, select View ➤ Guides from the menu. Here you can show, lock, edit, or clear your guides. Choosing Edit will open the Guides dialog where you can select a color for your guides, lock/unlock, hide/show, and even adjust snap accuracy as well as make your selections the default for all documents.

Snapping is a standard feature of many applications where "moving things around in a view" is part of the workflow. Flash is no exception. Snapping allows you to place objects accurately based on some rules. You can snap to guides, which means that guides will act like magnets when you get objects near them. Additionally, you can have objects snap to other objects and objects snap to a grid on the stage.

Property inspector options of the document window

Property inspector options for the document are divided into two sections, Publish and Properties, as shown in Figure 2-14.

The Publish settings are determined by what publish profile you have selected. (Using one of the Welcome Screen options selects a publish profile for you.) To change the Flash Player and ActionScript versions you wish to publish for, click the Edit button. This will open the Publish Settings dialog where you can change your settings. If you're chomping at the bit to set up custom profiles or dig deep into the publishing capabilities of Flash, jump to Chapter 18, where we cover the publish settings in detail.

The other option under Publish is the Class field. Use this to assign an ActionScript class to the document. We'll cover this and the Actions panel in Chapter 8.

There are three document properties that can be set in the panel: fps (frames per second, referred to as the frame rate), size, and stage color. You can also access these properties though the File menu by selecting Modify ➤ Document, or by pressing Ctrl+J (or Cmd+J on a Mac).

Figure 2-14.
The Property inspector
for the document window

Changing the document frame rate

The default frame rate is now 24 fps. To change it, use the methods described previously in the section "Changing numeric property values (new behavior!)" or open the Document Properties dialog by clicking the Edit button in the Size section under Properties.

Changing the stage size

Clicking the Edit button next to Size will open the Document Properties dialog, allowing you to adjust the document dimensions as well as the frame rate and stage color.

Changing the default document settings

If you commonly use specific dimensions, frame rate, and stage color, you can make those settings the default by clicking the Edit button in the Properties section of the Property inspector. In the Document Properties dialog, adjust the settings to match your preferences and click the Make Default button in the lower left of the dialog. Now every new document will have these properties!

> These are the "physical" characteristics of your document and will not impact the publish profile—which player and version of ActionScript your movie will target.
>
> Flash has historically shipped with a default frame rate of 12 fps in order to accommodate older, slower computers. The new default frame rate is 24 fps, so be sure to dial it down if your audience is known to have older equipment with slower processors.

The Timeline panel

Hated by some, revered by others—the timeline has been a point of contention in these later years of the evolution of Flash. Coders say, "I cannot use Flash. You can put code anywhere! And what's with the timeline?! What is that for?" Animators and designers say, "I cannot use ActionScript to draw and animate. I cannot see what I am doing." And really, we are all right. No matter what side of the fence you are on (including the middle), Flash may have some paradigms you don't "get" or need. But the cool thing about these paradigms is that they are not mutually exclusive worlds. If you don't need the timeline for what you do, don't use it. If you absolutely must have it, then by all means do. Somewhere in the middle there is a place where "timeliners" and coders work together in harmony, and it's much closer than you might think. In fact, we'd be able to see this common ground if we weren't all standing on it together.

Flash programmers will be quick to point out that if you use Flash as a tool for authoring Rich Internet Applications and take advantage of the power of ActionScript, you may need the timeline less than ever—if at all. However, the timeline remains an integral part of what Flash is at its core and is used extensively by a large community of Flash designers and animators, which is why it not only remains a table stake of the Flash interface, but also has been expanded (in a tangential way) by way of the new Motion Editor.

Even if you create an application in Flash with only code, you still need a target Flash source (FLA) file in order to publish it, and it will contain a stage—the fundamental display object container of every Flash movie (SWF file). The stage contains the main timeline of your application, also a display object container.

We discuss the display list in detail later in the book, but for now let's say that in AS 3.0, it's a list of things designed to help you manage the relationship of everything you see on that list. If you can see it, it's a display object. If it's a display object, it is the child of a display list container. And yes, some display objects can be display object containers at the same time, which results in nesting.

For character and motion graphics animators, being able to see the relationship of multiple events over time is critical to imparting personality into their work. The timeline does just that. For interface designers, the timeline can be used for organizing layout elements using layers and folders and representing view states of an application using frames. Prototypes of transition animations or special visual effects can be created by artists in the timeline to later be replicated and modified in code if need be.

Understanding the Timeline panel

The Timeline panel (see Figure 2-15) is the visual representation of the items on your stage over time. It lets you arrange and organize your stage during the authoring process (when you are building your movie or application). You can organize visual depth by using layers and folders much the way you might in Photoshop. You can then manage your visual composition over time by using frames.

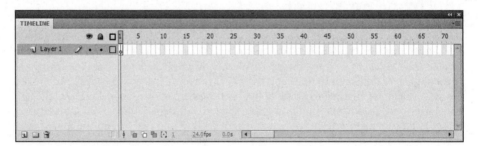

Figure 2-15. The Timeline panel

A significant change to the interface in this release is that when you have multiple documents open, the Timeline panel no longer holds the tabs for open documents. To switch between documents, you must select the document tab in the document window. The document window header displays the active document. Read "Understanding the document window" earlier in the chapter to learn more.

Controlling layers

Timeline layer options allow you to manage and organize your layers as well as give you control over settings for each layer independently. Following is a detailed discussion of each of these options.

■ **The layer strip**: The layer strip is the horizontal strip of space in the Timeline panel to the left of the timeline that shows (from left to right) whether the layer is a folder or not, the layer name, whether it is editable or not (if selected), hidden or not, locked or not, and the outline color setting. Double-clicking the layer icon will open the Layer Properties dialog and allow you to change all of the layer's properties (see Figure 2-16).

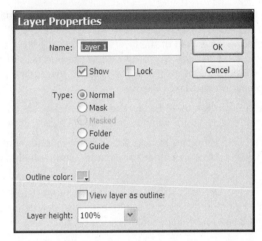

Figure 2-16.
The Layer Properties dialog

> *Folders are layers in the* Timeline *panel. Even though you can't put content in them, the interface treats them the same way it treats layers. Folders are a great way to organize your content layers into meaningful groups. You can also nest folders in other folders.*

■ Show/Hide layer: Clicking the eyeball icon at the top of the Timeline panel will affect all of the layers in the following way. If some or all layers are visible, clicking this icon will hide all layers. If all layers are hidden, clicking this icon will show all layers. In addition to this icon, you can show and hide layers individually by clicking the first black dot that appears beside the layer name under the eyeball icon. A red X indicates that the layer is now hidden.

> *Notice the pencil with the slash through it that appears next to the layer name when the layer is hidden. This indicates that the contents of that layer cannot be edited. You will only see this indicator on the active layer.*

- Lock layer: Clicking the lock icon at the top of the Timeline panel will affect all of the layers in the following way: If some or no layers are unlocked, clicking this will lock all layers. If all layers are locked, clicking this icon will unlock all layers. In addition to this icon, you can lock and unlock layers individually by clicking the second black dot that appears beside the layer name. A lock icon appears indicating that the layer is now locked.

> Notice the pencil with the slash through it that appears next to the layer name when the layer is locked. This indicates that the contents of that layer cannot be edited. You will only see this indicator on the active layer.

- **Outline layer**: Clicking the square outline icon at the top of the Timeline panel will affect all of the layers in the following way: If some or no layers are in outline view, all layers will be set to outline view. If all of the layers are in outline view, all layers will be set to normal view. When a layer is in outline view the outline indicator on the layer strip appears as an outline of a square. The color of the outline indicates what color outline the object on that layer will be.
- **Add layer**: Use the Add Layer button to add a layer to your timeline above the currently selected layer or folder. Layers are named sequentially Layer 1, Layer 2, etc.
- **Add folder**: Use the Add Folder button to add a folder to your timeline above the currently selected layer or folder. Folders are named sequentially Folder 1, Folder 2, etc.
- **Delete layer/folder**: Use the Delete Layer/Folder button to remove the selected layer(s) or folder(s) from the timeline. Deleting a folder will also delete any content within it as well, including layers, subfolders, etc.

The timeline

The ruler or timeline header side of the Timeline panel is where "time is measured"—or broken into equal parts we call frames.

- **Ruler or timeline header**: Moving to the right side of the Timeline panel, you will see at the top a row of numbers incremented by 5. These are frame numbers. Directly below them is a row of small ticks (short vertical lines). Together they make up a sort of frame ruler that gives you a visual indication of the frame numbers of the frames in the grid below. (You can always look at the current frame indicator, discussed a little later in this list, to see exactly what frame the playhead is on.)
- **Playhead**: On the timeline is a red rectangle with a red line extending down through the grid. This playhead indicates what frame on the timeline will be reflected on the stage in the document window.
- **The grid**: As you add frames to layers, you will begin to fill in the space under the ruler. Every fifth frame is shaded gray as a visual aid, and all of the frames are delineated by vertical lines (see Figure 2-17).

Empty   Empty
Keyframe   Frame   Keyframes

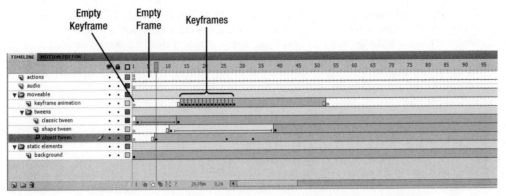

Figure 2-17. Many of the types of frames and keyframes you will encounter on the timeline

- Frame View Options: This menu lets you adjust frame width, layer height, and frame tinting (discussed in the upcoming section "Persistence and tinting frames").

- Center Frame: This button horizontally scrolls the timeline so that the frame that the playhead is on appears centered in the Timeline panel.

- Onion Skin: Select Onion Skin to simultaneously see multiple frames of animation.

- Onion Skin Outlines: Click this button to display the onion-skinned frames as outlines.

- Current Frame: During playback of the timeline, this will show the position of the playhead. At rest, you can click to enter a value or use your mouse wheel as described in "Changing numeric property values (new behavior!)" earlier in the chapter. Entering a number will immediately move the playhead to that frame. Scrolling will move the playhead back and forth as you scroll.

- Frame Rate: During playback this indicates the *actual* frame rate of playback. At rest you can use it to set the document's target frame rate by using the methods described in "Changing numeric property values (new behavior!)" earlier in the chapter.

- Elapsed Time: During playback this shows the calculated elapsed time of the playhead based on frame 1.

> The Add Motion Guide *button has been removed from the bottom of the* Timeline *panel in this version of Flash. To read more about the new approach to guiding motion in Flash CS4, refer to Chapter 6.*

Adding frames/keyframes to the timeline

A new FLA document will have a single layer and a single keyframe by default when you open it. If you're interested in controlling the visual state of an application from the timeline or using it for linear animation, you'll want to know how to add frames to your timeline. First let's have a look at the various types of frames. Look back at Figure 2-17 for examples of an empty frame, empty keyframe, and keyframe.

Now there's also a sort of ready state the grid is in before it has any frames on it. The frame-like rectangles you see under the timeline are simply individual placeholders for where frames might eventually be. We'll call them "unpopulated" to keep them distinct from empty keyframes and empty frames, the difference being that you can't do anything to an unpopulated spot on the grid—you must have a frame of some kind there. In fact, you can't even move the playhead over them. (This is an easy way to tell whether you've got frames.) So enough already—let's add some frames to the timeline.

Persistence and tinting frames

Whether you use the timeline to keep things separated or for linear motion, you'll want to know at a glance where things exist—and how they persist—in time. One useful feature to aid you in this is frame tinting. With frame tinting turned on, any frame that has a symbol or shape on it will be shaded gray, distinguishing it from empty frames, which are white. With tinting turned off, all of the frames are white, which makes it difficult to see how content on stage persists over time.

To turn on frame tinting, use the Frame View Options menu at the top-right corner of the Timeline panel and make sure the option Tinted Frames is checked.

The timeline flows like water

This section is for brand-new users of Flash or folks who are having a hard time understanding how the timeline behaves. Let's imagine the keyframe is a lake or some other small body of water. Add a single empty keyframe to the timeline (see Figure 2-18).

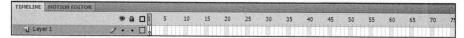

Figure 2-18. A single empty keyframe on the timeline

When you add a symbol or shape to the stage when that keyframe is selected, think of this as adding water to your lake. See Figure 2-19 to see a single keyframe with content. If you have no frames on that layer, you have no place for the water to flow.

All of the water stays in the lake. Adding frames to your layer is like adding a river to that lake, and when you do, all of the water flows from it down the river (that is, the content moves into every frame on that layer) until it meets another keyframe.

If there is already a keyframe on your layer, the content from your first keyframe cannot continue into it. Each keyframe carries its own distinct set of content (see Figure 2-20).

2

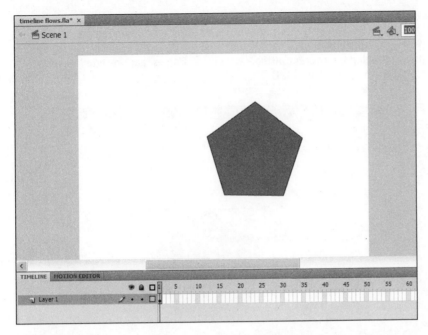

Figure 2-19.
A single keyframe with content

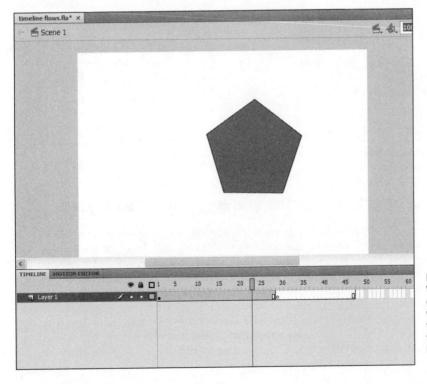

Figure 2-20.
What happens when you add content to a keyframe on a layer with a preexisting (empty) keyframe further down the timeline. Note that the frames following the second keyframe remain empty.

That being said, if you add a lake to a river (that is, you add a keyframe after a set of frames), the lake will fill up with water from the river—or collection of symbols and shapes that made up the original keyframe; you can then change the contents of the newly added keyframe without changing the content of the keyframe or frames that preceded it—only on the frames that follow (see Figure 2-21).

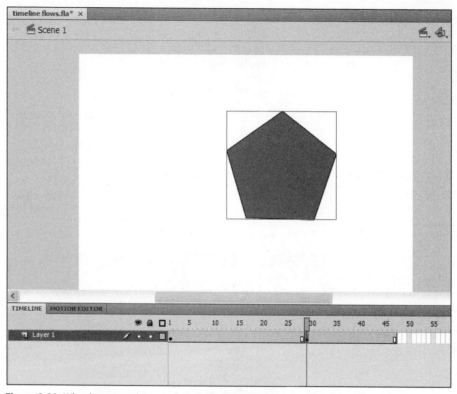

Figure 2-21. What happens when you insert a keyframe to a layer with content

Adding and inserting frames and keyframes to layers

The easiest way to add frames to the grid is to click anywhere under the timeline where there is a layer (selecting where there is no layer will only give focus to the Timeline panel) and pressing F5 (or selecting Insert ➤ Timeline ➤ Frame). This will add frames on that layer from the point at which there is a frame to the point at which you clicked under the timeline. For instance, if you click in the unpopulated placeholder under the number 50 on the timeline, you'll see that that placeholder turns a nice green, indicating that it is selected. Pressing F5 will populate every placeholder between frame 1 up to and including frame 50 (we're assuming that frame 1 is the closest frame—not placeholder—to the placeholder under 50). Pressing F6 will add an empty keyframe in the placeholder (or last placeholder) you have selected (look for the green) on that layer and fill the rest with empty frames.

You made frames!

If the current timeline has more than one layer, you can add frames to multiple layers by dragging under the timeline to include all of the layers you'd like to add frames to. You will notice the placeholders turn that lovely green to let you know they've been selected. Press F5, and you'll have frames on all of the layers you selected—from the first at which there is a frame to the position you selected. Pressing F6 will add an empty keyframe to the point (or points) you have selected on all of the layers you have selected (look for the green) and fill the rest with empty frames.

> Don't worry too much about selecting more than one column of placeholders when adding frames to empty layers. Flash will add frames up to the furthest column.

Adding and inserting frames and keyframes to all layers

So selecting placeholders on all of the layers of a timeline can get to be a drag if you're working on a timeline with many layers; but there is an easy way to add or insert frames and keyframes to every layer in the timeline.

To add frames to the end of the timeline to all layers, position the playhead at the last frame of the timeline, making sure none of the grid is selected (look for the green). Now press F5 to add a frame to the end of every layer. To add a keyframe, press F6 instead. To remove a frame, press Shift+F5. If the last frame on any layer happens to be a keyframe, it will also be removed.

> Grid selection takes precedence, and clicking the playhead or placeholders won't deselect, so make sure your timeline doesn't show any green before adding/removing frames and keyframes from all layers. To deselect everything in the timeline, click any dead space under the last layer or click away from the Timeline panel.

Inserting frames willy nilly

That's right—willy nilly. It sounds better than "multiple noncontiguous selection" don't you think? Let's suppose you have a timeline with three layers (each with 15 frames), and you want to insert 5 frames into the middle of Layer 1 and add 2 frames to the end of Layer 3. To do this, follow these steps:

1. Drag over 5 frames on Layer 1.

2. Press Ctrl (Cmd on a Mac) and drag over the last 2 frames of Layer 3.

You should now have a selection that looks like Figure 2-22.

Figure 2-22.
Multiple discontiguous
selections

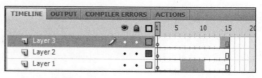

3. Press F5 to insert frames or F6 to insert keyframes.

Just remember the following:

- Green indicates a selection.
- Press F5 to add/insert frames.
- Press F6 to add/insert keyframes.
- Press Shift+F5 or Shift+F6 to remove frames or keyframes.

> *Pressing F5 with multiple frames selected on a layer or layers will insert as many frames as you have selected on as many layers as you have selected.*

Copying/pasting frames

As in any creation process you will at some point want or need to duplicate or move your work. Copying frames is a quick way to duplicate your efforts on the timeline.

To copy a frame select it on the timeline and press Ctrl+C or Cmd+C. This places all of the contents of that frame (all of the symbols on the stage) on the clipboard. Pressing Ctrl+X or Cmd+X will "cut" or remove everything from your selected frame and place all of the contents on the clipboard. Doing this will *not* remove the keyframe itself, just the stage content.

To paste the content of your clipboard back onto the stage, select a keyframe on the timeline (or create one) and press Ctrl+V (Cmd+V on a Mac). There will be times when you might want to paste everything into its prior position on the stage. To do this press Ctrl+Shift+V (Cmd+Shift+V)—or select Paste in place from the Edit menu.

> *These operations on a frame are executed on the closest keyframe that precedes the frame you have selected.*

Controlling the timeline

In order to see what you have on stage at any given time (or in any given frame), you will need to be able to move the playhead along the timeline. During authoring the playhead can be either playing or stopped. When it is playing it will move across the screen from left to right, and items on stage will reflect this. When it is stopped the stage will show only the items for that frame.

When the playhead reaches the last frame of the timeline, it will stop. You can change this by selecting Menu ➤ Control ➤ Loop playback. You can also extend playback in the authoring environment to multiple scenes by selecting Menu ➤ Control ➤ Play all scenes.

There are several ways to change the position of the playhead on the timeline:

- Press the Enter key to toggle play/stop.
- Drag the playhead.
- Use the less than and greater than keys, scroll/drag the current frame, or use elapsed time controls on the timeline (during authoring).
- Use the Controller.
- Use ActionScript.

Figure 2-23.
The Tools panel

The Tools panel

We think it should be required in every instructional book to say at least once, "You must have the right tool for the job." So there it was. And it's true—really! The Tools panel (see Figure 2-23) is where most of them live. We will be investigating each tool in more detail throughout the book.

Customizing the interface

Each and every one of us is different. We will all use Flash CS4 a little differently than everyone else. And so chances are you might want to customize this tool in some way and make it your own. Fortunately for all of us, Flash CS4 will let us do just that. You can create workspaces for customizing the collection and location of panels. You can modify the Tools panel to include the tools you need—and even tools you create yourself. You can adjust the general preferences of the software to reflect what is important to you through the nearly 100 options in the Preferences dialog (see Figure 2-24).

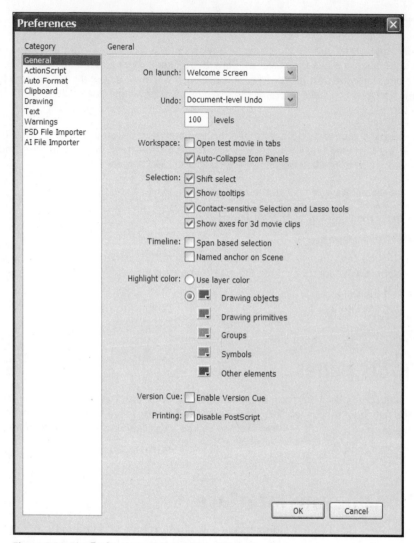

Figure 2-24. The Preferences dialog of Flash CS4

Working with workspaces

Why workspaces? No matter how many monitors you can plug into the back of your computer or how lovely that 30-inch cinema display is, there will be times when rearranging the workspace improves the pace of your work for the task at hand. For instance, you may find that for some tasks having the Tools panel horizontal makes work much faster than having it vertical. Setting up workspaces specific to regular work activities might wind up saving you loads of time (not to mention an unknown number of miles in mouse motion).

Customizing the interface with workspaces

To create a new workspace, follow these steps:

1. Arrange the workspace to your liking. From the menu bar select Window ➤ Workspaces ➤ New Workspace. (You can also open this menu by clicking the Workspace button in the upper-right corner of the application window.) You will see the New Workspace dialog shown in Figure 2-25.

Figure 2-25.
The New Workspace dialog

2. Enter a name for your workspace and then click OK to save or Cancel to exit the dialog without saving.

Switching between workspaces

To change workspaces, click the Workspace button in the upper right of the application window. You should see the name of the workspace you just created in the top section of the menu, Default in the middle section, and the options Reset [name of the current workspace], New Workspace, and Manage Workspaces in the bottom section. To change workspaces simply select any custom workspaces from the top section or Default from the middle section of the menu.

Managing workspaces

Managing workspaces really boils down to deleting or renaming workspaces. To delete a workspace, click the Workspace button in the upper right of the application window and select Manage Workspaces from the menu. In the dialog that opens, select the workspace you wish to delete from the list on the left (as shown in Figure 2-26) and click Delete.

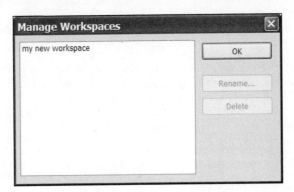

Figure 2-26.
The Manage Workspaces dialog

To rename a workspace, click the Workspace button in the upper right of the application window and select Manage Workspaces from the menu. In the dialog that opens, select the workspace you wish to rename from the list on the left (as shown in Figure 2-27), click the Rename button, enter the new name in the Rename Workspace dialog that appears, and click OK. You can also just double-click the workspace name to open the Rename Workspace dialog.

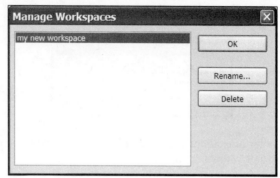

Figure 2-27.
A custom workspace
selected in the Manage
Workspaces dialog

Modifying existing workspaces

There will be times when the workspace you crafted for a task just doesn't work out the way you intended and you want to tweak it a little bit but keep the workspace name the same. To do this, change to the workspace you want to update (as described previously in "Switching between workspaces"), make any changes you want, and then follow the steps given earlier for creating a new workspace, being sure to keep the name the same. Clicking Save in the New Workspace dialog will open a warning dialog telling you that a workspace with that name already exists and asking if you want to overwrite the existing workspace. Click Yes to update the existing workspace.

Customizing the Tools panel

To customize the toolbar select Edit ➤ Customize Tools Panel (or Flash ➤ Customize Tools Panel on a Mac). This will open the dialog shown in Figure 2-28. There are only 18 spaces on the Tools panel, and while leaving some empty will remove the corresponding spaces from the Tools panel, you cannot add more.

Select a square on the Tools panel diagram on the left of the dialog. You will see the tools assigned to this space appear in the right-hand column under Current selection. To add tools to that space, select a tool from the Available tools column and click the Add button. (You can add up to ten tools per space.) To remove a tool from a space on the Tools panel, select the space you wish to remove the tool from. Select the tool you wish to remove from the Current selection column and click the Remove button.

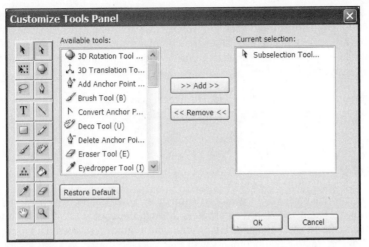

Figure 2-28. The Customize Tools Panel dialog

Customizing keyboard shortcuts

To customize your keyboard shortcuts, select Edit ➤ Keyboard Shortcuts. A few sets are preloaded, and as their names indicate, they are meant to be (as close to) the default keyboard settings of the applications that they are named after.

The first thing you need to do is to duplicate a set of keyboard commands by clicking the Duplicate set button. Enter the name of your new keyboard command set and click OK. This will close the dialog completely. Reopen it, and your new command set will be selected. You may now change the keyboard commands as you wish.

As you attempt to create new commands, you will notice that the dialog will post warnings about limitations and preexisting assignments.

Browse to a command you wish to add or change a shortcut to by selecting the command's category from the Commands drop-down and then the command itself from the tree in the list box below (see Figure 2-29). Once selected the + button will be enabled (next to Shortcuts). Click the + button to add a shortcut. Press the key or key combination you wish to assign to that command. If you get a "not" symbol (red circle with slash through it), you cannot proceed. If you get a caution symbol, you may go ahead and click the Change button.

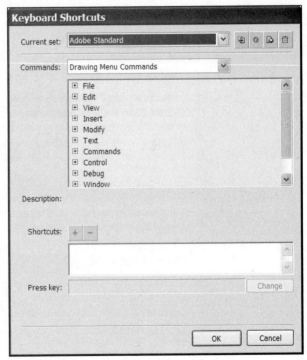

Figure 2-29.
The Keyboard Shortcuts dialog

To rename a command set, click the Info button (circle with an "i" in it). Type in the new name for the command set and click OK. To delete a command set, click the Trash Can button. This will open a dialog with all of the command sets (except for Adobe Standard, which you cannot delete). You can select one or more command sets from the list and then click Delete to remove them.

The last option in this dialog allows you to export your keyboard commands as HTML, which is a nice feature if you'd like to print them out.

Summary

The goal of this chapter was to give you enough of an orientation with the Flash CS4 authoring environment so that as you progress through the book you will feel comfortable reaching for the tools you need and finding your way around. We covered a lot of ground, including how to create new documents with the Welcome Screen. We also explored how to use the Flash CS4 authoring environment:

- How to work with panels and windows
- The timeline
- The Tools panel
- The Property inspector
- Customizing the Flash CS4 interface

If you have specific questions about publishing and the publishing settings, refer to Chapter 18 where we explore these topics in detail.

CHAPTER 3

DRAWING WITH FLASH'S VECTOR TOOLS

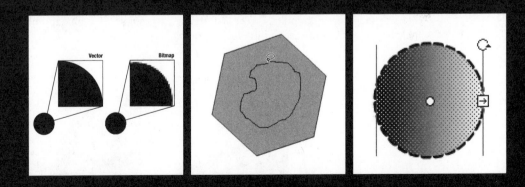

Now that you have familiarized yourself with the "kitchen," it is time to start opening up a few drawers and taking a look at the tools you will have at your disposal to cook up the necessary ingredients to dish up some Flash.

From the simplest of Flash advertisements to the most exquisite of all Flash applications, all have two things in common: graphics and colors. Here you will get familiar with the basic tools to create vector graphics, apply colors, and add a little extra flavor to your creations by spicing things up a bit.

Understanding graphic types

One of the driving themes throughout this book is Flash's ability to work with many different types of data and media. Graphic elements are certainly no exception to this theme. In order to make the best decisions about what types of graphics to use in your Flash projects, it is important to understand the two primary types of graphics and their pros and cons. Understanding these basic fundamentals will translate into better-looking applications and smaller file sizes.

By default, Flash is a program designed to animate vector images. However, it is possible to effectively integrate various types of bitmap graphics to enhance the user's experience as well. Before we get started, you need to understand the difference between bitmap and vector images.

Bitmap graphics

Bitmap graphics are made up of tiny dots or pixels (px). Each pixel is assigned a color value and coordinate that represents its placement within the image. You can think of bitmaps as mosaics that use many different colored pebbles to create a larger image. Because of the fine detail that can be achieved using this method, bitmap graphics work best for photos and artwork with a lot of colors and/or gradients. The disadvantages of bitmap graphics are file size, editing, and scalability. Bitmap graphics typically have a larger file size than vector graphics. Figure 3-1 shows an example of a bitmap image and the negative side effect of scaling this type of graphic.

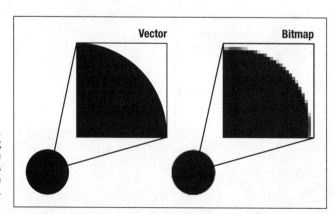

Figure 3-1.
The difference in scaling vector and bitmap images. The vector image will maintain its smooth edge, while the bitmap becomes jagged.

Vector graphics

Vector graphics are defined by points. These two points are used to create a line, which is also called a vector, hence the term "vector graphic." Vectors are also commonly referred to as **line segments**. The points that define a line segment are also responsible for determining whether that line is curved or straight. One or more segments joined together make up a **path**. Multiple segments and paths can be joined together to create shapes.

To understand the initial advantage of vector graphics, picture a 100 × 100 px square. If this square were a bitmap graphic, we would have a total of 10,000 px (100 by 100), each defining a color, coordinate, and alpha value (transparency). If the square were a vector graphic, each corner of our square would be defined by a point. These points would subsequently be connected, forming segments (vectors). Therefore, our picture would be defined by a total of 4 points, as opposed to 10,000. Further, if we increased our picture to a size of 200 × 200 px, our total would be increased to 40,000 px. Our vector image, however, would still be constructed with 4 points. This as you can see lends itself to a considerable file size difference.

Figure 3-1, shown previously, demonstrates the effects of scaling on both a vector and bitmap image. As you can see, vector images allow for a greater degree of scalability.

Working with vector graphics

In Adobe Flash CS4 a number of different tools are available to you for creating vector graphics. Here you will learn what those tools are and what each one of them does. It is important to gain familiarity and become comfortable with using these tools. As you learned in Chapter 1, Flash is first a vector-based drawing tool, and you will be using this tool for most of your Flash projects.

Drawing modes: Merge Drawing vs. Object Drawing

Before we begin you have to understand a little bit about how Flash handles vector graphics on the stage. There are two drawing modes used in Flash: **Merge Drawing** and **Object Drawing**. If you are a veteran Flash user, the first is probably all too familiar to you. The second, though not a new feature in CS4, was introduced in Flash 8 and is often overlooked.

Merge Drawing

Merge Drawing is how drawing in Flash has been handled since its early years. This mode gets its name from its behavior of overlapping shapes. If you come from other design programs such as Adobe Illustrator or Adobe Photoshop, you are aware of the concept of arrangement, where each vector element on the stage is either in front of or behind other elements on the stage. In Flash, when in Merge Drawing mode, there is no concept of arrangement on a single layer. All shapes on the stage occupy the same plane of existence.

So what happens when two shapes overlap? For shapes of the same color, the shapes will merge together as one shape. For shapes of different colors, the selected shape wins dominance and "knocks out" its shape in the shape it is overlapping as shown in Figure 3-2. This was a common frustration among Flash designers, who would oftentimes inadvertently merge shapes together or knock out portions of other shapes by dropping them on top of each other. To avoid this, designers would draw a shape and then group it. Grouped objects in Flash behave as separate objects and introduce the more familiar concept of arrangement. Obviously somebody was listening to the Flash community and introduced the second drawing mode to compensate for this: Object Drawing.

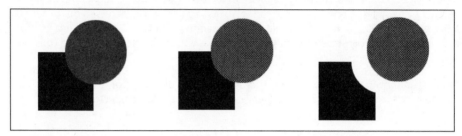

Figure 3-2. In Merge Drawing mode, overlapping shapes will knock out one another.

Object Drawing

When Adobe purchased Flash in 2005, it wanted its principal programs to have an integrated feel. One of the first enhancements that was discussed was the concept of Object Drawing. Because so many of the graphic elements that were used in Flash were created in both Illustrator and Photoshop, Adobe wanted to capture some degree of cross-software familiarity. Object Drawing was Adobe's answer to Flash designers the world over.

When drawing in Object Drawing mode, shapes are automatically grouped and treated as individual objects called **Drawing Objects**. Drawing Objects occupy space on their own plane of existence. This means that overlapping shapes have no effect on each other. The overlapping portions are simply hidden from view by the object in front of it as shown in Figure 3-3.

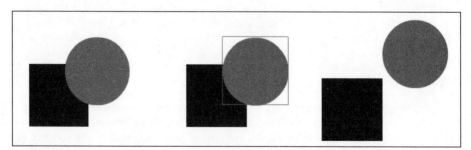

Figure 3-3. Object overlapping

By default, Flash is in Merge Drawing mode. To change drawing modes, click the Object Drawing button that appears at the bottom of the Tools panel as shown in Figure 3-4. You can also easily access this feature by pressing the J key when you have a drawing tool selected.

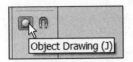

Figure 3-4.
Object Drawing button located at
the bottom of the Tools panel

Unless otherwise noted, we will be working in Merge Drawing mode for the examples and exercises in this chapter.

Creating and manipulating lines

Lines are the simplest forms in design and the basic building blocks of shapes. To create lines in Flash, you can use the Line tool and the Pencil tool. A line in Flash is nothing more than a segment, or vector, that can have color applied to it.

The Pen tool is another tool that can be used to create lines, as well as complex paths and shapes; we will cover this tool in the section "Advanced drawing," which comes later in this chapter.

The Line tool

The Line tool is used for creating straight line segments. To draw a line using the Line tool, select the Line tool from the Tools panel. You should see your mouse cursor turn into a set of crosshairs. Now click the stage and drag the mouse with your mouse button still pressed. You will see the length and angle of the line change as you move your mouse around. As you can see, you can create a line of any length and at any angle. To set the line, simply release the mouse button.

Now, you may or may not have tried to draw a horizontal or vertical line. If you did, you may have noticed it required a fairly steady hand. To make things easier, you can hold down the Shift key to constrain a line's angle at 45-degree increments. Draw another line, but this time draw it at a 45-degree angle.

Again, select the Line tool if it isn't already selected and click the stage. Now hold down the Shift key and drag the cursor down and away. You may notice as you are dragging that the line will jump back and forth between horizontal, vertical, and 45-degree angles. Release the mouse button to set the line.

The Shift key is known as a **modifier key** because you can use it to change the behavior of a tool. In general the Shift key and the Alt key (Option on the Mac) are used as modifier keys for a lot of the drawing tools in Flash. The Alt key switches the point of origin to the center of the shape you are dragging. We highly recommend you play around with the modifier keys for each tool we cover to see what they do.

> *Although not technically considered a modifier key, the spacebar can be held down to activate the* Hand *tool temporarily and navigate around the stage. This is a useful shortcut when portions of the stage are offscreen. Note that the spacebar shortcut key only works when the mouse button is not being pressed.*

It is a common belief in art and design that the first line is always the hardest one to draw. However, unless you are a pure minimalist, you may want more than just straight lines.

Selecting and manipulating lines

Now that you have your first line on the stage, let's go over some basics about selection tools and manipulating lines.

The most common tool used, the Selection tool, is the black cursor arrow in the Tools panel. It is used to select objects as a whole on the stage. Select the Selection tool from the Tools panel. You should see your mouse cursor change into a black cursor arrow. Click one of your lines to select it. You will notice that the line will become highlighted.

You can also press the mouse button and drag to select multiple objects. When you drag, you will see a bounding box; any object within this bounding box will be selected.

If you place the cursor over the selected line, you will see the cursor change with four-way directional arrows appearing next to it (see Figure 3-5). This indicates that you can move the line. To move the line, press the mouse button and drag the line to a new location. Releasing the mouse button will "drop" the line at the new location. To deselect the line, simply click anywhere on the stage not occupied by another object. Do this now.

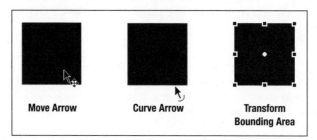

Move Arrow   **Curve Arrow**   **Transform Bounding Area**

Figure 3-5. The move and curve arrows, and the transform bounding area

Again, when you are moving an object using the selection tools, you can press and hold down the Shift key to constrain the movement of the object to 45-degree increments.

With your line deselected, again place your mouse cursor over the line. Do not click the mouse button to select it. You will notice the cursor again changes, with a small arc shape appearing next to the cursor arrow as shown in Figure 3-5. This indicates that you can manipulate the curve of the line. To do this, press the mouse button and drag the line. You will see the line form a curve.

The next tool that you will use quite often is the Transform tool, which allows you to scale, rotate, and skew objects. Select the Transform tool from the Tools panel and select one of your lines. You will notice a bounding box with eight control points appear, as shown in Figure 3-5.

The control points at each corner of the bounding box can be used to scale both the height and width of the object at the same time. The control points that appear on the lines in between each corner are used to manipulate the height and width separately, with the points along the horizontal manipulating the object's height and the points along the vertical controlling the width.

When placing the mouse over these control points, you should see two-way directional arrows that indicate you can scale the object (see Figure 3-6). To scale, press the mouse button and drag the control point. Release the mouse to set the new size.

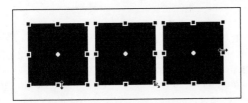

Figure 3-6.
The scale cursor

If you mouse over the lines of the bounding box, you will notice the cursor change to two arrows pointing in opposite directions, as shown in Figure 3-7. This indicates that you can skew the object. Just like you did when scaling, press the mouse button and drag to skew the object.

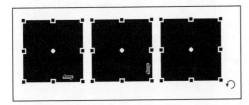

Figure 3-7.
The skew and rotate cursors

Lastly, you can use the Transform tool to rotate an object. In order to rotate the object, place the mouse cursor close to the outside edge one of the control points on the corner of the bounding box. You will see the cursor change to include a small circle arrow next to the cursor arrow (see Figure 3-7). Again, press the mouse button and drag to rotate the object.

The other tools used for selecting and manipulating objects are the Subselection tool, the Lasso tool, and the 3D Rotation tool. We will introduce these tools where appropriate throughout the rest of this book.

The Pencil tool

The Pencil tool works, as its name suggests, in much the same way a pencil works. It allows you to draw freeform lines using your mouse or other pointing devices such as a graphics tablet.

The Pencil tool works in three different modes: Straighten, Smooth, and Ink (see Figure 3-8). Each mode affects the final outcome of the shape you draw and is there to assist you in creating cleaner lines.

- Straighten mode straightens lines and angles you draw.
- Smooth mode smoothes lines and angles you draw.
- Ink mode leaves the lines you draw unchanged.

Figure 3-8.
Straighten, Smooth, and Ink options

To draw using the Pencil tool, select it from the Tools panel. You should see your mouse cursor turn into a little pencil icon. Click and drag to draw your line. Try changing the Pencil tool mode to see how the lines it creates are affected. As was the case with the Line tool, holding down the Shift key while drawing a line with the Pencil tool will constrain the line to either a horizontal or vertical path.

Drawing shapes

Shapes are made from closed paths. A **closed path** is simply a path consisting of three or more points, where one of these points serves as both the beginning and the end of the path. Closed paths, in addition to having a stroke, can be filled with color. This color is known as the fill. Flash provides some tools for drawing the most common shapes: rectangles, ovals, polygons, and stars.

Anatomy of a shape

Shapes are comprised of two primary parts. In Flash these two parts are known as strokes and fills. You have already been using the Line and Pencil tools to create line segments. Ultimately these line segments can be closed to create shapes. When color is applied to the segment, it is referred to as a **stroke**.

The second part of a shape is a byproduct of closing the path. When a path is closed, you are then able to work with all of the area that exists within the path. When color is applied to the inside of a shape, it is referred to as the **fill**. For example, when you create a square, the stroke is the outline of that square and the fill is the inside of the square.

These two elements of a shape can be colored and manipulated independently from one another. Figure 3-9 demonstrates the concept of the stroke and the fill in terms of a total shape.

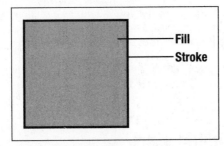

Figure 3-9. Stroke and fill of a shape

Drawing squares and rectangles

If you want to draw a square or rectangle, the quickest way to do it is by using the Rectangle tool. Select the Rectangle tool from the Tools panel. You should see the mouse cursor change into a set of crosshairs. Take a look at the Property inspector. Notice at the bottom a section titled Rectangle Options, as shown in Figure 3-10. You can add rounded corners to your rectangles by changing the values in this section. If you can't find the Rectangle tool, press R to toggle the Oval tool to the Rectangle tool.

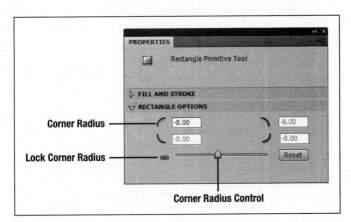

Figure 3-10. Rectangle options

Press the mouse button and drag out a rectangle on the stage. Now use the Selection tool to select the rectangle you just drew. Notice that the Rectangle Options area is no longer available to you. If you want to change the roundness of the corners of your rectangle, you will need to delete the rectangle and start again. We will show you a way around this a little later.

Drawing ovals, donuts, and pie shapes

The Oval tool allows you to draw all things round: Ovals (circles), donuts, and pie shapes. Select the Oval tool from the Tools panel, and again you will see the cursor change into a set of crosshairs. In the Property inspector you will notice a section called Oval Options. The options in this section can be used to draw donuts and pie shapes. If you cannot find the Oval tool, press O to toggle the Oval tool on in place of the Rectangle tool.

Just as before, press the mouse button and drag out an oval shape. Use the Selection tool to select your oval, and again you will see that the Oval Options area is not available in the Property inspector.

Drawing polygons and stars

What is a polygon? If you were a little distracted in geometry don't worry—so were we. A polygon is basically a shape with three or more sides (or a closed plane figure bound by three or more line segments). A star is uh . . . a little bit more complicated—look it up on Wikipedia, you'll see what we mean. Besides—you know—it's a *star*.

What then is a polystar exactly? It's a made-up thing Adobe used to combine two similar tools into one and it's a lot of fun. Regardless of definition, this is the tool for drawing them. We'll cover the basics here but by all means experiment and have fun.

To draw a polygon, follow these similar steps:

1. Select the PolyStar tool from the Tools panel. You'll notice an Options button in the Tool Settings area of the Property inspector. Click this to launch the dialog shown in Figure 3-11.

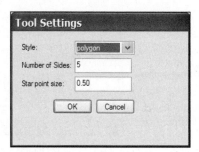

Figure 3-11.
Polystar Tool Settings dialog

2. Use the Style drop-down to select polygon. Choose a number of sides (three will make a triangle, four will make a square, etc.).

> The Star point size *setting has no effect when the* polygon *style is selected.*

3. Drag on the stage, and a polygon with the number of sides you selected will be drawn there. If you chose a large number of sides, you may wind up with a shape that resembles a circle. Experiment and have fun!

To draw a star, follow these similar steps:

1. Select the PolyStar tool from the Tools panel. Again, you'll notice an Options button in the Tool Settings area of the Property inspector. Click this to launch the dialog shown in Figure 3-11.

2. Use the Style drop-down to select star. Choose a number of sides. For the star style this really means number of points, and the Star point size setting here has a huge impact on the shape you get. Setting number of sides to 3 and point size to .01 will render a shape resembling a modern wind turbine, whereas those same three sides with a point size of 1 will look almost like a triangle.

3. Drag on the stage, and a star with the number of sides you selected will be drawn there. Experiment and have fun!

The primitive tools

You may have noticed that after drawing your rectangles and ovals the options are no longer available in the Property inspector. This is somewhat of an inconvenience if you decide at a later time that you want to change the radius of a rounded corner or the inner radius of your donut.

Let me introduce now the Rectangle Primitive tool and Oval Primitive tool. The **primitive tools** maintain the options you set in the Property inspector and make them available for editing after creation. The primitive tools also draw your shapes as **primitive objects**, meaning they are on separate planes and can be arranged in front or behind other objects on the stage. Other than that, they work in much the same way as objects created by the Rectangle and Oval tools.

Selecting and manipulating shapes

Once you've created some shapes on the stage, you will more than likely need to select them so you can move them around and make any necessary changes. We've already covered the Selection tool and Transform tool. These tools work in pretty much the same way with shapes, except that you can select both the stroke and the fill of a shape. Two things to make note of: Simply clicking the fill once will only select the fill. If you want to select both the fill and the stroke, double-click the fill of the shape.

Clicking a stroke once will select all segments in between two corner points. This means that if you click the stroke of a square, you will select only the stroke of the side you clicked because each point in a square is a corner point. If a curve point appears between two corner points, the two segments that make up the curve will be selected. Clicking a circle once will select the full path because all of the points in a circle are curve points. In order to select the full path of a square, simply double-click its stroke.

The next tool that can be used for selection is the Lasso tool. At times you may want to make a selection that doesn't conform to a perfect square. This might be a section of a shape, or it could be a group of items mixed in with other items. The Lasso tool allows you to hand-draw the bounds of your selection, as shown in Figure 3-12.

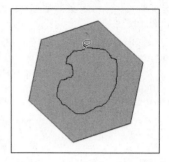

Figure 3-12.
Lasso tool selection

Early in this chapter you learned that shapes are just a collection of points. These points can be manipulated in order to change the path that defines a shape. This is one of the many uses of the Subselection tool, depicted as a white cursor arrow in the Tools panel.

Draw a polygon on the stage using the PolyStar tool. Click the Subselection tool in the Tools panel to select it and place the cursor over the path of the polygon. Notice there is a small black box that appears next to the mouse arrow, as shown in Figure 3-13. This indicates you are selecting a path. Click the path to select it.

Figure 3-13.
Polygon with path selection
showing black square

Once the path has been selected, notice little white squares at each joint in the polygon; these are the anchor points defining the polygon's shape. Place the mouse arrow over one of the points of the polygon. The mouse arrow shows a small white box next to it. This is the indicator that you are selecting a point on a path.

When you click a point to select it, the white square changes to a solid-colored square. The color of the square will depend upon the outline color set for the layer the polygon is on. Press the mouse button and drag the point to move it. Notice the shape changes.

The Subselection tool works a little bit differently for the Rectangle Primitive and Oval Primitive tools. For the Rectangle Primitive tool, dragging a point will manipulate the corner radius of the rectangle as shown in Figure 3-14.

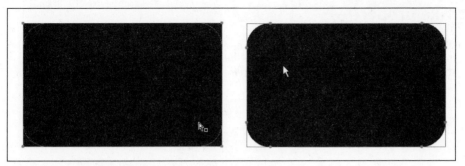

Figure 3-14. Corner radius points

For the Oval Primitive tool, there are three points. One is at the center point of the circle and controls the inner radius of the circle. The other two points, depending upon the Oval Option settings, appear to be one point along the edge of the circle, usually at the 90 degree or three o'clock position. These points control the start angle and end angle of the circle and can be move to create pie shapes (see Figure 3-15).

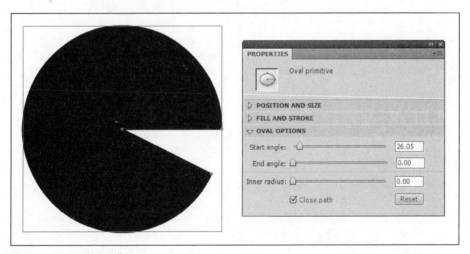

Figure 3-15. Angle handles

Strokes and fills

Now that you know how to create and edit the paths of lines and shapes, it's time to move on to editing the strokes and fills of your shapes. You may remember that the stroke of a shape is the visible outline of that shape, and the fill of a shape is the color that appears inside of the shape.

Stroke properties

At times you may require a solid hairline. At other times you may want to make a statement with a nice bold dotted or dashed line. All of this can be achieved by editing a stroke's properties in the Property inspector (see Figure 3-16).

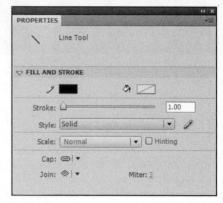

Figure 3-16.
Property inspector

The best way to take a look at how a stroke's properties affect its appearance is with a star shape. Create one on the stage by using the PolyStar tool and changing the PolyStar tool's Style setting to allow you to draw stars.

1. Select the PolyStar tool from the Tools panel.

2. In the Property inspector under Tool Settings, click the Options button to bring up the Tool Settings window.

3. Select star as the Style setting and click the OK button to close the Tool Settings window.

4. Drag out a star shape. You can hold down the Shift key while dragging out the star shape to constrain the rotation.

5. Select the star's stroke by double-clicking it. Remember, clicking once will only select one of the line segments of the star since all of the star's points are corner points.

6. In the Property inspector under Fill and Stroke, change the value of the Stroke property to 5. Notice that this changes the thickness of your star's stroke.

7. Skip down to the bottom of the Property inspector where it says Cap, Join, and Miter. These settings control the shape of the stroke at each point. **Cap** refers to the shape of the cap that is added to the ends of an open path. **Join** is the shape of the joint between two line segments.

8. Set Join to each of the three options to see how they affect the look of your star's points.

9. Set Join to Miter if it isn't already set to this option.

10. You will now see that the Miter value is editable. The Miter property controls the size of the miter. Set this property to 0 and then set it to 8 to see its effect.

11. Click the Style drop-down and select Dotted. You will see that your stroke has changed to a dotted line. You can click the Custom button to edit each style's options and further refine the look of your stroke.

> The term **miter**, as discussed in the previous example, refers to the joining of two line segments into a single joint. Flash uses the miter settings to allow designers to create pointed or beveled joints when two segments join at an angle.

The Scale option controls how the stroke scales when your artwork is converted into a Library item. You can have the stroke not scale, scale horizontally only, scale vertically only, or scale both horizontally and vertically. We will discuss the Library in more detail in Chapter 4.

The last property is Hinting. At times when you are creating shapes with curves or odd angles, you will notice the stroke gets a little fuzzy. This often occurs with a thin line when it is in between pixels. By enabling Hinting, Flash will adjust the line's anchor points to fall on full pixels, preventing the lines from becoming fuzzy.

Color properties and fills

There are several avenues to take when setting colors in Flash. For some it can be a little confusing. The good news is whichever route you take, the end result is the same. You may have noticed two of the ways of changing colors as you've gone through this chapter: color pickers for stroke color and fill color appear in both the Tools panel and the Property inspector. You can use either one of these two quickly to change the color of your artwork. The stroke color picker is depicted with a little pencil icon and the fill color picker is depicted with a paint bucket icon (see Figure 3-17).

Figure 3-17.
Color pickers

Clicking either one of these color pickers will bring up a Color palette with web-safe color swatches you can choose from. You can also use the mouse to sample any color on the screen. Yes, if you really like the gray used for the Flash interface, you can sample that color too. NICE!

You will also see options to enter a hex value to set color, as well as set the transparency or alpha of the color. If you want a little more control over your color selection, you can click the Colors icon in the Color palette, which is represented by a multicolored circle. This will bring up the Colors dialog with a variety of different palettes, color wheels, and color spectrums to choose from.

Lastly, if you want to clear the fill or stroke color, you can click the No Color button, depicted by a white square with a red diagonal line going through it.

The Color panel

Another way of choosing colors is with the Color panel. If the Color panel is not already open, you can open it by selecting Window ➤ Color in the menu bar or by pressing Shift+F9.

Again, you will see the color pickers for the stroke and fill. If you click the pencil icon, you will make the stroke active, and any color settings you set in the Color panel will be applied to the stroke color. The same goes for clicking the paint bucket icon.

Under the color pickers for the stroke and fill, you will see three more icons (see Figure 3-18). One should look familiar; it is the No Color button. The other two, which are also available under the color pickers in the Tools panel, are the Black and White button and the Swap Colors button.

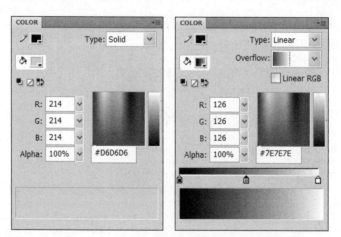

Figure 3-18. The Color panel. On the right, the Color panel has the gradient options activated.

The Black and White button resets the fill and stroke colors to their default values, black stroke and white fill. The Swap Colors button does just as its name suggests: it swaps the fill and stroke colors, so the fill color becomes the stroke color, and the stroke color becomes the fill color.

To set your colors you have several options. You can click the color picker, set the RGB values for the color, set the hex value for the color, or select the color from the color spectrum. You can also set the alpha transparency of the color by specifying a percentage, where 100% is opaque and 0% is completely transparent.

Next, notice the Type drop-down. This is where you can specify the stroke or fill type. The options you have here are None, Solid, Linear, Radial, and Bitmap. None and Solid are pretty self-explanatory. Linear and Radial are types of gradients. You would use Bitmap if you need separate pixels that can be manipulated individually. Bitmaps will be covered in more detail in the next chapter.

Select Linear from the Type drop-down, and you will notice a gradient bar appear. You will use this bar to define your color gradient. Under the bar you will see little arrow sliders with colored squares in them—this is where you set the colors in your gradient.

Click one of the arrow sliders and use the color spectrum to select a new color. You can set the color using any of the options available to you in the Color palette. You can also double-click the arrow slider to set its color as well.

To add another color to the gradient bar, simply click anywhere on the bar there isn't already a slider arrow. You can move any of the slider arrows by dragging it. Doing this adjusts the length of the gradient transition from one color to the next.

The Overflow drop-down gives you options for specifying how the gradient fills to the edges of a shape. The Extend option will extend the first and last color to the edge of the shape. The Reflect option will start another gradient using the adjacent color as the start color (A ➤ B ➤ B ➤ A). The Repeat option will simply repeat the gradient all the way to the edge (A ➤ B ➤ A ➤ B).

The Panel Options button, located in the top-right corner of the panel, gives you two options. The first is the ability to change the Color Mode setting for the Color panel. The default is RGB (red, green, blue), which most people are familiar with. The other is HSB (hue, saturation, and brightness). The second option is Add Swatch, which allows you to add the current color to the Swatches panel.

The Swatches panel

The Swatches panel is another tool you can use to set colors, and it consists of a collection of color swatches called a **color set**. The Swatches panel makes it easy to quickly select predefined colors. To open the Swatches panel, select Window ➤ Swatches or press Ctrl+F9 (Cmd+F9 on the Mac).

As shown in Figure 3-19, the default colors in the Swatches panel are web-safe colors and a couple of gradients. The Swatches panel also allows you to add your own color swatches and save them for use later.

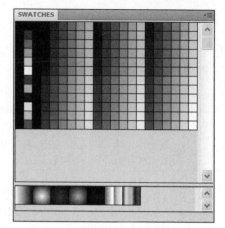

Figure 3-19.
The Swatches panel

There are several ways to add colors to the Swatches panel. To add the currently selected color to the Swatches panel, you can click the Color Panel Options button and select Add Swatch.

1. Open the Color panel (Window ➤ Color).

2. Click the paint bucket icon to select the fill color.

3. Select your favorite color by editing the RGB or hex values, or select your color from the color spectrum.

4. Click the Color Panel Options button and select Add Swatch as shown in Figure 3-20.

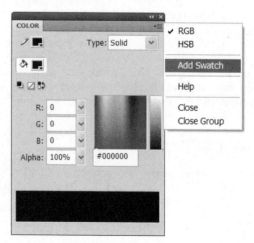

Figure 3-20.
Selecting the Add Swatch option from the Color Panel Options menu

5. Open the Swatches panel. Notice that your color was added to the collection of color swatches. You may need to resize the Swatches panel or scroll down to see your newly created swatch. This swatch will also be available when using the color pickers in the Color panel or Tools panel.

6. In the Swatches panel, notice that the far-right column is all gray. This is an empty area of the Color panel. Position your mouse over this gray area, and your mouse cursor should change into a paint bucket (see Figure 3-21). This indicates you can click to add the currently selected color. Click the gray area to add another color swatch.

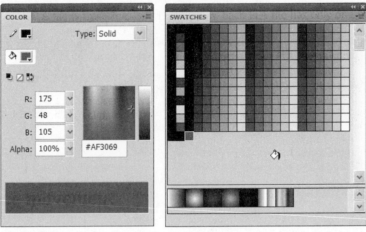

Figure 3-21. How the Color panel (left) can be used to add a swatch to the Swatches panel (right)

7. You should now have two custom color swatches in your Swatches panel. Position the mouse cursor over one of these newly created swatches. Your mouse cursor should change into the eyedropper icon. This indicates that you can select the color swatch. Click the color swatch to select it.

8. To delete a color swatch, select a color swatch in the Swatches panel, click the Options button at the top right of the Swatches panel, and select Delete Swatch.

9. To duplicate a color swatch, select your other color swatch in the Swatches panel. Click the Swatches Panel Options button and select Duplicate Swatch.

10. If you want to set the colors back to the default set, select Load Default Colors from the Swatches Panel Options menu.

If you add swatches to the Swatches panel, they will be lost when you close Flash. If you want to keep your colors for use later, you can save your color set by selecting Save Colors from the Swatches Panel Options menu. Provide a file name and location to save the file.

The next time you open Flash, you can load these colors by selecting Add Colors or Replace Colors from the Swatches Panel Options menu. If you don't want to have to load your colors every time you open Flash, you can choose Save as Default, and your color set will load automatically when Flash is opened.

If you want to start with a clean color set, you can select Clear Colors from the Swatches Panel Options menu. This will allow you to create a completely custom color set that doesn't include the swatches already included in the default set. These sets can then be added into the Swatches panel as needed.

The Paint Bucket tool

Now that you've learned how to choose colors, let's take a look at the tools for applying those colors to your artwork. The Paint Bucket tool allows you to fill shapes with color and can be employed to quickly fill multiple shapes with the same color. You can use it with solid fills, gradients, and bitmap fills. (We will cover bitmap fills in Chapter 4.)

1. Click the Black and White button in the Tools panel to set your stroke and fill to the default colors.

2. Using the Oval tool, draw three ovals on the stage. Notice that the ovals are created with a black stroke and a white fill.

3. Select the Paint Bucket tool and using one of the fill color pickers on the toolbar, as shown in Figure 3-22, to change the color of your fill.

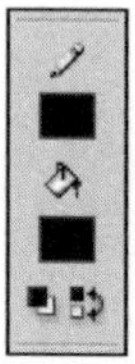

Figure 3-22.
Fill color pickers
on the tool bar

4. Using the Paint Bucket tool, click the fill of each of your three ovals to apply the new color.

5. The Paint Bucket tool can also be used to fill in empty shapes as well. Click the Selection tool and select the fill of one of your ovals. Press Delete to delete the fill.

6. Select the Paint Bucket tool again and click inside of the oval whose fill you just deleted. Again, you will notice your new color has been applied to your fill.

7. You can apply gradient fills to your shapes with the Paint Bucket tool as well. In the Color panel, select Linear from the Type drop-down and set the start and end color for your gradient, as shown in Figure 3-23.

8. Click the fill of one of your ovals. Notice that the gradient is applied horizontally across your oval, and the gradient is evenly distributed. If you want more control over the direction of your gradient and distribution of colors, you can press the mouse button inside the oval where you want your gradient to start and drag in the direction you want your gradient to run. You will notice a line that runs from your starting point to the Paint Bucket tool. This line indicates the direction your gradient will run.

Figure 3-23.
The Gradient Color panel
can be used to apply
gradient fills to shapes.

9. Release the mouse button to set your gradient.

10. You can drag the end point of your gradient out past the bounds of your shape. Click inside of the oval that is in middle of your three ovals and drag out your gradient to one of the other three ovals. Release the mouse button in the center of the oval.

11. The Lock Fill modifier, depicted by a gradient bar with a lock on it, is located at the bottom of the Tools panel (see Figure 3-24). The Lock Fill modifier locks the gradient you just dragged out and will treat your gradient as if it filled the whole stage. This allows you to apply gradients across multiple shapes on the stage. Click each of the ovals to set their new fill. Try this with five or more shapes on the stage to better see the transition.

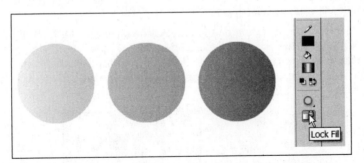

Figure 3-24. Three circles with Lock Fill applied, linking their fills

12. Click the Lock Fill modifier again to deselect it.

Another modifier for the Paint Bucket tool is the Gap Size modifier (see Figure 3-25). Using this modifier you can fill in open paths that have small gaps in them. This works well for hand-drawn shapes that might not quite be closed.

Figure 3-25.
Gap Size
modifier button

13. Select the fill of one of your ovals and delete it, leaving just the stroke.

14. Using the Selection tool, drag out a selection to select a small portion of the stroke, between 5 to 10 pixels. Delete this selection to create a small gap in the stroke, as shown in Figure 3-26.

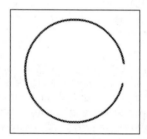

Figure 3-26.
Oval with gap in stroke

15. Using the Paint Bucket tool, click inside of the circle with the gap in its stroke. Notice the fill color was not applied.

16. Hold down the mouse button on the Gap Size modifier button. You will see four options pop up: Don't Close Gaps, Close Small Gaps, Close Medium Gaps, and Close Large Gaps, as shown in Figure 3-27. Select the Close Large Gaps option. You will see the icon for the Gap Size modifier change from a closed circle to a circle with a gap in it.

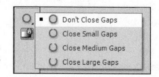

Figure 3-27.
Gap Size modifier options

17. Click inside of the oval from which you just you deleted a section of the stroke. This time the color is applied.

18. Save your file (File ➤ Save) as 3circles.fla. You will continue using this file in the next section.

The Ink Bottle tool

In much the same way the Paint Bucket tool works for fills, the Ink Bottle tool is used to apply stokes to shapes. Whereas the Paint Bucket tool is strictly used for applying color, the Ink Bottle tool can be used to apply stroke properties such as stroke weight, style, and color.

The Ink Bottle tool is grouped with the Paint Bucket tool in the Tools panel. If you look at the Paint Bucket tool icon, you will notice a small black triangle in the bottom-right corner. You will also notice this same black triangle on some of the other tools in the Tools panel. The black triangle indicates that there are tools grouped together in a fly-out. To access these tools, simply click and hold down the mouse button on the triangle icon, and the fly-out will appear.

1. If it is not already open, open the file 3circles.fla that you were using in the examples in the preceding section.

2. Select the Ink Bottle tool from the Tools panel. If the icon for this tool is not showing, click and hold down the mouse button on the Paint Bucket tool to access it (see Figure 3-28).

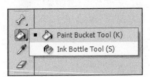

Figure 3-28.
Ink Bottle tool fly-out

3. In the Property inspector you will see all of your stroke properties. Change the stroke color, set the stroke width to 5 px, and select Dashed from the Style drop-down.

4. Click one of your oval shapes. You will see the stroke change for the shape.

The Gradient Transform tool

The Gradient Transform tool is used to scale and rotate the gradient fill of a shape. When you select a gradient fill with the Gradient Transform tool, you will see a couple of transform handles that allow you to edit the way your gradient looks (see Figure 3-29).

At the center is a small white circle. Dragging this circle will move the gradient center point and shift your fill. The two lines indicate where the start and end colors of your gradient are at 100%. Along one of the lines is a white square with an arrow in it. Dragging this square will scale the transition of your gradient. At the end of the same line you will see a circular arrow; dragging this transform handle will rotate your gradient.

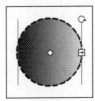

Figure 3-29.
Gradient Transform
tool transform handles

The Kuler panel

If you find it hard to make it through your work day without a small dose of the social Web, the Kuler panel (shown in Figure 3-30) is your ticket to getting that fix. As the About section of the Kuler panel states, "kuler is an online community for colors and inspiration, to explore, create, and share color themes." This can be an excellent resource for you right inside of the Flash IDE in putting Color palettes together for your projects.

The Kuler panel makes available an extensive collection of user-created Color palettes that you can browse and search through. When you find palettes you like, you can save them for easy access. You can also use the color wheel to create your own palettes and save them locally or to the kuler web site.

The Kuler panel requires an Internet connection to access the kuler web site but does allow you to save your favorite Color palettes locally and even transfer those Color palettes to the Swatches panel.

The Kuler panel can be accessed by selecting Window ➤ Extensions ➤ Kuler.

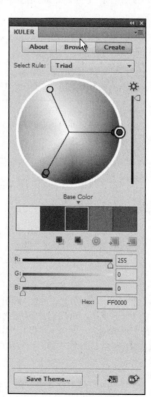

Figure 3-30.
The Kuler panel

Advanced drawing

Now that you are familiar with the basic tools and drawing skills in CS4 Flash, let's look at some more advanced topics that will let you become a Flash artist extraordinaire, or at least put you on the right "path," pardon the pun.

The anatomy of a path

As mentioned previously, a path is a collection of two or more points connected by lines. The points that make up a path are referred to as anchor points. The area between two anchor points on a path is known as a segment. The anchor point in between two segments on a path is known as a joint.

Each point within a path can be either a corner point, a curve point, or a corner-curve point. The type of points that make up a segment determines the shape of the line between two points and the shape of the joint between two segments.

- **Corner points**: These create straight lines and sharp corners between segments. The four points in a square are all examples of corner points.

- **Curve points**: These create curved lines and curved corners between segments. Manipulating curve points affects the segments on either side of the point. This means that when you change the curve of one segment, it affects the curve of the opposite segment. This creates a nice, fluid transition between the two sections. The four points that make up a circle are all examples of curve points.

- **Corner-curve points**: As you might guess, these are a combination of the two preceding types of points. They are used when you want to independently control the curve of each line segment.

When you select a curve point with the Subselection tool, you get curve handles that are used to manipulate the shape of the curve, as shown in Figure 3-31. You can manipulate the curve handles by moving the tangent points at the end of each curve handle. Each curve handle corresponds to one of the segments adjacent to the selected curve point. For corner-curve points, you will see only one curve handle. Yes Martha, even curves have corners.

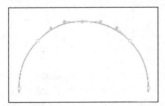

Figure 3-31.
This figure represents a rounded path with curved corner points.

The Pen tool

The Pen tool is used in Flash to create complex paths. The Pen tool gives you more control over the shape of a path during and more notably after creation. This gives the Pen tool a considerable advantage over the Pencil tool in creating paths, especially when "tracing" an image for illustration. Even if you feel you have more control creating shapes using the Pencil tool and a stylus or you don't plan on doing much tracing, it is important to get comfortable with the concepts we describe here, as they are the basis for working with and manipulating points of other shapes as well.

1. Open a new Flash file (File ➤ New ➤ Flash File (ActionScript 3.0)).

2. Click the Black and White button in the Tools panel (see Figure 3-32) to change your colors to the default colors.

Figure 3-32.
Black and
White color
defaults button

3. Select the Pen tool from the Tools panel. It is depicted as a fountain pen tip (see Figure 3-33).

Figure 3-33.
Pen icon

4. Click the stage to set the first point of your path.

5. Create two more points on the stage by clicking to set your points. Create an open triangle shape with your three points, as shown in Figure 3-34. Keep the Pen tool selected—you aren't finished creating your path just yet. You will see the shape of the path you are creating as you add points. So far, you have just created three corner points. Notice the joint created by the second point is sharp.

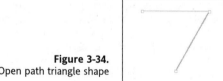

Figure 3-34.
Open path triangle shape

6. Create another point on the stage, but this time instead of simply clicking, hold down the mouse button and drag. You will see a curved path is created. Drag out a curve that you are happy with and release the mouse button to set the point.

7. You can edit the path while you are creating it by using modifier keys. Holding down the Ctrl key (Cmd on Mac) will allow you to move points. The mouse cursor will change into a black arrowhead. Do this now and move some of your points around. Move the curve handles to change the shape of the curve you just created. Notice that moving one curve handle also changes the curve handle on the opposite side of the anchor point. You just created a curve point.

8. Create another point on the stage and again hold down the mouse button and drag out a curve. At times you will want to create a straight line after you create a curve. To do this you need to create a corner-curve point. Place the mouse over the point you've just created. A small "V" shape will appear next to the pen cursor. Clicking the point will convert the point to a corner-curve point. Notice your anchor point now has only one curve handle (see Figure 3-35).

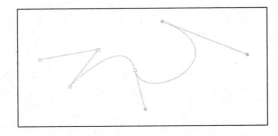

Figure 3-35.
Corner-curve point

9. Click the stage to create another point. The line that you just created is straight.

10. Now let's back up two points. Counting the point you just created, follow the path back to the third point (it will be the curve point you created earlier). Remember that when you moved the curve handles on this point, both curve points moved in tandem. If you want to unlink the two curve handles so they can be moved independently, hold down the Alt key (Option on the Mac). The cursor will change into a "V" shape. With the Alt key held down, drag the curve handle to move it. The curve handle now moves independent of the curve handle on the opposite side of the point and only affects the curve on the same side of the point as the handle you moved (see Figure 3-36).

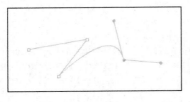

Figure 3-36.
Independent curve handles

11. The Alt key can also be used to convert a curve point to a corner point, or a corner point to a curve point. You do this by holding down the Alt key and clicking the point you want to convert. Click the curve point now to convert it to a corner point. You now have a sharp corner (see Figure 3-37).

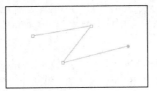

Figure 3-37.
After conversion to a corner point

12. Back up two more points to the second point you created, the peak of your "tri-angle." Holding down the Alt key, click, and drag the point to drag out the curve handles. You now have a curve point (see Figure 3-38).

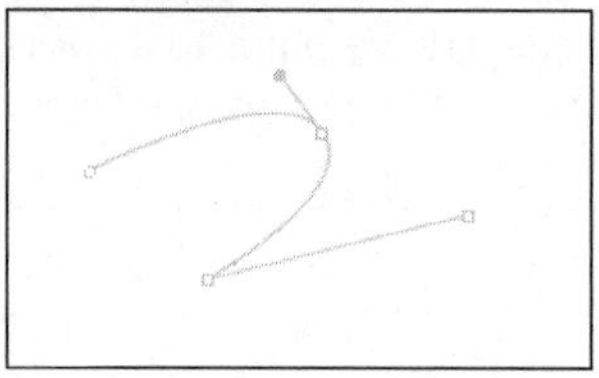

Figure 3-38.
After conversion
to a curve point

13. To close off a path, place the mouse over the first point on your path. You will see a small circle appear next to the Pen cursor, as shown in Figure 3-39. This indicates that you are closing the path. Click the point to finish off your path.

Figure 3-39.
Close path cursor

Manipulating paths

So you just learned how to use the Pen tool to create a complex path and how to edit the points and paths during creation. What if you want to edit the path after you've created it? The same tools you accessed using the modifier keys during the creation of your path are also available in the Tools panel.

The first tool is the Subselection tool, which we covered earlier in this chapter. You can use the Subselection tool to move your anchor points and curve handles to change the shape of your path. The same modifier keys you used earlier are available when editing paths with the Subselection tool.

The next tool is the Convert Anchor Point tool. You can access this tool by holding down the mouse button on the Pen tool icon to bring up the fly-out. The Convert Anchor Point tool is used to convert your curve points to corner points, and vice versa. It works in the same manner as the Alt modifier key used earlier.

The other two tools are the Add Anchor Point tool and Delete Anchor Point tool, accessible in the same fly-out under the Pen tool. As their names suggest, these tools are used for adding and deleting points on your path.

To add a point, select the Add Anchor Point tool and click where you want to add a point on your path. Again, you have access to the modifier keys to edit the point using this tool. To delete a point, select the Delete Anchor Point tool and click the point you want to delete.

Summary

In this chapter we covered an incredible amount of ground with respect to creating shapes with vector tools in Flash. This should come as no surprise since Flash is a vector drawing tool. You learned about the following topics:

- Vector vs. bitmap
- Drawing modes
- Object drawing
- Drawing tools
- Drawing shapes
- Strokes and fills
- Color properties
- Manipulating lines

3

In the previous chapter we took an in-depth look into the creation of vector-based graphics using the Flash IDE. Though Flash is natively a vector drawing program, it is certainly not limited to that type of asset. Depending on the need, Flash specialists may find that they want to incorporate other types of external assets such as bitmaps, sounds, and videos.

In the first half of this chapter we will focus on how Flash works with bitmap graphics. As discussed in Chapter 3, bitmaps offer a greater degree of visual detail over their vector counterparts. Therefore, this type of graphic is very useful when dealing with items like photographs or video game sprites. And, when used in tandem with vector-based images, bitmaps will help establish a more effective user experience.

You will also learn how to create symbols from graphical elements and manage them with the Library panel. The symbol is one of the key ingredients in any Flash project and could be considered the cornerstone of the Flash design process. Symbols allow you to organize and implement graphical elements with a greater degree of efficiency. With symbols you can easily replicate graphics that not only reduce the overall file size of your SWF, but also make it easier to update your working file.

Let's get started with using bitmaps in Flash.

Using bitmaps in your Flash projects

Bitmaps are an integral part of any application. In fact most, professional-grade user interfaces such as video games, business-tier software applications, and even operating systems all use bitmaps as the primary graphical assets for their user experience. Though Flash does not natively possess the power to create bitmaps—as a program like Photoshop would—it is certainly poised to work with dozens of different industry-standard bitmap file types. In addition, the manner in which Flash does work with bitmaps is virtually seamless when considering the workflow of many design/development processes.

Importing external bitmaps into Flash

To begin working with bitmaps in Flash, all you need to do is simply import that bitmap to either the stage or Library panel. Fortunately, Flash makes this task quite easy. As shown in Figure 4-1, you can import an external asset by selecting File ➤ Import.

You will notice that a fly-out menu appears with the following four options:

- Import to Stage
- Import to Library
- Open External Library
- Import Video

From these four choices you have the ability to import quite a collection of external files ranging from bitmaps, to sounds, videos, and vector graphics. Giving the complete list at this time would probably do more harm than good. For now we will focus on importing bitmaps. And, when you get to Part 5 of this book, we will discuss importing other types of media such as sound and video.

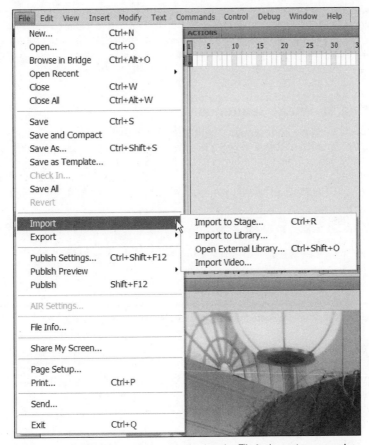

Figure 4-1. Bitmaps are easily imported using the File ➤ Import command.

Importing to the stage or library

If you select Import to Stage or Import to Library, you will get a File Open dialog that will enable you to browse for a rather hefty number of different file types. And you can select any graphical or audio file type that is included in the File of type drop-down menu. Once you select the item you want to import, you can complete the import by clicking OK. The only major difference in using Import to Stage and Import to Library is the destination of the imported file.

If you import an external asset to the stage, you can move it around and manipulate it as if you had drawn it within Flash. Well, this is not exactly true—the ability to manipulate an asset depends on the type of asset. Bitmaps will initially behave like bitmaps, vector shapes will behave like vector shapes, and so on. The point is, graphical assets that are imported to the stage are immediately available for use in the design of your application and offer similar functionality to those you create in Flash. Further, if an item is imported to the stage, it is automatically placed in the Library panel. More on that in a bit.

There are also some fairly intricate options used for importing other CS4 files from programs like Photoshop, Illustrator, and Fireworks. For more on CS4 integration, please see Using Imported Artwork found on the left side of Adobe's Using Flash CS4 companion website (http://help.adobe.com/en_US/Flash/10.0_UsingFlash/).

Importing an image sequence

When importing images to the stage, if you select a file that has a trailing number such as an_image_0.jpg and an_image_1.jpg, Flash will search for other assets in that directory with the same name. Trailing numbers are commonly used in the naming of frames in an image sequence or animation. If Flash detects that there are other items with the same name and an incrementing trailing number, it will open the dialog shown in Figure 4-2.

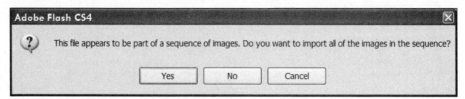

Figure 4-2. Flash automatically detects image sequences that could be animations.

Clicking Yes in this dialog will import all the images in the sequence. Again, Flash will be assuming that these images are associated with an image sequence or animation. Because of this it will not only import all the graphics associated with this sequence, but also place each image in its own sequential frame of the timeline. Basically, Flash will reconstruct an image-based animation simply by detecting a possible sequence.

More to come on animation in Chapter 6!

Opening an external library

Open External Library, the third import option available in Flash, allows you to open an external library. You can open the library of any other FLA file without opening the FLA itself. This becomes extremely useful for the management of reusable assets. As a Flash designer you could create an FLA file for containing groups of assets that you can use in future projects. For example, if you were a sprite designer in a Flash game development shop, you may have an FLA that contains nothing but a collection of bullet images. You might have another that contains a bunch of different spaceship graphics. Without question, using external libraries is extremely useful for project organization.

We realize that we have not discussed Import Video, the fourth option in the Import flyout menu. See Chapter 17 for a discussion of the Video Import Wizard.

Importing your first bitmap into Flash

Now, we'll take you through the steps for importing a few external items to the stage and Library panel. As discussed earlier, bitmaps can be an extremely valuable aid to any Flash project. Subsequently, Flash makes importing these bitmaps a walk in the park.

1. Create a new Flash file by selecting File ➤ New and choosing Flash File (ActionScript 3.0).

2. Select File ➤ Import ➤ Import to Stage.

3. Browse to the working directory for Chapter 4 and select the file art_BG001.jpg. Click Open.

You should immediately notice the image of a flower being placed on the stage similar to that in Figure 4-3.

Figure 4-3.
Images imported to the stage are
immediately available for use in Flash

We're not done yet. We need to import the counterparts for our first graphic. This time we will import them to the Library panel.

1. Select File ➤ Import ➤ Import to Library.

2. Browse to the working directory for Chapter 4 and select the files art_BG002.jpg and art_BG003.jpg. You can select both of these files simultaneously by holding down the Shift key and clicking both files.

3. Click Open.

You should now have one image on the stage and three different flower images in the Library panel. In order to view the contents of the Library panel, press Ctrl+L (or Cmd+L on a Mac) or select Window ➤ Library. This brings up the panel, where you will see the three imported files, as well as the one on the stage. Take notice how that graphic has been placed not only on the stage, but also in the Library panel (also shown in Figure 4-4).

Figure 4-4. Images imported to the stage are also placed in the Library panel.

Setting bitmap properties in the Library panel

From within the Library panel you can edit several properties of any bitmap image. To access the Bitmap Properties dialog, as shown in Figure 4-5, right-click (Windows) or Ctrl-click (Mac) on an image from within the Library panel and select Properties from the context menu. Go ahead and try this with one of the graphics in your current library.

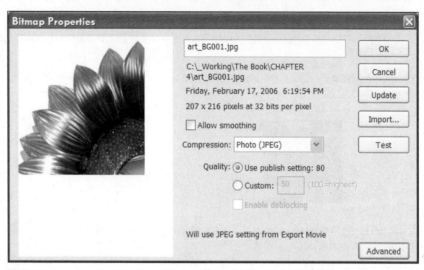

Figure 4-5. Custom compression and rendering properties can be set for each bitmap in the Library panel.

From within this dialog, designers have the ability to control the manner in which the bitmap renders. This can ultimately play a significant role in how the final application performs. Selecting the Allow smoothing check box improves the overall quality of bitmaps as they are scaled. Likewise you have the ability to set the compression of the bitmap.

There are two basic types of bitmap compression in the Bitmap Properties Compression drop-down.

- Photo (JPEG) is the default setting for bitmap compression in Flash. As the name indicates, this is the best option when working with photographic images. It offers several options to customize the compression quality.

  The following two options are available for Quality settings when the Photo (JPEG) option is selected:

  - Use publish setting uses the bitmap compression settings as determined in the Publish Settings dialog, which will be discussed in Chapter 18.

  - Custom allows you to select a number between 1 and 100 representing the quality of the image as a percentage. When you select this option, the Enable deblocking check box is made active. Selecting this will smooth the look of the bitmap's appearance.

- Lossless (PNG/GIF) actually does not discard any information from the image. This option is best when working with simple shapes and a minimal number of colors.

You can test how the bitmap will render by clicking the Test button after adjusting your settings.

From the Library panel's context menu, it is also possible to access an external editing program like Photoshop or Fireworks to edit bitmaps from within Flash. This is an extremely invaluable feature for Flash to have, as it is not a native bitmap editor itself. Having the ability to edit images in an external editor is basically like bringing all the features of that program into Flash. Follow these steps to edit an image externally:

1. Right-click the image in the Library panel.
2. From the context menu select Edit with.
3. When the Open External Editor dialog appears, browse to your favorite bitmap editing program and click Open.
4. The image will automatically be opened in the external editor. From here edit the image as needed and save it.

Once the image has been edited and saved in the external editor, it will automatically update its appearance in Flash.

Breaking apart bitmaps

Breaking apart bitmaps opens up a lot of useful functionality for working with them. Recall from earlier in this chapter that we said imported assets behave like any other asset you created in Flash. This feature actually proves the truth in our statement. When you break apart a bitmap, the bitmap is converted to a shape that effectively makes it editable using the Flash drawing tools. In addition, you have the ability to select the bitmap as a fill with the Eyedropper tool. This gives you the ability to use the bitmap as a fill for other shapes or as the fill color for tools used to create fills.

To break apart the bitmap, first select it on the stage. Then select Modify ➤ Break Apart. When the bitmap breaks apart, it will change to a hashed pattern similar to that of a selected vector shape, as shown in Figure 4-6.

Figure 4-6. Breaking apart bitmaps allows you to treat them as vector shapes.

Once the shape has been broken apart, there are a number of options that become available for further use. What actually occurs when bitmaps are broken apart is that the bitmap is converted to a vector shape with the bitmap's image applied as the fill color. You can then treat the shape itself as a vector shape, exactly as it would be had you drawn it with the Flash drawing tools. The bitmap fill is then tiled across the face of the shape.

The ability to use bitmaps as fills made its first appearance in Flash MX 2004 and over the years proved to be very useful. You can use bitmaps as the "color" for fills and stroke. Flash CS4 makes this process pretty easy. There is no special procedure for getting bitmaps ready to be applied to shapes. As soon as a bitmap is imported into Flash, it is able to be applied as a color.

Let's give this a whirl:

1. Select one of the Flash drawing tools (Rectangle, Oval, or Pen).

2. If it is not already accessible, open the Property inspector and select a new stroke color, as shown in Figure 4-7.

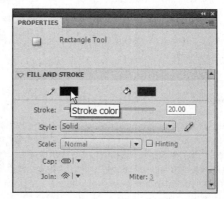

Figure 4-7.
To apply a bitmap to a stroke, you must first select the stroke color chip.

3. When the color picker opens, you will notice that any available bitmaps are displayed at the bottom, as in Figure 4-8. Select one of the imported bitmaps to use as your stroke color.

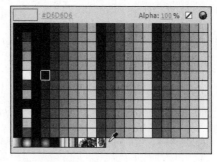

Figure 4-8.
Bitmaps appear as color options in the bottom of the color pickers.

4. Next, adjust the stroke to a value like 20. This will allow you to notice the bitmap pattern that has been applied to the stroke.

5. Draw a shape on the stage. You should have something that resembles Figure 4-9.

Figure 4-9.
Bitmaps can easily be applied to shapes as fill or stroke colors.

Using the Trace Bitmap feature

The Trace Bitmap feature in Flash allows designers to convert any bitmap image into a vector-based graphic. Though this sounds similar to breaking apart images, it is actually different. When you break apart a bitmap image, the image is just converted into a vector shape with the bitmap applied as a fill color. When you trace the bitmap, the bitmap is converted into many vector shapes that are created based on color. The benefits to this process are both decreased file size and increased vector editability.

> *We should point out here that tracing bitmaps that are very complex or not accurately adjusted in the Trace Bitmap settings can create an excessive number of vector shapes, resulting in a larger file size. You should take some time and tweak each trace to achieve the optimal results.*

Tracing bitmaps in Flash is extremely simple. Using the file we have been working with, let's walk through this process. You should have a couple different elements on your stage from previous examples. We will want to get rid of this excess before we begin.

1. Select Window ➤ Select All to select all elements on the current stage. Press Delete to delete all selected items.

2. From the Library panel select one of the bitmaps that you previously imported and drag it to the stage.

> *Dragging items from the Library panel to the stage does not remove them from the library; instead, it creates a copy of this item. This copy is known as an **instance**.*

3. With the Selection tool, make sure that the instance of your bitmap is selected. Then select Modify ➤ Bitmap ➤ Trace Bitmap. This will bring up the Trace Bitmap dialog, as shown in Figure 4-10.

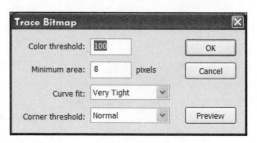

Figure 4-10.
The Trace Bitmap dialog allows you to define settings for an accurate trace.

4. Using Table 4-1 as a guide, adjust the parameters of the Trace Bitmap dialog to achieve optimal results.

5. Check your settings by clicking the Preview button. When you feel the settings are where they need to be, click OK to complete the process.

Table 4-1. The options in the Trace Bitmap dialog for tweaking the bitmap conversions settings

Parameter	Effect
Color threshold	This setting compares the color values of two adjacent pixels. If the difference in these values is less than the selected threshold value, the colors will be considered the same. Increasing the threshold ultimately decreases the number of colors.
Minimum area	This parameter sets the minimum, in pixels, of any shapes that are created. Therefore, if this option is set to 5, there will be no shapes created that are less han 5 pixels in size.
Curve fit	In the conversion process, many tiny squares are being converted into vectors (lines). This setting determines how closely the vector created conforms to the original bitmap pixels.
Corner threshold	This setting determines how sharp edges are treated, working in a manner similar to that of the Curve fit option. Because Flash is creating vectors (lines) from bitmaps (a checkerboard of square pixels), it needs a way to discern the edge of a pixel from an edge that exists in the graphic.

Once the bitmap is converted, it will be comprised of several vector shapes that represent the primary groups of color. Figure 4-11 gives an excellent look at how these colors have been grouped into independent vector shapes that can be modified like any other vector shape created in Flash.

Figure 4-11.
The Trace Bitmap feature converts the image into editable vector shapes.

Swapping bitmap images

Finally, you have the ability to substitute any bitmap on the stage with another that exists in the FLA's library. When a bitmap image on the stage has been selected, the Property inspector will change to accommodate bitmaps. As shown in Figure 4-12, you can click the Swap button to open the Swap Bitmap dialog.

> You can also click the Edit button (Figure 4-12) to automatically open a bitmap's default external editor.

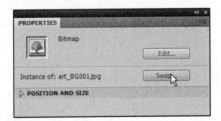

Figure 4-12.
The Swap button in the Property inspector allows you to switch between bitmap images.

The Swap Bitmap dialog, shown in Figure 4-13, allows designers to select from any bitmap that happens to be in the library.

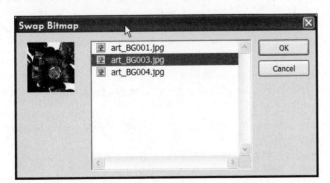

Figure 4-13.
Switch between images from within the Swap Bitmap dialog.

Through your work with bitmap images, you have been introduced to how Flash organizes assets into the library. In addition, you were briefly exposed to the idea that library items can be used over and over through the concept of instantiation. Now we will expand on both of these concepts by showing you how to use symbols and further organize them within the Library panel.

Using and organizing symbols

The concept of symbols is the cornerstone of Flash design and development. A **symbol** is a type of reusable asset that can be used throughout your Flash project. Any visual asset that is created or imported into Flash can be converted to a symbol. Once a symbol is created, it is added to the Library panel. As with other elements in the Library panel, you can create an unlimited number of instances of that symbol. (Instances are discussed later in this section.) Further, some symbols can be set up to be used with ActionScript.

The primary benefit to using symbols is the efficiency that is gained by creating an asset only once. Because all symbol instances are derived from one single symbol (also referred to as a **symbol definition**), the size and performance of the Flash movie are greatly optimized. Further, since symbols serve as blueprints for symbol instances, changes or updates to the symbol will propagate through all symbol instances.

Imagine you need to create an animation that involves dozens of snowflakes falling to the ground. By using symbols, you would only need one actual snowflake image. Once that image was converted to a symbol and available in the Library panel, you could make tens or hundreds of snowflakes from that single snowflake image.

Let's take a look at the types of symbols available.

Types of symbols

There are four types of symbols that are available to Flash designers, as outlined in the following list. In this chapter we will be discussing the first three, which are associated with graphic elements. Font symbols will be discussed in detail in Chapter 13.

- **Graphic symbols** constitute the most basic symbol type available for use with Flash. Graphics are used for creating simple graphic assets like background images. Graphics cannot be used with sound, video, interactivity, or animations involving an independent timeline. This reduced functionality is beneficial because it allows graphic symbols to be inherently smaller than buttons and movie clips.

- **Button symbols** are used to create simple interactive elements. This type of symbol offers a unique four-frame timeline for establishing different graphical representations for each state of the button.

- **Movie clip symbols** are the most widely used type of symbol. They have their own timelines, which can run independently of the main timeline. In addition, movie clips are capable of the full range of interactivity that is offered by the button symbol. The main timeline in Flash is actually an instance of a movie clip.

- **Font symbols** are employed to embed fonts into a Flash movie for use with ActionScript or other SWF files.

There is a fifth type of symbol, the sprite. **Sprites** can be thought of as a hybrid of the graphic and movie clip symbols. They are also often referred to as one-framed movie clips. The benefit of sprites is that the absence of a timeline reduces file size, but they still retain the interactive aspects of movie clips. Sprites are typically used only in ActionScript development.

Creating and managing symbols

Any one of the previously mentioned symbols can be created directly from the stage. The stage is typically the most logical place to create symbols as it is usually integrated within the workflow of the design process.

The quickest and easiest way to create a symbol is to simply convert a vector or bitmap that is located on the main stage to a symbol. The following example will get you started with creating various symbols:

1. Open ch04_02.fla. On the stage you should see both a vector-based red rectangle and one of the previously imported flower bitmaps.

2. Right-click (Windows) or Ctrl-click (Mac) the image of the flower. From the context menu select Convert to Symbol. The Convert to Symbol dialog, shown in Figure 4-14, will display the default options for defining a symbol.

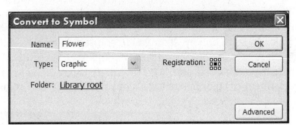

Figure 4-14. The Convert to Symbol dialog allows you to create graphic, movie clip, and button symbols.

3. Set the fields as follows to define the symbol:

   - The Name field allows you to define a custom name for your symbol. It is important to understand that there can only be one symbol in your library for any given name. For this example, we have named this symbol Flower. Therefore, there can be no other symbols with the name Flower.

   - The Type drop-down menu gives us the ability to select from the three primary types of visual symbols. In this case, because this is a basic image and you will not be using animation or interactivity, set this to Graphic.

   - The Registration point determines the location of the symbol's (0,0) coordinates. By default this will be set to the center point. You can change this setting to any one of the nine points shown. These points indicate the corners, sides, and center of the symbol. A selected registration point will be black.

   - The Folder option determines which folder in the library should contain the symbol definition. Since there are no folders in the library as of yet, this symbol will be placed in the library root, or topmost location.

4. Click OK.

You have successfully created your first symbol. Check the Library panel; you should now see the Flower symbol, in addition to the bitmaps that were imported from earlier in this chapter.

Creating symbol instances

An instance of a symbol is basically a copy of a symbol definition that is active in the Flash movie. The symbol definition is the actual symbol that resides in the library. You can create as many copies (instances) of this original symbol as your application dictates. Again, the benefit of this approach is demonstrated in both application performance and ease in the ability to update.

Creating symbols is a fairly straightforward task. The easiest way to accomplish this is by simply dragging an instance of the symbol from the Library panel to the stage as we did with bitmaps. Go ahead and drag three instances of the Flower symbol to the stage.

Once you have an instance of a symbol on the stage, Flash allows you to edit various properties of each symbol instance independently of the symbol definition or other symbol instances. Through the Property inspector and transform tools, you have the ability to edit each symbol instance to give it some degree of uniqueness.

1. Select one of the three symbol instances you created from the last section.

2. Open the Property inspector by selecting Window ➤ Properties. Figure 4-15 shows the various options that are available to a designer when a symbol instance is selected. The Position and Size options allow you to adjust the height, width, and general position of the asset. In the Color Effect settings you have the ability to adjust the Brightness, Tint, Advanced, and Alpha (transparency) settings. Advanced is a combination adjustment of color percentage, alpha percentage, and color offset.

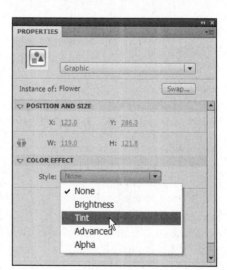

Figure 4-15.
The properties of symbol instances can be adjusted using the Property inspector.

3. Select Tint from the Style drop-down menu in the Color Effect section of the Property inspector.

4. Adjust the Tint setting to experiment with different outcomes.

5. Select another symbol instance. This time choose Alpha from the Style drop-down.

6. Change the Alpha setting to 15%.

7. Finally, select the third symbol instance.

8. Select the Free Transform tool from the Tools panel.

9. Adjust the size and rotation of the symbol instance.

As you can see from this exercise, all three symbol instances can be adjusted independently from one another and from the symbol definition itself.

Creating button symbols

Buttons symbols allow you to quickly create interactive objects with states. All the symbol types that we are discussing in this chapter are nothing more than movie clip symbols. Graphics are movie clips with limited functionality. A button is also a special kind of movie clip that contains only four frames to govern the states of the button.

1. Select the red rectangle that is on the stage.

2. Right-click (Windows) or Ctrl-click (Mac) and select Convert to Symbol.

3. Name the symbol Red Button and select Button from the Type drop-down.

Excellent, now that the button symbol has been created, we will need to set up the button to have states. To accomplish this, we will need to edit the symbol.

Editing symbols

Editing symbols can take some getting used to. The best thing to do is think of each symbol as its own SWF file inside of your main SWF. There are three primary methods by which you can edit your Flash symbols:

- Edit in Place allows you to edit a symbol definition directly from the instance of the symbol on the stage. To edit a symbol through this option, you simply double-click any instance of the symbol that resides on the stage. You will then notice that all other visual assets become dimmed.

- Edit in New Window opens a new tab in the Flash IDE, allowing you to edit the symbol definition in a separate window.

- Symbol-Editing Mode (Edit) opens the symbol definition in the same window as the stage.

> When you edit a symbol in Flash you are actually editing the symbol definition. As a result, editing a symbol in Flash will automatically update all instances of that symbol that are used in your Flash project.

Preparing to add states to the button

Now we can add the state to our button symbol by editing it in place. Start by double-clicking the red rectangular button symbol. This will take you inside the red button symbol and allow you to edit its special timeline.

Flash helps you keep track of which symbol you are actually working in through a series of icons located on the top of the document window. These icons are arranged from left to right to also indicate the nesting order of each symbol instance. Figure 4-16 shows icons for Scene 1 and Red Button. Red Button is the rightmost icon, which is the current symbol we are working on. The fact that Scene 1 is to its immediate left tells us the symbol instance we accessed is currently nested in Scene 1. Selecting the Scene 1 icon would take us back out of the symbol and return us to the main stage.

Figure 4-16.
The document window displays icons that
allow designers to navigate among symbols.

The next thing to notice is that the red rectangle on the stage is actually the original vector rectangle that was used to create this symbol. And because it is a vector shape, we can edit this shape, and the changes will update in every symbol instance used in our Flash movie.

Finally, the timeline that is used for button symbols is quite different from the timeline used for movie clips and graphic symbols. This timeline, as shown in Figure 4-17, contains the four following frames. Three of these frames represent the states of this button; the last frame is the hit area.

- Up is used for when the button is in the up state.
- Over is used for when the mouse is over the button.
- Down is used to define what will happen when the button is pressed.
- The hit area defines the active clickable area for the button.

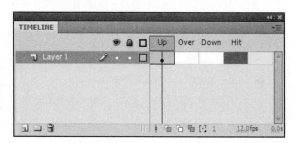

Figure 4-17.
Button symbols have a
special four-frame timeline
that contains a frame for
each state of the button.

So, what is a button without states? Adding such a button is actually your first step in creating interactivity in Flash. Although no significant reaction will occur from pressing this button, it is no less interactive. Therefore, your application will, in a way, respond to a user's input.

1. First test the movie by clicking Control ➤ Test Movie.

2. Try to click the red button. You will no doubt notice that nothing happens. This is because the button has no state and no hit area.

3. Close the test movie.

4. In the timeline, select the frame under the Over label and press F6. This will add a new keyframe to allow us the ability to change the appearance of the button when we select it.

5. Select the red rectangle shape on the stage and change its color to blue.

6. Now select the frame labeled Down and press F6.

7. Select the blue rectangle on the stage and change its color to green. You should now have a red rectangle on the Up frame, a blue rectangle on the Over frame, and a green rectangle on the Down frame.

8. Finally, select the frame under the Hit label and press F6. You will not need to change the color here because there is no visual representation for this frame. It simply defines the interactive area of the button.

9. Test the movie again, and now try to click the button.

You should now notice that the button will react to all states that have been defined in this exercise. Later in this book, you will learn how to make buttons like this accomplish more meaningful tasks.

Swapping symbols

In some cases a designer may need to swap symbol definitions. Doing so can give a designer the ability to change the symbol that is linked to a specific instance. This is often helpful when dealing with last-minute tweaks and proofing. To accomplish this, select a symbol instance on the stage of a Flash movie and click the Swap button (see Figure 4-18) from within the Property inspector. This opens the Swap Symbol dialog, as shown in Figure 4-19, allowing you to pick the new symbol to be used with that symbol instance.

Figure 4-18.
In the Property inspector,
click Swap to swap symbols.

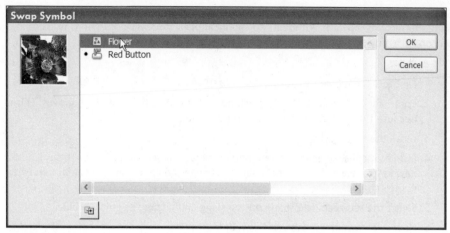

Figure 4-19. The Swap Symbol dialog lets you select a new symbol definition to be used for an instance.

Breaking apart symbol instances

Similar to the way that you break apart bitmaps, you can also break apart symbols. When you break the symbol instance apart, the link to the symbol definition is broken, and the instance is converted back to the internal graphic of the symbol. The symbol definition remains in the library.

To break apart a symbol, right-click (Windows) or Ctrl-click (Mac) the symbol and select Break Apart from the context menu.

Duplicating symbols

When creating Flash projects, it can sometimes be necessary to create duplicates of symbols. For example, if you want to create a group of buttons that all looked the same but have different textual labels on them, you might want to make duplicate symbols. The conundrum with symbols is that many new Flash designers often think they can change the labels (or other internal graphical elements) from within the symbol instance. The problem is that instances are linked to the definition. If you edit the instance, you are really editing the symbol definition. If a symbol contains a text label inside of itself and that label is changed, the change will be implemented across all symbol instances. For this reason, it is necessary to create a duplicate symbol.

When you duplicate a symbol, you are taking an existing symbol definition and creating a completely new and independent symbol definition from it. Do not confuse this with creating a symbol instance. A symbol instance is a copy of a symbol definition. A duplicate symbol is an entirely new symbol altogether. Therefore, this process creates a new symbol definition in the library.

To duplicate a symbol, right-click (Windows) or Ctrl-click (Mac) on any symbol and select Duplicate Symbol from the context menu. This will bring up the New Symbol dialog, allowing you to set the properties for the new duplicated symbol.

The Library panel

The Library panel is probably the single most important panel used in Flash design and development. It is used to organize all assets that are employed in a Flash project. Libraries can also be used to store and access assets for other projects as well. From here you can quickly access the elements of your project to make edits or change specific settings. Nonetheless, both designers and developers alike will find the Library panel beneficial to their efforts.

So far in this chapter you have had some minimal exposure to this panel, but it is worth covering in more detail.

Getting familiar with the Library panel

The Library panel is not as complicated as some of the other panels used in Flash. It is actually quite intuitive to use, as it possesses some aspects common to file browsers found on most computers. Taking a closer look at the Library panel, you can see that it is comprised of two primary sections.

The first of these sections, as shown in Figure 4-20, is the preview pane. The preview pane occupies the upper portion of the Library panel and is used to get a quick glimpse of items as you are browsing the library. From this area you also have the ability to preview sounds and animations as well.

The second key area of focus in the Library panel is the item browser, which occupies the majority of the lower half of the panel. In this area you will find icons and details that represent each symbol, sound, video, or other asset in your project. From this section you can organize, edit, and remove the various elements of your Flash project.

Finally, there are several other elements shown in Figure 4-20 that are worth mentioning:

- The Panel menu contains options that allow you to create, edit, and remove symbols.
- The New Library Panel button opens additional Library panels that can be used to browse external libraries.
- The Pin Library button locks the currently selected library to the currently selected Library panel.
- The library browser allows you to browse all libraries that are currently open in Flash.

- The Search Library field allows you to browse the library for assets.
- The New Symbol button will open the New Symbol dialog and allow you to create a new symbol.
- The New Folder button creates a new folder in the Library panel.
- The Properties button opens the Properties dialog for the currently selected library item.
- The Delete feature (represented by a trash can icon) will remove the currently selected library item.

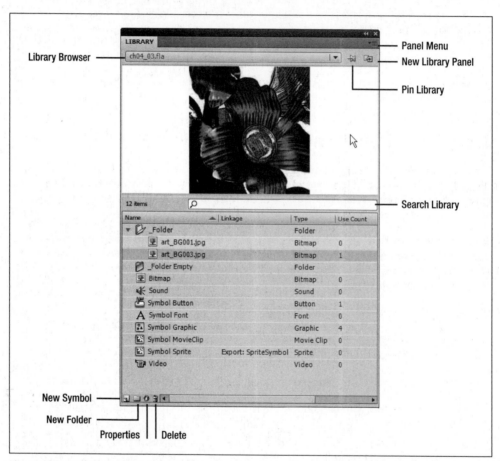

Figure 4-20. The Library panel offers an efficient way to organize the assets used in a Flash application.

Examining library items

You have been working with library items from the first couple pages in this chapter. A **library item** is any asset (symbol, sound, video, font, etc.) that is stored in the Library panel. As you learned, it is very simple to import items to the Library panel or add items to the Library panel when creating symbols. You can also add these items (and instances of these items) to your projects by simply dragging them onto the stage.

Organizing with folders

Folders are an invaluable resource. If you are a regular computer user (this is certainly assumed), you will no doubt be familiar with the benefit of organizing your files in folders. Folders in the Flash library offer this same degree of higher organization as you would expect from folders on your computer's hard drive.

Folders can be created using the New Folder button located at the bottom of the Library panel. Once created, you can drag items to these folders for organization. Figure 4-21 demonstrates that items located within a folder will be indented. Folders may contain any item located in the library including other folders. For further organization, folders may be expanded or collapsed by pressing the gray arrow located to the left of the folder's icon.

Figure 4-21. Folders can be used to organize the library.

Sorting and searching

Sorting and searching library items are both new to Flash CS4. Though users had the ability to sort items by type in Flash CS3, it was nowhere nearly as effective as the sorting method in this release. It is now possible to sort in ascending or descending order from any of the columns in the Library panel simply by clicking on a column's header.

Searching, on the other hand, is completely new to this version and in our opinion long overdue. Using the Search Library field gives you the opportunity filter the library based on an item's name. Figure 4-22 shows that typing Bitmap into the Search Library field will prompt the library to show only those items with "Bitmap" in their names. All other items will be hidden.

Figure 4-22. Use the Search Library field to locate specific items in the library.

To clear the search and restore the other library items to visibility, click the X located in the right side of the Search Library field.

Finding unused library items

Over the course of a project's life cycle, it is possible for the project to accumulate a number of library items that are no longer used or required. Similar to cleaning out a closet or a junk drawer, it can be useful to perform a bit of spring cleaning on your projects. For this Flash offers the Select Unused Items feature in the Library panel menu.

Rather than have you go through every item in your Flash project and try to determine which are in use and which are not, Flash will do all the work for you. By selecting Select

Unused Items from the Library panel menu, Flash will automatically select all library items that are not being used or referenced in your project. It will then highlight those items in gray as shown in Figure 4-23. From here you can simply click the Delete button at the bottom of the Library panel, and all useless items will be removed from your project.

Figure 4-23.
Useless library items can be removed using the Select Unused Items command.

Updating imported library items

Updating library items can be particularly useful if you work from a central graphics repository or have imported items from an external library. Updating files can be useful because it maintains the integrity of the existing library item. Therefore, rather than reimporting (which could cause a naming conflict), you can simply update external items if their original files have been changed.

To update a library item, select it in the Library panel. Then select Update from the Library panel menu.

Summary

In this chapter we continued to lay the foundation for things to come. Bitmaps and symbols are going to be inherent to the majority of Flash projects you work on. Having a conceptual understanding of how symbols and symbol instances relate to one another will also give you a leg up when it comes time learn ActionScript.

In this chapter we discussed the following key topics:

- Basic use of bitmap images
- Importing external graphic assets into Flash
- Using the library
- Symbol creation and management

4

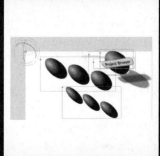

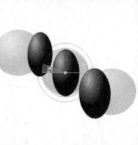

Now that we have given you a tour of the kitchen and its basic tools, we need to start adding some hot sauce.

In previous chapters you learned about the basic tools for creating graphics and colors. Here you will get familiar with the basics of spicing things up a bit more using blends, filters, and 3D tools. So in this chapter we will show you the following:

- Blends
- Filters
- 3D transformations

Blends

Blend modes let you create composite images or images with varying transparency or color interaction of two or more overlapping objects. Blending allows you to create unique effects by blending the colors in overlapping shapes, as well as adding a control to the transparency of objects and images. You can use Flash blend modes to create highlights or shadows that let details from an underlying image show through, or to colorize a grayscale image.

A blend mode contains these elements:

- **Blend color**: The color applied in the blend mode
- **Opacity**: The degree of transparency applied in the blend mode
- **Base color**: The color of pixels underneath the blend color
- **Result color**: The result of the blend's effect in the blend

Because blend modes depend on both the underlying "base" color and the color of the object to which you're applying the blend, you'll need to experiment with different colors to see what the result will be. Try the different blend modes to achieve the effect you want. Some samples follow.

Flash provides the following blend modes:

- **Normal**: Applies color normally, with no interaction with the base colors.
- **Layer**: Blends colors normally but sets the blend object at 100 percent opacity prior to blending. This prevents internal movie clips of the blend object from bleeding through one another.
- **Darken**: Replaces only the areas that are lighter than the blend color. Areas darker than the blend color don't change.
- **Multiply**: Multiplies the base color by the blend color, resulting in darker colors.
- **Lighten**: Replaces only pixels that are darker than the blend color. Areas lighter than the blend color don't change (opposite of darken mode).
- **Screen**: Multiplies the inverse of the blend color by the base color, resulting in a bleaching effect, often similar to lighten mode.
- **Overlay**: Multiplies or screens the colors, depending on the base colors.

- **Hard light**: Multiplies or screens the colors, depending on the blend mode color. The effect is similar to shining a spotlight on the object.

- **Difference**: Subtracts either the blend color from the base color or the base color from the blend color, depending on which has the greater brightness value. The effect is similar to a color negative.

- **Invert**: Inverts the base color.

- **Alpha**: Applies an alpha mask.

- **Erase**: Removes all base color pixels, including those in the background image.

Applying a blend mode

You use the Property inspector to apply blend modes to selected movie clips or shapes.

To apply a blend mode to a movie clip, follow these steps:

1. Select the movie clip instance (on the stage) to which you want to apply a blend mode.

2. Adjust the color and transparency of the desired movie clip instance using the Color pop-up menu in the Property inspector.

3. Select a blend mode from the Blend pop-up menu in the Property inspector. The blend mode is applied to the selected movie clip instance.

4. Verify that the blend mode you've selected is appropriate to the effect you're trying to achieve.

Figures 5-1 through 5-5 show the results of applying various blend modes to a movie clip.

Figure 5-1.
Normal blend mode produces no effect.

Figure 5-2.
With hard light blending mode, the shadows and light source become sharper.

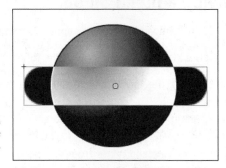

Figure 5-3.
With darken blend mode, the
lighter areas of overlap are replaced.

Figure 5-4.
With invert blend mode, the base
color is inverted in the overlap areas.

Figure 5-5.
With subtract blend mode, the base
color is subtracted from overlapped areas.

You will likely find you need to try varying both the color and transparency settings of the movie clip and then try applying different blend modes to achieve the effect you want. For information on adjusting the color of a movie clip, go to http://help.adobe.com/en_US/ Flash/10.0_UsingFlash. Select Using Flash and in the left-hand pane, expand Using symbols, instances, and library assets, **expand** Working with symbol instances, **and select the link** Change the color and transparency of an instance.

Working with filters

Filters let you add visual effects such as drop shadows, blurs, glows, and bevels to text, buttons, and movie clips. You may apply these filters using motion tweens that are unique to Flash and with which you can animate the filters. For example, if you create a ball (or sphere) with a drop shadow, you can simulate the look of the light source moving from one side of the object to another by changing the position of the drop shadow from its beginning and ending frames in the timeline.

After you apply a filter, rearrange the order of filters or change filter options at any time to experiment with combined effects. You can disable filters or enable or delete them in the Property inspector. When you remove a filter, the object returns to its previous state. You can view the filters applied to an object by selecting it, automatically updating the filters list in the Property inspector for the selected object.

Applying filters

You can apply filters to selected objects using the Property inspector. Each time you add a new filter to an object, it is added to the list of applied filters for that object in the Property inspector. You can remove filters that have been previously applied, as well as apply multiple filters to an object. Applying different filters affects the appearance of a movie clip instance (see Figure 5-6).

Figure 5-6.
A drop shadow applied to multiple objects

For information on how using filters can affect the performance of your SWF files, see the following sections of Flash Online Help: "Filters and Blends" (located at http://help.adobe.com/en_US/Flash/10.0_Welcome under Using Flash ➤ Using Flash CS4 Professional ➤ Filters and Blends) and "Filtering Display Objects" (which you'll find at http://help.adobe.com/en_US/ActionScript/3.0_ProgrammingAS3 located to the left).

You can apply filters only to text, button, and movie clip objects. To apply a filter, follow these steps:

1. On the stage, select a movie clip, button, or text object to which you want to apply a filter.

2. Select the Filters tab in the Property inspector.

3. Click the Add Filter (+) button in the lower-left corner and select a filter from the Filters pop-up menu (see Figure 5-7). The filter you select is applied to the object, and the controls for the filter settings appear in the Property inspector (see Figure 5-8).

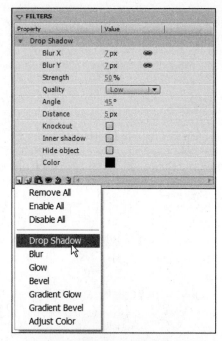

Figure 5-7.
Adding a filter to the Filter tab
in the Property inspector

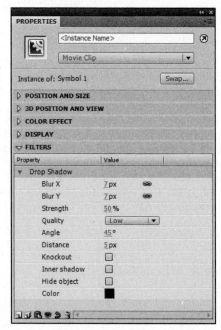

Figure 5-8.
Setting your filter properties

Vary the filter settings until you get the look you want. For details about the settings available for each filter, see the following sections in Flash Online Help (http://help.adobe.com/en_US/Flash/10.0_Welcome), all of which can be accessed by first selecting Using Flash, expanding the Special effects node, and then expanding the About filters node:

- Apply a Drop Shadow
- Apply a Blur
- Apply a Glow
- Apply a Bevel
- Apply a Gradient Glow
- Apply a Gradient Bevel
- Apply the Adjust Color Filter

To remove a filter, follow these steps:

1. Select the movie clip, button, or text object that you want to remove a filter from.
2. Select the Filter tab in the Property inspector.
3. Select the filter you want to remove in the list of applied filters.
4. Click the Remove Filter (–) button to remove the filter.

You can create a filter settings library that allows you to easily apply the same filter or sets of filters to an object. Flash stores the filter presets you create in the Property inspector on the Filters tab in the Filters ➤ Presets menu. You can delete or rename any presets as desired.

The filter configuration file stored in your Flash configuration folder can be used to share libraries of preset filters with other developers.

For more information, go to http://livedocs.adobe.com/flash/10.0/UsingFlash/. Select Using Flash, expand Special effects, expand About filters, and click the link Creating preset filter libraries.

To enable or disable a filter applied to an object, click the enable or disable icon next to the filter name in the filter list in the Property inspector. Alt-click the enable icon in the filter list to toggle the enable state of the other filters in the list. If you Alt-click the disable icon, the selected filter is enabled and all other filters in the list are disabled.

To enable or disable all filters applied to an object, click the Add Filter (+) button in the Property inspector and then select Enable All or Disable All from the pop-up menu. You can Ctrl-click (Cmd-click) the enable or disable icon in the filter list to enable or disable all the filters in the list.

5

At this point, you may want to try applying a basic filter effect yourself. There are many examples in the Flash documentation, as indicated earlier. However, an easy example to start with is applying a drop shadow, so try it out by using the following steps:

1. Select the movie clip, button, or text object that you want to apply a filter preset to.

2. Select the Filter tab in the Property inspector.

3. Click the Add Filter (+) button and select Presets from the Filters pop-up menu.

Select the filter preset you want to apply from the list of available presets at the bottom of the Preset menu. When you apply a filter preset to an object, Flash replaces any filters currently applied to the selected object(s) with the filter(s) used in the preset.

Creating a skewed drop shadow

To create a more realistic look, use the drop shadow filter's Hide object option when skewing the shadow of an object (see Figure 5-9). To achieve this effect, you need to create a duplicate movie clip, button, or text object, apply a drop shadow to the duplicate, and use the Free Transform tool to skew the duplicate object's shadow. Next, hide the original object with the skewed shadow and remove the drop shadow from the other copy.

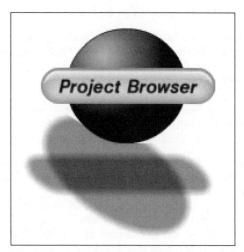

Figure 5-9.
Skewing the drop shadow filter to
create a more realistic shadow

The effect is the original object has a shadow that is skewed to one side as if the light source casting the shadow were offset.

Introducing 3D transformations

Flash CS4 allows you to create 3D effects by moving and rotating movie clips in 3D space with a z axis in the properties of each movie clip instance. You add 3D perspective effects to movie clip instances by moving or rotating them along their z axis using the 3D

Translation and 3D Rotation tools. In CS4, moving an object in 3D space is called a **translation** and rotating an object in 3D space is called a **transformation**. Once you have applied either of these effects to a movie clip, you get the z axis that makes it a 3D movie clip.

When you move an object along its z axis with the 3D Translation tool or the Property inspector, that object will appear nearer or further away from the viewer. When you rotate the movie clip around its z axis with the 3D Rotation tool, you give the impression of an object that is at an angle to the viewer. Through using these tools, you get the impression that the objects they are applied to are in 3D space, which is made even more apparent with movement.

You can use the 3D Translation and the 3D Rotation tools to manipulate objects on the entire stage (global) or movie clip (local) 3D space. For example, if you have a movie clip containing three nested movie clips as shown in Figure 5-9, local 3D transforms of the nested movie clips are relative to the drawing area inside the parent movie clip. The default mode of the 3D Translation and 3D Rotation tools is global. To use them in local mode, click the Global toggle button in the Options section of the Tools panel.

Vanishing point

The vanishing point property (see Figure 5-10) of an FLA file controls the orientation of the z axis of 3D movie clips on the stage. The z axis of all 3D movie clips in an FLA file recedes toward the vanishing point. By relocating the vanishing point, you change the direction that an object moves when translated along its z axis. By adjusting the position of the vanishing point, you can precisely control the appearance of 3D objects and animation on the stage, as shown in Figure 5-11.

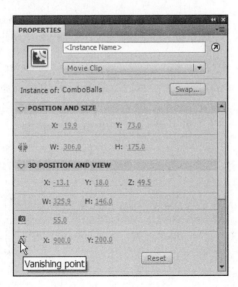

Figure 5-10.
Setting vanishing point properties

5

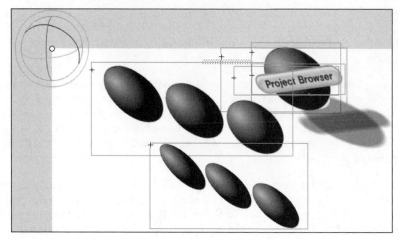

Figure 5-11. Global 3D showing a vanishing point for all movie clips on the stage

For example, if you locate the vanishing point at the upper-left corner of the stage (0, 0), increasing the value of the z property of a movie clip moves the movie clip away from the viewer and toward the upper-left corner of the stage.

Because the vanishing point affects all 3D movie clips, changing it also changes the position of all movie clips that have a z-axis translation applied.

The vanishing point is a document property that affects all movie clips that have z-axis translation or rotation applied to them. The vanishing point does not affect other movie clips. The default location of the vanishing point is the center of the stage.

To view or set the vanishing point in the Property inspector, a 3D movie clip must be selected on the stage. Changes to the vanishing point are visible on the stage immediately.

To set the vanishing point, follow these steps:

1. On the stage, select a movie clip that has 3D rotation or translation applied to it.

2. In the Property inspector, enter a new value in the Vanishing Point field, or drag the hot text to change the value. Guides indicating the location of the vanishing point appear on the stage while dragging the hot text.

To move the vanishing point back to the center of the stage, click the Reset button in the Property inspector.

Figure 5-12 shows three balls with a vanishing point and the 3D Rotation tool's controls with the combined movie clip rotated slightly compared to the same three balls not rotated in the figure. Keep in mind that you are *not* actually rotating 3D objects but only 2D objects with 3D effects. See Figure 5-13 a little later in the chapter for what happens if you rotate too far.

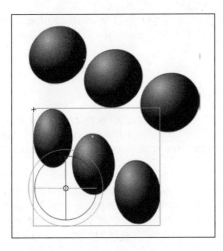

Figure 5-12.
The three balls
selected with the 3D
Rotation tool

5

Rotating a multiple-object selection in 3D space

To rotate a selection of multiple objects in 3D space, follow these steps:

1. Select the 3D Rotation tool in the Tools panel (or press W).

2. Verify that the tool is in the mode that you want by checking the Global toggle button in the Options section of the Tools panel. Click the button or press D to toggle the mode between global and local.

3. Select multiple movie clips on the stage.

4. The 3D Rotation controls appear overlaid on the most recently selected object. Place the pointer over one of the four rotation axis controls. The pointer changes when over one of the four controls.

5. Drag one of the axis controls to rotate around that axis or the free rotate control (outer orange circle) to rotate x and y simultaneously.

6. Drag the x-axis control left or right to rotate around the x axis. Drag the y-axis control up or down to rotate around the y axis. Drag the z-axis control in a circular motion to rotate around the z axis.

The 3D center point, which appears at the center of the rotation guide, controls all of the selected movie clips.

To relocate the 3D rotation control center point, do one of the following:

- To move the center point to an arbitrary location, drag the center point.

- To move the center point to the center of one of the selected movie clips, Shift–double-click the movie clip.

- To move the center point to the center of the group of selected movie clips, double-click the center point.

The location of the rotation control center point for the selected object appears in the Transform panel as the 3D center point. You can modify the location of the center point in the Transform panel.

Rotating objects in 3D space

You rotate movie clip instances in 3D space with the 3D Rotation tool. A 3D rotation control appears on top of selected objects on the stage. The x control is red, the y control is green, and the z control is blue. Use the free rotate control to rotate around the x and y axes at the same time.

The default mode of the 3D Rotation tool is global. Rotating an object in global 3D space is the same as moving it relative to the stage. Rotating an object in local 3D space is the same as moving it relative to its parent movie clip if it has one. To toggle the 3D Rotation tool between global and local modes, click the Global toggle button in the Options section of the Tools panel while the 3D Rotation tool is selected. You can temporarily toggle the mode from global to local by pressing D while dragging with the 3D Rotation tool.

The 3D Rotation and 3D Translation tools occupy the same space in the Tools panel. Click and hold the active 3D tool icon in the Tools panel to select the currently inactive 3D tool.

By default, selected objects that have 3D rotation applied appear with a 3D axis overlay on the stage. You can turn off this overlay in the General section of Flash Preferences.

Rotating a single object in 3D space

Select the 3D Rotation tool in the Tools panel (or press W). You'll get a result similar to what you see in Figure 5-13.

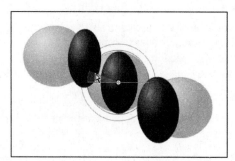

Figure 5-13.
The three balls with the 3D
Rotation tool handles

But of course that *may* be what you wanted.

If you need a variety of graphic effects without duplicating movie clips in the library, the 3D properties of movie clip instances in your FLA file may be sufficient. If you edit a movie clip from the library or in edit-in-place mode, the 3D transforms and translations that have been applied are not visible. When editing the contents of a movie clip, only 3D transforms of nested movie clips are visible.

If you have 3D objects on the stage, you can add certain 3D effects to all of those objects as a group by adjusting the perspective angle and vanishing point properties of your FLA file. The perspective angle property has the effect of zooming the view of the stage. The vanishing point property has the effect of panning the 3D objects on the stage. These settings only affect the appearance of movie clips that have a 3D transform or translation applied to them.

In the Flash authoring tool, you can control only one viewpoint, or **camera**. The camera view of your FLA file is the same as the stage view. Each FLA file has only one perspective angle and vanishing point setting.

To use the 3D capabilities of Flash, the publish settings of your FLA file must be set to Flash Player 10 and ActionScript 3.0. Only movie clip instances can be rotated or translated along the z axis. Some 3D capabilities are available through ActionScript that are not available directly in the Flash user interface, such as multiple vanishing points and separate cameras for each movie clip.

For a video tutorial about 3D graphics, see "Working with 3D Art" at www.adobe.com/go/lrvid4059_fl.

3D space movement

When you want to move movie clip instances in 3D space, you do it with the 3D Translation tool. Select a movie clip with the tool, and you will see its three axes, x, y, and z, appear on the stage on top of the object. Figure 5-14 shows this tool; although you can't see the colors in this figure, on your screen the x axis is red, the y axis is green, and the z axis is blue.

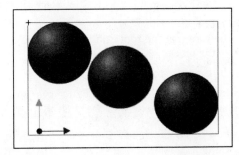

Figure 5-14.
The three balls with the 3D Translation tool off palette, left of the stage

The 3D Translation tool default mode is global. Moving an object in global 3D space is the same as moving it relative to the stage. Moving an object in local 3D space is the same as moving it relative to its parent movie clip. You can temporarily toggle the mode from global to local by pressing D while dragging with the 3D tool or by clicking the Global toggle button in the Options section of the Tools panel while the 3D

Translation tool is selected. Figure 5-15 shows the three balls after changes with the 3D Translation tool.

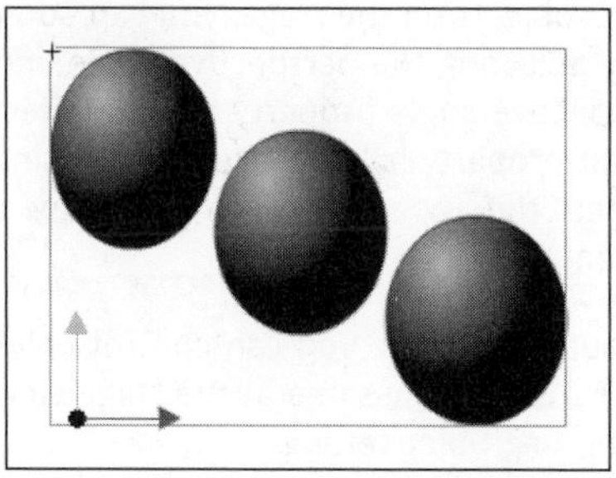

Figure 5-15.
Use the 3D translation tool to apply a translation to the three balls.

As mentioned previously, the 3D Translation and 3D Rotation tools occupy the same icon.

In the Tools panel, click and hold the active 3D tool icon in the Tools panel to select the currently inactive 3D tool.

By default, selected objects that have 3D translation applied appear with a 3D axis overlay on the stage, which you can turn off in the General section of Flash Preferences.

Moving a single object in 3D space

The 3D effects are most effective with apparent movement; here is how to get started. There are many ways to add spices, and the only limit is your creativity.

To move an object in 3D space, follow these steps:

1. Select the 3D Translation tool in the Tools panel (or press G to select it).
2. Set the tool to local or global mode. Check the Global toggle button in the Options section of the Tools panel to be sure that the tool is in the mode you want. Click the button or press D to toggle the mode.
3. Select a movie clip with the 3D Translation tool.
4. Move the object by dragging with the tool. Move the pointer over the x-, y-, or z-axis controls. The pointer changes when over any of the controls.

The x- and y-axis controls are the arrow tips on each axis. Drag one of these controls in the direction of its arrow to move the object along the selected axis. The z-axis control is the black dot at the center of the movie clip. Drag the z-axis control up or down to move the object on the z axis.

To move the object using the Property inspector, enter a value for x, y, or z in the 3D Position and View section of the Property inspector.

Move an object on the z axis, and its apparent size changes. The apparent size appears in the Property inspector as the Width and Height read-only values in the 3D Position and View section. Note in Figures 5-14 and 5-15 that the apparent size changed from left to right as we position on the z axis.

Moving multiple objects in 3D space

When you select multiple movie clips, you can move one of the selected objects with the 3D Translation tool, and the others move in the same way. Try it yourself:

1. Set the 3D Translation tool to global mode to move each object in the group in the same way (in global 3D space), and then drag one of the objects with the axis controls.

2. To move the axis controls to another object, shift–double-click one of the other selected objects.

Set the 3D Translation tool to local mode to move each object separately in the group in the same way in local 3D space, and then drag one of the objects with the axis controls. Shift–double-click one of the selected objects to move the axis controls to that object.

You can also move the axis controls to the center of the multiple selection by double-clicking the z-axis control. Shift–double-click one of the selected objects to move the axis controls to that object:

1. Verify that the tool is in the mode that you want by checking the Global toggle button in the Options section of the Tools panel. Click the button or press D to toggle the mode between global and local.

2. Select a movie clip on the stage.

3. The 3D Rotation controls appear overlaid on the selected object. If the controls appear in a different location, double-click the control center point to move it to the selected object.

4. Place the pointer over one of the four rotation axis controls. The pointer changes when over one of these controls.

5. Drag one of the axis controls to rotate around that axis: Drag the x-axis control left or right to rotate around the x axis. Drag the y-axis control up or down to rotate around the y axis. Drag the z-axis control in a circular motion to rotate around the z axis. Or use the free rotate control (outer orange circle) to rotate x and y simultaneously.

6. To relocate the rotation control center point relative to the movie clip, drag the center point. This lets you control the effect of the rotation on the object and its appearance.

7. Double-click the center point to move it back to the center of the selected movie clip.

The location of the rotation control center point for the selected object appears in the Transform panel as the 3D Center Point property. You can modify the location of the center point in the Transform panel.

5

Transform panel rotation

To use the Transform panel for rotation, follow these steps:

1. Open the Transform panel (Window ➤ Transform).

2. Select one or more movie clips on the stage.

> *In the* Transform *panel, enter the desired values in the* 3D Rotation X, Y, *and* Z *fields to rotate the selection (see Figure 5-16 in the next section). These fields contain hot text, so you can drag the values to change them. The 3D rotation takes place in global or local 3D space, depending on the current mode of the* 3D Rotation *tool in the* Tools *panel.*

3. To move the 3D rotation point, enter the desired values in the 3D Center Point X, Y, and Z fields.

Perspective angle

The perspective angle property of an FLA file controls the apparent angle of view of 3D movie clips on the stage.

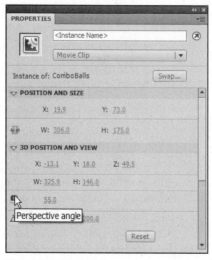

Figure 5-16. Setting the perspective angle in the Property inspector

The apparent size of 3D movie clips and their location relative to the edges of the stage are adjusted by increasing or decreasing the perspective angle effects. By increasing the perspective angle, you make 3D objects appear closer to the viewer. By decreasing the perspective angle, you make 3D objects appear further away. The effect is like zooming in or out with a camera lens, which changes the angle of view through the lens.

All movie clips with 3D translation or rotation applied to them are affected by changes to the perspective angle property. The perspective angle does not affect other non-3D movie clips. The default perspective angle is 55 degrees of the view, like a normal camera lens. The range of values is from 1 degree to 180 degrees.

To view or set the perspective angle in the Property inspector, as shown in Figure 5-16, a 3D movie clip must be selected on stage. Changes to the perspective angle are visible on the stage immediately.

The perspective angle changes automatically when you change the stage size so that the appearance of 3D objects does not change. You can turn off this behavior in the Document Properties dialog box.

To set the perspective angle, follow these steps:

1. On the stage, select a movie clip instance that has 3D rotation or translation applied to it.

2. In the Property inspector, enter a new value in the perspective angle field (currently 55.0 in Figure 5-16) or drag the hot text to change the value.

Figure 5-17 shows two perspectives of the same image, with Figure 5-18 showing changes in one of those perspectives.

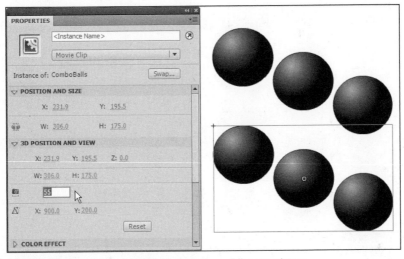

Figure 5-17. Showing two different perspectives of the same image

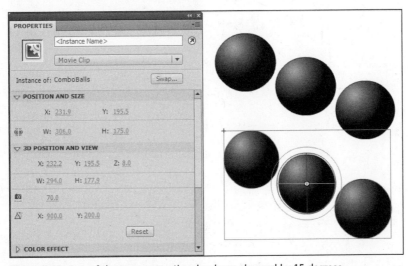

Figure 5-18. One of the two perspectives has been changed by 15 degrees.

121

Summary

Now you should have plenty of spicy flavors to add to your Flash soup: in this chapter we showed you how you can blend two or more objects in a number of different ways and apply filters to get special effects. Then we demonstrated how to add another perspective, literally, with 3D so you can make things look more like they do in the real world and less like a flat painting.

In this chapter, we covered the following topics:

- Blends
- Filters
- 3D transformations

PART TWO
ANIMATION

CHAPTER 6
BASIC ANIMATION IN FLASH

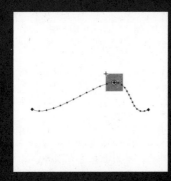

In this chapter we'll consider the following questions:

- When is animation appropriate?
- What can be animated in Flash?
- What specific properties of an object can be changed over time?
- What are some of the limitations of various types of symbols during animation in Flash?
- "Where" does animation happen in Flash?
- How do you control the animation by fine-tuning the tween?

We also want to talk a little about why animation is important. We'll discuss ways to engage users in an experience. We'd also like to explain the role of animation in the presentation of information and how it relates to the importance of Flash as an application platform.

Animating to convey information

It can be asserted that basic animation is at the core of why the Rich Internet Application has taken hold of late. On the one hand, other web technologies have static page after page of lists and lists of information. Yes, sortable, filterable, savable: all very necessary functions for dealing with information. On the other hand you have Flash, now with its powerful programming language and data connectivity, that can take information and do all of that sorting, filtering, and saving as well as present it in a form with which human beings can easily identify. Check out www.gapminder.org to see what we mean.

Human beings respond to cues about dynamic relationships between things in space and apply meaning to them. We can use animation in the presentation of information systems to help users keep track of where they are within that information, how the information relates to itself and the other elements, or what types of information appear in the interface.

We can also use animation to help users keep track of where they are within the structure of our web sites and presentations as well. You'll even find this type of animation used on the desktop, as evidenced by the "genie" effect on the Mac and minimize animation on PCs. These effects tell users "Here I am! You didn't close me all the way, and if you need me, just click down here where you saw me *move* to, and I'll just pop right back up."

Finally, we can suppose that the reasons that moving pictures were invented and translated to computers are the same. It's a natural thing for us to want all of what we interact with in the virtual world to emulate the things we interact with in the real world.

Animation for impact and emotion

Other obvious uses of animation are impact and emotion, as devices for driving your point home or telling a story. Combined with sound, motion is a powerful tool for creating an "experience," an event that people will remember and then associate with a feeling. This is important because this feeling, as advertisers well know, is the key to selling—not just products, but also ideas and concepts. People's decisions are generally either supported by emotion or dictated by it, in spite of the facts.

The disciplines of animation

A distinction should be made between types of animation, and we don't mean from a technology point of view, but from a craft point of view. Here are some common types of animations:

- Interface animation
- Character animation
- Game-play animation
- Motion graphics for video

They're all different. Any of these disciplines of animation could be (and have been) a book unto themselves, so keep in mind that what we're talking about here is the Flash CS4 tool and how it applies to animation and not necessarily the craft of animation itself.

Now that we have given you some ideas about how you can use animation effectively, let's have a look at the nuts and bolts of animation in Flash.

Understanding animation in Flash

Some major changes have occurred to the way animation happens in Flash with CS4, so even if you're a seasoned Flash professional, you may want to become acquainted with the new approach.

Motion tweening vs. frame-by-frame animation

Tweens are mathematical interpolations of the change in a symbol (such as a movie clip instance) over time. You tell Flash what that movie clip instance looks like on frame 1 (a keyframe). Then you tell Flash what that movie clip instance is supposed to look like on frame 10 (another keyframe). Finally, Flash tells you what it thinks the movie clip instance should like on frames 2 through 9.

6

We'll discuss the following types of tweens:

- Shape tweens
- Motion tweens
- Classic tweens

The benefit of tweening has always been, and largely remains, a reduction in the file size of your animation and an increase in speed of development. For the most part this works great. It's fast and easy and gets the job done; but keep in mind that what is lost is complete control over the "in-betweens"—the frames between keyframes. While you can add keyframes where you need them to tweak your animations, this quickly adds file size to your Flash movie and just as quickly renders your animation unmaintainable. There are times when complete control over the in-betweens is of paramount importance—in character animation, for instance.

> A tween changes the properties of a single object: where it is, how big it is, its rotation, its color, and its transparency (alpha). Frame-by-fame animation creates many discrete shapes or objects.

The shape tween

Shape tweening is useful for applying a smooth morphing effect to shapes or other drawing objects in your design that don't warrant the creation of a symbol. You cannot apply a shape tween to a symbol or group. You can only do so to drawing objects or shapes. Figure 6-1 shows a shape tween on the timeline.

Figure 6-1. A shape tween

> We should also point out that drawing objects and shapes cannot be motion tweened.

Introducing the new motion tween

The motion tween has been an invaluable tool for the Flash designer and developer alike. This version of Flash brings a significant change to how the motion tween is approached in the authoring environment. Figure 6-2 shows the new motion tween as it appears on the timeline.

Figure 6-2. The new motion tween

Since ActionScript 2.0, the developer has been able to create tweens using code and therefore use and reuse that code, applying it to different objects at will, even changing the properties of that tween dynamically. This version of Flash applies that paradigm to the stage and timeline. You can now give your motion tweens instance names, because that's what they are—instances of a tween object. You can then access those motion tweens via ActionScript just like any other named instance on the stage.

Many character animators rely on the motion tween as a way to encapsulate their animation. Because their characters are actually complex collections of other movie clips or graphics symbols, it allows them to animate each element separately without affecting the other. For instance, an animator could change the speed at which his or her character moves from left to right across the stage while leaving the animation of the legs (a separate clip nested within the character clip) alone. You cannot do this using drawing objects or shapes, which utilize the shape tween.

Classic tween

If you would rather continue on motion tweening the way Flash has done so well for so many years, you are free to do so with the classic tween, shown here in Figure 6-3. Creating these classic motion tweens has not changed from previous versions of Flash.

Figure 6-3. The classic tween

Now that you have an idea of the different types of tweens, let's get to the business of making one in real life.

Creating a motion tween—a step-by-step primer

This demonstration might seem elementary to you, but we want to take some time to really dig into the root of animating in Flash. For the moment, let's forget that we can use shape tweens and that we can continue to tween discrete instances of objects on the timeline by using what are now called classic tweens.

Right now we want to focus on the new approach to tweening in Flash CS4, and that is motion tweening (object-based tweening). Don't confuse this to mean tweening *of*

6

objects—what we are talking about here is *the tween as an object* of its very own with many malleable parts. We will come back to the shape tween and classic tween methods of creating motion in Flash, but for now we want you to brave this strange new idea, step by step:

1. Create a new Flash file with one layer, no frames, and your document frame rate set to 24 fps.

2. Create a symbol on the stage.

3. Right-click your symbol and select Create Motion Tween from the context menu.

4. Move the playhead to another frame.

5. Move your symbol.

You made some basic motion in Flash. Notice that your layer has been converted to a tween layer and it now has 24 frames (see Figure 6-4). A **tween layer** is like a guide layer and a layer with a classic tween on it all rolled into one, and it is cool. Play your timeline or test the movie (Ctrl+Enter or Cmd+Return on a Mac) to see your motion, well, in motion.

Figure 6-4. The tween layer is like a guide layer and a layer with a classic tween combined.

Flash CS4 has a few rules about this type of tweening, but it does an excellent job of helping you out. If you are trying to create a tween on a shape or drawing object, Flash displays the dialog shown in Figure 6-5 and offers to convert your shape into a symbol. If you have multiple symbols selected or a mix of symbols and shapes, you will get the same dialog.

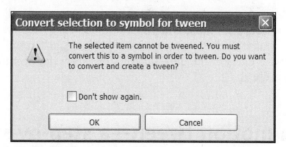

Figure 6-5. Convert selection to symbol for tween dialog

Flash CS4 does a few cool things for you at this point. If you have no frames on the layer that your symbol of interest is on, Flash will create 1 second's worth of frames from the keyframe where your symbol instance is. If you select a symbol instance on a layer that has other objects on it as shown in Figure 6-6, Flash will create a tween layer for you. Flash will then move your symbol to the new tween layer it created, as shown in Figure 6-7. Pretty sweet!

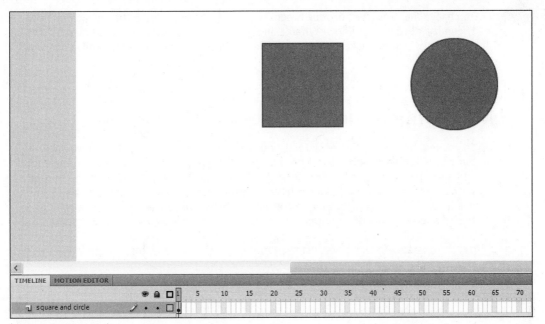

Figure 6-6. Two symbols on one layer

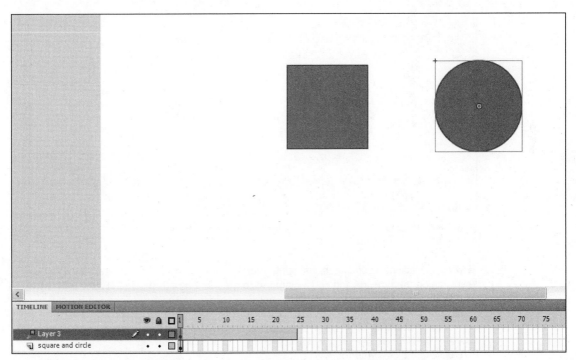

Figure 6-7. The motion layer created by Flash with the nontweened symbol remaining on its layer

To change the properties of your tween, simply select any point on the timeline on your tween layer between the first keyframe and the last frame of the tween, and then use the Property inspector to make changes. Next we'll look at the many ways to modify your new motion tween.

Modifying a motion tween

So you may be less than impressed with your moving box (or circle, or whatever you made), but fear not, there's more. Notice on stage that there is a line with diamonds on the ends and small pluses (they may look like dots) distributed over the line. This is the **motion path**, or the path that your symbol takes over time, and it's illustrated in Figure 6-8. The diamonds are the endpoints, which are keyframes in the *animation*, not of the *timeline*, and the other dots represent each frame that your motion tween occupies on the timeline.

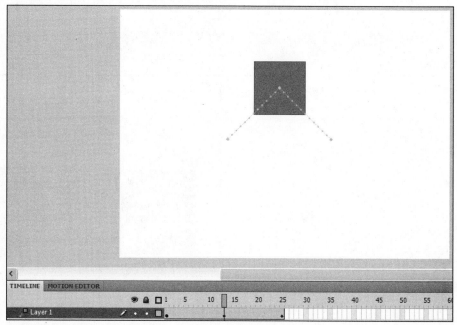

Figure 6-8. New animation keyframes are added to the tween span in the timeline as well as the motion path.

Moving the playhead and then changing your symbol's position will create a new tween keyframe on the timeline and add a diamond to the motion path shown in Figure 6-7. Once you do this, that value for your symbol's position persists to the end of the motion tween.

> On the timeline, keyframes are represented by circles. Animation or tween keyframes are represented by diamonds.

Moving a motion path

Occasionally you may want to move the location of your tween. Everything about it could be perfect aside from where it is on stage. No problem! With the Selection tool, you select all of it and just move it. Or just grab a segment and change the curve or change the position of the line segment joint or endpoint. Figure 6-9 shows the entire motion path while being moved.

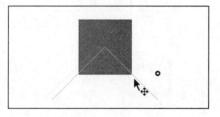

Figure 6-9.
Moving the entire motion path

Changing the curve of a motion path

With the Selection tool active, hover over the motion path until you see the curve indicator as shown in Figure 6-10 and modify the motion path as you would a line. With the Subselection tool, select the motion path and modify the motion path using handles or endpoints.

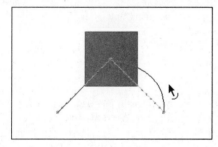

Figure 6-10.
The small curve next to the cursor indicates what will happen when you drag the motion path. As you drag, the original path and future path are drawn.

To rotate, scale, or skew the motion path

With the Transform tool active, select the motion path. Transform it as you would any other shape. Figures 6-11 through 6-13 show the rotate, scale, and skew of a motion guide.

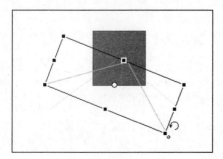

Figure 6-11.
Rotating a motion guide

6

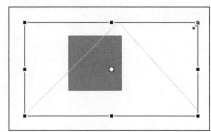

Figure 6-12.
Scaling a motion guide

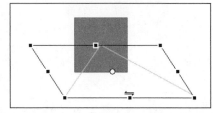

Figure 6-13.
Skewing a motion guide

As you can see, the motion path gives us the same creative control over the path of our symbols that the guide layer does when applied to a symbol in the classic tween, without the extra overhead of another layer in our timeline.

There are quite a few ways to tweak your tween right on stage. Now let's look at how you can change the speed of your tween over time using easing.

Understanding easing

Easing is how your animation is distributed over time. In plain language, when you ease in to an animation, you sort of take it easy to begin with, start off slow, and make up for it at the end of the animation. Most of your time is spent at the beginning of your tween. Easing out is the opposite. You start quickly and then change less and less as your animation slowly winds to a close. Most of your time is spent at the end of your tween.

Easing in and easing out are the very basic of eases. All of the complex types are combinations of these two, and we'll look briefly at them when we explore the Motion Editor later in this chapter. For the most part, experimentation will serve you well in understanding easing.

Changing the easing of your tween

To change the easing of your tween, select either your motion path or the tween span in the timeline so that the motion tween properties appear in the Property inspector, as shown in Figure 6-14. You'll see the motion tween symbol in the Property inspector.

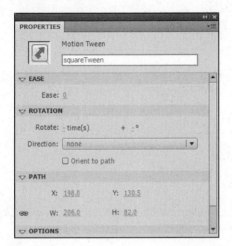

Figure 6-14.
The Property inspector for the new motion tween. The field for inputting an instance name for your motion tween is new in Flash CS4.

If you have worked in Flash before, you may be asking yourself, "What happened to my easing options in the Property inspector*?" The answer is that they grew up and moved out. They're in the Motion Editor, which we talk about in the section "Introducing the Motion Editor" later in this chapter.*

The easing value can be anywhere between -100 and 100, and you can interpret this range as follows:

- 0 means your animation is distributed evenly over time.
- -100 means most of your time is spent in the beginning of the tween (easing in).
- 100 means most of your time is spent at the end of your tween (easing out).

Play with this value and take note of how the plus marks on the motion path change, remembering that marks on the path represent individual frames on the timeline, and that frames on the timeline (for purposes of our discussion here) represent equal chunks of time.

With the ease set to 0 (shown in Figure 6-14), you'll note that the small pluses on your motion path (indicating individual frames on the timeline) are evenly distributed. This means time is evenly distributed, as shown in Figure 6-15.

Figure 6-15.
The motion guide with easing set to 0

With the ease set to -100 (shown in Figure 6-16), you'll note that the small pluses on your motion path (indicating individual frames on the timeline) are squished at the beginning. Much time is spent at the beginning of your tween.

Figure 6-16.
The motion guide with
easing set to -100

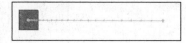

With the ease set to 100 (shown in Figure 6-17), you'll note that the small pluses on your motion path (indicating individual frames on the timeline) are squished at the end. Much time is spent at the end of your tween.

Figure 6-17.
The motion guide with
easing set to 100

> This is obviously a simplification of the complex math behind easing but is meant to explain how you might expect your tweens to behave.

To exaggerate the effect this value has on your animation, extend the duration of your tween as explained next, or better yet lower your frame rate until you see what's going on.

Changing the duration of your motion tween

To change the duration of your tween, hover over the end of the tween span in the timeline. When you see the cursor change into the horizontal double arrow (see Figure 6-18), you may drag the end of the tween span in or out to the desired length as shown in Figure 6-19. Keyframes that follow the tween span on that layer are moved in or out depending on how you changed the length (duration) of your tween.

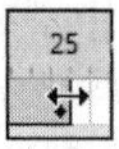

Figure 6-18.
The horizontal double-arrow cursor

Figure 6-19.
Dragging the end of a motion
tween on the timeline

It's important to note that this is a significant difference from the classic tween where changing the duration required adding frames between the beginning and ending keyframes of a motion or shape tween. Because the property keyframes belong to the tween object (and not the instances of the symbol as in the classic tween), you have more control over their behavior as you change the duration of the tween.

If you right-click the tween span, at the bottom of the context menu, you will see the three following options for modifying your motion path:

- Switch keyframes to roving
- Switch keyframes to non-roving
- Reverse Path

The third option will actually reverse the property keyframes of your tween! Figure 6-20 displays these options.

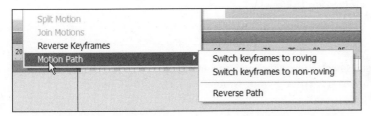

Figure 6-20.
New tween
keyframe options

Roving keyframes vs. nonroving keyframes

When you change the duration of your tween, **nonroving keyframes** will stay put. A keyframe that was on frame 50 will remain on frame 50. A **roving keyframe** will move so that it occurs in the same relative time. For instance, a roving keyframe placed at the halfway point of an 80-frame tween (frame 40) will move to frame 60 when that tween is lengthened to 120 frames.

As you can see, this approach to motion tweening gives you unprecedented control over the path and easing of your tween. This next section goes beyond the path and easing and looks at how to make changes to the symbol that you're tweening in the first place.

Modifying your symbol

So far we've been talking about ways in which you might change the path that your symbol takes on stage over time, but you can also, and will likely want to, change some properties of the symbol itself as well.

Changing the position of your symbol

While the position of your symbol can be modified by manipulating the motion path, you can also simply move your symbol to the position on stage where you'd like it to be at a given time, and Flash will modify the motion path for you.

If your motion path is a straight line and you drag your symbol to a new place on stage, the resulting motion path will be two straight lines, as shown in Figure 6-21. If your motion path is a curve and you drag your symbol to a new position on stage, the resulting motion path will be a more complex curve like the one in Figure 6-22.

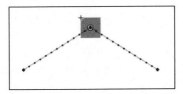

Figure 6-21.
A straight motion path after
changing the position of the
symbol being tweened

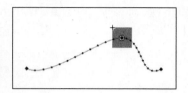

Figure 6-22.
A curved motion path after making the same change of the position of the symbol being tweened

Alternatively, you can select your symbol on stage and use the Property inspector to change the value of the x and y properties of your symbol.

Changing the rotation of your symbol

Things spin, so Flash gives you the ability to change the rotation of your symbol in three easy steps:

1. Activate the Transform tool.

2. Select your symbol on the stage.

3. Rotate your symbol as shown in Figure 6-23.

A new motion keyframe will be added to your motion tween.

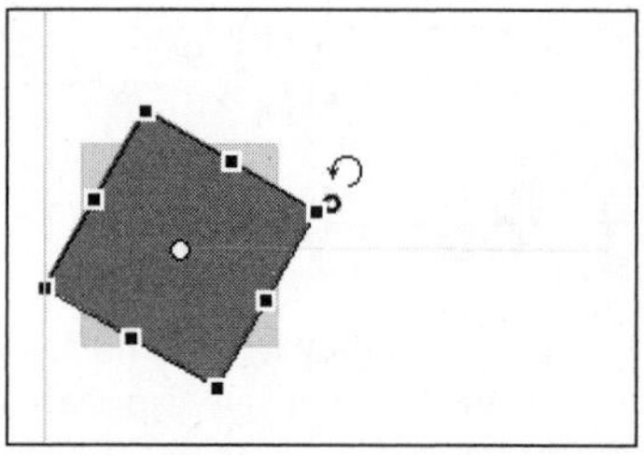

Figure 6-23.
Rotating a tweened symbol

Alternatively, you can select your motion tween from the timeline and use the Property inspector to change the value of the rotation properties of your symbol. Figure 6-24 shows the rotation section for the Property inspector of the motion tween.

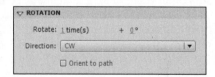

Figure 6-24.
The rotation section for the Property inspector of the motion tween

This is kind of an odd bird in that you are changing the rotation of a symbol, but you do so by changing the properties of its motion tween. Your options include the following:

- Rotate tells Flash how many times to rotate your symbol over the time span of your motion tween.

- Additional degrees tell Flash *how much further* than the number of rotations to turn your symbol. If you enter 360 as the additional degrees value, Flash will change it to 0 and add 1 to your rotate value.

- Direction choices are CW (clockwise), CCW (counterclockwise), or None. CW is selected by default. Selecting None will reset rotation and additional degrees to empty values.
- Orient to path negates all of the other settings and rotates your symbol to follow your motion path.

Experiment with these options. It's fun—seriously.

Color animation

Changing color over time can be instrumental in fine-tuning animation. The subtle change in the intensity of a shadow to indicate changes in button state or adding a hint of red to that reflection effect can make all the difference between "things that move" and a living interface. To animate changes in color, follow these steps:

1. Create a symbol on stage.
2. Right-click (Option-click) your symbol and select Create Motion Tween.
3. You should have 1 second's worth of frames in your timeline with the playhead positioned at the last frame.
4. Select your symbol. Notice the Property inspector. With the exception of Blending, *any* of these properties can be changed over time.
5. In the Color Effect section of the Property inspector, choose Tint from the Style drop-down menu.
6. Select a color from the color picker. (Click the color chip next to the drop-down menu.)
7. Notice that an animation keyframe has been added to the timeline.

Filter animation

You can also use animation to change the following filters:

- Drop shadow
- Blur
- Glow
- Bevel
- Gradient glow
- Gradient bevel

To adjust color filters over time, simply move the playhead to a desired location in time and select the symbol you wish to affect. For example, from the Property inspector add a drop shadow filter, as shown in Figure 6-25.

6

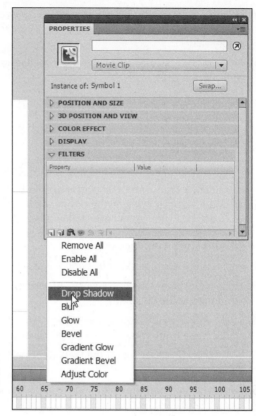

Figure 6-25.
Selecting Drop Shadow from
the Filters drop-down menu
in the Property inspector

You might observe that no animation keyframe magically appears on the timeline as it would if you had changed your symbol's position. While your symbol has values for its position merely by being on stage, your symbol doesn't automatically have values for the filter you just added. Therefore, it can't tween from nonexistent to some other value. So when you add a filter to your tween, Flash applies the initial values to the first frame of the keyframe your symbol is on.

Change some values for that filter and also change the x and y values and notice the change on stage. If you test your movie, you will see the drop shadow changing over time on your symbol.

You can add more than one of each type of filter as your project requires. Move the timeline and make adjustments as needed as explained in the previous sections of this chapter.

To this point you've been using the Timeline panel and Property inspector to craft your animation—a traditional approach to animation in Flash. Next we're going to introduce you to the brand new Motion Editor—a completely new way to edit motion in Flash.

Introducing the Motion Editor

The Motion Editor is brand new in Flash CS4, and it provides you with an expanded interface for changing symbol properties over time independently. The Motion Editor is broken into five main sections, shown here in Figure 6-26.

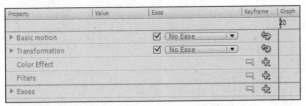

Figure 6-26. The layer information half of the Motion Editor with all sections collapsed

You'll notice that each of the five sections addresses the properties that can be changed over time. You should be familiar with them because you've seen them earlier in this chapter. Top to bottom they are as follows:

- Basic Motion: Holds controls for changing values of the x, y, and z properties of the object being animated as shown in Figure 6-27.

- Transformation: Manages controls for changing skew and scale values for the object being animated, shown here in Figure 6-28.

- Color Effect: Manages controls for alpha, brightness, tint, and advanced transformation values for the object being animated. (Advanced transformation gives you independent control over RGB, RGB offset, and alpha offset values.)

- Filters: Manages controls for drop shadow, blur, glow, bevel, gradient glow, gradient bevel, and adjust color and each of their properties.

- Eases: Represents a bit of a special case, as indicated visually by the darker, heavier line that separates it from the other sections of the Motion Editor as shown at the top of Figure 6-29. It manages the various types of eases you can apply to all of the other sections of the editor.

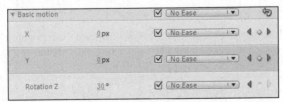

Figure 6-27. The Basic Motion section of the Motion Editor. Here, the y property layer is active as indicated by the darker gray color.

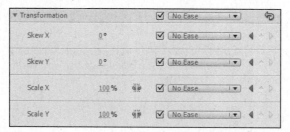

Figure 6-28. The Transformation section of the Motion Editor

Figure 6-29. The Eases section of the Motion Editor shown with the default ease—Simple (Slow)

Each of these sections is distinguished in a manner consistent with the Property inspector and other panels of the interface. Main sections have a slightly darker gray and an arrow to the left for collapsing and expanding that section.

> *You may notice that* Basic Motion, Transformation, *and* Eases *have subsections by default and that the* Color Effect *and* Filters *sections do not, but the latter two do have a feature not on the other three—the* plus *and* minus *buttons for adding and removing sections of their own, which we cover shortly.*

Understanding the Motion Editor

We'll discuss the sections of the Motion Editor in detail in a moment, but we wanted to point something out if you have not already noticed it. Not only can you control each of these areas independently, you can control *every property* of each of these independently, all from a single editor. Without the Motion Editor, you would have to create and make changes to a new instance of an object on the timeline *every* time you wanted to change *any* of the properties, which as you can imagine gets out of hand rather quickly.

If you don't get how extremely cool this is right now, don't worry about it. By the end of this chapter, you will be wondering how you got along without the Motion Editor.

> *This approach is similar to that of many video editing systems, such as Adobe After Effects and, from what we hear, the (now defunct) Adobe Live Motion. It is also the next logical step in the custom ease editor interface from Flash CS3.*

In order to actually use the Motion Editor, you must have created a motion tween using the new method of object tweening detailed earlier in this chapter in the section "Creating a motion tween—a step-by-step primer." Once you have created a tween, you can switch to the Motion Editor view, as shown here in Figure 6-30.

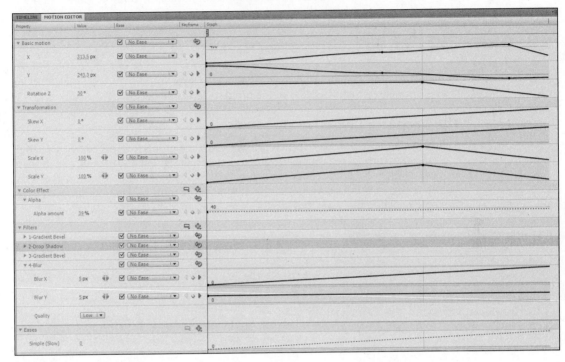

Figure 6-30. The Motion Editor

You must have only one tween selected from the timeline or only one object on stage that is being tweened in order to edit a tween with the Motion Editor. Think of it as an auxiliary Property inspector on steroids just for animation.

The Motion Editor interface

Being a type of extension of the timeline, the Motion Editor is laid out in much the same way, with a section on the left for the property layers and a grid on the right showing the property curves over time. You can use both the controls found in the property layers and the property curves to interact with the values of properties.

Under the Ease column of the Motion Editor you will notice a check box (checked by default) and a drop-down menu with the default value No Ease on every property layer. These controls on the section headers serve as master controls for all of the property layers that fall under that section. The check box enables and disables easing for every property or effect within that section. The drop-down will change the method of easing for all properties within that section at the same time.

> *The* Color Effect *and* Filters *section headers will not have these controls. These override controls will appear on the header of the color effect or filter added to their section of the Motion Editor and will manage all of the individual properties of that color effect or filter.*

To the right of the Ease drop-down you'll notice an arrow turning back on itself. Clicking this button will reset all the values of the property layers below it.

The property layers

If you expand the Basic Motion section, you will see three property layers below in a lighter gray: one each for x, y, and rotation z values, as shown in Figure 6-31. Clicking one of these property layers will both expand that property layer's height and make it a darker gray, indicating that it is the active portion of the Motion Editor. Clicking the property layer again will minimize that layer, but it will remain selected.

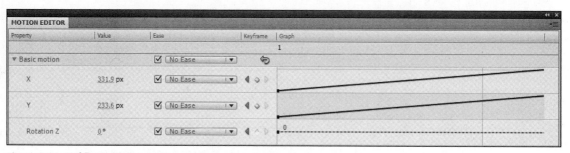

Figure 6-31. The Basic Motion section and its property layers

The headers along the top of the Motion Editor indicate the following:

- Property: The name of the property. This cannot be changed.
- Value: The value of the property. This can be changed either via the numeric hot text or property curve on the graph.
- Ease: Easing controls, as described in the previous section (enable/disable check box, easing type drop-down).
- Keyframe: Previous Keyframe, Add Keyframe, and Next Keyframe buttons. Use these buttons to jump to the next or previous keyframe on the layer or to add a new keyframe where the playhead is when clicked.
- Graph: The property curves, visual representations of the changes in value over time of any given property.

The Eases section

We're going to talk about this section of the property layers first, even though it appears at the bottom of the Motion Editor, because it acts as a tool that lets you determine what eases are made available to the rest of the property layers.

This may be one of the coolest parts of the Motion Editor. Now, you can apply different easing to various properties of your tween. You can apply a bounce ease to your color effect while applying a fast ease in to your rotation while adding a custom ease to your motion blur. How sweet is that?!

Here's how it works. The Eases section of the Motion Editor shows you which eases are available for the tween you are editing. By default only Simple (Slow) is available, shown expanded in Figure 6-32.

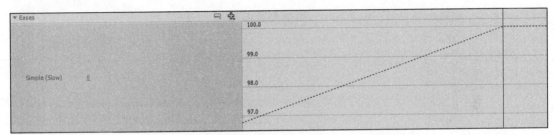

Figure 6-32. The default Eases section of the Motion Editor with Simple (Slow) expanded

To make eases available to your motion edit, click the plus icon in the Eases header and select from the drop-down as shown in Figure 6-33. (We'll choose Custom.)

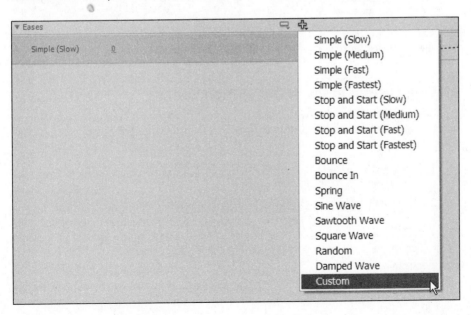

Figure 6-33.
All of the prebuilt eases in the Motion Editor and a custom ease for you to make your own eases with

You'll notice in Figure 6-34 that the custom ease layer is the only one with keyframe controls—this is because it is the only type of ease that is editable. Don't worry, though, you can make as many as you want.

Figure 6-34.
The custom ease has keyframe controls. None of the premade eases do.

You'll notice in Figure 6-35 that any ease added to the Eases section of the Motion Editor will be available to you in the drop-down Ease selector of the other sections of the editor.

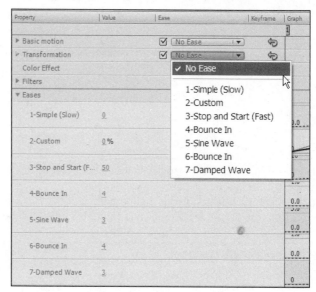

Figure 6-35.
All of the eases added to the Eases section are available for use on the properties of your tween.

Making custom eases in the Motion Editor

Even though Flash CS4 comes with a healthy number of eases, we can never tweak animation enough—so we have the custom ease. Follow these steps to create and edit a custom ease:

1. Add a custom ease to the Motion Editor by clicking the plus icon on the Eases section header.

2. Add a keyframe to the value line on the graph. Right-click the point of the line where you want a new keyframe (shown in Figure 6-36). As an alternative, move the playhead to that point and click the Add Keyframe button located at the right side of the layer information portion of the Motion Editor.

3. Select the handles that appear when you click the line and edit your line as a Bezier curve (see Figure 6-37). You can also click and drag any keyframe to modify your curve.

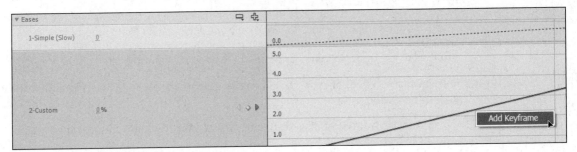

Figure 6-36. Adding a keyframe to a custom curve

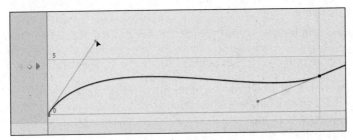

Figure 6-37. Handles on the Bezier curve of the custom ease

The graph

The graph shown in Figure 6-38 should look a little familiar to you now. With the playhead and frame numbers across the top, it should resemble the timeline, and for good reason. Figure 6-38 shows frames 15 through 23, with the playhead on frame 23.

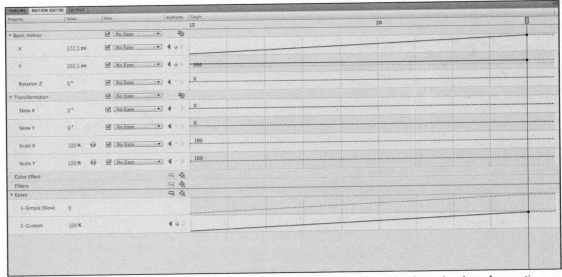

Figure 6-38. The graph appears on the right-hand side of the Motion Editor and shows the change in values of properties over time.

As you make changes to the properties of a symbol over time, those changes will be represented on the graph as a line. If there is only one keyframe for that property, the line will be dotted. If there is more than one keyframe for that property, the line will be solid. All properties have by default one keyframe where its symbol is instantiated on the stage.

You can change values of properties in one of the following ways by interfacing with the graph:

- **Add keyframes**: Adding keyframes creates discrete points in time where values can be changed.
- **Move keyframes**: Moving a keyframe horizontally changes when a property's value changes. Moving a keyframe vertically changes the value of a given property at that time.
- **Move graph lines**: Moving a graph line horizontally will change the time at which the keyframes at either end occur by the same amount. Moving it vertically changes the value of the keyframes at either end by the same amount.

If you happen to drag a keyframe vertically out of visual range of the property layer, the graph for that portion of the layer will begin to scroll. You'll notice the numbers on the left of the graph begin to change with it, indicating the value range of the current view of the property layer's graph.

When you release that keyframe, the property layer will immediately adjust to include the entire range of values in the visible timeline. For instance, if the x values of an object range from 0 to 50, the property layer will indicate this with horizontal lines on the graph labeled 0 and 50. If, however the range is from 0 to 2300, the property layer would reflect this with horizontal lines on the graph labeled 0, 500, 1000, 1500, and 2000. In both cases, the property layer will take up the same vertical real estate in the Flash interface.

Figure 6-39 shows the value line of the x property being tweened from 0 to 2500 over a period of five frames.

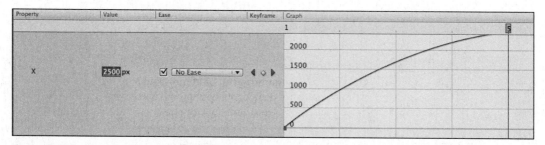

Figure 6-39. The horizontal lines that make up the graph are labeled with the range of values for that property.

Because the property layer updates immediately, this process may take some getting used to. A better way of making large changes in values is through the numeric hot text on the layer information side of the Motion Editor.

To create a new keyframe on the fly, simply move the playhead where you want a change to occur and then change the property's value using the numeric hot text. A new keyframe will be created for you.

Adding a color effect

To add a color effect to your tween by way of the Motion Editor, click the plus icon of the Color Effect section. This presents the drop-down shown in Figure 6-40. You can choose to add an alpha, brightness, tint, or advanced color effect to the tween.

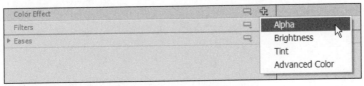

Figure 6-40. Adding a color effect to the Motion Editor

Just as with adding these effects from the Property inspector, you can have only one per motion tween. If you have one selected and change to another type, the first is replaced.

To remove the effect, click the minus icon (shown in Figure 6-41) from the Color Effect section header and select your effect from the drop-down. (There will be only one to choose from.)

Figure 6-41. Removing the color effect in the Motion Editor

Adding filters to your tween

To add a filter to your tween by way of the Motion Editor, click the plus icon of the Filters section. This presents the drop-down menu shown in Figure 6-42. You can choose to add a drop shadow, blur, glow, bevel, gradient glow, gradient bevel, or adjust color filter to the tween.

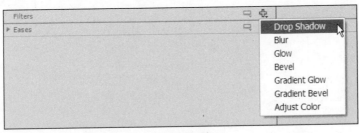

Figure 6-42. Adding a filter to the Motion Editor

Just as with adding these filters from the Property inspector, you can have many on one motion tween (even multiple filters of the same type). Filters are stacked on one another under the Filters section header, and each has its own easing master controls as do the Basic Motion and Transformation sections and operate as described previously.

As you add filters you'll notice that each one can be expanded to reveal property layers of its own. Each section changes to reflect the available properties of the filter you have added. Figure 6-43 shows what the properties of the glow filter look like in the Motion Editor.

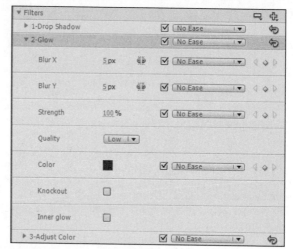

Figure 6-43.
The expanded view of the glow filter shows all of the properties that can be edited in the Motion Editor.

You can use all of the tools and methods described earlier to modify the properties of the filters you have added to the tween. To remove a filter, click the minus icon from the Filters section header and select the filter you wish to remove from the drop-down. Choose Remove All to remove all filters at once as shown in Figure 6-44.

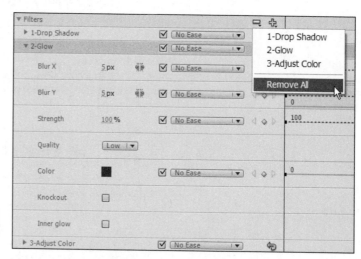

Figure 6-44.
Removing all filters at once

Something to keep in mind

The Motion Editor is a very powerful interface enhancement that provides new control over all of the properties of your tween from a single interface. Just keep in mind that all of the properties accessible through the Motion Editor are the very same properties that you may already be used to accessing through the Property inspector.

The Motion Editor is a convenient and powerful way to modify many properties quickly and with real-time feedback—but none of the properties themselves are new to Flash.

Now that you know about the many ways of creating and modifying motion in Flash, let's talk about making it easy get the most from your hard work by reusing it.

Reusing animation

Duplicating motion in CS4 is a pretty straightforward operation, and you have the following methods to choose from:

- Duplicating a tween from the timeline
- Saving animation as ActionScript
- Saving animation as XML
- Using motion presets

The rest of this chapter is dedicated to explaining these ways of reusing animation.

Duplicating a tween from the timeline quickly

In many cases you may want to repeat an animation but not necessarily need or want to nest it in its own timeline. Here's how to quickly repeat a tween from the timeline:

1. Select a tween.
2. Right-click (or Ctrl-click on a Mac) and select Copy Frames (see Figure 6-45).

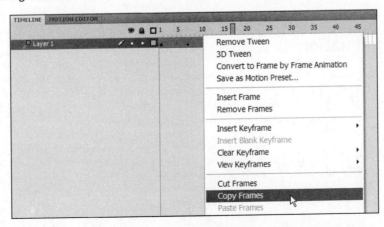

Figure 6-45.
The context menu of the motion tween

3. Select a frame on the timeline and right-click (Option-click on a Mac).

4. Select Paste Frames.

Voilà! A copy of your tween (see Figure 6-46).

Figure 6-46. Pasting frames at the playhead position

You can now drag this tween around the timeline at will when selected, as shown in Figure 6-47. Your tween will also stay on your clipboard until you replace it with something else.

Figure 6-47. Dragging a motion tween on the timeline

> Pasting a motion tween on top of already populated frames will delete the content from those frames.

Saving animation as ActionScript

To save your motion as ActionScript, right-click a tween span on the timeline and select Copy Motion as ActionScript from the menu. Now that it's on your clipboard, you can paste the ActionScript version of your motion into the editor of your choice—it's just text at this point. You could even e-mail it to a friend or post it on your blog. Of course, the real power here is having Flash write the complex code for your animation and then using that code over and over as you see fit without having to reanimate it every time.

Saving animation as XML

To save your motion as XML, select a tween span on the timeline. From the Commands menu select Copy Motion as XML. Now that it's on your clipboard, you can paste the XML version of your motion into the editor of your choice—again, it's just text at this point, and the real advantage to doing this is the reusability and portability.

> Explaining the XML generated by this process falls outside the scope of this chapter. See Chapter 12 for more on using XML with Flash.

Using motion presets

Motion presets are animations stored as XML files on your computer. The motion presets in Flash CS4 are a set of commonly requested animations put in one convenient place. Your operating system user name and installation drive name will dictate exactly where the motion presets are stored. Browse to the following location in your file system to find these files. (User installation and user name values are substituted with *<harddisk>* and *<user>*, respectively.)

- **Windows**: *<harddisk>*\DocumentsandSettings*<user>*\Local Settings\ApplicationData\Adobe\FlashCS4*<language>*\Configuration\Motion Presets\

- **Mac**: *<harddisk>*/Users/*<user>*/Library/Application Support/Adobe/FlashCS4/*<language>*/Configuration/Motion Presets/

Applying motion presets

Follow these steps to apply motion presets to a symbol:

1. Open the Motion Presets panel if it is not already open by selecting Motion Presets from the window menu.

2. Select the symbol instance on stage you wish to apply motion to or drag one from your library if one is not already on stage. You must have something selected on stage in order to apply animation to it.

3. With a symbol instance selected, choose the motion preset you wish to apply, and then click Apply.

4. If you want to apply a different animation to that symbol, simply select that symbol or the tween span in the timeline, select a new preset from the Motion Presets panel, and click Apply. The new preset will be applied to your symbol, replacing the old motion.

> *Motion presets are a specific length. If you apply a 10-frame preset and overwrite a 20-frame motion, the new motion will be 10 frames and everything on the layer that followed it will shift 10 frames earlier, since 10 frames will have been removed from that layer.*

Saving your animation as a custom preset

To save your motion tween as a custom preset, right-click your motion tween in the timeline and select Save as Motion Preset from the menu as shown in Figure 6-48.

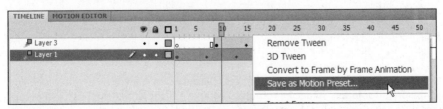

Figure 6-48. You can save motion presets right from the timeline.

You will be prompted with a dialog (see Figure 6-49) asking you to name your new preset. Enter the name of your new preset and click OK to save or Cancel to stop the process.

Figure 6-49.
The Save Preset As dialog

To verify your animation has been saved, look in the Motion Presets panel under Custom Presets as in Figure 6-50.

Figure 6-50.
Your custom motion
saved as a preset in the
Motion Presets panel

Managing motion presets

You can manage motion presets much in the same way you manage your symbol library. The Motion Presets panel comes with two folders, Default Presets and Custom Presets, that cannot be renamed or deleted. However, you can create your own folder hierarchy under the Custom Presets folder, which might come in handy if you have some signature animations you want to keep separated, or perhaps different clients have specific animations that they use and reuse. Figure 6-51 shows a sample custom preset folder hierarchy.

Figure 6-51.
A sample custom
preset folder hierarchy

When you save your motion as a preset, it gets placed in the Custom Presets folder. You can then drag it into any folder or subfolder you have made under the Custom Presets folder. You cannot drag custom presets into the Default Presets folder.

One nice feature is the search function. Below the motion preview and above the preset folders is a search field marked by a binoculars icon, as shown in Figure 6-52. Enter text to search on, and the presets list gets filtered as you type.

Figure 6-52.
Searching motion presets

To clear your search and restore the list, click the X at the right of the search field.

> *At the time of this writing, if you choose to consolidate animations in a subfolder but don't include the subfolder name as part of the preset names themselves, searching on that name will only show you the folder and none of the presets within it.*

Converting motion presets to frame-by-frame animations

You can use the motion tweens as starting points and then convert them to frame-by-frame animations to customize if you choose to. After applying a preset, just right-click your motion tween on the timeline and select Convert to Frame by Frame Animation from the menu shown in Figure 6-53. This will change every frame of your motion tween to a discrete instance of your symbol as well as change the layer to a normal layer as shown in Figure 6-54.

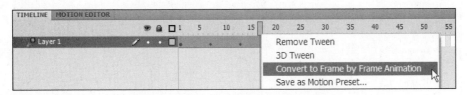

Figure 6-53. Converting a motion tween to a frame-by-frame animation

Figure 6-54.
The motion tween after conversion to frame-by-frame animation

Exporting and importing motion presets

Since motion presets are stored as XML files on your system, they are easily shared among the people you work with and other developers and animators in the community.

Here's how to export a motion preset:

1. Choose the preset in the Motion Presets panel that you want to export.

2. Select Export from the panel menu located in the upper-right corner of the panel or right-click a preset to bring up the menu shown in Figure 6-55, and select Export.

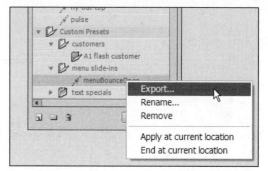

Figure 6-55.
Context menu for a
motion preset

3. In the Save As dialog box (see Figure 6-56), pick a name and location for the XML file and click Save.

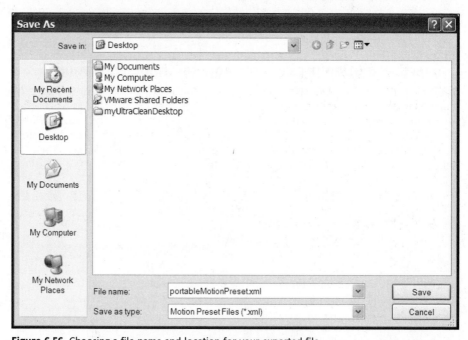

Figure 6-56. Choosing a file name and location for your exported file

Follow these steps to import a motion preset:

1. Select Import from the panel menu located in the upper-right corner of the Motion Presets panel, as shown in Figure 6-57.

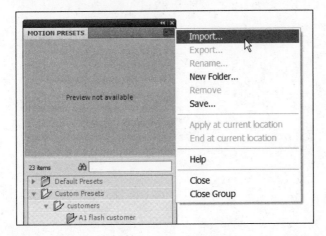

Figure 6-57.
Choosing to import a file

6

2. Browse to the preset file, select it, and click Open. The preset will appear in the Motion Presets panel under the Custom Presets folder as shown in Figure 6-58.

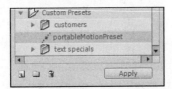

Figure 6-58.
A newly imported preset in the Motion Presets panel

> *It's important to note that the XML schema used for motion presets is different from the XML generated using the steps under "Saving animation as XML." For that reason, XML generated by using the Copy Motion as XML command will not be able to be imported as a motion preset.*

Summary

In this chapter we talked about why animation is important. We discussed when it might be appropriate to use animation in your project. You learned the following:

- Basic animation with the new motion tween
- How the classic motion and shape tweens work
- How to use the new Motion Editor
- How to use, create, and share motion presets

CHAPTER 7
PLAYING WITH DOLLS: INTRODUCING FLASH IK

One of the most highly anticipated features to be included with Flash CS4 is the addition of inverse kinematics (IK) for aiding animation. Inverse kinematics is something that has been eagerly awaited and widely considered long overdue for Flash designers. Up to now it was something only achievable in Flash using advanced ActionScript. IK tools are staples in many other 3D and animation programs used in professional multimedia development. Typically, IK systems are used to animate complex anatomies such as those of humans, animals, and machinery. Fortunately, the developers of Flash have answered the cries of the many animators out there and added a set of tools for governing kinematics with great ease. And the benefits of this technology can now be harnessed in the Flash design environment.

In this chapter we will explore how this new functionality benefits Flash designers. You will be introduced the Bone and Bind tools, which are the two primary tools used to create IK systems. We will then use these tools to apply IK systems to symbols and shapes.

What is kinematics?

Kinematics is the area of mechanics associated with the motion of objects, without consideration for that object's own mass or the external forces acting on that object. Wow, seems intimidating—but don't worry, it is not. In everyday language, kinematics simply describes how objects move.

Inverse kinematics

Though there are several types of kinematics, as far as Flash designers are concerned, we only need to concern ourselves with inverse kinematics. As mentioned previously, kinematics primarily focuses on the motion of objects. Inverse kinematics is a type of kinematics that explains the motion of specific systems. A **system** is essentially a group of connected parts (like a skeleton, hence the bone analogy). And, kinematics is responsible for governing how those parts move in relation to one another.

For example, an arm, along with the hand and shoulder, is a system comprised of three primary segments (hand, forearm, humerus) and three primary joints (wrist, elbow, shoulder). The movement of one of these parts affects the position of the others. It is also important to point out that these systems also must have a base, or fixed end, like a shoulder is fixed to the torso. And, they must have a free end, like a hand.

Inverse kinematics is then specifically responsible for explaining how these systems move when a change is applied to the *free* end. Think of this like a paper doll, marionette, or even an action figure to some extent. When the free end of an appendage is moved or positioned, the rest of the system needs to move as well, like pulling on a chain.

It is through these principles of IK that Flash designers are granted a greater degree of control when working with complex systems. Once applied, the IK functionality in Flash makes animating these complex structures as simple as positioning a paper doll.

An arm or a leg: Experimenting with IK

Now that you are an expert in the concept of IK, it's time to put that knowledge to good use. First, we are going to take a look at building a basic, three-segment IK structure. Here we will discuss the ins, outs, and subtleties of using this tool set. This example will also get you ready to animate a more complicated humanoid system later in this chapter.

Getting started with the arm

You can start off by opening ch07_01_start.fla found in the Chapter 07 folder of the book's source file samples. You will notice a single black rectangle on the stage. This rectangle is a movie clip symbol that we have created for you to use in this example. It represents one of the three segments that we will need to create our three-part IK system. What you are going to need to do here is create two additional segments.

As shown in Figure 7-1, the best way to achieve this is to simply use the original segment and clone or duplicate it across the stage. The easiest way of doing this is to hold down the Alt key (Option key on a Mac) and select the original segment. While still holding the down the left mouse button, you can then drag the new segment out on the stage. Go ahead and repeat this to create all three segments.

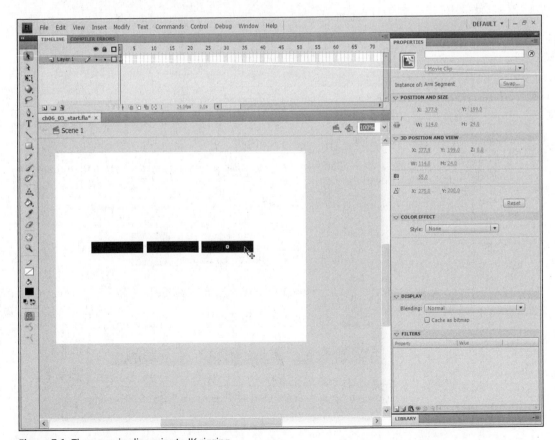

Figure 7-1. Three movie clips prior to IK rigging

Now that we have all three segments on the stage, we can simply link them together using the new Flash IK Bone tool.

The anatomy of a bone

For those of you who have never done any animation before, we cannot begin to explain the amount of time the Flash IK Bone tool is going to save you now that it is available. In addition to being a time saver, it also offers a cleaner and more organized approach to the way animations are produced.

The IK bone, as illustrated in Figure 7-2, is comprised of these three primary components, which are listed in the order of their creation:

- **Parent joint**: The parent joint is the circle located near the larger end of the triangle.
- **Bone**: The bone is the triangular shape that connects the two joints.
- **Child joint**: Subsequently, the child joint is the circle located at the smaller end of the triangle.

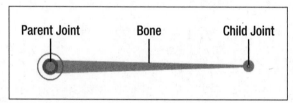

Figure 7-2. IK bones are comprised of three main parts: a parent joint, a bone, and a child joint.

Adding bones to the arm

Now, let's take a crack at adding IK bones to the segment created earlier in this section. To add bones, follow these steps:

1. Select the Bone tool, shown in Figure 7-3, from the Flash Tools panel.

Figure 7-3.
The Bone tool is used to add IK
bones to symbols and vector shapes.

2. Using Figure 7-4 as a reference, move the cursor to the center of the leftmost edge of the left segment.

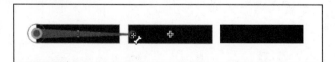

Figure 7-4. Bones can be applied by dragging the Bone tool from one symbol to another.

3. Press and hold the left mouse button to begin drawing the first bone of your IK system.

4. With the left mouse button still held down, move the cursor to the center of the leftmost side of your second segment and release the mouse button. You should now see your first bone connecting the first two segments of your system.

By repeating the process and dragging out a second bone between the second and third segments, you will successfully link all three of these segments into one structured IK system. Once you have completed the linking of the three segments, try selecting each of them with the Selection tool and moving them around the stage. You should notice that all elements in the system move with respect to one another depending on which segment you try to move.

You should also take particular notice of the fact that after completing the process of rigging an IK system, all symbols used in that system will be moved to one new layer as shown in Figure 7-5. This new layer—denoted by a running character in the Layers panel—is referred to as an **armature**.

Figure 7-5.
IK structures are grouped together into an armature and moved to a new layer.

> *The term "armature" is classically used in sculpture to refer to a wireframe pose around which clay is applied to produce a sculpture. You will later see that keyframes used in IK animations are also referred to as **poses**. Hence the reason behind this brilliantly used metaphor.*

Controlling the motion of specific bones

You have just seen how quickly and efficiently you can create a simple three-segment system using the new Flash IK tools. And though it may not be something worthy of hanging on the refrigerator, it certainly is your first step toward animation mastery. Before we get into the heavy lifting, there is one more thing we would like to show you with regards to the specific nature of individual IK bones.

Like most other elements in the Flash development environment, individual IK bones are able to have specific parameters applied to them through the use of the Property inspector. This functionality becomes incredibly advantageous when a designer begins to develop more sophisticated systems—like humanoids or octopods. In order to access this functionality, you will need to select a specific bone within your armature. When the bone is selected, it will turn a color that is complementary to the color of the entire system.

> *In this instance, the term "complementary" is used as it would be in color theory. Essentially, this means that a selected bone will become the opposite color of the rest of the bones in a system. For example, if the system is orange, the selected bone will be blue. Likewise, if the system is cyan, the selected bone will be red.*

7

Upon selecting a specific bone, the Property inspector will change to reflect the specific parameters of that particular bone. It is important to understand that the parameters applied to a specific bone in the Property inspector directly influence that bone's parent joint. As noted earlier, the parent joint is the circular part of the bone located next to the larger end of the bone's triangular shape. Therefore, if we adjust the rotation of a bone, it will control how the bone rotates around its parent joint.

As shown in Figure 7-6, four types of parameters can be applied to a bone through the Property inspector once it has been selected:

- **Joint location**: Though the Location section gives specific information relative to the position of the selected bone, you are unable to change the position from the Property Inspector. What can be changed here is the Speed parameter. The speed at which a bone can move will give the bone the illusion of weight in an animation.

- **Joint rotation**: The set of parameters under Joint: Rotation allows you to control the rotation of a bone around its parent joint. You have the ability to enable, disable, and constrain or limit the range of motion.

- **Joint x translation**: The set of parameters under Joint: X Translation allows you to control a parent joint's motion along the x axis, which is horizontal or left-to-right motion.

- **Joint y translation**: The set of parameters under Joint: Y Translation allows you to control a parent joint's motion along the y axis, which is vertical or top-to-bottom motion.

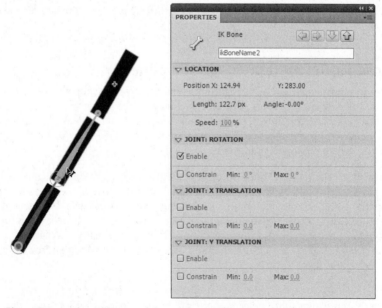

Figure 7-6. A selected bone and the subsequent Property inspector parameters

Let's apply constraints to some specific bones.

Applying constraints to specific bones

For starters, go ahead and select the first bone in your system from ch07_01.fla. Remember, when a bone is selected, it will highlight with a color complementary to the rest of the bones in that system. Now pay close attention to the parent joint. You may have noticed a thin circle that surrounds it. This circle, as shown in Figure 7-7, indicates that joint rotation has been applied to this particular joint.

Figure 7-7.
The constraint indicator is used to show which contraints have been applied to a bone.

Let's go ahead and remove this joint's ability to rotate.

1. In the Property inspector **under the** Joint: Rotation section, uncheck the check box next to the word Enable. You should notice that the constraint indicator circle disappears.

Try to move the system by dragging its various segments. You will see that arm no longer has motion from what we will call the shoulder joint.

Next let's change the parameters on the second bone in our system.

2. After selecting this bone, disable the joint rotation by unchecking the check box next to Enable under Joint: Rotation in the Property inspector.

3. Enable the y translation by checking the check box next to Enable under the Joint: Y Translation section in the Property inspector.

Again, you should notice that the circle around this joint has disappeared. You will also notice that a small line with two arrowheads has now appeared along the parent joint's vertical axis. If you haven't already guessed, this line is the constraint indicator for y translation.

As you learned earlier, x translation and y translation parameters are responsible for constraining the motion of a parent joint to a linear motion in either a vertical or horizontal direction. Try moving the system now. You'll see that the first segment basically does nothing, the second segment is now restricted to moving up and down, and the third segment still freely spins in 360 degrees.

Constraining bone movement

Finally, notice that the Joint: Rotation, Joint: X Translation, and Joint: Y Translation sections of the Property inspector all contain a Constrain check box option. With these parameters, you can limit the range of motion for any parent joint associated with the Constrain.

For example, the second segment in our system can move up and down with no apparent limitation. Select the bone associated with that section. Then check the check box next to Constrain under Joint: Y Translation in the Property inspector. You should immediately note two specific changes. The arrowheads on the orange line that indicate y translation on the parent joint of that bone have changed to straight lines. You should also notice that the Min and Max values next to the Constrain check box have become active. It is now possible to edit the Min and Max values to limit the total range of motion for that joint. This is also true for joint rotation.

> The Min *value can be set to any value between 0.0 and –5760. The* Max *value can be set to any number between 0.0 and 5760. The* Joint: X Translation Constrain *values operate in the same fashion for a horizontal direction, and the* Joint: Rotation Constrain *values can be set to any number between –360 and 360 degrees.*

Now that you are familiar with controlling bones and the IK system, let's try animating the arm.

Creating motion with an IK system

All right, we think it's about time you saw something move on its own, don't you? This is where the real power of the Flash IK tools comes to light. So far in this chapter we have primarily focused on the construction of a simple three-segment IK structure. And so far, it probably doesn't seem terribly difficult to work with the Flash IK tools. We hope this is the case.

In this section we are now going to examine how IK animation is different from traditional methods of Flash animation. Then we will apply these techniques to the arm we created in the previous section.

Comparing IK to motion tweening

Let's briefly examine the file ch07_02.fla, found in this chapter's working files. This file is more or less the same arm system you have been experimenting with. The primary difference is that it has been constructed using traditional (motion) tweening methods. And though the tweening model in Flash CS4 is significantly easier to work with than previous versions, it still poses a tremendous amount of difficulty when trying to articulate complex systems.

When examining ch07_02.fla, you should immediately notice that it looks pretty much exactly like the ch07_01_start.fla file you have been working with so far in this chapter. There are three black rectangles that need to be animated to mimic the motions of an arm.

The first primary difference to point out is the presence of two additional layers, as shown in Figure 7-8. Unlike the IK system that automatically organizes all three segments on one layer, motion tweening requires that each symbol reside on its own layer.

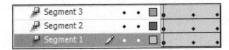

Figure 7-8.
Animating with traditional tweening methods requires a more complicated layer structure.

> Remember, when tweening by regular methods, each symbol needs to reside on its own layer. So, even with a system as simple as a three-segment arm, the efficiency of organization immediately takes a hit.

Imagine how complicated this would become if you were animating several human characters. Even the simplest human character would need between five and eight parts working in tandem to achieve the illusion of animation. Add more characters, and the complexity of the layer structure alone becomes a nightmare.

Next, take a moment to see how the ch07_02.fla animation works by moving the playhead slowly from frame 1 to frame 10. You should notice that as you approach frame 3, the three segments of this animation begin to overlap. This is definitely not very effective. Therefore, in addition to increased layer management, a designer would also be responsible for an increased number of intermittent tweaks to get the animation to behave in the desired manner. You may close ch07_02.fla.

Animating the arm

Fortunately, we now have the ability to control animation quickly and efficiently with the Flash IK tools. Let's go ahead and animate the arm in ch07_01_start.fla.

> We realize that, through the various experimentations in this chapter, your version of this file may not be the best starting point. If you need a fresh start, you may use ch07_03_start.fla. It should look familiar to you when you open it.

Remember that in animation we need keyframes. When dealing with IK armatures, keyframes are referred to as *poses*. Therefore, we will need to pose our armature in the manner in which we would like it to look. You have the option here to pose your armature in any manner you see fit. And, if you would like, please feel free to play with the Property inspector parameters for each bone to help you gain more familiarity. For the sake of comparison, the sample files ch07_03_start.fla and ch07_03_finish.fla will be improving on the throwing animation demonstrated in ch07_02.fla.

Your armature should be set in the proper starting point, as decided by you. The next thing that you will need to do is set an end position. Animation, of course, is the change of state over time. So we will need to add a few frames. This has been made extremely easy in Flash CS4, as you will see by following these steps:

1. Position your mouse over frame 1 of the Armature_1 layer of your current working file. Your mouse cursor should change from a white arrow to a short black line with two arrowheads, which are pointing left and right.

2. Go ahead and select frame 1 by clicking your mouse. Frame 1 should now be highlighted in blue.

3. With the mouse button still pressed, you can drag to the right and highlight additional frames to add to your animation. We suggest highlighting to frame 10.

4. Once you have highlighted the desired number of frames, you may release the mouse button, and additional frames will be added to the timeline.

5. Make sure the playhead is at the last frame of your animation. For example, we have set our playhead to frame 10. Once you have done this, arrange your armature in a different pose. Move the playhead back and forth across the timeline, and see what you get.

Not bad. Let's add an intermittent pose. Position the timeline approximately halfway between the beginning and end of your animation. As shown in Figure 7-9, we have positioned our playhead to frame 5. Now we can add a new pose.

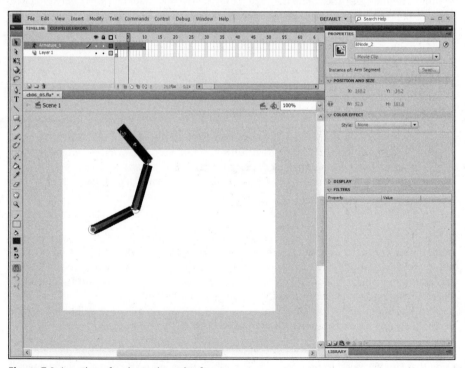

Figure 7-9. Insertion of an intermittent keyframe

As you learned earlier, in order to achieve a change in an animation, you need a keyframe. Remember, keyframes in IK animations are called poses. There are a few ways you can add a new pose to the timeline in Flash. We will explain the two most commonly used and efficient methods to do this.

The first method is to right-click (Ctrl-click on a Mac) a frame:

1. Move the mouse cursor over a frame in the timeline where you would like to place a new pose.
2. Right-click (Windows) or Ctrl-click (Mac).
3. Select Insert Pose from the context menu.

As an alternative, you can also add a pose simply by adjusting the armature as follows:

1. Move the playhead to the desired position for adding a new pose.
2. Reposition the armature as needed, and a keyframe is automatically added.

Since the repositioning of the armature is required for all other methods of adding poses to armature animations, the second option should be considered the most efficient way to perform this task.

Using one of the aforementioned methods for including poses in an armature animation, you may now add a second pose to your animation. Sticking with the examples from earlier, ch07_03_finish.fla demonstrates a simple throwing motion.

That's it! You have successfully created an animation using the Flash IK tools. It may not seem like much yet, but you will be applying these techniques to a more complicated structure very shortly. And, though it may not be immediately evident, these techniques will save you hours in production.

Author-time versus runtime IK animation

Before all this newfound knowledge can be brought together into something useful, there is one more thing that is worth mentioning. Flash IK tools have the ability to be set for either author-time use or runtime use. If you are not familiar with the terms "author time" and "runtime," don't worry. **Author time** simply means something that happens while you are creating or authoring your Flash projects in the Flash IDE, and **runtime** refers to something that happens when you play or run your Flash movies.

If you still have your file open from the previous example, you are going to use it for one last example. If you happened to close it, don't worry—you can simply open ch07_03_finish.fla.

To switch between author-time and runtime IK animation, all you need to do is select any frame in the Flash timeline on the Armature_1 layer. You will notice that the entire timeline associated with this layer is highlighted blue. When this happens, you should also notice that the Property inspector reflects various parameters that can be applied to this specific animation. This is demonstrated in Figure 7-10.

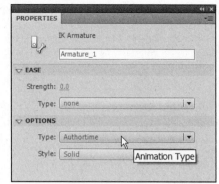

Figure 7-10.
The timeline properties
for a pose layer in the
Property inspector

> *You should already be comfortable with the* Ease *section from Chapter 6.*

For now, take a look at the Options section. The Style drop-down menu allows you to determine the type of bones that are used in your armature:

- Wire: Displays bones in the familiar triangular fashion. The primary difference is that these triangles are represented by outlines also known as **wireframes**.

- Solid: Serves as the default display setting for bones. It is what you should be used to working with in this chapter. Bones are represented by filled triangular shapes of varying color.

- Line: Simply displays bones as single individual lines of varying colors.

The other drop-down menu shown in the Options section of the Property inspector is the Type drop-down. It is here that you have the ability to set the IK animation to Authortime or Runtime. Select Runtime from the Type drop-down.

Oops! You may have noticed the screen prompt shown in Figure 7-11 warning you of an error with your animation. This is actually quite all right.

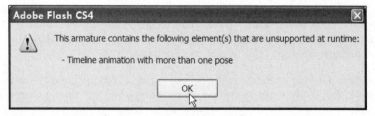

Figure 7-11. An alert window is triggered when runtime animation is used improperly.

The reason for this error is that IK animations that are to be set for runtime are not allowed to have more than one pose. Why, you ask? Well, if the armature is set to be used at runtime, you will have the ability to pose and interact with it when the Flash movie is playing. If there are several poses defined at author time, the armature will want to animate itself. You can't move an object and have it move itself at the same time.

To remedy this you will need to do the following:

1. Delete frames 2 through 10 of the Aramture_1 layer in your movie.

   You can do this by selecting frames 2 through 10, right-clicking (Ctrl-clicking on a Mac), and then selecting Remove Frames from the context menu.

2. You may now return to the Property inspector and change the Type drop-down from Authortime to Runtime.

3. Test this movie.

You are now able to move your IK armature in your published SWF files just as you were able to on the stage. If you tried this with Authortime still selected, you would be unable to move your armature.

Using IK with complex anatomies

There is no doubt that the true purpose of the Flash IK tools is for use with complex anatomies such as human character animations. In the next section we are going to rig a simple cartoon character to help you better understand this concept. When we finish, you should have a thorough understanding of this process and how to apply IK rigs to even more complex systems in the future.

Simple anatomy: A little help from Leonardo

Setting up a human IK rig is going to be a bit more complicated than that of an arm. After all, the human design has two arms! Additionally, your human armature will introduce you to the concept of **branching**. Though this is not a particularly difficult concept to understand, it may not be obvious for those who have no prior experience with this sort of animation. Therefore, we are going to take a second to examine the anatomy of the human IK rig before we begin.

Using the popular drawing of Leonardo da Vinci's *Vitruvian Man* as our model, we have the ability to examine just how one would begin to apply an IK system to a human being. If you have ever spent time in a gym training for a sport or watching ESPN right before the sun comes up, you may have heard the term "power core." Also referred to as the core or powerhouse in Pilates, the **power core** refers to the center of the body. This area is traditionally comprised of the abdomen, lower back, and often the buttocks and inner thighs. It is referred to as the power core because it is responsible for the stabilization of the entire body. Essentially, the human body's mechanics are grounded in the abdomen.

We are always amazed by the apparent unintentional nature of art imitating life. You could, for example, start constructing your IK armature from the head of a figure and get it to work to some degree. You could also begin your armature in the chest area, and that would probably work pretty well, too. This may, however, create a rotation problem later in the hips of many armatures. If you plot your first bone at about the belly button, that will give you the most efficient apparatus. Even in the designing of an IK animation, the abdomen serves as the best center.

7

This principle, of course, applies only to humanoids. If you were to create an octopus, for example, the head would be the best place to start your IK system.

Subsequently, all other bones in the armature branch out from this center point. As you can see from Figure 7-12, this armature is comprised of three primary branches. The first of these is the parent, or root, bone, which starts at the belly button and traverses to the chest, the neck, and finally the head. The other two primary branches are the legs. For these, bones travel through the hips, thighs, lower legs, and joint at the ankle.

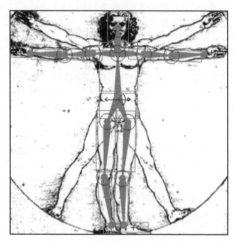

Figure 7-12.
An IK armature applied to Leonardo da Vinci's *Vitruvian Man*

Finally, you may now be wondering the obvious question about the classification for the arms. Well, the obvious answer is that they are secondary branches off of one of the primary branches. These systems can become quite sophisticated if necessary. Imagine that you are going to detail the armature of a human to the finger level. Fingers are a three-part system in their own right. Therefore, your child branches would have child branches (grandchildren). And, the chances of getting three levels of branching are probably a little better than you might think.

Applying IK to a human character

To begin adding an IK rig to a character, the first thing to do is familiarize yourself with the assets that will be used in the file. In the real world, you will want to have this planned out in advance. In this case, we have supplied you with a file that contains all the graphical elements that you will need to create this animation.

For this example, we will start with the working file ch07_04_start.fla. Open this file and explore the layer structure as shown in Figure 7-13. You should notice that the graphics for this file have been organized as a head, a torso, a hip, two legs, and two arms. The layers have also been organized with respect to the physiology of the character. That is, the front arm pieces are in front of the torso, and the back arm pieces are behind the torso. This stacking order also holds true for the head, legs, and so forth.

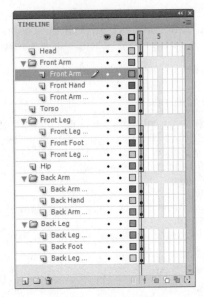

Figure 7-13. Body parts of any character should be arranged logically.

Before we get started, it is important we point out that the most complicated part of this process will be keeping the character organized. As you add pieces to the armature, Flash will automatically pull pieces off of their respective layers and add them to the armature layer. This will, without question, change the preestablished stacking order of each graphic.

Additionally, it will also be somewhat difficult at first to get the feel for adding each new bone. Until you have become comfortable with this process, you will probably feel that each graphic is getting in the way of the others. Because of this, we will offer the following suggestions.

- Utilize the outlining feature for each layer.

  While you are rigging the character, we suggest that you immediately turn on outlines for the armature layer so you can see the pieces that have not yet been added. This will also help you position the bones more accurately.

- Move pieces out of the way.

  You should notice from Figure 7-13 that several pieces overlap. For example, the front arm overlaps the hip piece and top portion of the front leg. You will more than likely want to move the front arm out of the way to get access to the underlying pieces.

- Reorder layers as you work.

  As mentioned earlier, adding graphics to the armature will change the stacking order of the original layout. It may be advantageous to manually change the position of layers as you work. This will also make it easier to access certain graphics throughout the process.

- Lock and unlock layers as needed.

  To avoid confusion and inadvertent symbol selection, it is recommended that you utilize the locking and unlocking of layers as you work.

Now that we are ready, let's get started!

Setting up the core

The first thing we will want to do is establish the root of our structure. As discussed earlier, the best place to start is in the abdomen area. In this case, our character's midsection is broken into two primary parts: the torso and hip symbols. Of these two pieces the most centrally sound is going to be the hip symbol. The hip will give us direct access to both the legs and upper body.

You can begin your armature by doing the following:

1. With the timeline open, unlock the Head, Torso, and Hip layers of the character.

2. Hide the front arm graphics by clicking the Show/Hide layer button for the Front Arm folder's layer.

3. Make sure the Property inspector is open to allow you to add constraints.

4. Select the Bone tool from the Tools panel and draw your first bone from the hip graphic to the upper portion of the torso graphic.

> It is recommended that you immediately switch the Armature_1 *layer to outlines to help you keep organized.*

Once your first bone is added, your stage should look similar to Figure 7-14. The center of the hip has been connected to the torso right near the center. The Armature_1 layer has had the outline option selected so that items will become transparent as they are added to the armature.

Figure 7-14.
The first step when creating an IK rig is establishing the parent, or core.

5. Draw a second bone from the child joint of your first bone to the head symbol just at the base of the neck.

6. Select this second bone. In the Property inspector, uncheck the box next to Enable under the Joint: Rotation options.

7. Select the first bone. Check the box next to Enable under the Joint: X Translation options. This will later allow you to move the character from left to right.

Adding the arms

Next we will want to add the arms for the character. The arms will be secondary systems that originate from the joint that is located on the character's chest. For this we will also be adding more constraints for the shoulders, elbows, and wrist joints.

To add the arms, follow these steps:

1. Unlock the Back Arm layer, and drag that layer above the Armature_1 layer.

2. With the Bone tool selected, drag a bone from the chest joint to the top of the upper portion of the back arm as shown in Figure 7-15. When the cursor changes to a white bone with the plus sign (also shown in Figure 7-15), this signifies the ability to add a new bone.

Figure 7-15.
When the Bone tool cursor changes to a white bone, a new bone can be added.

3. Add a bone for this arm that connects the shoulder to the elbow.

4. Add a bone from the elbow to the wrist.

5. You want to constrain the motion of the elbow. To do this, select the bone going from the elbow to the wrist. In the Property inspector, check the box next to Constrain under the Joint: Rotation options. Set the Min property to -85 and the Max property to 0.

6. Repeat the preceding steps to add the bones to the front arm. Make sure that the layers are unlocked and visible.

Once you have finished rigging both arms, we strongly suggest that you move them out of the way so they don't impede the rigging of the rest of your character. When you have finished with the arms, you should have a character that resembles the image shown in Figure 7-16.

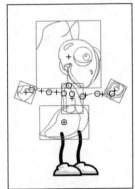

Figure 7-16.
The arms of the character are moved to help the rigging process.

Adding the legs

Adding legs to the IK system is actually very similar to adding the arms. When adding the legs, we are going to use the hip bone as the parent. Adding the legs will be a bit more difficult, as the graphics are very close together.

To add the legs, follow these steps:

1. Unlock the Front Leg and Back Leg folders' layers.

2. Starting with the front leg, create a new bone by dragging the Bone tool from the hip to the upper leg. Figure 7-17 shows that a bone can be started by mousing over any part of a symbol. Figure 7-18 shows you how to apply this bone.

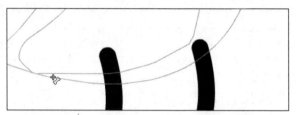

Figure 7-17. The add bone icon will appear when mousing over any symbol with a bone already applied to it.

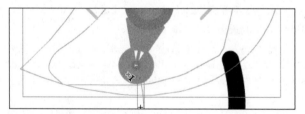

Figure 7-18. The hip bone is connected to the leg bone. We know!

3. Create a bone that connects the upper leg joint to the lower leg at the knee.

4. Add the bone that connects the lower leg to the foot at the ankle.

5. Select the bone that connects the lower leg to the foot. In the Property inspector check the box next to Constrain under the Joint: Rotation options. Set the Min property to -60 and the Max property to 135.

6. Repeat these steps to add bones to the back leg.

Once you have added the bones to both legs, you should have a character like the one shown in Figure 7-19.

Figure 7-19.
All bones have been
added to the character.

Cleaning up your character

Before we can begin the animation process, we will need to do a bit of tidying up. The process of adding an IK system to your character has no doubt wreaked havoc on the general organization of things.

1. Delete all layers in your timeline except the Armature_1 layer. All of your graphics have been moved to this layer. Therefore, none of the other layers are needed.

2. Turn off the outlines option for the Armature_1 layer. You will now see how crazy everything has really become.

3. To fix the stacking order of the character pieces, right-click (Ctrl-click on a Mac) each symbol and select Adjust from the context menu. Using a combination of Bring to Front and Send to Back, rearrange the stacking order of each symbol so that it is restored to its original position.

4. It may also be necessary to slightly adjust the positions of specific symbols. To adjust the positions of a specific symbol, select that symbol with the Subselection tool while holding the Alt key (Option key on a Mac). You can also use the Transform tool to tweak the symbol's transform point if needed.

Animating the character

Animating your Flash IK character is actually the easiest part of the whole process. All you need to do is add some frames and position the armature in a new pose, and the character will animate.

To animate the character, do the following:

1. Pose the armature in a desired starting position.

2. As shown in Figure 7-20, add frames by mousing over frame 1 of the timeline. When the cursor becomes the double arrow, drag out more frames on the timeline.

Figure 7-20.
The double arrow allows designers to
quickly add frames to the timeline.

3. To create movement, simply move the playhead to a different frame on the time-line and change the position of your character to create a new pose as shown in Figure 7-21.

Figure 7-21.
To add a new pose, simply
reposition the armature.

4. Finally, once you have created several positions for your character, test your movie. You will see your character animate across the stage (see Figure 7-22).

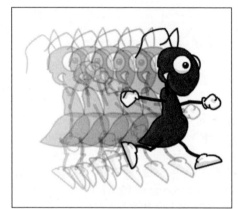

Figure 7-22.
Characters will easily
animate using the IK tools.

Now that you have seen how easy it is to animate a complex structure, experiment a bit. Try adding different constraints and new intermittent poses to see what you can come up with.

Using IK with shapes and the Bind tool

Another exciting feature of the Flash IK tools is the ability to use bones with vector shapes. This gives designers an incredible amount of increased control over the animation of vector shapes. Unlike symbol instances, which only allow one bone per symbol, shapes allow you to add as many bones as you need to create the animation you desire.

In addition to the ability to add multiple bones to a shape, designers also have the ability to add bones to multiple shape fills and strokes at the same time. In fact, during our research with this new functionality, we were able to add an IK system to a vector-based butterfly that was comprised of over 600 individual shapes! And, in a similar fashion to the way symbols are grouped, all shapes associated with a shaped-based IK system are grouped together on their own new pose layer.

Working with bones and vector shapes

Creating an IK shape object is an extremely easy process that can be summed up in the following steps:

1. Select a vector shape in Flash.

2. Select the Bone tool from the Flash Tools panel.

3. Add a bone in exactly the same manner that you would add a bone to a symbol instance. Similarly, you can add bones to multiple shapes by simply selecting all shapes that are required for the animation, and then applying the bones using the Bone tool.

Selecting shapes for IK

To get some practice with this technique, let's take a look at ch07_star_start.fla, located in the sample files for Chapter 7. As you can clearly see, this is a very simple file comprised of one shape, which resides on one layer, which spans one frame. To add an IK system to this star, as shown in Figure 7-23, you need to make sure that the star is selected. So, go ahead and select the star with the Selection tool found in the Flash Tools panel. You will by now recognize that it is selected by the hash pattern that appears within the fill color.

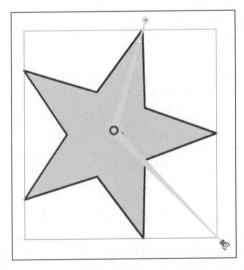

Figure 7-23.
An IK bone being applied to a vector star shape

For just a moment it is worth drawing attention to the fact that the star has a blue stroke. If you were to add a bone to the star shape at our current point in this discussion, the blue stroke would be excluded. It is important that when you are using the Flash IK tools with vector shapes, you make sure that everything you want to animate is selected. For now, selecting the blue stroke with the star is simply a matter of double-clicking the star with the Selection tool. If in the future your shapes did happen to be independent from one another, you could simply draw a selection rectangle with the Selection tool or Shift-click all your shapes with the Selection tool.

Applying bones to a vector shape

Once your shapes are selected, you may add a bone using the Bone tool in the Flash Tools panel. In the exact same fashion as you would when adding bones to symbols, select the Bone tool and click the selected shape where you would like the root of your armature to be. Once you have clicked your shape, you can drag out a new bone in any direction.

One of the primary differences between shape bones and symbol bones is the fact that when dragging out bones with shapes, you do not have to attach the bone to anything else. Figure 7-23 shows that the child end of your IK bones can be positioned virtually anywhere.

Now that you have bones connected to your shape, you will notice that a new pose layer was created in Flash. You can also experiment with how the bones affect different aspects of the shape. Try experimenting with adding more bones and seeing how they too affect the transformation of the overall shape.

Further, you have the ability to create complex armatures with shapes. Figure 7-23 demonstrates a couple simple bones being added to the star shape. Imagine if you were to construct a human armature for the star like the one you constructed earlier for the cartoon character. You could theoretically animate a dancing star!

> Though we won't demonstrate this here, we will include ch07_human_star.fla with our example files for those curious as to how this would be done.

Regardless of what you do, it is inevitable that you will start to develop some fairly complicated armatures that may require some tweaking and adjusting. In many cases you may not have your joints in the exact place that they are needed. To adjust a joint's position, simply select that joint with the Subselection tool—also affectionately called the white arrow—and move the joint to the desired location. Should you find yourself in the unfortunate situation that a bone needs to be deleted, select the problematical appendage with the Selection tool and simply press Delete.

Using the Bind tool

As you no doubt noticed from your experimentations over the last few pages, working with IK and shapes sometimes delivers varying and unexpected results. To help with this issue and offer designers more control over their IK shapes, the fine people at Adobe have included a nifty little contraption known as the Bind tool. The Bind tool allows you to link various control points on your vector shape to specific bones within your IK rig. This tool can be used to link a bone to multiple control points or multiple bones to the same control point.

Accessing the Bind tool

To access the Bind tool, take a look at the Bone tool in the Flash Tools panel. You should notice a small black triangle in the lower-right corner of the tool. This triangle signifies that a tool is grouped with other tools or other sets of tools. In this case the Bone tool is grouped with the Bind tool. To activate the Bind tool, click the Bone tool and hold down the mouse button until a fly-out menu appears that contains both the Bone and Bind tools. From this fly-out menu, you may select the Bind tool shown in Figure 7-24. This tool can also be accessed by pressing Z.

Figure 7-24.
To access the Bind tool, hold down the mouse button while selecting the Bone tool in the Tools panel.

Applying binds to shapes

To apply binding to your armature, select your IK shape object with the Bind tool. If your armature is already visible, select a specific bone with the Bind tool. As shown in Figure 7-25, when you select a bone, it will be signified by a red line. All applicable surrounding control points will be highlighted yellow. By this, we mean that not all control points on the shape will be active for each bone. Therefore, when this bone is moved during animation, only the yellow control points and strokes associated with those control points will be affected. This is where the Bind tool comes into play.

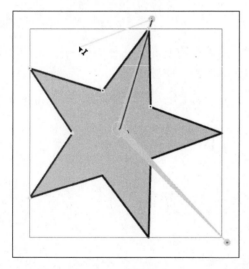

Figure 7-25.
The Bind towol is used to apply multiple control points to bones.

With the Bind tool, you can link other control points in the shape, which are not highlighted yellow, to a particular bone. There are two ways to add a control point to a bone:

- With the Bind tool selected, Shift-click any control point that is not highlighted yellow. As shown in Figure 7-25, you may also Shift-drag from the child, or tail end, of any given bone.

- In contrast, if you would like to remove control points from bones, you may use the Ctrl key (Cmd key on a Mac) instead of Shift. Using the Ctrl key, you may either click or drag to remove unwanted control points.

7

Finally, you may have noticed that some control points are squares and some control points are triangular. This small difference is an indicator for how many bones are connected to that particular control point. As we mentioned earlier, you have the option to link multiple bones to a single control point. The square signifies that this particular control point is connected to one bone. Consequently, a triangle lets the designer know that this control point is governed by two or more bones.

For great practice working with the Bind tool, try to bind the IK armature from ch07_human_star.fla that was discussed earlier. This file is found in the sample files directory for this chapter.

Summary

Well, you learned some pretty cool things in this chapter. And, we really only scratched the surface of the new and powerful capabilities now available through the use of the Flash IK tools. We trust that your creative interests have been stirred and hope you already have many uses for this newly acquired knowledge.

In this chapter we discussed

- Inverse kinematics
- Using the Bone tool to apply an IK system
- Animating complex systems and characters with IK
- Applying IK to vector shapes with the Bone and Bind tools

PART THREE
ACTIONSCRIPT

CHAPTER 8

THE PROGRAMMING PRIMER:
A FLASH DESIGNER'S INTRO
TO ACTIONSCRIPT 3.0

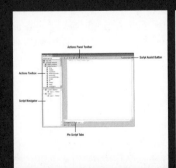

Welcome to the wonderful world of ActionScript programming. In the first two parts of this book, you have been exposed to what is classically considered the design side of Flash authoring. Throughout the duration of this book, you will gradually be introduced to the versatile capabilities of ActionScript, the developer side of Flash authoring.

In terms of programming languages, ActionScript is easily the most widely used language in new media. Its functionality is applicable in industries such as web design, game design, courseware development, and enterprise-level application development. Developers or graphic designers possessing a keen sense of proper ActionScript usage open a whole new level of opportunity for their career.

In this chapter you will be introduced to the most basic elements of ActionScript programming. You will gain needed insights and the proper foundation to adequately implement the various aspects of ActionScript that will be covered in the upcoming chapters. Even if you are an experienced programmer, this chapter will serve as your point of translation and allow you to quickly apply programming logic you may already know to ActionScript.

If you are someone transitioning to the world of Flash, it is important that you do not become discouraged or overwhelmed by the breadth of this topic. At any given point in this publication, it is possible to extract a section or chapter and have an entire book devoted to only the material covered in that section. In fact, because there are so many directions a Flash professional could take, Adobe once offered two certification exams to adequately represent a person's true understanding of the software.

Additionally, you should understand that programming, in its own right, is a topic that goes beyond the scope of Flash itself. Therefore, though you will be introduced to the language and some basic programming concepts, we encourage you to explore and reinforce your learning through additional reading and research.

Some excellent online resources for learning Flash and ActionScript include www.kirupa. com and www.actionscript.org. The benefit of online tutorials and forums is that it is very common for other developers to be seeking answers to the same problems as you. This is beneficial because it has a tendency to yield many solutions. We will also point out additional resources in later chapters as it becomes relevant.

Before we get started with the tools and elements of ActionScript, if you are a nonprogrammer or Flash designer, we would like to offer a few paragraphs to help you get in the right frame of mind.

Dreaming in metaphors

Programming is very much like creating a new world. As the programmer, you have complete control over that world. You decide what exists in that world and how things interact with one another. And, if you happen to be a really good programmer, you have the ability to create something that is virtually incomprehensible in the physical world we live in. Because of this complexity, that creation can often become extremely difficult to articulate using known concepts. So, it is ultimately necessary to illustrate a topic by relating it to another. Enter the metaphor. Actually, it entered a few sentences ago!

You can think of this in much the same manner as trying to describe color to a blind person. Color, in this case, would be considered something that is incomprehensible and abstract to a person who cannot see. How would you begin to describe color to a blind person? It would be something very hard to articulate. You would need to find a mediating idea, or metaphor, that would not only be familiar to the blind person, but also convey the idea of color. For example, you may try to use concepts like heat or anger to describe a color like red.

Nonetheless, if you want to be a great programmer, you will need to become an abstract thinker capable of dreaming in metaphors. And remember, if this book is your first step into programming, be sure to give yourself enough time to take it all in.

Now that you are in the right frame of mind, let's discover what ActionScript is and how it has matured with the various releases of Flash.

Following the evolution of ActionScript 3.0

Elements of Flash-based scripts can be traced back as early as Flash 2. However, the name "ActionScript" did not make an appearance until the release of Flash 5 in 2000 with the release of ActionScript 1.0. ActionScript was originally a scripting language built to aid in the navigation of the Flash animation environment. These simple scripts were nothing more than the ability to change frames or scenes. With each new release of Flash, however, ActionScript becomes more and more adherent to the ECMA-262 standard, which allows for an even greater degree of optimization.

> *Ecma International (formerly the European Computer Manufacturers Association) is an organization responsible for the standardization of information technology and communication. The ECMA-262 standard, also known as ECMAScript, is typically associated with the standardization of many popular web dialects such as JavaScript and ActionScript.*

The release of ActionScript 3.0 has been no exception. This version offers an ActionScript language that has been completely reconstructed from the ground up. Though much of the base syntax remains, it is often said that ActionScript 3.0 should be approached as an entirely new language, independent of previous releases of ActionScript.

The Flash-based release of ActionScript 3.0 saw many key architectural improvements such as a true object-oriented model, enhanced low-level access, and a revamped version of the ActionScript Virtual Machine (AVM2). All of these improvements combined to create blistering fast performance and a greater degree of optimization.

8

> *ActionScript 3.0 was actually formally introduced with the release of Adobe Flex 2.0 in the late spring of 2006. Flash didn't officially receive ActionScript 3.0 until spring 2007.*

Further, programmers were introduced to complete reconstructions of many core features including redesigns to the Events, Display, Loading, and XML classes. With Flash CS4, programmers can also reap the benefit of additional enhancements like a more robust Sound API and improvements to the Drawing API. Finally, developers are also introduced to the Vector data type, which allows for strict data typing of arrays.

> *Like many other commonly used modern languages such as C#, Java, and JavaScript, ActionScript derives most of its syntax from C-based languages. Therefore, a programmer moving from one of those languages should be able to get up to speed very quickly.*

Now that you have an idea of what ActionScript is, it's time to start creating ActionScript programs. In the next section, we'll take a look at a traditional example that will help you get your feet wet when working with ActionScript and the Flash IDE.

Crafting your first ActionScript application

In the course of computer programming history, there have been many great traditions passed down from programmer to programmer. One of the most famous practices of ritualistic behavior comes in the form of the Hello World application. The Hello World application is typically used as the very first example in a book or as the first computer program written by a new programmer. It is basically nothing more than the words "Hello World" being displayed on the screen. Though we contemplated skipping the Hello World app for this section, we wouldn't be honorable men if we chose to neglect such a fabled institution. We can think of no fewer than six titles we have read that have included a Hello World app.

This example will serve as an excellent lead-in for you to get exposed to the many aspects of this chapter. You will be introduced to some important tools like the Actions panel, Script Assist, and trace statement. Later in this chapter we will discuss these tools in greater detail. The exercise will then serve as your frame of reference. So without further ado, it's time for your first program to say "Hello!"

1. Open Flash CS4.

2. Create a New Flash file (ActionScript 3.0) by either choosing the Flash File (ActionScript 3.0) option on the Flash Welcome Screen or selecting File ➤ New and choosing Flash File (ActionScript 3.0) from the New Document window.

3. Once your new document has been created, open the Actions panel by selecting Window ➤ Actions or by pressing F9. (F9 is definitely a shortcut you should remember.)

4. Once the Actions panel is open, activate the Script Assist by clicking the Script Assist button, located in the upper right of the Actions panel as shown in Figure 8-1. At this point you will notice the expansion of the Script Assist above the script pane. You should also notice that not much is happening there at the moment.

Figure 8-1.
The Script Assist button

5. In order to use the Script Assist, you will need to add a code snippet from the Actions toolbox. The Actions toolbox is located in the upper right of the Actions panel. Using Figure 8-2 for reference, make sure that the scrollbar in the Actions toolbox is at the topmost position. Then select Language Elements, followed by Global Functions.

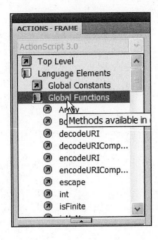

Figure 8-2.
The available features
in the Actions toolbox

8

6. One of the coolest features in the Script Assist is the fact that you can see what each function does before you use it. With Global Functions expanded, scroll down until you see the trace function. Single-click the trace function to see what it is used for.

7. Add a trace statement to your ActionScript by either double-clicking it or dragging it to the script pane. Immediately, your script is added to the script pane and a list of parameters is now visible in the Script Assist pane.

8. Now that the function has been added to your ActionScript, you will need to fill out the Arguments field to get it to work properly. As you will find out shortly, the trace statement is primarily used to write information to the Output panel in Flash. For now it will be sufficient for you to type "Hello World!" (including the quotation marks) as shown in Figure 8-3.

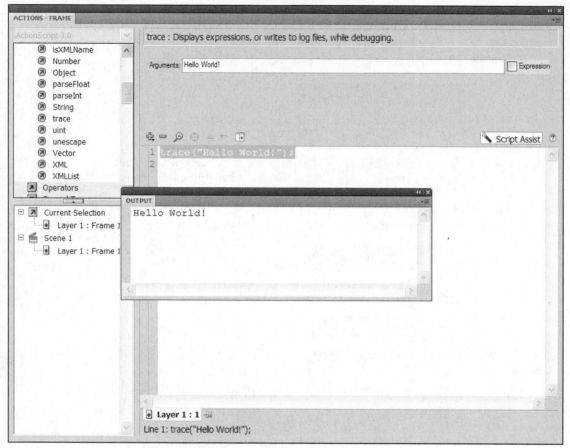

Figure 8-3. The `trace` statement's output to the Output panel

> You may have noticed a check box at the end of the Arguments *field. You will learn the difference between expressions and literals by the end of this chapter. For now you may leave this check box checked.*

9. Test your movie by selecting Control ➤ Test Movie or by pressing Ctrl-Enter/Option-Enter. This will publish your SWF file, and immediately you will see the Output panel appear with the phrase "Hello World!," as shown in Figure 8-3.

Congratulations! You have just written your first ActionScript program. Now we will take a closer look at the various components that were used to create this application. In the next section, you will be officially introduced to the `trace` statement, a tool that will help you communicate with your program.

The trace statement: Leaving breadcrumbs

In the last exercise you created the all-too-famous Hello World application. In that application you used a popular statement known as the trace statement. The trace statement is actually a special kind of statement known as a **top-level function**.

> Most ActionScript functionality can only be used in certain instances. The term "top level" is used to describe a type of functionality that is accessible from anywhere and at anytime in your program.

The primary function of the trace statement is to send any expression to the Output panel during author-time testing of your Flash movies. You may also send output to a log file during debugging. Typically, trace statements are used to check the execution timing and values of dynamic parts of any given program. If you're familiar with the children's fairy tale "Hansel and Gretel," the trace statement can be thought of as your bag of breadcrumbs to help you find your way home if you get lost in the programming woods.

As you saw in the previous section, the trace statement is actually quite easy to evoke. Simply type the keyword trace followed by a set of parentheses. Within the parentheses you type the item you would like printed to the screen. As illustrated previously in Figure 8-3, typing the phrase "Hello World!" between the trace parentheses printed "Hello World!" to the screen.

> A **keyword** is a special type of reserved word for which ActionScript has a specific purpose. When using the Actions panel in the Flash IDE, keywords will by default appear as bolded blue text.

With the trace statement you also have the ability to print multiple items to the screen at one time. To do this, simply type the values you would like to trace delimited by a comma. With the following example, the characters a, &, and b would all print to the Output panel.

```
trace("a","&","b"); //a&b
```

The trace statement is one of the most useful allies that any ActionScript developer can have. It will allow you to communicate with yourself as a program executes. You will certainly get plenty of exposure to the trace statement as you work through the rest of this book.

In addition to the trace statement, the single most important aspect of developing ActionScript from within Flash is the Actions panel. Let's have a look at the many benefits this tool has to offer.

8

Moving into the Actions panel: Your new home

When authoring ActionScript in Flash, all of your work will be done in one of two ways. The first of these is the use of external ActionScript files (which have the extension .as). As you become more familiar with the proper techniques of programming ActionScript, more and more of your work will be done in external files.

> At this stage in the evolution of Flash, external files are considered the best method for programming.

The second method for writing ActionScript is to apply actions directly to keyframes using the Actions panel (select Window ➤ Actions or press F9) in the Flash development environment. For this chapter a majority of the examples we will look at can be easily coded using the Actions panel.

Further, you will notice when migrating to programming with external files that they are opened in Flash using a document window that is very much like the Actions panel. Though this is not actually the Actions panel, you probably won't notice much difference. As a convention, we will refer to ActionScript written in external .as files as *external* and ActionScript placed on the timeline in Flash as *embedded*.

> Because Flash still possesses some limitation to the way external files are organized, many professional ActionScript programmers have turned to other programs for advanced ActionScript development. Some software solutions that are worth mentioning include FlashDevelop, SEPY, Flex Builder, and Eclipse.

Looking closely at the Actions panel

The Actions panel is comprised of several important sections as shown in Figure 8-4.

- The **script pane** is the primary section of the Actions panel positioned at the right. Within this pane, you will enter all scripts that will be used in your ActionScript program. As shown in Figure 8-4, the script pane currently has the script //This is ActionScript! on line 1.
- The **Actions toolbox** is located in the upper-left portion of the Actions panel. Within the toolbox you have access to all core ActionScript libraries that were included with your installation of Flash. From here you can access all objects including their properties (variables) and methods (functions). Double-clicking an element of the Actions toolbox will automatically add it to the script pane.

- The **Script Navigator** is located at the bottom left of the Actions panel. This feature will allow you to browse all embedded scripts for the FLA you are currently working on. All scripts are organized hierarchically by object and location. This pane is available only if you are authoring ActionScipt that is embedded on the timeline within an FLA. Therefore, if you are working on an external ActionScript file, you will notice that this pane has disappeared.

- The Actions **panel toolbar** is a list of tools to aid in the organization and development of ActionScript code. This set of tools is located directly above the script pane. These tools are available for both embedded and external ActionScript files.

- Pin Script **tabs** give developers the ability to quickly switch between various scripts in their ActionScript program.

- The Script Assist **button** is used to open the Script Assist pane in the Actions panel.

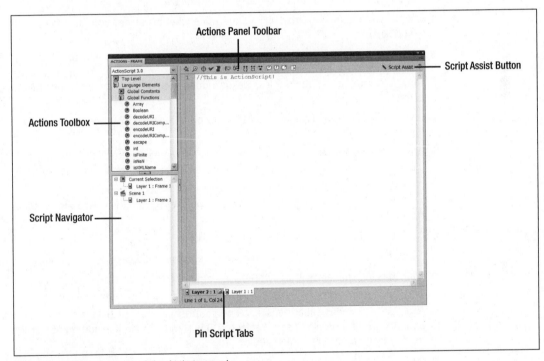

Figure 8-4. The main areas of the Actions panel

Though pointing out the primary sections of the Actions panel will certainly help you in learning your way around, it is probably more helpful to discuss a few of these sections in more detail. As you'll see in the following three sections, the Actions panel toolbar, Pin Script tabs, and Script Assist can all offer a greater degree of organization and efficiency when working with ActionScript.

Actions panel toolbar

The Actions panel toolbar offers developers a quick method to check, reference, and format their code. The following toolset is one that should definitely be made familiar to every ActionScript programmer.

- Add New Item to the Script is represented by the blue plus icon located at the left of the Actions panel toolbar. It works in the same manner as the Actions toolbox. Selecting this will open a drop-down menu containing all of the core libraries contained in the Flash installation. Selecting any item from this drop-down will add it to the script pane.

- Find gives you the ability to find and replace any text located in your ActionScript.

- Insert Target Path is only available for use with embedded ActionScript. This tool allows you to locate a symbol instance in your FLA file and reference its name in ActionScript. Paths can be either absolute or relative.

- Check Syntax allows you to quickly determine whether or not your scripts contain syntax errors.

- Auto Format formats your scripts so they are syntactically correct and are more easily read. This includes the addition of indents and semicolons. You can adjust the format setting using the Preferences window (Edit ➤ Preferences) under Auto Format.

- Show Code Hint will allow you to receive a code hint for the code you are working on.

- Debug Options allows you to set breakpoints for debugging your ActionScript files line by line. This feature is only available for embedded ActionScript files.

- Collapse Between Braces collapses all code that exists between curly braces. In addition, it will collapse all code between parentheses if that is where the cursor is currently located.

- Collapse Selection collapses all code that is currently selected.

- Expand All expands all code that has been previously collapsed.

- Apply Block Comment will add multiline comment markers at the beginning and end of currently selected code.

- Apply Line Comment will add a single-line comment marker at the current position of the cursor. If multiple lines are selected, it will add a single-line comment marker to the beginning of each selected line.

- Remove Comment removes all comments from currently selected code or the line containing the cursor.

- Show/Hide Toolbox toggles the Actions toolbox as either hidden or visible.

Pinning scripts so you don't lose them

Though it is becoming less common in ActionScript development, it is inevitable that at some point in your Flash career you will need to have multiple scripts embedded in several different locations of your FLA file. It is also more than likely that you are going to have to jump back and forth between these scripts. For such an occasion, the Actions panel comes equipped with the Pin Script feature.

As shown in Figure 8-4, the Pin Script feature is a series of tabs located at the bottom of the script pane in the Actions panel. The script that is currently active is always represented by the leftmost tab. However, if you browse to other scripts located on other keyframes in your FLA, you have the ability to pin this for easy access. Once you have navigated to the new script, simply click the pushpin icon located next to the first tab, shown in Figure 8-4 as Layer 1:1. After clicking the pushpin icon a new tab will appear, allowing you to jump directly back to this script at a later time.

Script Assist—taking it easy

For those professionals who are either new to ActionScript or only interested in learning just enough to get by, Flash offers a rather helpful tool, the Script Assist. You should have some familiarity with this from the previous Hello World example. The Script Assist is located at the top left of the Actions panel, inline with the Actions panel toolbar. You should notice a button labeled Script Assist with the icon of a magic wand.

The true benefit of this tool is that it allows developers to work in tandem with the Actions toolbox to quickly develop scripts that are meaningful to their program. As shown in Figure 8-5, once the Script Assist button is clicked, you will immediately notice that the portion of the Actions panel above the script pane extends to reveal the Script Assist pane. You can then browse for items in the Actions toolbox. By single-clicking items in the toolbox, the Script Assist will display a brief description of that item. Double-clicking an item will then add it to the script pane.

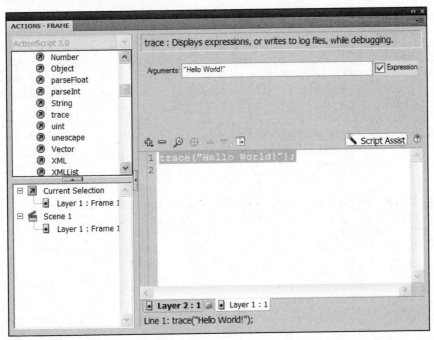

Figure 8-5. Proper use of the Script Assist

> *Once Script Assist has been activated, you can no longer edit scripts in the script pane. In order to be able to edit scripts in the script pane, the Script Assist must be deactivated.*

Once an item has been added to the script pane, the Script Assist then displays a list of fields that are relevant to properly constructing that section of code. Therefore, a beginner can quickly create well-formed ActionScript with a just few clicks and filling out a couple of fields.

Because the Script Assist is so user friendly, it is often an excellent starting point for someone wanting to learn ActionScript without the worry or hassle of proper syntax and formatting.

> *The Script Assist is meant for simple scripting. Therefore, it is only available through the* Actions *panel while creating embedded code.*

Now that you have been acquainted with the most important tools for working with ActionScript, let's now transition into the most basic elements of the ActionScript language itself and how to work with them.

Basic elements of ActionScript programming

Though we will be looking at the elements of programming as they apply to Flash and ActionScript, it is worth pointing out that most programming languages within a certain categorization operate in pretty much the same fashion. By "categorization," we mean the type of language. In this book we will be speaking about **object-oriented languages**. In fact, given the industry to which this book is associated, it is a pretty safe assumption to say that you are more than likely only going to ever use markup languages and object-oriented languages. Therefore, even though this book is directly specific to the ActionScript language, the programming basics that you will learn here are easily transferable to many other object-oriented languages.

> *Object-oriented programming is a style of programming in which code is organized into objects, also known as classes. Programs are then designed based on how these objects interact.*

Syntax

The **syntax** of any given language simply refers to the rules that govern how elements are structured or put together to form meaningful statements. In the English language the minimum requirements for a sentence are typically a subject and a verb as well as appropriate punctuation. Even in an exclamation such as "Run!," the subject is the person being spoken to and the verb is undoubtedly "run."

> *A **statement** can be thought of as a sentence in a computer program. A statement is any line of code that performs an action on a variable. The line c = a + b; is a simple statement.*

If we were to take a closer look at a sentence like "He runs," we can extract a few simple rules that determine whether or not this sentence is properly structured. There are basically four things that we are going to look at. Is there a subject, is there a verb, is there a punctuation mark, and is the first letter of the sentence capitalized? By now this stuff is more or less inherent; you probably can't even remember where you learned these rules.

Just like any written language, programming languages are also governed by a specific set of rules that need to be followed in order for the statements to make sense to the computer. Fortunately, this set of rules is infinitely less complicated than those applied to written language. And, without question, they will ultimately become as second nature to you as looking for a period at the end of a sentence.

Case sensitivity

ActionScript is classified as a **case-sensitive language**. The term "case sensitive" refers to the manner in which a programming element is physically entered into the computer by a programmer using the keyboard. The following example shows the declaration of two variables, mylist and myList. At first glance they may look the same, but the capitalization of the letter "L" in the second variable name is enough differentiation for these to be treated as completely different elements.

```
var mylist:String;
var myList:String;
```

Though this may not seem like a tremendous issue, it is the small details like this that wreak havoc on many programs. As a new programmer, case sensitivity will more than likely be the culprit for the majority of your programs not working properly.

> *In Flash development it has become commonplace for Flash programmers to use a typing technique called **camel casing**, which is applied to an element that is given a name comprised of several words not separated by spaces. The first letter of the first word is lowercase, and all subsequent words begin with a capital letter. For example, var camelCaseExample; is an example of camel casing.*

Dot syntax

In ActionScript, **dot notation** is used to perform two primary functions. First, as you become familiar with working with external class libraries, you can use the dot operator to import these libraries into your Flash program. As you begin to break a program into manageable chunks, you will want to begin to create ActionScript files externally. A library is nothing more than a collection of external ActionScript files that is stored in a centralized location.

8

If you were to try to gain access to this location from your computer's desktop, you would use slash notation (/). To access the same information from Flash, you would use dot notation (.). The next example shows the path to an AS called myasfile.as. This file is being stored in a folder called ASFiles, which is stored in MyDocuments. The first line shows how the file is addressed using slash notation, and the second line shows dot notation.

```
MyDocuments/ASFiles/myasfile.as
```

```
MyDocuments.ASFiles.myasfile
```

Flash installs with a rather robust set of core functionality that is also managed using external libraries. The following paths determine the location of the Flash core class libraries based on computer platform:

- **Windows**: Hard Disk\Documents and Settings\user\Local Settings\Application Data\Adobe\Adobe Flash CS3\language\Configuration\Classes
- **Macintosh**: Hard Disk/Users/user/Library/Application Support/Adobe/Adobe Flash CS3/language/Configuration/Classes

The second use for the dot operator is to access the members of a particular object. Again, don't be confused by the phraseology. As you will learn very shortly, objects used in object-oriented programming are comprised of properties, methods, and events. These items are known collectively as the **members** of the object. And, the dot operator will grant you access to some of these members for the benefit of your program.

For sake of simplicity, we will pretend that I (Paul) am an ActionScript object called Paul. As an object I could contain various properties like height, weight, and whether I have hair. Similarly, I could have a method for performing various tasks like eating, sleeping, and working. It is bleak, I know. Additionally, I could react to an event. If someone were to tickle my nose, I may react by saying "AH-CHOO!" In the next chapter, we'll demonstrate that events are nothing more than functions triggered under certain circumstances, as well as look more closely at the differentiation between properties, methods, and events.

Now if we wanted to access one of those properties or tasks, we would do so using dot notation. The following example shows access to various members of the Paul object:

```
Paul.height = 6.25;
Paul.weight = 225;
Paul.hair = true;
Paul.hair.color = "brown";

Paul.sleeping();
Paul.eating();
Paul.working();

Paul.addEventListener(Event, sneeze);
function sneeze (e:Event)
{
  trace( "AH-CHOO!");
}
```

Expressions and literals

Literals refer to values in a program that are typed (keyed in) and returned verbatim. In the following example the variable myName is assigned the literal value of "Paul". When the trace statement is used to print this variable to the Output panel in Flash, you will notice that it returns the value Paul exactly as it was assigned.

```
var myName:String = "Paul"; //String literal
var currentAge:int = 5; //Numeric literal
var birthday:int = currentAge + 1; //Numeric expression
trace(myName + " is " + birthday + " years old.");➡
//Paul is 6 years old.
```

Conversely, **expressions** are values that are resolved by the execution of a statement. The variable birthday in itself does not have a legitimate value. It is dependant on the value of the variable currentAge. Therefore, the expression currentAge + 1 must resolve to a legitimate value before any value can be assigned to birthday. If you were to delete the second line of the preceding program, you would notice that the expression would be unable to resolve, and an error would appear. Fortunately, in this case, the value does resolve to 6.

Finally, all of the items in the parentheses of the trace statement would also be considered an expression. Though there are several string literals present, the entire group of elements needs to resolve to a single value before it can be passed to the Output panel.

Semicolons

In Flash the semicolon is used to indicate the end of an executable statement. You should think of this as a period in your program. Though semicolons are not required, not using them could cause some unexpected results while programming. For example, omitting a hard return between two lines of code that are also not delimited by a semicolon would cause your program to fail to execute. Further, it is considered good practice to use them.

The following two code examples look almost identical to one another. The first example is missing the semicolon after the string "Paul". Without this semicolon, ActionScript cannot tell that each line actually contains two statements. Therefore, an error occurs in the first line.

```
var myName:String = "Paul"    trace(myName); // error

var myName:String = "Paul";    trace(myName); // Paul
```

Parentheses

The primary uses of parentheses are similar to the function they serve in basic arithmetic. That is, they are responsible for changing the order of operations in any given expression. Therefore, any expression or part of an expression that is encapsulated within parentheses is executed first. You may also continuously nest groups of parentheses to further control the order of operations.

8

The following example demonstrates several examples of parentheses usage. As the mathematical order of operations suggests, the contents of the innermost parentheses are executed prior to that of the outermost parentheses.

```
trace (2+2*3);  //8
trace ((2+2)*3);  //12
trace (((2+2)/6)*3);  //7
```

Similarly, you can use parentheses to execute a series of statements separated by a comma. The statements are executed sequentially, and the result of the final statement is returned.

In the following example, the first five lines of code are simplified into one statement using comma-separated statements encapsulated within parentheses.

```
var a:int = 1;
var b:int = 2;
a++; //the variable a is incremented by 1 (a = a+1)
b--; //the variable b is decremented by 1 (b = b-1)
trace (a+b); //3

//The preceding statements could be simplified as
trace ((a++, b--, a+b)); //3
```

Finally, parentheses are used to pass parameters to a subroutine, known in Flash as a **function**.

```
function passParameter(theParameter)
{
    theParameter++;
    trace(theParameter)
}

passParameter(3); //Traces 4 to the Output panel
```

Comments

Comments are an extremely important part of any program. Though you may only be writing a program for your own benefit, chances are you are actually writing the program for the benefit of a team or company. Regardless of the end result, it is more than likely that someone else will eventually have to go into your code and make some kind of tweak or edit. It is considered excellent practice and extremely courteous to properly comment your code.

Commenting allows programmers to type additional text among their program's code offering directions, instruction, or additional insights. Any line that is commented will be ignored by the compiler and will neither interact nor interfere with any part of your program.

In Flash, there are two ways to generate comments. For a single-line comment, a programmer can use double (//) slashes. All characters to the right of the double slash will be commented out.

The second method of commenting is the multiline comment. This is achieved by using the single slash and asterisk (/*) character combination to open the comment and the asterisk and single slash (*/) character combination to close the comment.

As shown in the following example, both double-slash and slash-asterisk notation are used to create a line comment and a block level, or multiline, comment.

```
//Use double slashes to create a single-line comment

/* Use a slash then asterisk to open a multiline comment
and use an asterisk then slash to close it */
```

This technique will also prove invaluable to you when testing various options while writing your programs. As shown here, multiple trace statements have been created to trace different options. Commenting can be used as a way of "turning off" trace statements.

```
trace("option1"); //option1
//trace("option2");  Will not trace
```

Variables

Variables are the most basic component of any given computer program. Technically speaking, a **variable** is a reference to a portion of memory that has been allocated for the storing of a particular type of data. Basically, this is a fancy way of saying it is a name given to a location where a specific kind of information will be stored. And a computer program is nothing more than a sophisticated way of manipulating information. In some capacity or another, every statement in a computer program must interact with a variable. Therefore, variables can be thought of as the subject or noun of the computer program.

To declare a variable in ActionScript, you must first use the var keyword. For example, the following statement declares the variable myVariable. Failing to use the var keyword in the declaration of a variable will result in an error in your program.

```
var myVariable;
```

As a programmer you have complete control over the names you give your variables. However, there are a few rules that need to be followed when creating a variable name:

- Variable names can contain any number or letter, dollar signs ($), and underscores (_).
- Variables names **cannot** begin with a number.
- They **cannot** contain spaces.
- Variable names must be unique. Two variables cannot share the same name within the same scope.
- Variable names are case sensitive. It is also recommended that you avoid using the same variable names with different case. For example, myvar is different from myVar but will probably create confusion.

Though it is not absolutely necessary, it is considered best practice to strictly type your variable by assigning it a data type. To strictly type a variable, add a colon (:) followed by the desired data type. As you will learn in the next section, data typing is beneficial for more efficient programming.

In the following code, we assign the variables myVariable and myNumber the respective data types of String and Number.

```
var myVariable:String;
var myNumber:Number;
```

Once a variable is declared, you can give it a value by using an assignment operator (=) followed by the value. As shown here, our previously defined variables are assigned the values of Hello and 4:

```
var myVariable:String;
var myNumber:Number;

myVariable = "Hello";
myNumber = 4;
```

You can also assign the value to a variable when it is created as follows:

```
var myVariable:String = "Hello";
```

Though it is also possible to instantiate multiple variables at one time using the comma delimiter, it is not considered best practice. In the following example, the variables myVar_1, myVar_2, and myVar_3 are all created in one statement using the comma delimiter.

```
var myVar_1:int = 1,  myVar_2:int = 2, myVar_3:int = 3;
```

Right now you are probably thinking of variables in terms of a **name-value pair**. For example, myName="Paul" is basically a variable for my (Paul's) actual name. And the variable has been given a name that more or less describes what the value is going to be, a name. So, the statement is really comprised of nothing more than a variable's name and the variable's value. As you become more and more familiar with using ActionScript, you will come to realize that variables become references to extremely complex objects that may also contain a number of additional variables.

Data types

If variables are thought of as the nouns of computer programming, data types can be thought of as the adjectives. A **data type** is used to describe what type of information is going to be stored in a variable. Though strict data typing is not required, it is considered excellent practice.

> *It is important to understand that regardless of whether you define the data type for a variable or not, Flash will. If the variable is in use, it has a data type.*

Practically speaking, data typing can serve several purposes. First, strict data typing reduces the amount of memory needed for using any given variable. Therefore, if you data type your variables, the variable will only accept information of a specific type. For instance, if a variable is typed String, you know the variable is going to be of the String data type and only store characters. Further, if a variable is type Number, you know that the variable will only accept numbers. Subsequently, if a variable is type String and you try to assign a value to it that is a number, you will receive a type-mismatch error from the compiler.

Second, typing your variables enables inline code hinting. Inline code hinting is a feature of the Actions panel whereby suggestions are made from the Actions panel as to what code should come next.

In ActionScript, data types can be classified into two categories:

- **Primitive**: Primitive data types are what you have been exposed to so far in this chapter. They include the most basic type of data that can be used in Flash programming. Table 8-1 gives a list and definition of the primitive data types.

- **Complex**: Complex data types are every other type of data used in Flash. They include common reference data types such as Array, Date, and Math. Where primitive data type can only contain primitive types of data such as numbers and letters, complex data types can contain many primitive values and other complex values at the same time.

Table 8-1. Primitive data types

Data type	Example	Description
Boolean	True/False	Values of this type can only be true or false. These are commonly used for comparison and decision making.
String	"Hello World"	This type is used for any text-based value or string of characters.
Number	1, 88, 4.3	This type is used for any numerical value including floating-point or decimal values.
int	0, -5, 3	This type is used for any integer or whole number.
uint	1, 2, 3 . . .	Short for unsigned integer, this type can contain any whole number that is not negative or a decimal.
void		This type is used if a function does not return any value.
*	untype	This type is used if a variable is not of a specified type.
undefined	undefined	This type indicates untyped variables that have not been initialized.
null	null	This type is used for variables that do not have a value at all.

8

Operators

Adobe defines **operators** as special functions that take one or more operands and return a value. An operator, though defined as a function, is usually nothing more than one, two, or three characters used to take two or more values and evaluate them. The best way to comprehend this is with simple arithmetic. If we were to take the math problem 2 + 2 and turn it into a computer program, it might look very similar to what you see here:

```
var answer:uint;
answer = 2 + 2;

trace(answer); // 4
```

> An **operand** is any value to the left or right of an operator. Operands represent the information that is being operated on, or manipulated. In the statement answer = 2+2;, answer, 2, and 2 are all operands.

These statements are pretty simple to understand. We have declared the variable answer and given it the data type uint because we are fairly certain the result will be a positive number. We then assign the value of answer the expression 2 + 2. Finally, we trace out the value of answer, and we are given 4. The operator in this series of statements is the plus sign (+), also known as the additive operator. What is happening here is that the additive operator (+) is evaluating the operands (2 and 2). And because the additive operator (+) is responsible for adding things together, it determines the type of data that is involved and joins them appropriately.

Further, had we attempted to add two strings together, the result may not be as expected. For instance, let's change the 2 and 2 to "two" and "two". As shown in the following code, you would then end up with something entirely different. Keep in mind that because strictly typed variables can only accept the data of one type, the data type will also need to be changed from uint to String for this to properly execute. In this case, the resulting join of two character strings is known as **concatenation**. Additionally, when an operator has the ability to change the way it reacts based on the type of operand it is dealing with, as the additive operator (+) did here, it is known as **operator overloading**.

```
var answer:String;
answer = "two" + "two";

trace(answer); // twotwo
```

As you can see, even the most basic use of an operator can become extremely convoluted. If we were to simply list all of the ActionScript operators and descriptions in tabular format, it would probably take about three or four pages. Further, if we were to take the time to explain them all in detail, it could easily be an entire chapter. As a general rule, most of the time operators behave intuitively; a plus sign will add things together, or an asterisk will multiply them. They maintain an order of operations similar to arithmetic. Because operators are such an integral part of a programming language, it is best to introduce them in the manner in which they are operating. This facilitates the best comprehension.

Postfix operators

Postfix operators are typically used to increment and decrement one numerical operand by 1. As shown in the following example, the variable a is incremented using the increment (++) operator. It is then decreased using the decrement (--) operator.

```
var a:uint = 0;
a++;
trace (a); // 1
a--;
trace(a); //0
```

Table 8-2 lists the postfix operators.

Table 8-2. Increment and decrement postfix operators

Operator	Name	Description
++	Increment	Increments a numeric variable by 1
--	Decrement	Decrements a numeric variable by 1

Multiplicative and additive operators

Multiplicative and **additive** operators perform similarly to their arithmetical counterparts. They are used to add, subtract, multiply, and divide various operands. The following example demonstrates a simple mathematical operation performed using the multiplicative operator (*):

```
var a:uint:Number;
a = 3 * 4;
trace (a);  //12
```

Table 8-3 lists the standard multiplicative and additive operators.

Table 8-3. Most commonly used multiplicative and additive operators

Operator	Name	Description
*	Multiplication	Multiplies numeric variables.
/	Division	Divides any two numeric values. If the variable is type Number, this will return a decimal. If the variable is type int or uint, the return value is truncated at the decimal, and only a whole number is returned.

Continued

Table 8-3. *Continued*

Operator	Name	Description
%	Modulo	Divides two numeric values and returns the remainder.
+	Addition	Adds two values together. Numeric values are added arithmetically. Strings are concatenated.
-	Subtraction	Subtracts numeric values arithmetically.

Relational operators

Relational operators are used to compare the value of two operands. The resulting value is Boolean, either true or false. The following sample checks to see whether the value of the variable a is greater than or equal to the value of the expression (1+2):

```
var a:uint = 2;
trace (a >= (1+2)); //false
```

Table 8-4 lists the standard relational operators.

Table 8-4. Standard relational operators

Operator	Name	Description
<	Less than	Checks whether the left value is less than the right value
>	Greater than	Checks whether the left value is greater than the right value
<=	Less than or equal to	Checks whether the left value is less than or equal to the right value
>=	Greater than or equal to	Checks whether the left value is greater than or equal to the right value

Equality operators

Equality operators work in much the same fashion as the relational operators in that they compare two values and return a Boolean value of either true or false.

In the next example the assignment operator (=) is used to give a value to the variable a. The first statement can be read a *is* equal to 2. Conversely, the trace statement uses the equality operator (==) to compare the values of a and the expression (1+2). Therefore, relational and equality operators can be thought of in terms of questions. *Is a equal to* (1+2)?

You can also use the NOT operator (!) to determine whether values are not related.

```
var a:uint = 2;
trace (a == (1+2)); //false
trace (a != (1+2)); //true
```

Table 8-5 lists the standard operators of equality.

Table 8-5. Most common operators of equality

Operator	Name	Description
==	Equality	Checks whether the left value is equal to the right value.
!=	Inequality	Checks whether the left value is not equal to the right value.
===	Strict equality	Checks for same values, as well as compares the data types of each value. If the left value and the right value are the same and the data types are the same, the expression returns true. Objects and arrays are compared by reference, not data type.
!==	Strict inequality	Checks for the same values, as well as compares the data type of each value. If the left value and the right value are not equal or the data types are different, the expression returns false. Objects and arrays are compared by reference, not data type.

Logical operators

The **logical operators** are also similar to the relational and equality operators in that they compare the values of two operands. The primary difference is they give programmers the ability to compare multiple comparative statements. The following sample checks to see whether the value of a is greater than 1 *and* less than 3:

```
var a:uint = 2;
if( a > 1 && a < 3)
{
    trace ("Yes"); //Yes
}
```

Table 8-6 lists the common logical operators.

8

Table 8-6. The AND and OR logical operators

Operator	Name	Description
&&	Logical AND	Allows you to perform a comparison on one or more expressions simultaneously.
||	Logical OR	Allows you to perform a comparison of several expressions simultaneously. Only one of the expressions needs to be true for the statement to execute.

Conditional statements

Conditional statements are one of the first logical needs in any programming language. Quite simply they allow a programmer, or more to the point the program, to make an intelligent decision based on a set of predetermined conditions. For instance, if it is raining outside, wear a raincoat or else you'll get soaked.

if . . . else statement

The if statement is the simplest and most commonly used conditional statement in programming. It can be thought of as the fork-in-the-road decision maker. As shown in the next example, the statement is comprised of four primary parts. The if keyword simply lets the program know that it is going to be entering the if statement. The second part, characterized by parentheses, is where the actual decision is made. The third part consists of two curly braces that signify a code block associated with the if statement. Finally, all statements within the curly braces are executed if the if statement evaluates to true.

```
if (weather == "rain")
{
   putOnRaincoat();
}
```

The if statement works by evaluating expressions that are encapsulated within these parentheses. There are only two possible outcomes for the evaluation of any given expression with respect to an if statement, true or false. Therefore, the preceding example asks, "Does the value of the variable weather equal rain?" Again, the outcome can only be true or false.

The else clause can be added to the end of an if statement to offer a desired outcome for the if statement evaluating false. Therefore, rather than having your program do nothing, you have the ability to have it act intelligently with respect to either decision. As shown in the following code, the else clause enables the if statement to have an alternative option in the event it evaluates to false:

```
if (weather == "rain")
{
   putOnRaincoat();
}
```

```
    else
    {
       putOnShades();
    }
```

else . . . if clause

A third option for working with if statements is the use of the else...if clause. The following example shows how this option gives you the ability to break your decision making into multiple branches.

```
    if (weather == "rain")
    {
       putOnRaincoat();
    }
    else if (weather == "snow")
    {
       putOnBoots();
    }
    else
    {
       putOnShades();
    }
```

> Though technically we could refer to an else clause as a statement, it is actually a clause because it cannot be used without an if statement.

Logical operators && and ||

Finally, by using the logical operators && and ||, you have the ability to create compound evaluations to check multiple conditions at one time. The following sample code shows the use of both types of logical operators to evaluate compound conditions:

```
    if ((weather == "rain") && (temperature == "4 degrees"))
    {
       stayHome();
    }

    if ((weather == "snow") || (temperature == "4 degrees"))
    {
       dressWarm();
    }
```

switch

The switch statement is a special kind of conditional that allows you to define a multitude of outcomes based on the evaluation of a single statement. Unlike the if statements, which check only whether an expression is true or false, the switch statement checks the actual value of the variable, compares it to the list of viable options, and determines the appropriate code block to execute.

As shown next, the switch statement is defined by the switch keyword followed by a set of parentheses that contain the expression to be evaluated. All execution options are then encapsulated within the curly braces. Each subsequent option is defined by the case keyword, followed by an option value and a colon. The colon is then followed by any code statements that are to be executed should this option be met. Each case statement is then closed with the break keyword.

```
switch (weather)
{
  case "rain":
    putOnRaincoat();
    break;
  case "blizzard":
    putOnBoots();
    break;
  default:
    checkWeather();
    break;
}
```

Loops

In addition to making decisions, it is also very common for a computer program to repeatedly execute a series of statements until a certain parameter is met. Loops are essentially statements that increment a variable a given number of times until a condition is met. In ActionScript the two most commonly used loops are the for and while loops.

for

The most common loop used in programming languages like ActionScript is the for loop. As shown next, the anatomy of a for loop is rather unique in that unlike other functions it uses the semicolon as the delimiter instead of the comma. The reason for this is that you are actually sending three statements to the loop as opposed to an expressed value.

```
var i:int; //i is classically used for the incrementing variables
for (i = 0; i < 5; i++)
{
    trace(i); // 0 1 2 3 4
}

for (var i:int = 0; i < 5; i++)
{
    trace(i); // 0 1 2 3 4
}
```

The first of these statements, i = 0, sets the starting value for our count. The second statement sets the ending value of our count to 4. Finally, the third statement uses the incrementing postfix operator to increment the value of i by 1. These statements can be read as "For i is equal to 0 and i is less than 5, add 1 to i."

The loop works as follows. With the first pass through the for loop, the value of i is 0. Therefore, the trace statement traces 0. When the loop has completed its first pass, i is incremented to 1. The loop compares this to the second statement. Is i less than 5? Yes! The loop runs again. The trace statement traces 1 and the cycle repeats until the variable has reached the value as predetermined in the second statement—in this case 4.

while

The while loop works in exactly the same manner as the for loop. As shown next, the first step is to define a base starting point for the incrementing variable. In this case, i will once again begin at 0.

```
var i:int = 0;
while (i < 5)
{
    trace(i); // 0 1 2 3 4
    i++; // Adds 1 to the current value of i
}
```

The while loop is a bit less complex than the for loop in that you now only need to give the while statement one conditional expression in the parentheses. Therefore, we again want this loop to run until it is less than 5, or 4. Finally, all code that we wish to have execute is placed in between the curly braces of the while function. As you can see, it is here that we tell our i variable to increment.

> *The while loop is not used as commonly as the for loop. Though it is easier to understand, it does have a greater chance of becoming stuck in an infinite loop. For instance, if the statement i++ were left out of the while loop, the variable would never reach 4, and the loop would never stop running.*

Functions

Functions are the part of the program that makes things happen. To continue the English-language metaphor we have also been using in this chapter, functions can be thought of as the verbs of the program.

Think about the trace statement, which should now be very familiar to you. As you learned earlier, the trace statement is a special kind of function that passes information to the Output panel. This information comes in the form of a variable that can be either a literal or an expression. Like the trace statement, other functions have the ability to accept variable information in the form of arguments, also known as parameters, through the use of parentheses.

Defining your own functions

Functions are defined using a special predefined keyword, function. This keyword works in the same manner as does the var keyword. Once a function is declared by using the function keyword, the function is then named under the same guidelines that govern the naming of variables. (See the section "Variables" earlier in this chapter for an explanation of these guidelines.) The function name is then always followed by a set of parentheses. These parentheses are used to pass information to the inner workings of the function in the form of variables. These variables can also be declared in the parentheses at the time the function is declared. The function body is then established using a pair of curly braces. Within the function body, all statements that define the execution of the function are placed.

The following sample shows the definition of a function called helloWorld. The helloWorld function accepts one parameter, message, of the String data type. The function will then pass the message variable value to the trace statement located in the function's body.

```
function helloWorld(message:String)
{
    trace(message);
}
```

In order to use a function, you simply need to type the function's name followed by the desired parameter value encapsulated in parentheses. The following example demonstrates how the helloWorld function can be used within the program. By passing Hello World! as the parameter, the helloWorld function will then trace the parameter to the Output panel.

```
function helloWorld(message:String)
{
    trace(message);
}

helloWorld("Hello World!"); // Hello World!
```

> The term "call" is often used to describe when a function is used in a program. It is often said that you can "call a function" or "make a function call."

Returning values from functions

For the time being we have been working with trace statements. The problem with the trace statement is that it always works. You put something in, you get something out. Given any logical parameter, the trace statement will give you some kind of meaningful feedback. Unfortunately, that is not indicative of how functions really work.

Functions can be thought of as a machine that operates on data. However, you don't always have to give it information. Additionally, it doesn't have to give you information back. In some cases, it will not want anything from you or give anything back. The trace statement, of course, is an elementary example of the other extreme.

You have learned how to pass information into a function. Remember, the parameters of functions that are defined in the parentheses allow you to pass information to the function. Now let's take a look at how to get things back. The following function performs a basic arithmetical process on a couple of variables:

```
function mathMachine (a:int, b:int)
{
  var c:int
  c = a + b;
}

trace(mathMachine(1,2)) //undefined
```

You will notice that when we try to trace the value of the mathMachine function, it returns the value of undefined to the Output panel. This is because the function is not returning any value. It is accepting two parameters, a and b. It is also, without question, adding a and b together and assigning that value to c. Right now, it simply isn't returning a value.

In order for a function to return a value, we have to use a special keyword, return. The return keyword does exactly what it says in that it returns the variable it is assigned to. To use the return keyword, enter it as you would keywords like var or function followed by the variable name you would like returned.

```
function mathMachine (a:int, b:int):int
{
  var c:int
  c = a + b;
  return c;
}

trace(mathMachine(1,2)) //3
```

After adding our return statement, you will notice that the function returns a value of 3, as expected. Did you also notice the addition of the :int data type? Yes, functions can be data typed as well. The purpose of data typing functions is to make the program aware of what type of value is going to be returned by the function. Again, it is not required but considered extremely good practice.

> Data types are discussed earlier in this chapter if you'd like more information about them.

Variable scope

Scope refers to what parts of a program's code have the ability to reference a variable. Scope is always assigned automatically based on where the variable is declared. In ActionScript variables are defined by two different types of scope, global and local.

Global variables

A **global variable** is one that can be accessed by all parts of your code. Global variables are defined independently of functions—that is, they reside outside of the body of any function. In the following example the variable myVar is declared outside of the body of the function global. Therefore, it is accessible from any part of the program. As you can see, both trace statements are able to trace the value of the variable myVar, which is Hello.

```
var myVar:String = "Hello";

function global()
{
    trace(myVar); // Hello
}
global();

trace(myVar); // Hello
```

Local variables

Local variables, on the other hand, exist only in a small portion of your program. Local variables are declared within a function's body. They are only accessible directly by the function itself. As shown next, the myVar variable is declared inside the function's body. Therefore, when we try to trace the variable using a trace statement located outside of the function, we receive a compiler error.

```
function local()
{
    var myVar:String = "Hello";
}
local();

trace(myVar); // error 1120: Access of undefined property myVar
```

Shadowing global variables

It is also possible for a local variable to shadow a global variable. The term "shadow" is used to describe a situation in which the same variable name is employed for two separate variables that are defined in different scopes of the same program. In the next example myVar is used as the name of a variable declared outside of the function shadow. In addition, the same name is used to describe the variable declared inside the function. As you can see, the local trace statement uses the local declaration of the myVar variable.

214

```
var myVar:String = "Hello";

function shadow()
{
    var myVar:String = "There";
    trace(myVar); // There
}
shadow();

trace(myVar); // Hello
```

Finally, let's take a look at the last primary component of ActionScript development, the class.

Having a little class or a big one

The last stop in the development of an ActionScript program is going to be the construction of a class. A **class** is a collection of related properties (variables) and methods (functions) that are grouped together in one collection. If you think of classes in the same way you think of functions, they are a means by which you can group similar code into one well-organized package. The idea of grouping code to make it more efficient is referred to as **modularity**. To get an idea of how this is helpful, consider the following list:

- A variable is the most basic element in a computer program.
- Statements are used to manipulate and change the information stored in variables.
- A series of repetitive statements can be organized into functions for the sake of efficiency.
- For an even greater degree of organization, functions and variables can be grouped together into what is known as a class.

In Chapter 10, you will build a multiclass application. In this example, we are going to show you how to construct a simple one-class application so you gain familiarity with the basic structure of an ActionScript-based class.

Building your first application

Alright, now before we wrap up and move on to bigger and better things, let's take a moment and construct a simple application to give you a basic understanding of how you create one and what the important parts are.

First thing you need to do is open Flash, if you don't already have it open. Next, you need to create two new files. First, create a new Flash file by either selecting the Flash file (ActionScript 3.0) option from the Welcome Screen or by selecting File ➤ New and choosing Flash file (ActionScript 3.0) from the document window. Save this file as HelloWorld.fla in a directory that you are comfortable with.

8

The document class

The **document class** is a property of an FLA file that assigns any given class as the primary class to be used for this Flash file. Like all other document properties such as canvas size, background color, and frame rate, the document class can be set using the Property inspector. For this step we will need to have HelloWorld.fla as the active window in Flash.

To access the Property inspector, select Window ➤ Properties or press Ctrl+F3. To assign a document class, simply type the name of the ActionScript file you would like to use (without the .as extension) in the field labeled Class. In the case of this example, you will be using the HelloWorld class (which you create in the next section). Therefore, type HelloWorld in the Class field of the Property inspector, as shown in Figure 8-6.

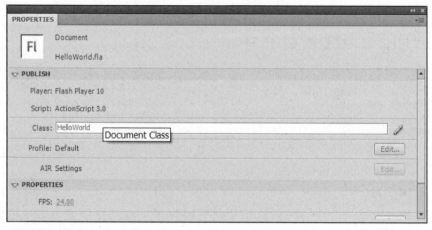

Figure 8-6. The Document Class field in the Property inspector

Packages and import statements

Now that your files are properly set up, you can start defining your class file. You will need to create an ActionScript file by selecting File ➤ New and choosing ActionScript File from the document window. Save this as HelloWorld.as in the same directory as the HelloWorld.fla file.

> *It is important that you save your ActionScript file in the same directory as your FLA; otherwise, Flash will be unable to locate it. In Chapter 10, you will learn to establish external libraries and define their locations using a source path, formerly called a classpath.*

The first step in defining a class is to properly define a package. In Flash, a **package** is nothing more than a collection of AS files. At this point, your AS file is located in the same directory as your FLA file, so it will not be necessary to give your package a name. However, it is a required element of any custom class, so it will need to be added. Go ahead and add the following lines of code to HelloWorld.as:

```
package
{

}
```

The next thing that you will need to do is import other packages for use in Flash. Recall that Flash installs with core functionality that is comprised of hundreds of classes. In order to use any functionality from another class, you will need to import it. To do this, you will use the import statement followed by the location of the class. Because you will need to use some of the functionality from the display and text packages, you will need to import those.

```
package
{
  import flash.display.*;
  import flash.text.*;
}
```

The preceding example uses the import statement to import the classes from the display and text packages. In the preceding code, flash represents the physical location of those files on your computer's hard drive. display and text represent folders in that location. These folders are what we referred to as packages. Inside each package is a varying number of AS files. The asterisk here represents "all" of the AS files in that package. Therefore, these two statements have imported all of the classes from both the display and text packages.

Class definition

The next thing that you need to do is define your class. As you can see in the next example, you'll have to add quite a bit of text in the form of keywords. For now, all you really need to be concerned with are the words class and HelloWorld. The rest, though necessary, will be explained in more detail in Chapter 10. Declaring a class is actually the same process as declaring a variable or function. You need the reserved keyword, class, to let the compiler know that this is indeed a class. And you need an appropriate name. The naming of a class is extremely important. It must be the exact same name as the AS file that it resides in, case and all. Therefore, because this class is being written in the HelloWorld.as file, it needs to be called HelloWorld.

```
package
{
  import flash.display.*;
  import flash.text.*;

  public class HelloWorld extends MovieClip
  {

  }
}
```

8

217

> *Classes in Flash are typically named using standard title case with no space. The first letter of every word is capitalized. This is not required, only common.*

Constructor functions

Constructor functions are the last absolutely necessary piece of any given class. When a class is instantiated, or declared in the program, the **constructor function** is responsible for what happens. It is the initializer of the class's functionality. It is the first domino, so to speak.

Like any other function in ActionScript, the constructor is declared using the function keyword and named appropriately. As with the class, the naming of the constructor is crucial. It must be the same as the name of the class and the file it resides in. For this example, the constructor must be HelloWorld.

```
package
{
  import flash.display.*;
  import flash.text.*;

  public class HelloWorld extends MovieClip
  {
    public function HelloWorld()
    {

    }
  }
}
```

> *Pay no attention to the word* public *behind the curtain! At this point, several keywords are being overlooked. The* public *keyword, for example, denotes permission to a class and its members. For now, it is sufficient to learn the basics of class construction and study the details later.*

Wrapping it up

To finish up your first class, you need only add the nuts and bolts to the constructor function. By now this should be a fairly simple task. What you are doing here is emulating the trace function. Because the trace function does not render anything to your published SWF file, you are going to need to fake it using a simple text field.

In this chapter, you worked with primitive data types such as String, int, and Boolean. In the upcoming example, you will create the variable helloText and give it a data type of TextField. A TextField is considered a complex data type. Complex data types are named so because they can contain complex sets of data. This means that they can represent entire classes. As you know, classes can contain members, which can consist of properties (variables) and methods (functions). Therefore, in direct contrast to a primitive data type like int, which is simply a whole number like 3, a complex data type can contain an abundance of information ranging from primitive data types or other complex data types.

When you assign a value to helloText, you will use the new keyword followed by the TextField() function. In this process, you are instantiating an object based on the TextField class. So, when you use the new keyword to assign a value to helloText, you are actually referencing the constructor function of the TextField class to create a new text field.

You also learned that an object, like a TextField, can have properties. These properties can be accessed using dot notation. In this case, text fields have a property called text, which is nothing more than a variable that represents the text displayed in the text field. So, the second statement in your constructor function will essentially take a TextField object named helloText and set the value of its text property to Hello World!

Finally, to get this TextField to display on the stage of your SWF, you need to add it to the display list. This is accomplished using the addChild() method. Therefore, you will add the helloText TextField to the stage with the statement addChild(helloText);.

The following shows the addition of the three previously mentioned statements to the HelloWorld constructor function:

```
package
{
  import flash.display.*;
  import flash.text.*;

  public class HelloWorld extends MovieClip
  {
    public function HelloWorld()
    {

      var helloText:TextField = new TextField();
      helloText.text = "Hello World!";
      addChild(helloText);

    }
  }
}
```

8

Go ahead and save your HelloWorld.as file and press Ctrl+Enter/Option+Enter to publish your SWF. You should see the text "Hello World!" publish to the stage!

Summary

In this chapter you were exposed to quite a bit of information. Though it may have seemed overwhelming, it is important to keep in mind that it was a mere overview of what is to come. In much the same fashion that you would need to learn the alphabet before you can write an epic, so must you learn the basics of ActionScript.

It is true that much of the syntax will become second nature as you learn other aspects of ActionScript. However, there is no replacement for having a good understanding of the basics. Be sure to utilize tools like the Script Assist and Actions panel, as mentioned in this chapter.

Remember, variables are the building blocks of any ActionScript program. Variables are references to memory that are used to store information. You can manipulate this information using statements. Repetitive statements can be grouped into collections, called functions. Finally, groups of related variables and functions can be grouped into even larger collections called classes.

The following are the most important topics from this chapter:

- Using the Actions panel
- Using Script Assist for easy ActionScript
- Proper ActionScript syntax
- Creating and data typing variables
- Manipulating variables through statements
- Using functions to group repetitive code
- Further organizing and modularizing your code via classes

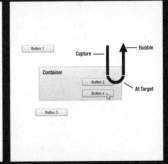

In this chapter we will take a closer look at properties, methods, and events—the three primary elements used to define how classes live and breathe in a programming world.

In ActionScript, all executable information is managed into classes that are used as templates to create objects or instances of that class. You can think of the concept of instantiation as a Xerox copy machine. The class is the original document that is placed on the glass and copied. The objects are the copies that are made. Therefore, if the Xerox machine were making copies of a document, such as a job application, you could make as many copies as you wanted and give them to as many people as you wanted, who would fill them out any way they wanted, and still not destroy the integrity of the original.

It is this fundamental principle that gives the object-oriented approach to programming its power. All functionality can be programmed once, in one location, and instantiated when needed. Within the class exists all the required functionality needed by the object (copy) that is created.

From a technical perspective a class is nothing more than a collection of variables and functions grouped together for a specific purpose. Remember, classes define things. As you might expect, things have the ability to be described, things have the ability to perform various tasks, and things have the ability to let other things know what they are doing. For example, a human being has the ability to be described. It can have height, weight, hair color, or any number of other traits that offer information about it. Human beings can also perform acts such as running and jumping. And, human beings have the ability to alert others of things they have done—"Honey, I'm home!"

Officially, the elements that have just been mentioned are known as properties, methods, and events. It is through these three vessels that an object can communicate with other objects in the programming world. **Properties** are used to describe an object, **methods** are used to allow the object to perform an action, and **events** give objects the ability to notify other objects of an action. In this chapter we will be looking more closely at these components so you can gain a better understanding of how classes function.

First stop, properties!

Properties: I unpacked my adjectives

You know that properties are the part of the class that describes the object. Functioning like adjectives, properties are just variables that have been defined within a class. Properties and variables use the same syntax—in fact, both are defined using the var or const keywords. The difference, however, is in the usage. Some variables, like local variables used for counting loop iterations, will be defined in your classes without being properties of the classes. Therefore, it is best if you think of properties as variables that have been specifically tasked with describing the object.

For example, a box may have properties like color, height, and width. These are all values that have some kind of descriptive meaning to the box itself. They only describe the box, not what the box can do. Properties are also typically a reference to a primitive data type such as int, String, and Boolean values. A box may have a height of 20 and a color of red.

You may not have realized it, but you have actually been working with object properties for several chapters now through the Property inspector, which is the panel used for editing an object's properties. And though it is not obvious to a designer at author time, the values of a symbol's properties that are set in the Property inspector are the values of those same properties in ActionScript. All that remains for you to do is learn to translate what you know about the Property inspector so you can apply it to ActionScript.

Translating properties from stage to ActionScript

The easiest place to draw a correlation between items created during author time and those same objects in ActionScript is by examining display objects. Because Flash is also a design tool, it is common practice for most users to become familiar with the design aspects of Flash prior to becoming involved with ActionScript, much like you have done in this book. Therefore, you are already very familiar with adjusting the properties of display objects by working with the design aspects of Flash in previous chapters. Because of this, you now have a tangible point of reference for manipulating those properties in ActionScript, while understanding how they ultimately affect the original object.

> *As a vernacular, most people refer to display objects in Flash as movie clips. In reality, a movie clip is a type of display object. Display objects can actually be any visible object in Flash, including bitmaps, movies, buttons, and a variety of others. Because movie clips are the most widely used type of display object, it is very common to hear all types of display objects referred to as movie clips. Try to avoid this habit. See Chapter 10 for a discussion of display objects.*

To further expand on this principle, consider the Property inspector along with the Transform tool and 3D Transform tool. These three tools are the primary ones used to adjust the size and position of display objects in Flash at author time. At any given point during the creation of a graphical asset, a designer can use these tools to adjust an object's rotation, position, scale, and more. In the case of the red box shown in Figure 9-1, a designer has the ability to adjust several properties of this object. Essentially, the tools in the Flash design environment give the designer complete control over an object's properties at author time.

9

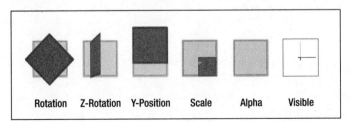

Rotation   Z-Rotation   Y-Position   Scale   Alpha   Visible

Figure 9-1. Display objects can be edited at author time using the Property inspector, Transform, or 3D Transform tools.

It is, however, also possible to manipulate these same properties using ActionScript. Just as a red box has an x property on the stage, it also has that same property within ActionScript.

Changing properties with ActionScript

Now that you are aware of the relationship between author-time graphical elements and ActionScript, it should be no tremendous feat to try and manipulate those elements. For this we are going to need to employ the services of ch09_01.fla. Go ahead and open ch09_01.fla.

Upon opening this file, you should see a red square in the middle of the stage. At this point, this box is no more than a simple movie clip. In order for us to be able to use this in ActionScript, it will need to be given an appropriate name.

Fortunately, the naming of individual symbol instances can easily be accomplished using the Property inspector. There is an input field at the top of the Property inspector with the words <Instance Name> in it. In this field you have the ability to assign a name to any symbol instance on the stage by selecting that instance and typing a unique name in the field. This instance name will serve as the variable reference for the selected display element, giving you the ability to access your symbol via ActionScript. In Figure 9-2, the instance name of redBox has been assigned to a movie clip.

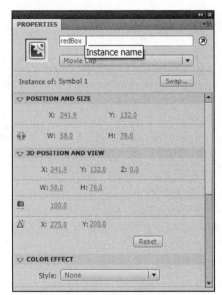

Figure 9-2.
An instance name entered into the Property inspector

1. Open the Property inspector by selecting Window ➤ Properties or by pressing Ctrl+F3.

2. As shown in Figure 9-2, add the name redBox in the <Instance Name> field of the Property inspector.

Now that the movie clip has a name, we can make reference to it in ActionScript. And because of this name, we now have the ability to manipulate its properties as well. It is also worth mentioning that the values assigned to this movie clip in the Property inspector will be the same starting values for these properties in ActionScript.

With that in mind, the second thing you will want to do is create a new layer for your ActionScript. Typically, when you are writing ActionScript directly to the timeline of your FLA, you will want all scripts to reside on a single layer of the FLA.

3. With the timeline open, create a new layer above the Red Box layer and label it Actions.

> For cleanliness' sake, it is also a good idea to lock the layer containing ActionScript so no visible elements are accidentally placed on its keyframes.

Next, we will want to add ActionScript to the Actions layer.

4. Select frame 1 of the Actions layer and open the Actions panel by pressing F9. In the script pane, enter the following two lines of code:

```
var redBox:MovieClip;
redBox.rotation = 20;
```

I should point out that the first line of code is more or less redundant. As discussed earlier, when you create a movie clip symbol in Flash, it is given all the functionality of a movie clip in ActionScript as well. In addition, when you give it an instance name, you are also giving it a reference or variable name to use in ActionScript. This item is also strictly typed as a movie clip. In fact, if you removed the first line of code, your code would execute exactly the same. It is more or less unnecessary.

In the real world, I have never heard the use of an instance variable being considered good practice. I will also say that it is more common for this line to be omitted when working with elements that have been given specific instance names. Why should we then bother to discuss this? Well, it does offer a few advantages to professionals just becoming familiar with ActionScript.

First it will greatly increase your understanding of working with variables in their true environment. From a programming standpoint, the declaration of variables is required. And, data typing is considered excellent programming practice. Much like the semicolon, just because it is not required at this point doesn't mean it isn't a good thing to use.

Secondly, and more tangibly rewarding, declaring variables enables inline code hinting. As shown in Figure 9-3, strictly typed variables are included in a drop-down menu that appears showing all the available members of that object type. A **member** is a term used to describe all properties, methods, and events contained in a class.

9

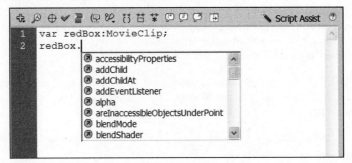

Figure 9-3. Code hinting while typing in ActionScript

> *In Chapter 8 we discussed dot notation, one of the primary purposes of which is to access the members of objects. In the preceding example, rotation is a property of redBox. Therefore, we use dot notation to access that property and change its value to 20.*

As you may have guessed, the previous two lines of code are going to rotate the redBox movie clip 20 degrees. Test your movie by pressing Ctrl+Enter (or Cmd+Enter on a Mac). As you can see, redBox does indeed rotate 20 degrees. You have just successfully edited an object's properties in ActionScript.

Incrementing ActionScript with frame loops

Still working with ch09_01.fla, we will now create a simple loop using keyframes to further manipulate the properties of the redBox movie clip. Creating a loop with the timeline is simple. You only need to add more frames to the timeline. Though recent years have seen more and more ActionScript development being done in external files, it may still be necessary for a developer to incorporate timeline-driven actions.

Now, because this movie has a frame rate of 24 frames per second, we will add 12 frames to the movie. This will give us a timeline that loops approximately every half second.

> *The fact that a movie has a specific frame rate does not mean the movie is necessarily going to execute at that speed. Many factors such as computer processor speed or network speed also play a role in how quickly a frame rate is executed.*

Next, you can simultaneously select frame 12 of both the Actions layer and the Red Box layer by clicking frame 12 of the Actions layer and dragging down to frame 12 of the Red Box layer. You will notice that both frames highlight blue.

1. With both frames selected, press F5. This will add new frames to both layers through frame 12, as shown in Figure 9-4.

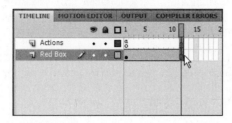

Figure 9-4.
Simultaneous addition of frames to the timeline

2. Once the new frames are added, select frame 1 of the Actions layer and open the Actions panel.

Right now, the ActionScript for the rotation property of redBox simply tells the redBox to rotate to 20 degrees. What we actually want to happen instead is to have redBox rotate in 20-degree increments. This is achieved by a special incrementing operator, +=. This operator takes the current value of a variable and adds an amount to it. In the following code, every time our movie passes through frame 1, the statement will take the current value of redBox.rotation and add 20 to it.

3. Change the code on frame 1 to the following:

```
var redBox:MovieClip;
redBox.rotation += 20;
```

This is all that is required for the creation of a simple ActionScript timeline loop. You can test the movie by pressing Ctrl+Enter (or Cmd+Enter on a Mac). You should see the redBox now rotating clockwise. You can further experiment with this loop to get familiar with the various properties of movie clips. For example, if you use the following code, your redBox movie clip will spin off like the Phantom Zone from *Superman*. You can also change the speed by adjusting the total frames and frame rate of your movie.

```
var redBox:MovieClip;
redBox.rotation += 20;
redBox.rotationY += 40;
redBox.x += 10;
redBox.y -= 5;
redBox.z += 40;
redBox.alpha -= .025;
```

Now that you are familiar with properties, what they do, and how they can be manipulated, it's time to take a look at the parts of the class that perform action. The first of these, methods, is the real doer of any procedural or object-based application.

9

Methods: Just do it!

Methods are functions that have been defined within a class. Like properties, they perform specific tasks that are relevant to the instance of the class. They more or less describe what an object can do or have done to it. For instance, if we create the class Human Being, it might have methods like walk(), run(), and sleep().

As we progress further through this chapter, you will be introduced to a number of basic methods that are associated with movie clips. And, by the end of the book, you should be extremely familiar with the concept of methods and how to use them.

The final player in the functionality of class-based programming is the event. In the past few years ActionScript has been moving toward a more event-based structure.

Events: Are we there yet?

Events are a special kind of method. Unlike regular functions and methods that are specifically called when they are needed, events actually wait for something to occur within the program and react to it. This quality makes events a bit more complicated than other aspects of programming. For example, they can require multiple objects to execute, including objects that put out or broadcast events and objects that "listen" for those events. Events are truly the magic that makes modern interactivity possible.

Event handling has always reminded me of the little kid in the back seat of a car—"Are we there yet? Are we there yet? Are we there yet?" Without events, a computer program constantly needs to check the status of an object to determine whether something has changed. Much like that little kid in the back seat of that car, a computer program would continually be asking, "Has it changed yet? Has it changed yet? Has it changed yet?"

Fortunately, someone in the computer world wised up and created the mother in the front seat. You know, that lady who finally screams, "I will tell you when we get there!" Events are similar to this. Not that they completely flip out and yell at the rest of the computer program, rather they take charge of the notification. So instead of your program constantly checking for a change in state, the event notifies the program when the change has occurred. Kind of like mom, only nicer.

The more mature ActionScript gets, the more event-driven it becomes. The release of ActionScript 3.0 is definitely no exception to this trend. With this version, Flash event handling was completely rearchitected to offer a more streamlined approach to the way Flash processes events. The following section outlines some of the more common event types and the theory behind them.

EventDispatcher class and the Flash event model

The EventDispatcher class is responsible for controlling all functionality associated with the execution of events in Flash. Though not new to ActionScript, it has now been restructured into the lower-level functionality of Flash as a base class from which other objects inherit its functionality.

The Flash event model

To better understand the way in which events function, let's first take a look at the three main components of the Flash event model:

- **Event listeners** are special methods that are used by other objects to detect when an event has occurred. A button would therefore be "listening" for when the mouse click has occurred.
- **Event handlers** are functions that are evoked by the listening object. These functions are able to respond appropriately to the event that has occurred.
- **Event dispatchers**, also commonly referred to as **broadcasters**, are responsible for letting the program know that an event has occurred. For instance, when you click a mouse button, the mouse notifies Flash the button has been clicked.

Though the construction of custom event dispatchers is a bit advanced for the scope of this book, using event listeners and event handlers is something that is easily implemented into everyday ActionScript programming.

> *Most of the events that you, as someone new to Flash, will be working with will deal with listening for user-driven events and interactivity. Many events occur behind the scenes, used by the application to also detect events involving the environments (browsers and computer) and different forms of data.*

Event listeners and handlers

Let's talk about using event listeners with mouse events. When you run a Flash movie, every time the mouse is clicked, it dispatches or broadcasts an event. Though you have no idea this is taking place, it nonetheless is happening. Other objects in Flash then have the ability to listen for that event.

Now let's look at an example of an event listener. Figure 9-5 shows an instance of a simple button used in the ch09_02.fla sample file. This button has also been given the instance name of button1 in the Property inspector.

Figure 9-5. A simple button armed with a CLICK event

9

If you select frame 1 of the Actions layer and open the Actions panel, you will notice the following code, which will be responsible for detecting and responding to the CLICK event:

```
//Event listener
button1.addEventListener(MouseEvent.CLICK, clicked);

//Event handler
function clicked(e:MouseEvent)
{
    trace("Button 1 clicked!");
}
```

The first two lines of code demonstrate what is needed for the invocation of the event listener. Remember, many events are automatically being dispatched from the Mouse object. You only need to be concerned with capturing that specific mouse event and responding to it. Therefore, in order to capture an event, it is necessary to assign an event listener to an object that will respond to that event. In this case, button1 is going to be the object interested in responding to the mouse event.

To assign an object the ability to listen for events, we use the addEventListener() method. The addEventListener() method serves a few purposes in the event model. It is more or less a liaison between the event and the response to that event. As a requirement, it accepts two parameters. The first of these defines the kind of event the object would like to listen for. In this case, button1 will be listening for a MouseEvent.CLICK event.

The second parameter in the addEventListener() method is the name of a function that will execute when the event is detected, in this case clicked(). This function is known as the event handler, and it reacts to the event as dictated by the event listener. Event handlers are nothing more than simple functions that require the passing of one parameter. This parameter is the event object that contains information about the event that was dispatched. As shown in the preceding example, the function clicked() will trace the string Button 1 clicked! whenever the event occurs.

Event objects

Event objects are objects that store information about an event when it is dispatched. In the event model, the event object is what is passed from the event dispatcher to the event listener and eventually the event handler. When you create an event listener, the event object is what is defined in the first parameter. This event object is then passed to the event handler as its parameter.

In the next example, we will take another look at the code from earlier in this chapter. Now we are specifically looking for a MouseEvent object that is of the type CLICK. Once this is detected, the event object is then passed to the event handler as the parameter e. This adjustment can be found in sample file ch09_03.fla.

```
//Event listener
button1.addEventListener(MouseEvent.CLICK, clicked);

//Event handler
function clicked(e:MouseEvent)
{
  trace(e);
  trace(e.target);
}
```

Event objects are incredibly useful in programming because they contain all relevant information about a particular event. If you were to click the button from the preceding example, the following information would be printed to the Output window. This output is all the information that is associated with this particular event object.

```
[MouseEvent type="mouseDown" bubbles=true cancelable=false➡
eventPhase=2localX=36 localY=9 stageX=267 stageY=200➡
relatedObject=null ctrlKey=false altKey=false➡
shiftKey=false buttonDown=true delta=0]
```

Mouse events

Depending on the type of event, you could be presented with an assortment of different information. Some of the more common mouse events are as follows:

- type: A string value indicating the type of event
- target: The target object of the event, typically buttons
- localX: A horizontal reference to the mouse's position relative to the target at the time of the event
- localY: A vertical reference to the mouse's position relative to the target at the time of the event
- stageX: A horizontal reference to the mouse's position relative to the stage at the time of the event
- stageY: A vertical reference to the mouse's position relative to the stage at the time of the event

Event targeting

The second trace statement in the previous example's event handler demonstrates access to another important property of the event object, the **target**. The target of an event is the object that actually receives the event. In this case, button1 is the target. If you happened to click the stage of the movie, the stage would be the target. You would not see anything happen, though, because the stage is not currently listening for mouse events.

The target property of an event is then a reference to the target object itself. Therefore, this reference gives you further access to information about the target as well. If the preceding event handler was changed to something like what you see in the following example,

9

the `trace` statement would then print the name of the button instance, button1, to the Output window.

```
function clicked(e:MouseEvent)
{
  trace(e.target.name); //button1
}
```

Event propagation

In previous versions of Flash it was impossible to have an interactive object within another interactive object. In other words, you could not have a button nested within another button. Any nested object that was located within another object would fail to receive its events. Fortunately, ActionScript 3.0 has introduced developers to the benefits of event propagation.

All visual elements in Flash are relationally organized in a system known as the display list. When a targeting event such as a mouse click or keystroke is used in Flash, the event object is not dispatched directly to the target of the event, but instead dispatched to the display list. The event enters the display list at the topmost level and ultimately traverses the hierarchy until it reaches the target object. Once the event object has reached the target, it will then make its way back to the top of the display list. This process, known as **event propagation**, is demonstrated in Figure 9-6. Event propagation is a rather elegant solution to an otherwise menial task.

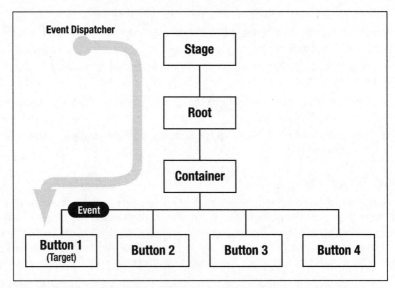

Figure 9-6. An event entering the display list and propagating to the target object

You will be introduced to display objects and their hierarchy in Chapter 10.

Event phases

As mentioned earlier, when an event is dispatched to the display list, it makes its way down through the display hierarchy until it reaches the target object. Once the target object has been reached, the event then returns, or bubbles, back to the top of the display hierarchy. This process is broken into the following phases to describe where the event is in the event flow:

- **Capturing phase**: This phase represents the event passing through all parent objects of the target object.
- **At-target phase**: This phase represents when the event flow has reached the target of the event.
- **Bubbling phase**: This phase is when the event makes it way back to the topmost object of the display list.

Welcomed side effects of event propagation

Event propagation actually creates two extremely useful situations when dealing with ActionScript. The first, which is demonstrated in ch09_04.fla, will show you how selecting one target will trigger events of other objects within the flow. This example contains three event listeners and three event handlers. The elements will trace mouse clicking for the stage, root, and button1 objects, respectively.

```
stage.addEventListener(MouseEvent.CLICK, sclick);
root.addEventListener(MouseEvent.CLICK, rclick);
button1.addEventListener(MouseEvent.CLICK, bclick);

function sclick(e:MouseEvent)
{
  trace ("Stage");
}

function rclick(e:MouseEvent)
{
  trace("Root");
}

function bclick(e:MouseEvent)
{
  trace("Button 1");
}
```

If you then test this movie and click the stage, you will see the word "Stage" traced to the Output window. If you then click button1, you will see the words "Button1," "Root," and "Stage" traced to the Output window. What you are seeing here is that even though you clicked the button, the event has been dispatched to the target through the display list and is now bubbling its way back to the top.

9

At this point you are only seeing the events as they reach the target and bubble back. In order to detect the capture phase of the event flow, you will need to use an optional parameter for the event listener known as useCapture, which is a Boolean variable set to false by default. Therefore, listeners by default are not detecting the capture phase of the event flow. If you add the two lines of code shown next in bold, you will then be detecting the capture phase for the event flow as well. Therefore, if you now test your movie and click the button, you will see the complete journey of the event in the Output window: Stage, Root, Button 1, Root, Stage. You should take notice of the extra parameter in the new event listeners, both of which are used to set useCapture to true.

```
stage.addEventListener(MouseEvent.CLICK, sclick);
root.addEventListener(MouseEvent.CLICK, rclick);
button1.addEventListener(MouseEvent.CLICK, bclick);
stage.addEventListener(MouseEvent.CLICK, sclick, true);
root.addEventListener(MouseEvent.CLICK, rclick, true);
```

Assigning events to parent objects

A second useful trick when working with events and event propagation is assigning an event to a parent object. In the sample file ch09_05.fla, also shown in Figure 9-7, four button symbols are arranged in the parent movie clip, Container.

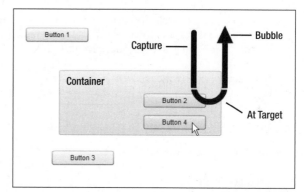

Figure 9-7. For more efficient programming, you can assign a single event listener to a parent object.

In previous versions of Flash, you would need to define event listeners and handlers for every button on the stage. However, because targeted events must travel to the target before they can complete the event phase, it is possible to assign listeners to parent objects. You can then manage the functionality for multiple targets with one event.

The following code demonstrates that rather than adding event listeners to multiple objects on the stage, it is possible to add an event listener to a parent object instead. And, simply by being the target, the button will receive the event. This becomes very useful when setting up navigation schemes.

```
buttonContainer.addEventListener(MouseEvent.MOUSE_DOWN, drag);
buttonContainer.addEventListener(MouseEvent.MOUSE_UP, drop);

function drag (e:MouseEvent)
{
  e.target.startDrag();
}

function drop (e:MouseEvent)
{
  e.target.stopDrag();
}
```

In the preceding code we create two sets of event handlers and listeners to determine when the mouse button is being held down and when it is released, or up. By using the target property of e, our event object, we can then use the startDrag() and stopDrag() methods to drag and drop the buttons.

So far we have looked closely at the use of mouse events. In ActionScript we are not limited to the use of events with the mouse. The event model actually ranges across dozens of events and event types. Two other types of event, which we will be looking at next, are frame- and time-based events.

Frame and timer events

Flash, by design, is a tool used for developing products that generally require the passage of time. As you learned in Chapter 1, Flash was first developed as a drawing and animation tool. Therefore, at its very core, it is necessary for Flash to be able to not only set up animations and state changes, but also control those changes at runtime. For this Flash uses the Frame and Timer event types.

Frame events

As you will continue to learn throughout your career with Flash, a significant amount of functionality goes on behind the scenes. For the most part, you will never need to employ the majority of this functionality in your day-to-day Flash development. One of these occurrences that is worth mentioning is the execution of frame scripts. Much like the previous example where we used the frame loop to increment the properties of the red box, ActionScript will detect the entering of frames on the timeline.

In ActionScript, you have the ability to listen for a special type of event known as the ENTER_FRAME event. The ENTER_FRAME event is dispatched in conjunction with the current frame rate for the document. Regardless of the number of frames in your document, this ENTER_FRAME event will be dispatched at a rate that is directly related to the frame rate of the document. This will happen even if the playhead has been stopped with the stop() method.

9

The following example shows code from ch09_06.fla:

```
addEventListener(Event.ENTER_FRAME, loop);

function loop(e:Event)
{
  var time:Date = new Date();
  var seconds:uint = time.getSeconds()
  var milliseconds:uint = time.getMilliseconds()
  trace(seconds + " : " + milliseconds);
}
```

As you can see, the event listener for the ENTER_FRAME event has been added directly to the stage, which is the topmost display object and itself a movie clip. The function loop simply creates a new Date object from which the seconds and milliseconds properties are used to generate a time signature that is traced to the Output panel. This function, as a handler, is then fired every time the ENTER_FRAME event is detected.

When you run this file by pressing Ctrl+Enter (or Cmd+Enter on a Mac), you will see that the Output panel is registering a time signature for the detection of events about 12 times per second. This, of course, is the current frame rate assigned to this file.

Because ENTER_FRAME events are directly connected to the frame rate for a given document, they serve as an excellent tool for creating ActionScript-driven animation. The file ch09_07.fla demonstrates how regularly updating an object's properties, in this case x, will grant the illusion of the object having movement.

```
ball.addEventListener(Event.ENTER_FRAME, mover);

function mover (e:Event)
{
  e.target.x += 5;
}
```

Timer events

Because the ENTER_FRAME event is directly related to the execution of the frame rate, it may not always be the best solution for working with events that need to occur on a regular interval. For these occasions, ActionScript offers the Timer event. Where the ENTER_FRAME event executes with the frame rate, the Timer event executes in terms of milliseconds.

To use a timer you first need to create an instance of the Timer class. The following line demonstrates the instantiation of the Timer class:

```
var timer:Timer = new Timer(delay, repeatCount);
```

Note that the constructor function of the Timer class can accept two parameters. The first of these, known as delay, sets the amount of time that passes between the dispatching of Timer events in milliseconds. The second parameter, which is optional, allows you to set a total number of intervals that will occur. For example, if delay were set to 1000 and repeatCount were set to 6, the timer would dispatch six events, one event every second.

In the next example file, ch09_08.fla, the timer object has been declared and given a delay value of 50. This will cause the timer to dispatch an event every 50 milliseconds. The optional repeatCount property has been omitted. Omitting this property will cause a timer to execute infinitely.

```
var timer:Timer = new Timer(50);
timer.addEventListener(TimerEvent.TIMER, mover);
timer.start();

function mover (e:TimerEvent)
{
   ball.x += 2;
}
```

The second line in this example is the assignment of the event listener. Because the timer is both the dispatcher and listener for a given event, the addEventListener() method is assigned to the timer object.

The third line of code used here adds an even greater degree of flexibility when working with timer-based intervals. Unlike the ENTER_FRAME event, which is always firing, the Timer event only begins when you tell it to. When using the start() method of the Timer class, you have the option of starting your timer at any given point in your program. Similarly, the Timer class also offers the stop() and reset() methods to allow complete control over when a programmer uses the timer.

Finally, the event handler mover is used to execute the code that is used for the Timer event. In this case, the ball movie clip is having its x property incremented by two every 50 milliseconds. This creates the illusion of motion.

Next, let's learn how to give our users the ability to control our applications using the keyboard.

Accepting keyboard input

The final type of event we will be looking at is the keyboard event. The KeyboardEvent class in Flash makes it easy for a developer to assign events for the purpose of capturing keystrokes.

9

For this example, we will take a look at the ch09_09.fla:

```
stage.addEventListener(KeyboardEvent.KEY_DOWN, mover);

function mover (e:KeyboardEvent)
{
  switch(e.keyCode)
  {
      case Keyboard.LEFT:
          ball.x -= 5;
          break;
      case Keyboard.RIGHT:
          ball.x += 5;
          break;
      case Keyboard.UP:
          ball.y -= 5;
          break;
      case Keyboard.DOWN:
          ball.y += 5;
  }
}
```

In the first line we set up the event listener for the various keyboard events. As discussed during the "Event propagation" section of this chapter, we can assign a single event listener to the stage that will effectively listen for all events dispatched from the keyboard. In this case, we use KeyboardEvent.KEY_DOWN to detect when a key is down.

Once the event is detected we can then call the mover function to efficiently handle the event. Within the mover function, we can use the switch() statement to filter through the keys as they are pressed and determine the right response to each one. This is made possible by checking the keyCode value of the event object. In Flash all keyboard keys are given a numeric value between 8 and 126. This value is assigned to the keyCode property of the event object that is passed from the event listener.

Flash also offers the Keyboard class, which is used to assign these keyCode values to constants that are more easily recognized by humans. Therefore, we can use a switch statement to determine whether the current keyCode is equivalent to a desired value.

When testing the movie, you will be able to move the ball about the screen with the arrow keys.

Removing events and listeners

If you don't remove events when you're done using them in Flash, they will continue to respond to interactions even if you don't want them to. Further, events like ENTER_FRAME are processor intensive and can cause significant lag in performance. Event listeners can also take up a decent amount of memory, which will increase the resources needed by your program. Needless to say, failing to properly manage event handlers can dramatically affect the efficiency of your program.

To remove an event listener, evoke the removeEventListener() method as shown here:

```
//Event listener
button1.addEventListener(MouseEvent.CLICK, clicked);

//Event handler
function clicked(e:MouseEvent)
{
  trace("Button 1 Clicked");
  button1.removeEventListener(MouseEvent.CLICK, clicked);
}
```

To properly use this method, simply apply it exactly as the addEventListener() method was used to create the listener, reflecting the example earlier in this chapter in the section "Event listeners and handlers." The preceding code shows the proper evocation of the removeEventListener() added to the initial sample. Just as the addEventListener() was used as a method of the button1 object, so must the removeEventListener() be used. In addition, the removeEventListener() method accepts the same two required parameters as the addEventListener() method. The first is the event type, and the second is the name of the event handler.

Summary

In this chapter we were able to look at the three primary components of developing ActionScript interactivity. Regardless of the complexity of your ActionScript program, everything will be based on what you have learned in the previous two chapters.

The following topics were covered in this chapter.

- Using properties

- Using methods and events

- Event listening and handling

- Event propagation

- Mouse events

- Frame and timer events

- Keyboard events

- Removing event listeners

9

CHAPTER 10

LEARNING THE DISPLAY MODEL AND BRINGING IT ALL TOGETHER

Working with visual elements in ActionScript 3.0 has become incredibly more efficient. This efficiency is due largely to the new way Flash handles visual elements at runtime. If you ever had the pleasure of working in previous versions of Flash and ActionScript, you would no doubt remember the complex way that Flash handled adding various objects to the stage. This complicated process involved several methods of actually adding elements to the stage. It was difficult to manage these graphics and keep track of layer depths.

The new display list model makes working with visual elements a whole lot simpler. By organizing elements in a hierarchical structure and using a few basic, streamlined methods, developers are no longer faced with the convoluted task of figuring out the best way to add items to the stage.

In the first part of this chapter we will be examining the way in which ActionScript now handles visual elements in Flash. Once you have learned how to manage visual elements with ActionScript, you will then apply this new knowledge to what you have learned in previous chapters and create the multiclass interactive game Germaphobe.

Let's begin by gaining mastery over display objects.

Working with display objects

Display objects represent everything that is associated with visual elements in Flash. Visual elements in Flash can be any kind of asset that has a graphical representation or is used as a container for graphical elements. As you have learned in previous chapters, these graphical elements can be vector shapes, bitmaps, or symbols.

Though it is possible to have visual objects that are not on the display list, the display list is responsible for governing all elements in Flash that have the capability of either being visible or containing visible objects. Visual objects are then organized hierarchically into the display list for that application. In Figure 10-1, you can see various elements arranged on the stage of a Flash movie.

When working with display lists, the stage always represents the topmost, or **parent**, container for the entire application. The stage is a representation of the main Flash Player that is responsible for displaying all other visual elements. Figure 10-2 demonstrates the display list hierarchy for the same group of images demonstrated in Figure 10-1.

The next element in the display list is the main timeline of the application. All Flash applications must contain a timeline. Even if the application is of the sprite type (one frame), it still contains a timeline. Therefore, if you were to publish a movie clip with nothing on the stage, you would still have at least two objects in the display list—the stage and the main timeline.

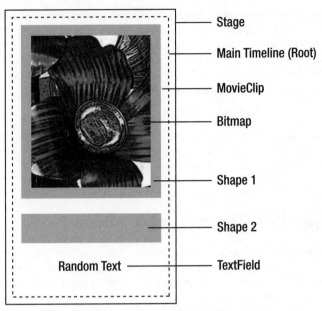

Figure 10-1. The arrangement of graphics on the Flash stage

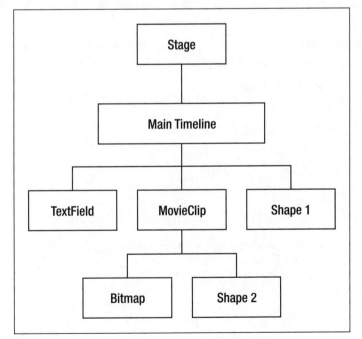

Figure 10-2. The display list hierarchy of a sample Flash file

When you begin adding items to the stage, you are adding **children** to the timeline of the display list. In the examples shown in Figures 10-1 and 10-2, three children have been added to the main timeline:

- The text field
- The orange rectangular shape (Shape 1)
- The movie clip containing the photograph (bitmap)

The movie clip contains two children itself, the bitmap photograph and a blue rectangular shape. The fact that this movie clip contains children, or child display objects, automatically classifies it as a display object container.

Traversing the display list

The Flash online help documentation (http://help.adobe.com/en_US/ActionScript/3.0_ ProgrammingAS3/) offers an extremely helpful way of tracing out the entire display list. In this section we will be discussing a loose adaptation of this function that we will call the listChildren() function. By using listChildren(), shown in the following code, you can get an accurate listing of all display objects that are available in the visible display list. In addition, this function introduces the concept of *display list containers*. Display list containers are a type of display list object that is capable of containing other display list objects.

The following example file, ch10_01.fla, corresponds to the graphics portrayed in Figure 10-1:

```
function listChildren ➥
(cont:DisplayObjectContainer, tab:String = ""):void
{
  var child:DisplayObject;
  for (var i:uint=0; i < cont.numChildren; i++)
  {
    child = cont.getChildAt(i);
    trace(tab, child, child.name);

    if (cont.getChildAt(i) is DisplayObjectContainer)
    {
      listChildren(DisplayObjectContainer(child), "    " + tab)
    }
  }
}

listChildren(stage, "|----");
```

On the AS layer of that file, you will also notice the preceding code segment. As mentioned, this function is used to trace the existing elements from the stage to the Output window in order of their hierarchical structure.

The first line of code defines the function listChildren(). This function accepts two parameters. The cont parameter represents the parent container, the children of which we will display. The second parameter (tab) represents a string variable that will be used to indent the list to give it better readability in terms of its structure.

Once the function is declared, we then create the variable child, which will serve as a reference for the child objects of the parent; in this case, the parent will be the stage. The for loop, shown next, is then used to loop through all the children contained within the parent display object.

```
for (var i:uint=0; i < cont.numChildren; i++)
{ ...
```

In this for loop we declare an incrementing variable, i, to serve as the counter and set its initial value to 0. The second statement of the loop then determines the maximum count for the loop. For this we are using the property numChildren. numChildren is a special type of property used by all display object containers. In this case our display object container is the cont object that was passed as the first parameter in the listChildren() function. Therefore, this number will resolve to the total number of child display objects that are contained in the cont display object container. The i variable is then incremented until the loop has reached the predetermined maximum value, cont.numChildren.

The next two lines of code set the value of the child variable to the current child of the cont container using the getChildAt method. Like the numChildren property, all display object containers also have the method getChildAt to reference a child container based on its index. When children are added to display object containers, they are indexed numerically based on when and how they were added to that container. Therefore, we have the ability to reference these child items based on that numerical index.

As the loop iterates and cycles through the code, we can use the i variable to determine each child located at that particular index. Once the reference is established, we then trace out information about the child object, as shown here:

```
child = cont.getChildAt(i);
trace(tab, child, child.name);
```

In the preceding trace statement, we first trace out the tab string. Remember the tab string will be used to indent the children of containers to aid in readability. Secondly, we trace the child itself. Then we trace out the type of object the child is. Finally, we trace the child name.

There are several elements in Flash that you can name using the Property inspector. However, there are many objects, like shapes, that you do not have the ability to name. If an object does not have a name when the program is instantiated, Flash will automatically

10

name that object. Therefore, many of your objects will have generic names such as instance2.

The first pass through this loop will detect the main timeline and trace out something like this:

```
|---- [object MainTimeline] root1
```

Here |---- is the indent string, [object MainTimeline] is the child, and root1 is the name of the child. So MainTimeline is the first child of the stage.

The remaining lines in the listChildren() function are used to determine whether the child object is a display object container itself. The is keyword is a type of operator used to determine whether an object is a specific type of object. In this case we are checking to see if the objects are of the DisplayObjectContainer type. If a display object has children, it is most certainly a display object container. Therefore, this statement will evaluate to either true or false:

```
if (child is DisplayObjectContainer)
{...
```

If the preceding statement does evaluate to true, we enter a rather interesting situation. You may have noticed that the code located in the if statement is actually another call to the listChildren() function. Essentially, we have a function calling itself from within itself. This phenomenon is known as **recursion**, or **recursive execution**. If the child object is indeed a display object container, we would want it to list its children as well. Subsequently, we can then call the listChildren() function within itself and pass it child as the container parameter. We also add more space to the front of the indent string to create further indenting of the child elements. This is demonstrated in the following statement:

```
listChildren(DisplayObjectContainer(child), "    " + tab)
```

Finally, we call the listChildren() function and pass it the initial variable for the container and the tab string. In this case, we want to determine all visual assets of the ch10_01. fla movie, so we pass stage as the topmost cont parameter. We also pass the |---- string to help aid in the readability of the traced output, as shown here:

```
listChildren(stage, "|----");
```

If you test the movie, you will see a list of all visible display objects being traced to the Output window.

Examining display object containers

As you just learned, display object containers are special types of display objects that are capable of containing other display objects. In ActionScript, there are four primary types of display object containers:

- Stage
- Loader
- Sprite
- Movie clip

You should now be fairly familiar with all types of containers with the exception of the loader type. You will be introduced to the loader in Chapter 11.

Display object containers give you the ability to manipulate their children in a number of different ways, as you'll find out shortly. Because the display model in ActionScript 3.0 has been completely rearchitected, those migrating from earlier versions of ActionScript should find these methods a lot more efficient to work with. Additionally, this change will also give you a tremendous amount of control both inserting and changing the stacking order of your visual elements.

Adding children

Adding a child object to the stage is one of the easier things that you can accomplished in ActionScript. As demonstrated in ch10_02.fla, the only thing that is required is a variable for reference. Using the addChild method, you can then easily add an item to the display list using the variable reference.

As shown next, a new shape is created and given the reference name of shape1. We then use the addChild(shape1) statement to add the new shape to the stage. If you tested this movie, you may be wondering where the shape is. Well, there are no visible aspects to the shape at this point. However, if you were to trace the shape using its index in the display list, you would notice that the trace statement does in fact return an object of the Shape type.

```
var shape1:Shape = new Shape();

addChild(shape1);

trace(this.getChildAt(0)); //[object Shape]
```

In order to have a visible shape, we will now use some basic ActionScript to draw the red rectangle as demonstrated in ch10_03.fla. At this point, these new lines of code are of no tremendous consequence. They have simply been added to help you see what we are doing. Testing the movie will render a red rectangle in the upper-left corner of the SWF.

```
var shape1:Shape = new Shape();

shape1.graphics.beginFill(0xff0000);
shape1.graphics.drawRect(0, 0, 200, 100);
shape1.graphics.endFill();

addChild(shape1);
```

10

Adding shapes to the stage is just as easy. In the following example, you can see that when adding a second green rectangle to the stage, Flash automatically stacks display elements as they are added. Notice that shape2 is added to the stage on top of shape1.

```
var shape1:Shape = new Shape();
var shape2:Shape = new Shape();

shape1.graphics.beginFill(0xff0000);
shape1.graphics.drawRect(0, 0, 200, 100);
shape1.graphics.endFill();

shape2.graphics.beginFill(0x00ff00);
shape2.graphics.drawRect(100, 0, 200, 100);
shape2.graphics.endFill();

addChild(shape1);
addChild(shape2);
```

Inserting display objects at different depths

In many cases, you will want to insert display objects at different depths in your movie. ActionScript gives you complete control over this functionality as well. Using the addChildAt() method, you have the ability to add a child at whatever depth, or index, of the display list you would like. Using the previous example, also found in ch10_04.fla, you can now see that when using the addChildAt() method, you have the ability to place the green rectangle below the red rectangle. Unlike the addChild() method, the addChildAt() method accepts a second parameter in addition to the object name. This second parameter represents the index at which you would like to insert your object.

> With respect to display objects, indexes can be thought of as both the position in the order of the display list and the depth of the display object. Think of this as floors of a building. The second floor of a building is on top of the first floor, the third floor of the building is on top of the second, and so on. Flash stacks and numbers display objects in a similar fashion. This numbering is known as the **index**.

The following code demonstrates how the previous example can be changed to switch the depths of the red and green rectangles:

```
var shape1:Shape = new Shape();
var shape2:Shape = new Shape();

shape1.graphics.beginFill(0xff0000);
shape1.graphics.drawRect(0, 0, 200, 100);
shape1.graphics.endFill();
```

```
shape2.graphics.beginFill(0x00ff00);
shape2.graphics.drawRect(100, 0, 200, 100);
shape2.graphics.endFill();

addChild(shape1);
addChildAt(shape2, 0);
```

In this example you can see now that the green rectangle is inserted below the red rectangle by using the index position of 0.

Removing children

In much the same manner that you add children to the display list, you have the ability to remove them. In ch10_05.fla, you'll find an example that is very similar to the previous one. The primary difference is that we have changed the shapes to movie clips for the benefit of interactivity. As shown next, there are also two sets of event listeners and handlers to toggle between whether mc2 is on or off the display list. Using the removeChild() method, we can then effectively make the green rectangle disappear.

```
...
addChild(mc1);
addChild(mc2);

mc1.addEventListener(MouseEvent.MOUSE_OVER, over);
mc1.addEventListener(MouseEvent.MOUSE_OUT, out);

function over(e:MouseEvent)
{
    removeChild(mc2);
}

function out(e:MouseEvent)
{
    addChild(mc2);
}
```

Similarly, we also have the ability remove children at certain positions using the removeChildAt() method. By changing the removeChild() statement in the over event handler to removeChildAt(0), we can now target the child object that is located at the 0 index of this display list. When testing the movie, you should now see the blue rectangle disappear when you mouse over the red rectangle.

```
function over(e:MouseEvent)
{
    removeChildAt(0);
}
```

10

Swapping depths

Finally, developers have the ability to change the position of child objects by also referencing either the child name or the index position of the child. In ch10_06.fla, we again take the previous example and alter the statements within the event handlers to control the changing of depths between the green rectangle (mc2) and the blue rectangle (mc3).

```
function over(e:MouseEvent)
{
  swapChildren(mc2, mc3);
}

function out(e:MouseEvent)
{
  swapChildrenAt(0, 2);
}
```

In the over event handler, we are swapping positions based on the child names using the swapChildren() method. With the swapChildrenAt() method, we can reference the display list index for the same particular objects. In this case because we know mc3 is originally at index 0 and mc2 is originally at index 2, we can set this up so that these two objects toggle positions when the red rectangle is moused over.

By now you should have the necessary understanding to begin putting together basic ActionScript applications. What you have learned in the last three chapters has more or less been laying the foundation for everything else that you will learn in ActionScript. You have been exposed to the core tools for development. The rest of the book can therefore be thought of as various extensions of this basic foundation. You will certainly learn a tremendous amount of new material in the upcoming chapters, but the basic theory and manner in which you engage these elements will remain the same.

Germaphobe

The Germaphobe application, as far as computer programs go, is relatively simple. In this game a player will be responsible for clicking germs that appear on the stage. The game grows increasingly difficult as more germs are added to the stage over time. The game is over when the game board becomes overrun by germs, causing a total infestation. Therefore, a player will need to click as many germs as possible before the game board becomes infested. As an intended side effect, developing this game will allow you to bring your current ActionScript knowledge together in one place. Leaning heavily on the previous three chapters, you will gain a working understanding of the total sum of ActionScript's basic working parts.

The Hello World application you built in Chapter 8 showed you how to construct a simple one-class application but no doubt gave you very little insight into a real-world application or its theory. In Germaphobe we will take a look at a simple two-class application that deals with user interaction, multiple graphics, and plenty of moving parts.

Finally, we are going to leave this application a little open-ended to allow you to further modify the game with enhancements as you learn new tricks throughout the book. It is always good to continually remold an application to help you understand why something is done a certain way and how you may be able to make it more efficient.

Setting up the game

It is fairly common for production houses to be split into two sides, design and development. And as a developer, it is not uncommon to have graphical elements done for you. Before we ever wrote one lick of code for this example, we started with an FLA file that had four colored dots in its Library panel. Obviously, the dots were later changed to graphics of germs, but there was without question a clear definition between design and development.

To get started with the Germaphobe application, you will first need to open the Germaphobe. fla file from the sample files. This file is pretty bare bones. With the exception of containing four graphics in the Library panel, it has no ActionScript of any kind. In the general scope of things, this is about where a typical developer will begin the process of coding.

> *In the real world, you will want to properly plan out your applications. It is also pretty good practice to create a little mise en place. That is, after you figure out what kind of cake you want to make, get your ingredients together, and then make the cake. You should never try to make anything without first having your ingredients in place.*

Assigning the document class

10

Once you have acclimated to Germaphobe.fla, what is the next course of action? If you said create a document class for the application, you are absolutely correct. The document class is the primary class in our application, and it is responsible for managing everything that will be used in the application. As the foundation for our application, it is the best place to start.

To create the document class for the application, you will need to do the following:

1. Create a new ActionScript file by selecting File ➤ New. Then select ActionScript File from the New Document dialog window.

2. Save the new ActionScript file as Germaphobe.as in the same directory as Germaphobe.fla.

3. In the Property inspector, assign the document class by typing Germaphobe in the Class field as shown in Figure 10-3.

Figure 10-3.
Defining the document class
in the Property inspector

Defining the Germophobe class

The proper definition of a class is pretty straightforward. Recall from Chapter 8, where you defined your first class, that three main components are required for class definitions:

- **Package**: A package is a collection of classes that reside in the same directory because they share related functionality. Because this class is defined in the same directory as Germaphobe.fla, a package name is not required.

- **Class definition**: The class definition encapsulates all functionality of the class. It must have the exact same name as the AS file that it is defined in.

- **Constructor function**: The constructor function is the main method of the class. All functionality that resides within this function is executed when the class is instantiated. The constructor function must have the exact same name as the class it represents and the AS file it is defined in.

To define the Germaphobe class, enter the following code into the Germaphobe.as file:

```
package
{
  import flash.display.Sprite;

  public class Germaphobe extends Sprite //Class Definition
  {
    public function Germaphobe () //Constructor Function
    {

    }
  }
}
```

An additional element to take note of in the class definition is the use of import statements. The import statement is used to import functionality from other classes and packages. By default all document classes must import either the MovieClip or Sprite class. In this case, because the Germaphobe timeline will not have more than one frame, it is best to import the Sprite class.

We then use the extends keyword to allow the Germaphobe class to behave like a Sprite. Where the import statement allows a program to access certain functionality, the extends keyword makes that functionality an innate ability of the class. Therefore, all properties, methods, and events of the Sprite class are now active members of the Germaphobe class.

The ability of a class to inherit functionality from another class is known as **inheritance**— go figure.

Class and property attributes

As a developer, you will often want to control the level of access other developers and other elements in the program may have when dealing with a specific class. For this reason ActionScript 3.0 offers several modifiers that are used to control this level of access. For example, you may have noticed the modifying word public in the class definition. Table 10-1 gives the appropriate use for attributes that are employed for modifying class declarations.

Table 10-1. The modifying attributes for class definition

Attribute	Definition
dynamic	Allows a programmer to create and add custom properties to an object at runtime
final	Prohibits the class from being extended
internal (default)	Indicates the class can be referenced by other classes within the package
public	Indicates the class can be referenced anywhere in a program

10

It is also necessary to have the ability to modify the various members of classes. The primary function is to limit accessibility from outside programming. The best way to think of this is to consider many modern mechanisms or appliances. For example, a television has public functionality. The on/off button allows a person to switch the television on or off. However, the TV also performs functions that are not directly accessible to the viewer, like converting a signal into a picture. Rightfully so, this kind of functionality should stay out of the hands of the average viewer. The use of class and property attributes is established for exactly this reason.

Table 10-2 gives a list of the various class property definitions and their uses.

Table 10-2. The modifying attributes of class members

Attribute	Definition
internal (default)	Makes the member visible to references inside the same package
private	Indicates the member can only be referenced from within this class
protected	Indicates the member can be accessed from this class and any derived classes
public	Indicates the member can be accessed from anywhere
static	Labels the member as specific to the class and not the instance

> *For the most part, classes and members used in this book will only be modified using the public and private attributes where applicable. Attributes are fairly advanced programming topics and should be researched through additional resources.*

Setting up the germs

Now that the main class of the game has been created, it's time to start to add the bits and pieces that actually define the purpose of the game. The germs constitute the primary component, and are thus the namesake of the game. The primary purpose of the game is to try to stop the infestation of the game board from occurring. Before we can include our germs in the game, they will need to be created.

Defining the class

As you may have guessed, the first thing that needs to occur for the creation of germs is the defining of the Germ class. Creating a class for a germ is no different from creating a class for the Germaphobe game. It will involve all the usual suspects for class construction and follow the same rules.

Follow these steps to create the Germ class:

1. Create a new ActionScript file by selecting File ➤ New and choosing ActionScript File from the New Document dialog.

2. Save the file as Germ.as in the same directory as Germaphobe.fla and Germaphobe.as. Remember, naming is extremely important and so is letter case.

3. Create the class definition by entering the following code into the script pane of the Germ.as file.

The creation of the Germ class is going to follow the exact same procedure as the Germaphobe class with the exception of a few minor tweaks.

```
package
{
  import flash.display.MovieClip;

  public class Germ extends MovieClip
  {
    public function Germ ()
    {

    }
  }
}
```

The most obvious difference between this class and the Germaphobe class is the use of an appropriate name. Therefore, because we are working in the Germ.as file and defining a new classification of object, the name of the class and the constructor function should both be Germ.

The second, and not so obvious, change is the use of the MovieClip keyword as the imported class and class extension. Remember, the primary difference between the movie clip and the sprite is the existence of a multiframed timeline. The main application is only going to reside on one frame of the main stage, so Sprite is sufficient for the document class. However, as you will find shortly, the Germ class is going to be linked to a library asset. This symbol contains multiple frames, which we will need to access later. Therefore, we will need access to timeline functionality, which will require the use of Movie Clip as the parent class instead of Sprite.

Linking to a graphic symbol

In Chapter 9, we briefly discussed the concept of creating new symbols as being similar to creating new classes. At this point, now that you've attained a general knowledge of inheritance, we are going to revisit and wrap up that concept.

When a symbol is created and added to the library, in this case the symbol Germ, you are basically extending the MovieClip class with the new class Germ (Germ extends MovieClip, right). Though adding ActionScript to the timeline of the Germ symbol would not really be best practice in this case, if you were to add a function to the timeline of that symbol, you would indeed be creating a method of Germ.

You then have the ability to add instances of Germ to the stage of your Flash movie at either runtime or author time. Therefore, the concept for creating new library symbols is similar to creating new classes. You also have the ability to link an external class to various library symbols. In this case, the creation of the library symbol is in fact actually the same as creating a new class.

10

To link the `Germ.as` class file to the `Germ` library symbol, do the following:

1. Right-click the `Germ` symbol in the `Germaphobe.fla` Library panel to open the Symbol Properties dialog.

2. Check the box next to Export for ActionScript, as shown in Figure 10-4. The Class field should automatically fill in with the value Germ, which is based on the name of the symbol. This also represents the name of the AS file that you want to link to the symbol. It is required that this field and the AS file have the same name. It is also excellent practice to plan ahead to make sure your symbol will also have this name.

3. Select Export in frame 1 and click OK.

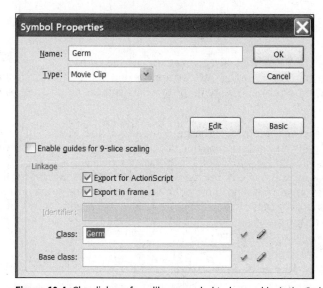

Figure 10-4. Class linkage for a library symbol to be used in ActionScript

Initializing the game

The initialization of your Flash application is always going to occur in the constructor function of your application's document class. In this case, the `Germaphobe` function of the `Germaphobe` class is going to be that point of initialization. The constructor function of your document class can always be thought of as the first domino. Therefore, as soon as the application is run, the document class will fire, and whatever is located in the document class's constructor function will fire.

A cleaner point of entry

As you will find, the first stages of an application such as a game can be a bit miscellaneous. They typically involve the creation of a few various tidbits that are responsible for getting the entire big picture rolling. As a personal convention, we usually don't like a lot of initial garbage in the constructor function of our applications. For this reason, we like to create a second function right off the bat. This method will handle all the initial functionality used to set up our application.

Directly below the constructor function in the next example, we will set up the private function init(). We set this to private because we want this function to be accessible only from our Germaphobe class. We then call this function in the constructor with the init(); statement.

```
package
{
  import flash.display.Sprite;

  public class Germaphobe extends Sprite
  {
    public function Germaphobe ()
    {
      init();
    }

    private function init():void
    {

    }
```

Randomly adding germs to the stage

To add germs randomly to the stage, we simply need to instantiate the Germ class and add it to the stage using the addChild() method of the DisplayObjectContainer class. As an added bonus, we will start scratching the surface of the Math class to help us further manipulate the position of our first germ.

Add the following code to the init() function of the Germaphobe class:

```
public function Germaphobe ()
{
  init();
}

private function init():void
{
  var germ:Germ = new Germ();

      germ.x = Math.random() * stage.stageWidth;
      germ.y = Math.random() * stage.stageHeight;

      addChild(germ);
}
```

The first line is the basic declaration and instantiation of the germ variable. Because the Germ class extends the MovieClip class, which is itself a distant descendant of the DisplayObject class, it has all the properties you would expect to find in a display object,

10

notably the x and y properties. With these two properties, we will have the ability to position the germs anywhere we like on the stage.

To give the game a more organic feel, we are going to randomly position germs on the stage as they are created. To do this we are going to use a simple statement involving the Math class. The Math class contains methods for performing basic numeric operations such as the elementary exponential, logarithm, square root, and trigonometric functions. It also contains several commonly used mathematic constants such as pi and Euler's e. In Flash, one of the most commonly used methods of the Math class is the random() method. The random() method generates a random decimal number between 0 and 1, but not including 1.

> The random() method is not actually random at all. The number is based on the time, in milliseconds, that the random() method was called.

In the next code sample, we are taking this randomly generated number and multiplying it by the height and width properties of the stage. We know that the stageWidth property is 550 because we can check it in the Property inspector of the Germaphobe.fla file. We know that zero times any number is zero. We also know that one multiplied by any number is that number. Therefore, by multiplying the stage width (550) by a randomly generated number between 0 and .99, we can effectively position the germ at any point from 0 to approximately 550. This holds true for the height (or y property) of the stage as well.

```
Math.random() * stage.stageWidth // is the same as (0 to 0.99) * 550
```

Finally, we use the addChild() method to place the movie clip on the stage. If you test your movie a couple of times, you should see that the germ appears in different places every time.

On a side note, the Target drop-down menu is used for targeting an FLA when working in external AS files. This is used to allow you to test an FLA directly from the AS file by selecting the file that you would like associated with the AS file. As shown in Figure 10-5, the target for the Germ and Germaphobe AS files is set to Germaphobe.fla.

Figure 10-5.
The Target drop-down for AS files

Picking the germ's face

You may have also noticed that when you tested the movie, the germ was changing all different shades of the color spectrum. This is because the germ image is comprised of a four-frame movie clip. You can see from Figure 10-6 that each frame of the Germ movie clip contains its own image of a different-colored germ. We can use these images to add a little variety in our game.

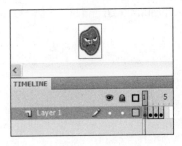

Figure 10-6.
The timeline of the Germ movie clip

At the moment the issue we have with the Germ movie clip is that its timeline plays and continues to loop while the game is playing. What we need to have happen is to have the timeline of the Germ movie clip stop on a frame to display a different-colored germ, seemingly at random.

To accomplish this, we are going to add a simple statement to the constructor function of the Germ class. Using the gotoAndStop() method, we can tell the timeline to jump to a specific frame in the germ's timeline and stop at that frame. The keyword this then targets the timeline of *this* germ.

```
public function Germ()
{
  this.gotoAndStop();
}
```

The gotoAndStop() method accepts one parameter, the frame. It can be either a string value that represents a frame label or a numeric value that represents the frame number. In this case, because we are not using frame labels, we will opt for the use of a numeric value. Once again, this puts us in the position to select the number at random.

To achieve the random number of the frame, we will again use the Math.random() method and multiply it by the total number of frames in the Germ timeline, 4, as shown here:

```
this.gotoAndStop(Math.random() * 4);
```

You may have been clever enough to pick up on the fact that this is not quite going to give us the values we need to select frames 1 through 4. Remember that the Math.random() method returns a decimal number ranging from 0 to 1, but not equaling 1. Therefore, this will never return a value of 4. The highest value we could ever hope to achieve from this statement is 3.999999999999999.

To get around this slight technicality, we will introduce the following method from the Math class, Math.ceil() (where ceil stands for ceiling). This method rounds any given decimal value up to the next whole number. Unlike standard mathematical rounding, which rounds up or down, the Math.ceil() method will round up no matter what the decimal value is. So, if the number happens to be 3.001, Math.ceil() will round it up to 4. Therefore, all numbers greater than zero will round to 1, all numbers greater than 1

10

will round to 2, all numbers greater than 2 will round to 3, and all numbers greater than 3 will round to 4.

```
public function Germ()
    {
        this.gotoAndStop(Math.ceil(Math.random() * 4));
    }
```

Test the movie a couple of times. You should notice that now when the first germ is placed on the stage, it is no longer flickering, but is a different color.

Making the germ scurry

Now that the germ is in our game, it is more than likely that we are going to want to get rid of it. Germs are bad, right? The unfortunate reality is that before we can kill the germ, we have to catch it. You're probably wondering what the difficulty will be in catching something that just sits in the same position. Well, before we can catch it, we have to make it scurry.

Creating random motion with the scurry event

Well, we have a germ. And, as exciting as that is, it is often said that "The fun is in the chase." Therefore, we need to give the germ the ability to try to escape its impending destruction.

Thinking back to Chapter 9, we discussed several ways to create animation using the help of events and event listeners. To create the motion for the germ, we will be using the ENTER_FRAME event, which will fire based on the frame rate of the main document. Because Germaphobe.fla has a frame rate of 24 fps, we should expect this to execute approximately 24 times every second.

In the following code we add the necessary framework for including an event in the Germ class. To use events we first import the events package using the import flash.events.* statement. By using an asterisk after the dot operator in this statement, we can import all classes in this package.

> For now, because the concept of importing packages may be new to you, it is okay to import an entire package. As you become more familiar with using packages, you will want to import only the classes you need. In the display import earlier in this chapter, you specifically imported the MovieClip class, and not the entire display package. You simply don't want to import what you don't need.

In the constructor function, we add the ENTER_FRAME event listener, setting the handler name to scurry. We then create the scurry() method of the Germ class to handle the movement of the germ.

```
package
{
  import flash.display.MovieClip;
  import flash.events.*;

  public dynamic class Germ extends MovieClip
  {
    public function Germ()
    {
      this.gotoAndStop(Math.ceil(Math.random() * 4));
      this.addEventListener(Event.ENTER_FRAME, scurry);
    }

    public function scurry (e:Event)
    {

    }
  }
}
```

Having set up the framework for the handling of the scurry event, we can now define exactly what it is for our Germ to scurry.

In my (Paul's) experience as an ActionScript instructor, the most common difficulty faced by new programmers is trying to translate complex human concepts into the programming realm. When we define a method such as scurry(), because the human thought process is so complex, it can conjure up a million different thoughts about what it means for something to scurry. In all actuality, scurrying in the Germaphobe world is nothing more than the germ moving around the board, trying to elude eminent doom. Therefore, scurrying is simply movement. And as you learned Chapter 9, you can create the illusion of movement simply by updating the position of an object at a regular interval. So scurrying is nothing more than regularly updating the x and y property of our germ.

In the upcoming code sample, we add four new lines to the Germ class. The first two lines are responsible for defining variables for xSpeed and ySpeed properties of our germ. When creating properties in a class, it is a common convention that all properties be defined first in the class before the constructor function.

We first create the dx and dy properties to control how fast the germ will move in any given direction. Speed, by definition, is the total change of distance over a certain interval of time. For our germ, the time is going to be handled by the ENTER_FRAME event. Therefore, the change in distance will be determined by the dx and dy properties.

> The variables dx and dy are commonly used for variables governing a change in distance. The d in these variable names comes from the Leibniz notation of calculus, where the letter "d" is synonymous with delta, or "change in." Essentially, these variables can be read as "delta-x" or "change in x" and "delta-y" or "change in y."

10

We again use the Math.random() method to add a more dynamic feel to the end product: every germ that is added to the stage will have the illusion of moving at a different speeds. We then multiply Math.random() by an arbitrary number, 10, to make the movement more significant.

The next two lines are added to the scurry function. The scurry function is the handler for the ENTER_FRAME event in the Germ constructor function. So, to give the illusion of motion, as we did in Chapter 9, we will increment the x and y properties of the Germ using the dx and dy properties. Therefore, every time the ENTER_FRAME event is fired, the scurry function will add the value of dx and dy to the current values of x and y, respectively.

```
public dynamic class Germ extends MovieClip
{

  private var dx:Number = Math.random() * 10;
  private var dy:Number = Math.random() * 10;

  public function Germ()
  {
    this.gotoAndStop(Math.ceil(Math.random()*4));
    this.addEventListener(Event.ENTER_FRAME, scurry);
  }

  public function scurry (e:Event)
  {
    this.x += this.dx;
    this.y += this.dy;
  }
}
```

Checking for walls

You may now notice that when you test your program, the germ does indeed move. And, as exciting as this may be, you will also no doubt notice that the germ eventually scurries off the screen, never to return. This of course would be the desired result if we did have an infestation of germs. Unfortunately, it doesn't make for a very exciting game. To avoid the problem of the ever-running germ, it becomes necessary for us to check the bounds of the stage to determine whether the germ has reached an edge.

To accomplish this, we add two very simple if statements to the scurry function. The first of these will check the horizontal bound of the germ's movement and then change the sign of dx. For a beginning programmer, this may look a bit complicated at first. However, reading it in layman's language, it becomes a little less sinister. The first line basically says, "If this (germ) x is less than 0 or this (germ) x is greater than 550 . . . " Logically, this is doing nothing more than determining whether the x position of the germ is less than zero (off the stage to the left) or greater than 550 (off the stage to the right). The second if statement in this code block works in the same manner as the first, only it governs the y property (vertical movement) of the germ.

```
public function scurry (e:Event)
{
    if (this.x < 0 || this.x > 550)
    {
        this.dx *= -1;
    }

    if (this.y < 0 || this.y > 400)
    {
        this.dv *= -1;
    }

    this.x += this.xSpeed;
    this.y += this.ySpeed;
}
```

Killing germs

The killing of germs is probably the most complicated part of the entire Germaphobe program. The reason for this is that it involves the authoring of code in both the Germ class and the Germaphobe class.

Setting up the kill

The first step to eradicating germs from the game is to create the mouse event. In the game, if you want to kill the germ, you simply need to catch it and click it. As you learned in Chapter 9, if you have many items within a display container, you can control targeted events to those items by applying the event listener to the parent object. In the Germaphobe game, the stage is going to serve as the parent container. Eventually, there will be hundreds of germs on the stage that you are going to have to try to catch and kill. Therefore, if we add the listener to the stage, all of the germs will receive the event through event propagation.

We add the listener for clicking germs in the init function of the Germaphobe class. The handler for this event will be the function kill, which is also going to be added to the Germaphobe class.

```
stage.addEventListener(MouseEvent.MOUSE_DOWN, kill);
```

The kill function does become a bit tricky because we must use the is operator to determine the type of object that is clicked. The first thing that needs to occur here is the filtering of target objects. When using event propagation, any interactive object that is a child of the container can be the target of the click. Since we are using the stage as the parent object, and it is the topmost container, all objects that are visible on the stage will be targets of the CLICK event and receive the event through propagation. Therefore, all Germs will receive the CLICK event. Because all display objects on the stage will receive this event, we will need to determine whether the item clicked is actually a germ.

10

The first line of the kill function is an if statement that is going to evaluate whether the target of the mouse click is in fact a germ. We can accomplish this using the is keyword, which is used to check the data type of any given object. The if statement then determines whether the item that was clicked is of the Germ data type. If the event target does happen to be a germ, or more specifically of the Germ data type, the if statement will be true. This then causes the if statement to execute its code block.

```
private function kill (e:MouseEvent):void
{
  if(e.target is Germ)
  {
    e.target.die();
  }
}
```

Within this code block we can then call the die method of e.target, which is really calling the die method of a Germ (the Germ that was clicked).

Things are killed, and then they die

The die() function is added to the Germ class and handles the germ being removed from existence and the memory of the game. In this function, we first remove the event listener for the scurry ENTER_FRAME event. Good garbage collecting dictates that when events are no longer needed, it's best to get rid of them.

The second thing this function does is remove the visual representation of the germ from the display list. We use parent to target the stage. We can then use removeChild() and pass the this keyword to target the germ. Therefore, the stage can remove its child, which is this particular germ.

```
public function die()
{
  this.removeEventListener(Event.ENTER_FRAME, scurry);
  parent.removeChild(this);
}
```

Allowing germs to reproduce

Alright, you are making excellent progress. When testing the game, you will now have a germ that scurries around the stage, is unable to escape the stage, and can be killed upon clicking. The next thing that we'll need to do is try to make it gradually more challenging for players. The best way to do this is to add more germs!

Adding by intervals

In games it is natural for the progression of the game to increase in difficulty. This increasing difficulty is usually managed with countdowns, new levels, or increases based on a player's score. Because this is your first attempt at making a Flash game, we will use a simple timer to add additional germs to the stage on a given interval. This will continually add germs to the stage until it becomes too much to handle.

The first step in adding a timer to the Germaphobe class is to import the Timer class from the flash.utils package.

```
package
{
    import flash.display.Sprite;
    import flash.events.*;
    import flash.utils.Timer;
```

Next, we will add three properties to the Germaphobe class. The first property will be a simple reference name for the timer object that will be used to add more germs to the stage. The second two properties, count and prevCount, will be used to store variables that will keep track of the number of germs that have been added to the stage.

```
public class Germaphobe extends Sprite
{
    private var timer:Timer;
    private var count:uint;
    private var prevCount:uint;
```

Once the properties have been added, we can then create a new timer object in the init function of the Germaphobe class. You should notice that we have set the required parameter of the timer to 5000 milliseconds, or 5 seconds. We also have the event listener set to trigger the addGerms() function when the event is detected. It is then required that the timer be started. This should give us a fresh set of germs every 5 seconds.

```
private function init():void
{
    var germ:Germ = new Germ();
    germ.x = Math.random() * stage.stageWidth;
    germ.y = Math.random() * stage.stageHeight;
    addChild(germ);

    stage.addEventListener(MouseEvent.MOUSE_DOWN, kill);

    timer = new Timer(5000);
    timer.addEventListener(TimerEvent.TIMER, addGerms);
    timer.start();
}
```

The addGerms function

The addGerms function is more or less the meat and potatoes of the Germaphobe game. As stated earlier, it is what controls the leveling in terms of difficulty. For the most part, implementing this function is not really any more complicated than when you added your first germ to the stage.

The first two lines are going to be responsible for managing the number of germs that will be placed on the stage. When we declared the count property, we set its initial value to 1. This represents the first germ added to the stage in the init function. When we enter the addGerms function, the first thing that happens is *prevCount* will be set to the value of count. The variable count is then added to itself. Therefore, the first time the timer fires and we enter this function, prevCount will be 1 and count will be 2. The second time through prevCount will be 2 and count will be 4. What is happening here is that we are defining a range that doubles every time addGerms is called by the timer listener. This will then set up the for loop to not only double every time the function is called, but also increment the number of germs based on the previous number of germs.

```
private function addGerms(e:TimerEvent)
{
  prevCount = count;
  count += count;

  for (var i:uint = prevCount; i < count; i++)
  {
    var germ:Germ = new Germ();
    germ.name = "germ" + i;
    germ.x = Math.random() * stage.width;
    germ.y = Math.random() * stage.height;
    addChild(germ);
  }
}
```

Keeping score

To keep track of how many germs we have killed, we will add a small scorekeeping scheme to the Germaphobe class. Though this is a relatively simple addition, there will be adjustments in four areas of the game code.

First off, we need to add the import statement to allow us to use the functionality for displaying text.

```
package
{
  import flash.display.Sprite;
  import flash.events.*;
  import flash.utils.Timer;
  import flash.text.*;
```

Next, we add two properties to the Germaphobe class. The scoreText variable will be used to control the actual text field that will display the text. And the score variable will be used to mathematically increment the value of the score before it is displayed.

```
public class Germaphobe extends Sprite
{
  private var timer:Timer;
  private var count:uint;
  private var prevCount:uint;
  private var scoreText:TextField;
  private var score:uint;
```

In the init function, we then set up the text field and its properties. We first define the appropriate position and width of the text field and add it to the stage.

```
private function init():void
{
  ...
  scoreText = new TextField();
  scoreText.x = 500;
  scoreText.y = 10;
  scoreText.width = 20;
  addChild(scoreText);
}
```

Finally, in the if statement of the kill function, we award points for killing the germ. The first line simply takes the current value of score and adds 10 to it. The second line then sets the text value of the scoreText text field to the value of the score variable. Because the text field's text is a string and score is a uint, we will need to convert the values of score from a uint to a String. To accomplish this, we use the toString method. This will effectively convert the value of score to a data type that is acceptable to the text property.

```
if(e.target is Germ)
{
  e.target.die();

  score += 10;
  scoreText.text = score.toString();
}
```

Ending the game by infestation

Finally, we need to determine when the game should end. By nature this is a casual game, and therefore there is no definitive purpose in actually winning the game. It is basically a situation where you play the game until the game beats you. How do we determine when the game has won? Well, in the case of this game, the game will need to win before there are so many germs on the stage that it causes the Flash Player to crash. We have determined that the safe number is at about 250 germs. So, we can use the numChildren property of display list containers to evaluate when the timeline has more than 250 children. At that point, we can say that a player has lost by infestation.

Checking for infestation

As it turns out, checking for an infestation is actually relatively simple. We can perform a check every time new germs are added to the stage. So, in the addGerms method, at the very end just before the closing curly brace, we will want to add a function call to the infested method. We add this function call here because it will allow the addGerms method to complete the process of adding new germs to the game. Once that process has

10

completed, we can check the number of germs on the stage. If there are too many, we then end the game.

```
private function addGerms(e:TimerEvent)
{
  ...
  infested();
}
```

Removing leftover germs

The final method for the Germaphobe game is actually a bit simpler than it may look. In the Germaphobe class, as the last method, you should add the following code:

```
private function infested()
{
  if (this.numChildren > 250)
  {
    timer.stop();

    var i:int = this.numChildren;
    while(i--)
    {
      removeChildAt(i);
    }
  }
}
```

The first line of this method opens with an `if` statement that immediately determines whether the main timeline has more than 250 children. As you know, this will evaluate to `true` or `false`. If it evaluates to `false`, nothing will happen. Should the statement evaluate to `true`, the end of the game is inevitable.

Immediately, the timer is stopped to prevent any more germs from being added to the stage. Next, an incrementing variable is established and set to the value of the total number of children on the stage. We then use that variable in a while loop that will decrement the `i` variable until it has reached 0. Within the while loop, we use the `removeChildAt()` method to remove all children on the stage. Keep in mind that the number of children in a display list is equivalent to the total number of indexes used to assign object depths. Therefore, as the while loop decrements, the display object at that index is also removed.

The final score

One unfortunate side effect of the previous effort to remove all the children from the timeline is that the text field used to display the score is actually a child of the timeline as well. This means that the score is also removed during this process. There is a quick solution to this problem: simply re-add the score as a child of the stage.

In the infested method, just after the while loop, simply add the scoreText text field back on the stage using the addChild method, as shown here:

```
private function infested()
    {
        ...
        while(i--)
        {
            removeChildAt(i);
        }

        addChild(scoreText);
    }
}
```

Summary

A lot of ground was covered in this chapter. You are now familiar with the construction of a working example of a multiclass application. From this basic foundation, you should now begin to see how the creation of objects and modular organization begin to benefit the efficiency of programming.

As mentioned at the onset of this chapter, everything you learn after this will be an enhancement to this basic foundation. Though many of the concepts to come will seem abstract at times, you should always revert to this foundation. Always remember to take it one section at a time.

Following are some of the important topics covered in this chapter:

- Display objects and display object containers
- The display list
- Adding and removing display objects
- Multiclass interaction and simple application development

10

CHAPTER 11

MANAGING EXTERNAL ASSETS
AND COMMUNICATION

The original intent of Flash (not SmartSketch) was to aid in the delivery of animation over the Internet. As its popularity grew, more and more designers and developers were using Flash for robust deliverables. And as the applications began to grow in complexity, the resulting SWF files began to increase in size. Once the fever spread from industry to industry, Flash started being used for a multitude of applications such as web intros, entire web sites, e-learning solutions, and later Rich Internet Applications. As a result, Flash was soon given the ability to manage external assets, like images and data, dynamically.

One of the biggest early contributors to the popularity of Flash, in addition to its ability to create vibrant content, was the fact that the files that it produced were so small. In addition to the need to alleviate size issues, Flash, in becoming a native web technology, was also rapidly developing the need to communicate with various web-based data sources. As Flash evolved from iteration to iteration, it gradually was granted more and more ability to manage content externally, as well as communicate with several standard web-based technologies. And though the content covered in this chapter is relatively brief, it is no doubt pivotal in the development of rich, data-driven applications.

Subsequently, this chapter will discuss the various capacities in which Flash communicates with external pieces of data. Whether it be loading a simple JPG image or a complex conversation with a server-side web script, Flash handles this communication in a very similar manner.

Working with external data

When a developer refers to external data in Flash, that data can represent any number of information types including sound, video, text, other SWF files, images, XML data, and much more. As you may have guessed, there are potentially a multitude of avenues for getting this data in and out of Flash. As with many other ActionScript features covered in this book, ActionScript 3.0 has taken the process of managing external data and streamlined it into a few easy-to-use classes. Therefore, unlike previous versions of Flash, all external data can be handled in one place. In this chapter we will take a look at the following data loaders and managers:

- URLRequest
- URLLoader
- URLVariables
- Loader
- LocalConnection
- SharedObjects

URLRequest—go get it pup!

Much like the Labrador or Golden Retriever is responsible for fetching ducks or the morning paper, ActionScript has a best friend that is responsible for going out and getting information about a specific URL. The term "URL," short for Uniform Resource Locator, is nothing more than a technical way of describing the location of a piece of information that is available over the Internet. For all intents and purposes, all external assets that are loaded at runtime are going to be classified as URLs. Whether it is a JPEG, video, or sound file found in a local directory or an XML file coming from halfway around the world, the first step in bringing that information into ActionScript is to go out and get it. For this very special task, ActionScript offers the URLRequest class.

The URLRequest class is used to retrieve all information about a given HTTP request and subsequent URL. Once the URLRequest has retrieved the desired URL, it can then be passed to any of the classes responsible for loading content. It is important to understand that depending on the kind of information that is retrieved by the URLRequest, ActionScript will use a class that has been specifically designed for handling that type of information. If the URL happens to represent a sound, the sound is then loaded via the Sound class. If the information happens to be textual, the URL is loaded via an instance of the URLLoader class. Though this may seem a bit complicated at first, it is actually very efficient. There are only a few ways in which you can load information into Flash. As you become more familiar with the types of data that can be loaded into Flash, these methods will seem as second nature.

In addition to capturing information to be loaded, the URLRequest can be set up to pass information to server-side programming such as PHP and ASP by packaging it with variables. This will be discussed more thoroughly later in this chapter.

By now you should be all too familiar with the way in which functionality is implemented in ActionScript. To use the URLRequest class, you simply create a new variable reference and instantiate it with the new keyword. The constructor of the new URLRequest accepts a single parameter. As shown in the following examples, this parameter is a literal string value representing the URL to be captured.

The URLRequest can be used to call a relative local URL, such as the name of a graphic residing in the same folder as your SWF file, as demonstrated here:

```
var req:URLRequest = new URLRequest("my.jpg");
```

It can also be used to call an absolute URL from a remote server:

```
var req:URLRequest = new URLRequest("http://www.anyurl.com");
```

Using the URLLoader

If the URLRequest is used to retrieve the URL, the URLLoader is the primary class for loading URL requests that are of a textual nature. That is, the URLLoader is responsible for loading items like TXT files, XML files, and external Cascading Style Sheets. Because of this versatility, the URLLoader becomes an integral part of many Flash applications.

Loading a simple data file

In the example in this section, you will see how the URLLoader is used in tandem with the URLRequests to load information into Flash dynamically. Using ch11_01_start.fla as reference, you will notice that the stage contains a simple TextArea component with the name ta. As you may have guessed, we will be loading a snippet of content into the text area by way of the URLLoader.

1. The first line of code, shown here, is used to instantiate the URLRequest object:

```
var req:URLRequest = new URLRequest("loaderinfo.txt");
var infoLoader:URLLoader = new URLLoader();
infoLoader.load(req);

ta.text = infoLoader.data;
```

Notice in the constructor function that the URLRequest is accepting the string parameter loaderinfo.txt. This value represents the name of a file that is located in the same directory as the ch11_01_start.fla file. Therefore, we will use the URLRequest to fetch the information about this file.

2. The second line of code defines the URLLoader object, infoLoader.

With the infoLoader we then have the ability to load the information that has been gathered by the URLRequest. To do this we use the load method of the URLLoader and pass it a single parameter, which is a reference to the URLRequest.

3. Finally, we can assign the text property of the text area the value of infoLoader. data.

The data property of any URLLoader, by default, is set as text. Therefore, we are simply assigning the information stored in the loaderinfo.txt file to the text property of the TextArea component.

Waiting for the data to arrive

At this point, if you test the previous file, you will notice that nothing loads within the text area, and you may also notice that an error is thrown in the Output window. The reason for this is that the data property of any loader is not set until the load method has completely finished with the loading of the URLRequest. Because loading external data in ActionScript works in the same manner as you may expect any form of data to load, it will then take an undetermined amount of time for the computer to parse the information. Granted, even though this example is taking nanoseconds to load, it is still loading. And because this example is executing sequentially, the fourth line of code will more than likely execute before the loader has finished loading. Because the computer can execute its code faster than the data will load, the previous example is trying to assign the loaderInfo.data information into the text area before that information has finished loading into ActionScript.

This is more or less the method of operations for the loading of external objects in Flash. To work around the previously mentioned execution problem, ActionScript allows for the listening of events on loading content. Therefore, whenever an object has finished loading in ActionScript, the COMPLETE event is dispatched. We then have the ability to assign a listener to the loader to detect this event. As shown in the following code, we can then place the `ta.text = infoLoader.data` line within the event handler, allowing us to wait for the URLRequest to fully load before ActionScript tries to use its information.

```
var req:URLRequest = new URLRequest("loaderinfo.txt");
var infoLoader:URLLoader = new URLLoader();

infoLoader.load(req);
infoLoader.addEventListener(Event.COMPLETE, loadText);

function loadText (e:Event)
{
   ta.text = infoLoader.data;
}
```

Finally, when the movie is tested now, the information from the `loaderinfo.txt` file is displayed in the text area as shown in Figure 11-1.

Figure 11-1.
Data from an external TXT file being loaded into a TextArea via ActionScript

Sending data to external places

When building web applications, it would be fairly ineffective to only be able to receive information from a given data source. Fortunately the URLLoader and URLRequest classes allow a developer the ability to pass information out to external sources using popular server-side languages like PHP, ASP.NET, and ColdFusion.

GET and POST methods

If you have ever worked with front-end HTML before, you will no doubt be familiar with the concepts of name-value pairs and the GET and POST methods of HTTP. If you are not yet familiar with these concepts, don't worry—they are not very difficult to understand.

The GET method sends its information by way of a query string stuck on the end of a URL. Though you may not be familiar with this, you may have noticed once upon a time information stuck on the end of a web page request. The following web request, www.webpage.com?name=value, demonstrates the sending of a variable in the form of a name-value pair, using the GET method.

11

The POST method also sends the same type of data in the form of name-value pairs. However, rather than send this information as part of the URL request, the POST method sends its information within the body of the request. Therefore, this information is actually hidden to the untrained eye.

It is often said that the difference between these two methods is a more secure transmission of information. The reality is that neither is really more secure than the other. And though both methods have the ability to send and receive information, it was originally intended that GET be used to get information from the server and POST be used to post information back to the server. At this point, however, it does not make much of a difference.

For the scope of this book it will be sufficient to know that the GET and POST methods are the way by which standard HTML sends variable data from page to server and back again. There are several other methods available, but these are the most commonly used.

Name-Value pairs

As mentioned previously, the standard method for passing variables from page to page on the Internet is in the form of name-value pairs. The name value pair is nothing more than a convention now used to describe the way variables are packaged. As the name would suggest, variables are sent as a variable name and a variable value that are paired together. So, *name* is the name of the variable and *value* is the value of the variable. Table 11-1 lists a few possible name-value pairs.

Table 11-1. A Series of Name-Value Pairs

Name	Value
Name	John Smith
E-mail	jsmith@email.com
City	Annapolis
State	MD

The concept may also be described using a standard contact form found on a number of web sites. Using Table 11-1 as reference, as a person fills out information on a web form, he or she is supplying the value for a number of predetermined variables, typically name, e-mail, etc. When that person clicks a Submit button, usually found at the end of the form, his or her information is collected and sent across the galaxy in the form of name-value pairs. If the GET method was used, the values would be arranged something like this:

```
http://www.apage.com/program.php?name=John%20Smith&email=➥
jsmith@email.com&city=Annapolis&state=MD
```

The page www.apage.com/program.php would then more than likely be set up to receive those variables and process them in some manner.

URLVariables

For the packaging, and possible unpackaging, of variables, ActionScript 3.0 introduces the URLVariables class. Like its previously discussed counterparts, URLLoader and URLRequest, the URLVariables class is incredibly intuitive and far superior to its AS2 counterpart. To create variables using the URLVariables class, you only need to create the object and start assigning variables to it in the form of properties. Here's an example:

1. The variable vars is created and typed as a new URLVariables object (as shown in the code example after the next step).

2. The name variable is then created as a property of the vars object and given the string value of John Doe.

```
var vars:URLVariables = new URLVariables();
vars.name = "John Doe";
```

Keep in mind the properties are arbitrary and thus able to be whatever you would like them to be.

The previous two lines of code could have just as easily been written like the following:

```
var vars:URLVariables = new URLVariables();
vars.firstName = "John ";
vars.lastName = "Doe";
```

It is also possible to pass the name-value variable as a parameter of the constructor function, in the form of a string.

```
var vars:URLVariables = new URLVariables("firstName=John");
```

Now that you are familiar with the way ActionScript packages variables, you have the ability to use this method in tandem with URLLoader and URLRequest to send those variables out of Flash.

There and back again: A variable's tale

In the file ch11_02.fla, we will take a look at how Flash has the ability to take a variable, send it to a remote location, and have that variable returned for further use. At first this task might seem a bit complicated. However, looking back on what you have learned so far, it is easy to break this down into four manageable parts.

1. Define your variables.

The first step to sending out variables is to actually define the variables. For this example, we are going to send a single variable out to an external location and hopefully get it back again. As shown here, we use the code from earlier and instantiate the URLVariables object. We then create an arbitrary property called name and assign it a value of John Doe.

```
var vars:URLVariables = new URLVariables();
vars.name = "John Doe";
```

11

2. Prepare the URLRequest for its trip.

The next thing that needs to happen is the creation of the URLVariables object. Remember, the URLVariables object is going to go out and collect information about a URL much like a probe that NASA would send into outer space. In order for the request to complete its work successfully, we need to make sure that it is properly configured.

The next four lines show you what you need to get the URLRequest ready to deliver and collect information to a specific URL. As usual, the first step is to create the object. We then define the destination URL. In the previous example of the URLRequest, we were passing the URLs as parameters of the constructor functions. However, URLRequest objects also give us the ability to set this using the url property of the object. In this example we will be communicating with a remote script that is hosted on this book's companion web site.

```
var req:URLRequest = new URLRequest();
req.url = "http://www.friendsofed.com/EssGuideFlashCS4/vars.php";
req.method = URLRequestMethod.GET;
req.data = vars;
```

The third line will define how the URLRequest will format the sending of its variables. As discussed earlier, the standard methods are GET and POST. For this example, we will be using the GET method, which will simply add the variables as name-value pairs to the end of the URL.

Finally, we assign, or package, information for the URLRequest using the data property of the URLRequest object. To this property we assign the vars object, which is the name of the URLVariables object that was created earlier.

3. Get the URLLoader ready.

Once the URLRequest has been properly established and has the URLVariables package with it, the next step is to create the URLLoader. The URLLoader used in this example is actually not that different from the example that was discussed earlier in this chapter. An object, ul, is created. An event listener is assigned to allow the information to load. And the load method of the ul object is used to load the URLRequest req. What is different is the existence of the second line. The dataFormat property of the URLLoader class is used to aid in the receiving of external information. It allows us to tell the URLLoader what kind of information to expect and how to deal with that information. In this example we are using the URLLoaderDataFormat.VARIABLES property to let the loader know that the information will be coming in via URL query string and that it should be ready to decode it.

```
var ul:URLLoader = new URLLoader();
ul.dataFormat = URLLoaderDataFormat.VARIABLES;
ul.addEventListener(Event.COMPLETE, loadComplete);
ul.load(req);
```

4. Define the handler.

Finally, the handler is created to coincide with the event listener that was attached to the URLLoader object. As you previously learned, this is used to allow external data sufficient time to load before it is used. The program is then notified using an event, and the external data can be manipulated.

In this case, the original variable, name, which was given the value of John Doe, has been sent to an external PHP script using the GET method. The PHP script performed a transformation on the variable and sent it back to Flash. The URLLoader then received that information and began loading it. When the loading had completed, the loadComplete handler is triggered by the dispatching of the Event.Complete event. The transformed variable can then be traced to the Output panel in Flash.

```
function loadComplete(event:Event):void
{
    trace(event.target.data.returningVariables);
}
```

Checking for program errors

Though we would like to tell you that the loading of external information into Flash is foolproof, we simply cannot. When dealing with the Internet, if something needs to be fetched and returned to a client's machine, there is still a strong possibility that many things can go wrong in the process. Though error handling quickly crosses over into the realm of advanced ActionScript development, it is definitely worth mentioning so that its presence is known.

For the handling of errors Flash incorporates the try...catch statements. In the following sample, we take the ul.load(req) statement, as used in the previous example, and set it up to handle possible errors. There are quite a few errors that can occur and ActionScript lets you test for them individually. For now, however, it will be sufficient for the program to check for all errors generically.

1. The first step in error handling is to create the try statement.

```
...
var ul:URLLoader = new URLLoader();
ul.dataFormat = URLLoaderDataFormat.VARIABLES;
ul.addEventListener(Event.COMPLETE, loadComplete);

try
{
    ul.load(req);
}
catch (er:Error)
{
    trace("There was a problem loading your URL");
}
...
```

The try statement does exactly as its name suggests: it tries to execute a specific code statement. In this case we will be trying to execute the ul.load(req) statement to load our URLRequest.

11

2. To handle errors, we then use the catch statement.

The catch statement will listen for specific errors and then allow the program to reroute or execute alternative code if an error occurs. The catch statement actually accepts a parameter, which is an error object to be detected. Similar to events, you have the ability to select different kinds of errors to handle such as I/O errors and security errors. In this example we used er:Error, which will check for all errors.

3. Finally, if an error is detected, the code statements contained within the catch statement will be executed. Therefore, if this program detects an error while trying to load the URLRequest, it will send us a notification in the Output panel: There was a problem loading your URL.

Loading external display objects

In Parts 4 and 5 of this book, we will take a look at loading various types of other information in ActionScript including the following:

- XML
- CSS
- Sound
- Video

For this chapter, we will take a look at one final type of loader, which is used for loading external display objects like bitmaps and SWF files. The Loader object is actually a type of display object container, like the Stage, Sprite, and MovieClip objects, which is used for containing externally loaded display objects.

The file ch11_03.fla demonstrates the difference between how the Loader and the URLLoader classes are used to load their respective content. Actually, the file demonstrates how similar the classes are when used to load such different content. When you first open the file, you will no doubt notice the blank white stage. There are no images on the stage or in the Library panel.

Here is the sequence for loading external display objects:

1. We start with the following two lines, which are virtually identical to those used earlier to load the loaderinfo.txt file:

```
var req:URLRequest = new URLRequest("flower.jpg");
var imgLoader:Loader = new Loader();
```

The only significant differences are that the URLRequest's parameter has changed to locate a graphic file and we are now using the Loader class instead of the URLLoader class. Other than that, the instantiation of these objects occurs the exact same way as before.

2. We then include the next two lines, which are also extremely similar to those found in the previous file:

```
imgLoader.load(req);
imgLoader.contentLoaderInfo.addEventListener(Event.COMPLETE, loadImg);
```

The first of these uses the load method of the loading object, in this case imgLoader. The second is a standard event listener. The only difference here is that instead of adding the listener directly to the loading object, the listener is added to the contentLoadInfo of the Loader class.

3. Finally, we use the event handler to add the image to the stage.

```
function loadImg(e:Event)
{
   addChild(imgLoader.content);
}
```

And though the nomenclature is a bit different from that used earlier, the concept is exactly the same. This time, instead of using the data property as we did in the previous example, we employ the Loader class to store the display information in the content property. Therefore, by using the content property of the imgLoader, we can effectively add the image to the stage.

When you finally test the movie, you will see a familiar image from Chapter 4 as shown in Figure 11-2.

Figure 11-2.
An external graphic being loaded into Flash using ActionScript

11

Now, let's discuss communication between two SWF files.

Communicating: SWF to SWF

One of the most commonly overlooked aspects of ActionScript development is the ability to have multiple independent SWF files on a client's machine communicate with one another. This option is so powerful that the SWF files do not even need to be located in the same parent application. For example, if you happen to be the kind of person who runs several different browsers on your computer, you could have two different SWF files running in two different browsers, passing information between each other. Further, this functionality can be extended to communicate with SWF files being run as Flash Projectors and Adobe AIR applications.

LocalConnection class

The communication between SWF instances, or SWF to SWF, is achieved through the use of the `LocalConnection` class. To properly use the `LocalConnection` class, you must first create an instance of the class in each SWF that will be used during the communication. Typically, the connection is established as one-way between two files. In order to complete the passing of data, one SWF will need to be set up to send information, and the other will need to be set up to receive it.

Send method

The send method is used to allow a SWF to send information to another SWF by means of a local connection. To set up the sender of a local connection, you first need to define an instance of the `LocalConnection` class. You can then call the send method of that object to establish the connection.

The send method has the ability to accept three types of parameters:

- Connection name
- Method name
- Optional parameters

In the following code example, connection_name is used as the first parameter, which also represents the name of the local connection. This name will be used by the receiving SWF as a means of detection for this connection. The second parameter, method_name, is the name of a method or function that exists in the receiving SWF that will be called once the connection is received. Finally, the send method can accept any number of optional parameters that can be used in the receiving SWF. Here is an example that uses these parameters:

```
var sender:LocalConnection = new LocalConnection();
sender.send("connection_name", "method_name", optional_parameters);
```

Connect method

The connect method is a type of listener that waits to hear from the sending SWF. As demonstrated in the following example, the receiving object of the local connection is set up in a similar fashion to the sending object. That is, both objects are instances of the `LocalConnection` class. The receiver, however, uses the connect method rather than the send method. In both cases the parameter, or name of the connection, will need to be the same.

```
var receiver:LocalConnection = new LocalConnection();
receiver.connect("connection_name");
```

Once the connection has been established, it is necessary for the receiver to have a function that corresponds to the second parameter of the send method. Remember, the sender is trying to execute a function that is contained within the receiver. Therefore, the second requirement of the receiving object is to have a function.

```
var receiver:LocalConnection = new LocalConnection();
receiver.connect("connection_name");

function method_name():void
{
  //function statements
}
```

Finally, as a measure of security, the client property of the LocalConnection object is used to assign which SWF contains the executable code. In this example, since the receiver does contain the function, the client property will be set to this, ultimately determining that **this** SWF contains the function.

```
var receiver:LocalConnection = new LocalConnection();
receiver.connect("connection_name");

function method_name():void
{
  //function statements
}
receiver.client = this;
```

SWF to SWF

Now let's take a look at actually getting two SWF files to communicate with one another. Figure 11-3 illustrates the concept that two independently running SWF files have the ability to pass information back and forth to one another over a simple local connection.

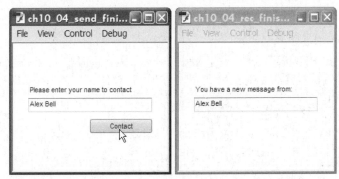

Figure 11-3. Information is being sent from one SWF to another using the LocalConnection class.

Setting up the sender

First thing that we will want to take care of in the creation of a SWF-to-SWF local connection is the creation of the sender SWF. For this example, we have supplied you with a base file, ch11_04_send_start.fla, for the benefit of focusing only on the ActionScript aspect of this exercise.

11

1. Open ch11_04_send_start.fla.

In this file you will find two primary elements that will be accessed via ActionScript. The first of these is a TextField, which has been given an instance name of nameText in the Property inspector. As shown in Figure 11-3, we will send information entered in this field to another SWF file. The second element is the Contact button. This button has also been given an instance name, contact_btn, so it can be referenced for use in ActionScript.

2. With frame 1 of the timeline selected, open the Actions panel by pressing F9 and enter the following code:

```
var sender:LocalConnection = new LocalConnection();
```

You first need to create an instance of the LocalConnection object to be used in this SWF. You can do this using standard protocol as demonstrated in previous examples in this book.

3. Create an event listener and assign it to the contact_btn button.

```
contact_btn.addEventListener(MouseEvent.CLICK, makeContact);
```

4. Create the event handler for the contact_btn listener.

Within this handler you will be evoking the send method of the sender object. As the first parameter of this method you will pass the string connection, which is used as the name of the local connection. Again, the first parameter is used as an identifier between the two SWF files so they are able to communicate with one another.

5. Pass the name of a method contained in the receiving SWF.

Though this method is not yet created, you can plan preemptively and give it an arbitrary name of ringRing.

6. Finally, pass a third parameter.

Now pay close attention here. This third parameter is actually going to be passed as a parameter of the ringRing function as well. For this value, use the text property of the nameText text field. This will allow you to send whatever text is present in the nameText text field as a parameter to the receiving SWF.

```
function makeContact(e:MouseEvent):void
{
    sender.send("connection", "ringRing", nameText.text);
}
```

Setting up the receiver

Once the sending SWF file has been configured, you then need to create a file that will be capable of receiving information. For this part of the exercise, you will be using the ch11_04_rec_start.fla. In a similar manner to the way the sender was set up, the receiving SWF file also has the needed visual components already in place.

1. Open ch11_04_send_start.fla.

For this segment, the important element to focus on is the TextField, which has been given the instance name callerId.

2. Select frame 1 of the timeline.

The Actions panel should already be open from the previous example. In the event that it is not, you can open it by pressing F9. In the Actions panel, create a new LocalConnection object. Notice that the LocalConnection object in this example is now called receiver.

```
var receiver:LocalConnection = new LocalConnection();
```

3. Next, create a connection to the LocalConnection object by using the connect() method of the receiver object.

For this method, you need to pass the name of an active LocalConnection. Since we already defined the name of the connection as the first parameter of the sender.send method in the ch11_04_send_start.fla file, you know that the name of this LocalConnection is connection. Therefore, you can pass that as the parameter of the receiver.connect() method.

```
receiver.connect("connection");
```

4. Define a function that will be executed. In the sending SWF file you created a reference to an undefined function ringRing. You now need to create that function in your receiving SWF. Enter the following code into the Actions panel:

```
function ringRing(caller:String):void
{
  callerId.text = caller;
}
```

When this function is created, you also set it up to receive a single parameter, which was also defined in the sender.send method of the ch11_04_send_start.fla file. This will allow the ability to pass the text from the nameText text field into the ringRing function as the variable caller.

Then, you can assign the value of caller, which was originally the value of nameText.text, to the text property of the callerId text field. Or, simply put, you can take the value of one text field and assign it to the value of another.

5. Finally, you need to set the client for the LocalConnection. Enter the following code in the Actions Panel:

```
receiver.client = this;
```

Remember, for security purposes you have to let the LocalConnection know which SWF file contains the method that will be executed. The this keyword is used to let the connection know that this SWF does indeed contain the method to be executed.

11

At this point, you may now test both SWF files at the same time. Enter some text into the text field of the sending SWF file and click the Contact button. As shown in Figure 11-3, your text should automatically appear in the text field of the receiving SWF.

> *It is also possible to communicate between ActionScript 2.0 and ActionScript 3.0 by using a LocalConnection. SWFBridge is set of third-party classes developed by Grant Skinner (www.gskinner.com) to offer a quick-and-easy method of implementation for this type of communication.*

Now that we have discussed sending information to remote locations, let's discuss storing information to a user's local machine.

Storing data to a local machine

In many web applications it becomes necessary for an application to be able to store data about session states and user information. Similar to an application written in any standard web technology, much of the heavy lifting can be handled by the application itself. Flash is certainly no exception. It does have the ability to communicate with various standard web technologies and store information in databases. But, as with other types of web programming methods that utilize cookies, you may need to store small amounts of information about applications on the user's machine.

The SharedObject in ActionScript is a special type of object that actually works in a similar manner as the standard web cookie. If you think about the commonly used "remember me on this machine" convention, a user has the ability to store small amounts of information about himself or herself to be used for the next time he or she arrives at that same web page. What the user does not typically notice is that information is stored on his or her local machine and not in a remote database. So, when the user returns to that page, the page automatically looks to see whether the cookie exists and uses that information to recall the user's information.

Similarly to the way web applications use these cookies, Flash has the ability to store various amounts of information to the local machine for later use through SharedObjects. And because browser-based Flash applications are set up to operate within a sandbox, SharedObjects cannot directly interact with the user's computer outside of the Flash Player. So, there is no threat of malicious activity.

> *By default, shared objects are restricted to 100K. Users have the ability to adjust the total size of their shared objects storage from 0K to an unlimited amount by navigating to www.macromedia.com/support/ documentation/en/flashplayer/help/settings_manager03.html and using the Settings Manager feature there.*

Taking a closer look at local shared objects

The file ch11_05.fla is aimed at helping you get a little familiar with the way that shared objects work. The trick with shared objects is that they typically don't save information until an application is closed. So, in order to examine the use of SharedObjects on your local machine or in the Flash IDE, you will need to test your Flash movie repeatedly to see the effects of those SharedObjects. By this, we mean that you will need to test your movie, close it, and then test it again.

As shown in Figure 11-4, the file ch11_05.fla logs the date every time the movie is tested. Therefore, whenever the movie is opened, the date is stored in a local shared object on the user's machine.

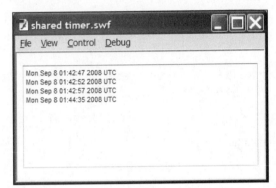

Figure 11-4.
Data being stored repeatedly over time to a SharedObject

Using shared objects is actually a rather easy thing to do. As shown in the next example, the most complicated part of the entire program is formatting the string that stores the date. Like every other data type you have experienced in ActionScript, the first thing to do is instantiate a variable that will store and reference your shared object.

1. In this example we start by using the variable shared.

```
var shared:SharedObject = SharedObject.getLocal("counter");
```

11

In the previous example we make use of the method getlocal. The getLocal method requires one parameter, which is the name of the shared object that is stored on the local machine. In the current example, the parameter counter directly refers to the file counter.sol, which is stored on the client computer. If the file does not yet exist, such as when you first test this sample program, the instantiation process will automatically create this file.

> When using shared objects, developers have the ability to access data both locally (on a client-side machine) or remotely (on a server). Because remote Flash programming is a bit out of scope for this book, our discussions will focus solely on local shared objects.

2. Next we add the following line of code, which simply creates a new date object, cleverly called date:

```
var date:Date = new Date();
```

The date object will be used to retrieve the current date and time to be used to store the time in which this movie was tested.

3. We then use an if statement to check and see whether the shared object exists:

```
if (shared.size == 0)
{
  shared.data.opened = date.toUTCString();
}
else
{
  shared.data.opened += "\r" + date.toUTCString();
}
```

This can easily be done by checking the size property of the object itself. The size property will return the size of the file in terms of bytes.

Keep in mind that when we originally instantiate a shared object, it does the following:

- Checks to see whether the data file exists
- Creates a file if one does not exist

In either case, the file will exist by the time you try to determine its size.

4. Therefore, we check to see whether the file size is equal to zero.

If the file size is zero, we know that it contains no information. As a result we can use the if statement to either write new information or simply add to information that already exists.

5. When adding information to the shared object, if we want that information to be saved, we always want to use the data property.

Once the data property is accessed, we can then create an arbitrary property name that will be used to label the information that will be stored in the shared object. In the following example, we use the property opened.

```
ta.text = shared.data.opened;
```

Once we have determined the existence of the shared object, we can either write the current date or add the new date string to the information that already exists.

6. In this case, we use the toUTCString method of the date object to retrieve the current date and convert it to a string that is easily recognizable by human eyes.

The UTC date is actually the absolute date at the prime meridian, so if you are following along, don't be alarmed if the date and time do not match your location.

7. If the shared object does exist, we use the else clause and simply add, or concatenate, the new date string to the old one.

As you can see, we also use the \r character string in the expression to add a carriage return before adding the new date string.

8. Finally, once we have determined the existence of the shared object's data and properly adjusted its value, we write that value to the TextArea component ta, which is located on the stage.

The greatest thing about shared objects is that they are automatic. Though you can have the ability to save, or flush, data to the shared object file, simply closing the program will do this for you.

Examining the .SOL file

To help you better understand the naming that is used and exactly what is involved in the creation of the shared object, let's take a brief sidestep and examine the inner workings of the shared object file that is stored on a user's local machine.

As shown in Figure 11-5, there is actually not much information stored in an SOL file. Using the previous example, remember during the instantiation process that we used the string value of counter as the parameter in the getLocal method. As you can see here, counter was used to name the file that is created to store the information. We also showed you that shared objects have many properties such as size and data. The data property is what is used to store and generate all the information you see in this file. This information can be broken into the following distinct parts:

- Header
- opened arbitrary property value
- Stored dates

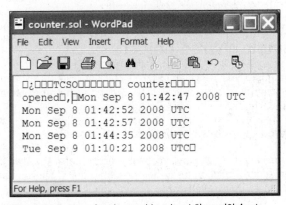

Figure 11-5. How data is saved in a local SharedObject

11

The first of these, which is of no particular consequence, is the header. The header is the first line in this file and is used to define the file in terms of type, size, and name. You should notice the object name `counter`, but the rest is illegible for a simple text reader. Not to worry, these other characters are used only for formatting and processing. They are not really meant to be read by humans.

> *For this example, we are using the simple text editor WordPad to view the inner workings of this file. And, though it is highly unlikely that you will ever want, or need, to edit a shared object directly, there are several third-party applications, such as SOL Editor, that would allow you to get a more detailed look at these files. An excellent free ActionScript editor that also has a built-in shared object reader is FlashDevelop (www.flashdevelop.org).*

The second item that you should immediately notice is the word `opened`. As you may recall, `opened` is the arbitrary property value that was created to store the date information in the `ch11_05.fla` file. Shared objects automatically take that property name and create a reference to it in the SOL file.

The final thing that should jump out at you is the list of dates that have been stored from the continuous testing of the SWF file. Shared objects store the information with the property names as comma-separated name-value pairs: "name" refers to the name of the property, in this case `opened`, and "value" is the date string created in the file.

Understanding how the information is stored in SOL files is a great start in understanding how to properly use them. You can see now that shared objects can be used to store much information about a specific user. For example, you could create a shared object called `userinfo` that could be used to store billing information about a user. You could then store all relevant information about the user in various properties of that shared object such as `name, John; cardNumber, 1234;` and `address, anyplace`. The best part about shared objects is that all information is stored locally on the client's machine, alleviating any concern of security issues during transfer or remote storage.

Creating a simple shared object

In the following example, you are going to take a crack at creating a shared object that will be used to store some basic form information. Storing form information is probably the most common use for basic shared object usage.

1. First thing you'll need to do is open `ch11_06_start.fla`.

As shown in Figure 11-6, the file contains a very simple form that will be used to store information about an individual on his or her local machine. Once you have examined the file and its graphical elements, you can proceed with the following steps to create the shared object.

Figure 11-6.
Storing of form data to
a local SharedObject

2. With the timeline open, select frame 1 of the actions layer and open the Actions panel (press F9).

3. Enter the following line of code in the script pane of the actions layer:

```
var shared:SharedObject = SharedObject.getLocal("userInfo");
```

As you are now fully aware, this line declares the variable that will be used to reference the shared object. The object is also instantiated using the SharedObject.getLocal method. You then need to pass it the parameter, which is the name of the shared object. For the purposes of this example we used userInfo, but this is an arbitrary value and can be whatever you like.

4. Next, define event listeners for the Remember Info and Clear Info buttons.

The two buttons on the stage have been prenamed for you in the ch11_06_start.fla file.

For the button labeled Remember Info, which is also named rememberInfo in the Property inspector, you need to create an event listener for the MouseEvent.CLICK event. This listener will also be set up to trigger the handler storeInfo. Similarly, the Clear Info, or clearInfo, button will also be set to listen for the MouseEvent.CLICK event. However, it will trigger the deleteInfo handler.

```
rememberInfo.addEventListener(MouseEvent.CLICK, storeInfo);
clearInfo.addEventListener(MouseEvent.CLICK, deleteInfo);
```

5. Now define the storeInfo function.

```
function storeInfo(e:MouseEvent)
{
  shared.data.firstName = firstText.text;
  shared.data.lastName = lastText.text;
  shared.flush();
}
```

The storeInfo() function is the listener for the rememberInfo button. This function is responsible for collecting the text data from the two text fields (firstText and lastText) and writing this data to the shared objects. You use this function to create two variables to be stored in your SharedObject.

11

The stage contains the firstText and lastText text fields. You then use the text property of these fields to retrieve whatever text is currently typed in those text fields. As demonstrated in previous examples, the text data can then be assigned to the appropriate shared.data variable using the assignment operator (=).

6. Finally, introduce the flush() method of the shared object.

The flush() method is used to force-save data to the SharedObject. As mentioned earlier, shared objects are automatically saved when a SWF file is closed. However, if need be, the flush() method gives developers the ability to save data instantly.

Creating the handler for the clearInfo button is much simpler than that used to save the data to the SharedObject.

7. Create the deleteInfo function and pass it the e event object, as the use of an event handler would dictate.

```
function deleteInfo(e:MouseEvent)
{
  shared.clear();
}
```

This function then contains one simple statement.

8. To remove information, or delete it, use the clear() method of the SharedObject class.

As its name dictates, the clear method is used to clear the shared object of any data. We can use this method to remove any previously stored form information that is associated with this application.

Lastly, you need to give the form the ability to repopulate the firstText and lastText fields when a user returns to your application. Once again, reflecting on previous sections of this chapter, you learned that it is possible to check the existence of a SharedObject's data by checking the size of that SharedObject. You know that, no matter what, the object exists.

9. Add the following code, the first line of which is responsible for either creating a new shared object or retrieving the object if it already exists:

```
if (shared.size != 0)
{
  firstText.text = shared.data.firstName;
  lastText.text = shared.data.lastName;
}
```

Therefore, the size property of the SharedObject must return a numeric value. If the size is zero, you know that there is no information stored in the object. If it happens to be something other than zero, you know there is information that can be retrieved.

To accomplish this check, you will need to create an if statement that will check to see whether the value of the shared.size property is zero. Actually, you will be using the logical NOT operator (!=) to determine whether the value of shared.size is not equal to zero. You do this because you want code to execute only if shared.size is not equal to zero. If it is equal to zero, this means you have no data. And, if there is no data, there is nothing to load.

10. Finally, once you have determined the existence of information in the SharedObject, load that data into the text fields.

11. In more or less a backward fashion to the storeInfo() event handler, take the value of the firstName and lastName properties of the shared.data object and assign those values to the text properties of the firstText and lastText text fields.

Once everything is in place, you can go ahead and test your movie as follows:

1. Fill out the form information and click the Save Info button.

2. Now close the movie and retest it.

Your information should automatically repopulate itself to the text fields.

3. Now click the Clear Info button and close the movie again.

When you test the movie a third time, you should notice that your information has been cleared; thus it is not loaded into the text fields.

Summary

In this chapter we took a brief look at the primary methods in which ActionScript communicates with the outside world. By using the URLLoader and URLVariables classes, you can effectively access any asset that is externally accessible to a Flash movie. In the upcoming chapters we will take a more in-depth look at specific types of data including sound, video, and XML.

The important classes covered in this chapter were

- URLRequest
- URLLoader
- URLVariables
- Loader
- LocalConnection
- SharedObjects

11

In the last chapter, we looked at several different ways Flash can incorporate various types of external assets. For the most part, the classes talked about in the last chapter are all that the average Flash user will need to effectively incorporate external content within the multimedia or web development world. With this information you will have the ability to access an abundance of data ranging from simple text files to complex imagery and web applications.

In this chapter, we are going to look at XML (Extensible Markup Language), a specific way of formatting data to make it more meaningful when interacting with ActionScript. The importance of XML is universal. It is able to be read and written by most major programming languages of the modern era. Much like Flash, it has the ability to be conformed to meet the needs of the project in which it is being used. Because of this, we felt it necessary to devote an entire chapter to the introduction of XML and ActionScript. Further, like so many other topics covered in this book, an entire book about using XML with Flash could easily be written. As a matter of fact, several already have.

For these reasons XML is one of the best companion technologies for working with Flash. The relative ease in which XML can be created and the XML support offered in ActionScript 3.0 make XML the best way for sending data in and out of Flash.

What is XML?

Whenever we have a discussion with a person who is familiar with XML, but never had the opportunity to use it firsthand, there always seems to be a degree of mystique that surrounds that discussion. More often than not, XML is immediately thought of as this sophisticated programming language capable of performing all of these magic tricks for the benefit of a given application. In reality, it is not really a programming language at all.

The true magic of XML is in how eloquently simple it is by design. It is used to give meaning and structure to an otherwise meaningless series of computer characters. Other than that, it does not really do anything. It can perform no program execution of its own. It is simply a liaison, passing a structured series of information from one program to another. The assumption can then be made that, by design, XML was developed for the systematic transportation of information. In addition to being more efficient, the data will always be accessible because it will be formatted using XML. This is true regardless of the server-side technology or primary programming language.

Though you may not realize it, you're probably extremely familiar with several modern uses for XML-based technology. The most common form of XML in use today is the **web service**. Web services are a way for many third-party users to access a company's information without compromising security. About now you are probably looking for a real-world example. Well, most online applications have some level of XML interaction that allows outside developers access to their records. Some of the more common ones are as follows:

- **Commerce**: Many popular commercial sites, such as Amazon.com and eBay, offer the ability for developers to access their products and listings through a collection of web-based functions known as application programming interfaces (APIs). With this functionality developers have the ability to access many of the products, services, and listings that are offered by these companies. The data is exchanged using XML.

- **Social networking**: In a similar fashion, leading social networking companies such as Facebook and Meetup.com offer the ability to access and communicate with member and group information through a similar series of APIs. This information is also passed from place to place in the form of XML.

- **News feeds**: The news feed is an idea that is almost as old as the Internet itself. It is a native feature for most blogs and community web sites. The most popular brand of feed is RSS (Really Simple Syndication). However, because news feeds are almost a web site staple in this day and age, they come in many forms. Additionally, larger news firms such as CNN, MSNBC, and FOX Sports all transmit their news through some type of news feed, usually RSS. The data sent from news feeds are commonly formatted as XML.

While the most common use for XML is communication via web service, the purposes of XML far exceed data transmission. XML can be used to define other markup languages as well. It is the foundational standard for all modern markup languages. The following web programming languages are some of the more popular languages that find their roots in XML:

- **ASP.NET**: Microsoft's standard web language
- **XHTML**: A strict XML-conformant form of HTML
- **MXML**: A markup language developed for use with Adobe Flex

XML is used as a standard for desktop applications as well. For example, Microsoft completely rearchitected its markup model for Word 2007 to include the new XML-based file format DOCX.

ActionScript 3.0 and E4X

E4X simply stands for ECMAScript for XML. Huge help, we know. Ecma International (formerly the European Computer Manufacturers Association) is a private nonprofit association devoted to the standardization of communications and information as it relates to technology.

Recall that ActionScript is a derivative of ECMAScript and the ECMA-262 standard. Well, the more ActionScript matures, the more compliant it will become with ECMA standards. The primary benefit to standards conformance is to ensure that programming is strict, well-formed, and common among different programmers. E4X is then the current standard for working with XML data in ECMA-based languages like ActionScript. With the addition of E4X in ActionScript 3.0, we saw a significant movement toward greater code manageability and data access.

12

In previous versions of Flash, a developer would need to access information through all of an element's parents. For example, let's say we had information about various cities around the world organized in an XML structure.

To access this information in early versions of ActionScript, you would need to use something like this:

```
World.NorthAmerica.UnitedStates.Maryland.Baltimore.population.
```

Actually, it would look something more like this:

```
World.childNodes[1].childNodes[1].childNodes[1].childNodes[1]➥
.attributes.population
```

You can see where this would become extremely inefficient.

Fortunately, ActionScript 3.0 and E4X do offer immediate help. To access the same information, as previously discussed, a developer can use a more condensed approached as shown here:

```
xml..Baltimore.@population
```

As you delve deeper into this chapter, you will get a better understanding of how Flash operates on XML. For now, it is sufficient to understand that Flash is now compliant with the standard method of operating on XML: E4X.

Let's get started examining the basics of the XML structure.

Learning to see XML

Much like any other type of computer language (markup or programming), when you first take a look at XML, it can be a bit overwhelming. Further, the more complicated the structure, the harder it becomes to discern data from syntax. Fortunately, there is no "doing" involved with XML as a language. Simply put, where ActionScript can perform computation and manipulation on various values, XML cannot. Therefore, there will be no added confusion associated with the learning of theory or interactive programming. Once a person learns a few very basic rules that govern the way XML is structured, developing and reading-in complex data structures becomes almost like riding a bike.

The most important thing that any new XML user needs to understand is that XML is self-descriptive. This simply means that the developer defines not only the data, but also the elements that contain the data. There are not an overwhelming number of reserved keywords or role-specific programming characters that need to be learned. With the exception of a few basic rules that we will discuss in this chapter, the entire document can be defined by the programmer. In essence, it then becomes a matter of not what is being organized but how.

As shown next, we have created an XML structure that organizes data relating to the members of a popular sports team into a structure that is more easily understood by both the human eye and a computer program. For sake of example, the structure defines a popular professional soccer team, the Red Devils. In the structure we are able to start defining information about the players on the team using the player tag. As you can see, this example actually defines three players. We then begin to have the ability to add further information about each player including name, pos, and number. This continual nesting of information is often referred to as the **XML tree**.

```
<red_devils>
  <player>
    <name>Van der Sar</name>
    <pos>Keeper</pos>
    <number>1</number>
  </player>
  <player>
    <name>Giggs</name>
    <pos>Midfielder</pos>
    <number>11</number>
  </player>
  <player>
    <name>Rooney</name>
    <pos>Striker</pos>
    <number>10</number>
  </player>
</red_devils>
```

Figure 12-1 gives an excellent graphical model to further understand what the preceding data structure is representing.

Figure 12-1. A graphical representaion of the defined XML structure

An XML tree must always contain a top-level node, or single element, which is commonly referred to as the **root node**. This element will contain everything else that exists in the XML data structure. In this example we used red_devils as the root node, which is also conveniently the name of the team. Because this is XML and self-descriptive, we could have just as easily used something like manchester, roster, or team as the root node. This becomes a powerful feature as the data and data structure are fully customizable.

Chapter 11 included a simple name-value pair data structure that sent data formatted as a query string to a remote PHP script. If you compare that example to the current one, you should see how much more powerful the XML approach becomes. Imagine trying to streamline this information in a name-value pair. Your variable-naming scheme would have to be pretty intricate. How would you define individual players? How would you associate attributes to those players? What about scalability? Right now, you are only working with three players. There are over 40 players on the Red Devils. Now imagine trying to pass information about the entire league. There are 20 teams registered this year. That's more than 800 players and a lot of statistics. Not to be obnoxious about the whole thing, but you can see where trying to organize this information into name-value pairs versus XML would become an absolute nightmare.

Conversely, using XML would be overkill in a situation as similar to that in the Chapter 11 form. XML is definitely better to use with complex data structures or data structures that have the potential for becoming complex.

Now, let's look a little more closely at how to create well-formed XML.

Using proper structure and syntax

To effectively work with XML, a developer only needs to become familiar with a few very basic syntactical rules to create a well-formed structure. Those rules pertain to the following:

- Elements
- Entities and escapes
- Attributes
- Empty elements
- Efficiency
- Comments

Elements

The **element** is the most basic part of the XML structure. An element is defined by an opening and closing tag. A **tag** is any descriptive text that is contained within the less than (<) and greater than (>) characters. To help you better understand this concept, go ahead and open player_01.xml located in the Chapter 12 folder of the working files directory.

> Though it is possible to open and edit an XML file in Flash, you may feel more comfortable in another program such as Dreamweaver or your computer's standard text editor. When you first open this document, you will notice that it is totally blank. This will give you the opportunity to see how easy it is to build a complex XML file from the ground up.

First thing you will want to do within the family.xml file is enter the following code, which will create an element. If you are familiar with working with HTML, you will no doubt feel right at home.

```
<family>

</family>
```

Notice that <family> is an opening tag that would also signify the start of the family element. The closing tag, </family>, is defined in the same manner and includes a forward slash (/) directly after the less than character (<). The entire element is then defined as everything located within these two tags, including the tags themselves.

Rules for working with elements

When working with XML elements, a few simple rules need to be adhered to. The ability to have self-descriptive items within a data structure is powerful indeed, but it is these rules that give the structure meaning.

- **Closing tags**: All XML elements must contain an opening and closing tag. Failure to properly tag your elements could result in a program error. The following is an example of an improperly tagged element. As you can see, there is an opening tag but no subsequent closing tag.

    <name>Van der Sar

- **Tags must match**: It is important, when establishing your elements, to make sure that the opening tag and the ending tag are exactly the same. Misspelling and case insensitivity will create program errors. The following opening and closing tags are not the same:

    <name>Van der Sar**</Name>**

- **Proper nesting**: One of the most important things associated with the XML structure is the structure itself. Improperly nested elements or broken structure will immediately create an error when the program tries to read in an XML document. The following example has the two closing tags out of order; this error completely undermines the XML structure.

    <player><name>Van der Sar**</player>**</name>

- **Proper naming**: There are a few things to also understand when choosing names for your element tags:

    - Element names may contain any alphanumeric character and most special characters with the exception of the reserved entities, which will be discussed shortly in the "Entities and escapes" section.

    - Names cannot start with numbers or special characters.

    - Names cannot begin with any derivative of the word "XML" (XML, xml, etc.).

    - Names cannot contain spaces.

Filling out the XML tree

Now that you have become familiar with creating XML elements, take a few minutes and flesh out a structure within the family.xml file. For this example you will want to create several members of your "family," much like the members of the Red Devils soccer team introduced earlier in this chapter. In addition to the members of the family, create several more elements to use to add description to each member. In the following example, such

12

elements include name for a name, hair for hair color, eyes for eye color, and rel for their relationship.

```
<family>
  <member>
    <name>Paul</name>
    <hair>Brown</hair>
    <eyes>Brown</eyes>
    <rel>Me</rel>
  </member>
  <member>
    <name>Erica</name>
    <hair>Red</hair>
    <eyes>Burnt Sienna</eyes>
    <rel>Wife</rel>
  </member>
  <member>
    <name>Kelli</name>
    <hair>Brown</hair>
    <eyes>Brown</eyes>
    <rel>Sister</rel>
  </member>
</family>
```

Entities and escapes

As mentioned earlier in this chapter, one of the greatest benefits to using XML is the lack of a complicated set of reserved keywords and characters. To create XML you simply need to know what data you want to organize and start organizing it. However, there are a few items that do have a specific meaning to the programs that digest the XML data. Take the following XML code, for example:

```
<math_problem> 3 + x < 10 </math_problem>
```

When a program begins to examine the structure of XML data, it knows that certain characters signify certain events. For instance, the less than (<) character lets the program know that a tag or closing tag is about to be defined. So, in the case of the aforementioned math problem element, the < character in the actual problem would make the parsing program think that a new tag was being defined. Because this is not actually a new tag and no other appropriate characters exist with it, the way that line is entered would create an error in the receiving program.

Fortunately, there is a simple workaround for this problem. To use a character that has been predetermined to perform a functional task in XML, you must employ the use of **character entity references**. The entity reference, also commonly referred to as an **escape sequence**, is a string of characters that is used in place of a specific character, or entity. There are only five reserved characters as defined by the XML specification, as shown in Table 12-1.

Table 12-1. The five primary reserved characters as dictated by the XML specification

Entity	Escape sequence	Usage
>	>	Greater than
<	<	Less than
&	&	Ampersand
"	"	Quotation mark
'	'	Apostrophe

The syntax of an escape sequence is actually also fairly straightforward. To initiate an escape you must use an ampersand (&), followed by a character code, followed by a semicolon (;). So to solve the problem from the earlier code snippet, we implement a standard escape sequence, using the character code for the less than (<) sign as demonstrated here:

```
<math_problem> 3 + x &lt; 10 </math_problem>
```

Attributes

Attributes give you the ability to add further information that is going to be associated with a specific element. An attribute is nothing more than a simple name-value pair that is added to the opening tag of any given element.

> *See Chapter 11 for a discussion of name-value pairs.*

Attributes also allow you to package, or encapsulate, information within one element for the benefit of increased organization. As demonstrated in the following example, you can see how adding attributes to a simple element lets you effectively associate more information with that element. The following element defines a collection of information about an apple:

```
<apple>
  <type>macintosh</type>
  <color>red</color>
</apple>
```

By using attributes we have the ability to add more descriptive information about the given element.

```
<apple type="macintosh" color="red"></apple>
<apple type="macintosh" color="red"></apple>
```

12

Here's a note of caution about attributes. As a personal approach, we try to organize ourselves as efficiently as possible. When working with XML, we like to use attributes as much as we can. However, there are a couple things to think about before you become too attribute crazy.

Because attributes are nested within the opening tag of an element, they are limited in the amount of information they can represent. Like the name-value pair, an attribute can only contain one value. When using elements, however, you have the ability to have that element contain many values, including text nodes, other elements, and attributes. This also gives you the future flexibility to edit the structure if needed.

The best way to approach this, as a developer, is to determine what the program requires. Remember, this is XML, so you can shape it any way you want. Therefore, don't limit yourself to what may or may not be considered best practice in this situation. Try to take an objective look at the problem you are faced with and determine the best solution.

Empty elements

Another tool that can be used as a medium of efficiency is the **empty element**. As you can see in the preceding code, moving all descriptive information to attributes has a tendency to make the use of text nodes and subsequent closing tags unnecessary. If you know that your elements will not require a text node, you have the ability to define them as empty elements.

To create an empty element, you simply remove the closing tag and insert a slash (/) just before the greater than (>) character in the opening tag definition. The following will be recognized as a complete element by the parsing program:

```
<apple type="macintosh" color="red" />
```

Efficiency

For further insight into how XML can become a more efficient structure, let's revisit the players example from earlier in this chapter.

```
<red_devils>
  <player>
    <name>Van der Sar</name>
    <pos>Keeper</pos>
    <number>1</number>
  </player>
  <player>
    <name>Giggs</name>
    <pos>Midfielder</pos>
    <number>11</number>
  </player>
```

```
    <player>
      <name>Rooney</name>
      <pos>Striker</pos>
      <number>10</number>
    </player>
  </red_devils>
```

If you were to take the previously mentioned structure and streamline it using only attributes, you could end up with something similar to what you see next. Notice how much more compact and efficient this information becomes while maintaining all the same information.

```
  <red_devils>
    <player name="Van der Sar" pos="Keeper" number="1" />
    <player name="Giggs" pos="Midfielder" number="11" />
    <player name="Rooney" pos="Striker" number="10" />
  </red_devils>
```

Commenting XML

In XML there are two primary methods of commenting text: standard XML-style commenting and using CDATA tags. Standard commenting is used in a manner similar to the way comments are employed in any other programming language. As shown next, a standard comment is exactly the type of comment found in HTML. Such comments are used to both describe areas of your coded document and serve as a vessel of communication between you and other developers.

Standard XML-style comment

The standard XML-style comment is initiated by the <!-- sequence of characters. It is then closed by the --> sequence of characters. Whatever text is typed between these two sets of characters will be ignored by the XML parser of the receiving program.

Here's an example:

```
  <!-- This is a standard comment typically used for instruction. -->
```

> *Flash has the ability to read in comments from XML documents and send them to the* Output *window.*

CDATA comments

CDATA comments are actually very similar to block-level comments used in ActionScript. The biggest benefit to using CDATA comments is that they maintain format and allow you to pass whatever characters you want to the parsing program as exact. Therefore you could pass any set of characters, including reserved entities, to ActionScript, and the XML would maintain the integrity of those characters.

Here's an example:

```
<xmlData>
  <a_cdata_comment>
    <![CDATA[

      function doSomethingCool(a:int, b:int)
      {
        var c:int;
        c = a + b;
        return c;
      }

      You may also type <b>any</b> manner
      of text here & it will still work!
      This includes reserved characters like >, <, and "".

    ]]>
  </a_cdata_comment>
</xmlData>
```

Now that you are familiar with the structure of XML, you can try your hand at loading this data into Flash via ActionScript.

Loading an XML file with ActionScript

In this section you'll take a crack at loading XML into Flash using ActionScript. For this example, you are going to load in the XML data you created earlier in this chapter with the family_02.xml file.

Loading XML data into Flash involves all of the usual suspects that you would expect to find when loading any other type of external data. Let's take a quick look at the following code used in ch12_01.fla:

```
var req:URLRequest = new URLRequest("family.xml");
var xml:XML;
```

URLRequest and URLLoader objects

After reading Chapter 11, you should be pretty familiar with the URLRequest object and what it is used for. In this example, it retrieves the family.xml file you created earlier. The second line is new, however. You should recognize it as a variable declaration. And based on its name, you have probably also assumed that this variable will be used to store your incoming XML data. You will not be assigning value to the variable at this point because there is nothing to assign.

See Chapter 8 for a discussion of variables.

The next three lines should be pretty straightforward. The first line creates the loader object that will be used to load the previously created URLRequest. The second line will be used to assign the event listener to the URLLoader object and set the handler as the loadXML function. Finally, the load method is called and passed the value of the URLRequest as its parameter.

```
var xmlLoader:URLLoader = new URLLoader();
xmlLoader.addEventListener(Event.COMPLETE, loadXML);
xmlLoader.load(req);
```

Event handler

The final piece of the puzzle is the event handler. There isn't really much variation from this handler and the ones we discussed in Chapter 9. Here, we assign a value to the xml object. As discussed a moment ago, you needed to wait until data was available before you could assign it to a variable.

```
function loadXML (e:Event)
{
  xml = new XML(e.target.data);
  trace(xml);
}
```

The other question that may also arise is why the variable was not simply declared in the event handler. Well, aside from being a cleaner way of coding, the answer has everything to do with the scope of the variable. Had the variable been declared within the event handler, we would have no way to access it outside of the event handler without creating some other form of external reference. Ultimately, the information loaded in from an external source will need to be used by other parts of the program. By declaring the variable at the root level, we make the XML data accessible to the whole program.

Once the necessary code is in place, you can test your movie (Ctrl+Enter or Cmd+Enter). You then see your XML data traced out perfectly in the Output window, similarly to Figure 12-2.

Once you have loaded an XML file into Flash, you will need to filter the information in the XML structure to use it in your application. In the next section we will discuss in detail the primary methods used to filter XML.

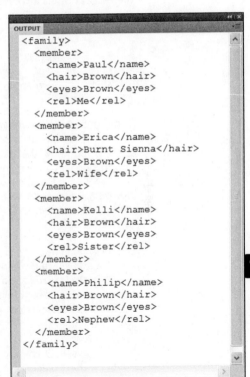

Figure 12-2. The Flash Output panel displaying XML data stored in the family.xml file

12

Reading the XML data

And now the real fun begins. So far we have looked at the creation structure for simple XML documents. We have also been able to access, load, and display an entire set of data stored within that XML document. At this time we will take a look at several methods for accessing that information for specific use in ActionScript.

XML and XMLList classes

For accessing the information stored in an XML tree, ActionScript offers two primary classes: the XML class and the XMLList class. For the most part, these two classes operate in a very similar fashion. Because of this, there is often some degree of confusion surrounding the best use of these classes.

The primary difference between the XML and XMLList class is that the XML class is used to work with a single, well-formed XML data structure, and the XMLList is capable of working with multiple XML objects including elements, text nodes, and attributes. Further, the XMLList offers increased functionality for handling lists of information. Ultimately, the XMLList class will aid you in the management of multiple sets of information like family members, players on a soccer team, or aggregated news feeds.

> *ActionScript 3.0 also offers the XMLDocument class as a legacy method for working with XML data in the traditional ActionScript 2.0 manner.*

In the previous example you used the XML class to create an object and load in a data structure that was descriptive of members of your family. Because you created it from scratch, you know that the data was both thorough and well formed. As a result your information was loading into ActionScript with no problem.

However, if you were to remove the root element of the structure as shown next, you would no longer have a single well-formed XML structure. Instead, you would have a list of many XML objects.

```
<member>
   <name>Paul</name>
   <hair>Brown</hair>
   <eyes>Brown</eyes>
   <rel>Me</rel>
</member>
<member>
   <name>Erica</name>
   <hair>Red</hair>
   <eyes>Burnt Sienna</eyes>
   <rel>Wife</rel>
</member>
<member>
   <name>Kelli</name>
```

```
        <hair>Brown</hair>
        <eyes>Brown</eyes>
        <rel>Sister</rel>
    </member>
    <member>
        <name>Philip</name>
        <hair>Brown</hair>
        <eyes>Brown</eyes>
        <rel>Nephew</rel>
    </member>
```

If you then tried to load this data, now referring to the file family_02.xml, using the standard XML object, you would be shown an error as demonstrated in Figure 12-3.

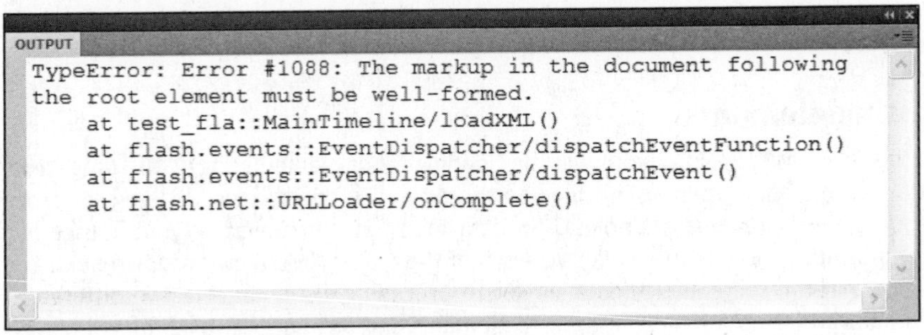

```
OUTPUT
TypeError: Error #1088: The markup in the document following
the root element must be well-formed.
    at test_fla::MainTimeline/loadXML()
    at flash.events::EventDispatcher/dispatchEventFunction()
    at flash.events::EventDispatcher/dispatchEvent()
    at flash.net::URLLoader/onComplete()
```

Figure 12-3. Output error generated by improper XML formatting

The error type Error #1088 is letting you know that the XML information that is being loaded into the XML object is not properly formatted. Recall that all well-formed XML must have a single root element or node that contains everything else in the structure. As a result of your data no longer having a root node, the family tag, ActionScript no longer accepts it as an XML object.

This minor setback is just what you need to get a glimpse at how the XMLList differs from the standard XML class. If you make a few minor edits to the code in ch12_01.fla (or jump right to ch12_02.fla) as shown next, you should now be able to load the XML data from family_02.xml with no adverse side effects. Because the XMLList is capable of handling multiple XML objects, it simply digests this information as a list of elements rather than one entire XML tree.

```
var req:URLRequest = new URLRequest("family_02.xml");
var xml:XMLList;

...

function loadXML (e:Event)
{
  xml = new XMLList(e.target.data);
  trace(xml);
}
```

12

Chances are, as a developer, you are not going to be dealing with malformed XML data coming from a remote source. In addition, as professionals, it is always a good idea to adhere to standards. Therefore, you will more than likely never have to use the XMLList object for loading XML information. The real purpose of the class is to allow you to work with different aspects of the information as a list. Therefore, though you may load the information from the family XML tree as an XML object, when you ultimately access that information it will be converted to an XMLList.

Accessing XML data

Thanks to the added benefit of E4X in ActionScript 3.0, accessing XML data has become significantly less difficult than in ActionScript 2.0. The primary reason is that you now have access to the various nodes (elements, attribute, and text) through the use of their names and the dot operator (.), as you would when accessing properties of ActionScript objects like Germ.height.

Accessing elements

Using the file ch12_03.fla, you will be loading and manipulating XML data from players_03.xml. Upon opening this file you should notice the standard loading sequence as used in several previous examples. The data found in the player_03.xml source is a slightly adjusted version of the earlier versions of the player XML files, as shown next. You will notice that this file contains data similar to preceding examples, the two differences being the mixed format offering both child elements and attributes and additional players for a more verbose data set.

```
<red_devils>
  <player name="Van der Sar">
    <pos>Keeper</pos>
    <number>1</number>
  </player>
  <player name="Giggs">
    <pos>Midfielder</pos>
    <number>11</number>
  </player>
  <player name="Rooney">
    <pos>Striker</pos>
    <number>10</number>
  </player>
  <player name="Rinaldo">
    <pos>Winger</pos>
    <number>7</number>
  </player>
  <player name="Vidic">
    <pos>Defender</pos>
    <number>15</number>
  </player>
</red_devils>
```

Now that you have had a quick look at the data you will be working with, you can begin to access that data directly. In the loadXML event handler in ch12_03.fla, enter the following line of code:

```
trace(xml.player);
```

In this trace statement, because you know that your XML data has been loaded into your xml object, you use that variable name to access the XML data. Because of the enhanced E4X capabilities, you can then access child nodes of the XML data's tree simply by using the node name as you would a property. Therefore, because you know that your data source contains a series of XML elements named player, you can access that information directly using xml.player. The trace statement would then send all information concerning the player nodes to the Output window as shown in Figure 12-4.

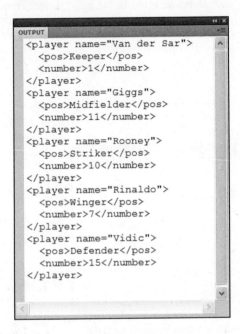

Figure 12-4.
The output of a trace statement referencing xml.properties

Drilling down into the structure

In a similar fashion you also have the ability to drill down into the structure and access child nodes of child nodes (think grandchildren) by continually using the dot operator (.). If you change the trace statement in your current working file to the following, you will then have the ability to access information associated with the pos elements, or position, of each player.

```
trace(xml.player.pos);
```

You then get an output of all nodes that match the request for the pos name, as shown in Figure 12-5.

12

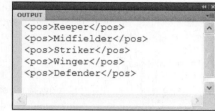

Figure 12-5.
The output of the request for the
xml.player.pos element name

Using the children() method

In the event that you are unable to access elements directly, you also have the ability to simply load all child elements of any particular node using the children() method. In this case let's assume that you know there are players or, more to the point, player elements within the XML data structure, but you are not sure what information, if any, is contained within those elements. You can then edit the trace statement, as shown next, to simply return all the child elements of any node that is named player.

```
trace(xml.player.children());
```

The resulting output would then contain a list of all child nodes and their values, as shown in Figure 12-6.

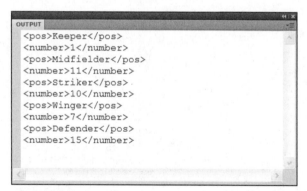

Figure 12-6. The trace output of values returned using the children() method

Retrieving text node values

When working with XML, the node name is important in order to access your information. However, because XML node names are typically repetitive, it is highly unlikely that you would ever want to use the node name as a valid piece of data. What is going to ultimately be important to the users of your application is the information stored in the text node element.

To access text node values in ActionScript, use the simple text() method, shown next. If you once again edit the trace statement of your working file, you can very easily get access to a valid text value stored in any of the existing nodes.

```
trace(xml.player.pos.text());
```

The resulting trace statement output, shown in Figure 12-7, is at this point probably not a very effective piece of data, but it does demonstrate the ability to access textual data that has been stored within an XML element.

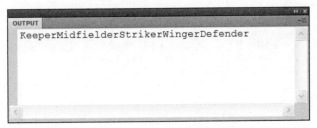

Figure 12-7. Text node values that have been captured using the text() method

Double dot notation

The double dot operator (..) gives developers the ability to bypass a long series of node names in the process of drilling into the XML structure. Earlier in this chapter we discussed the dot operator (.) as a means to access child nodes. This access was limited to parent-child relationships. With the double dot operator, you have the ability to jump to whichever node you wish to access. This is an incredibly valuable and effective tool for ActionScript programmers to now have the ability to use.

In the following example, the double dot is used to bypass the player node name.

```
trace(xml..pos.text());
```

Though this particular example is a relatively small leap, imagine if you need to access a more complex structure like the animal kingdom. To get to a dog, you would have to traverse a structure like Kingdom.Phylum.Classes.Orders.Families.Genera.Species. The double dot operator gives you the ability to bypass complex structures and go right to Kingdom..Species.

Accessing attribute values

As you may have guessed, because attributes have special placement within the XML structure, they do require a special method for reading their values. There are actually several ways to access XML attribute values. We'll discuss the following:

- Attribute identifier operator (@)
- attribute() method
- attributes() method

To access attributes directly by name, you may use the dot syntax that has been discussed so far in this chapter. However, you will be required to use the attribute identifier operator, @, as a prefix to the attribute name. In your current XML structure, all player elements have an attribute name that contains the last name of each player. If you then use the @ character followed by the attribute name name, you can directly access the value of that node just as you would any other node.

12

Here's an example:

```
trace(xml.player.@name);
```

You then get an output of all attribute values as shown in Figure 12-8.

Figure 12-8. The output of the attribute values from the name attributes

The second method for accessing values is using the `attribute()` method. The `attribute()` method can be used in a similar fashion to the attribute identifier operator, where the targeting of a specific attribute name is taking place. As shown next, this method accepts one parameter: a string value representing the name of the attribute. When this file is tested, you will notice exactly the same output as was achieved in Figure 12-8.

```
trace(xml.player.attribute("name"));
```

The final method for accessing attribute values works as the `children()` method did when retrieving the information about an element's children. This method is also used to search for attributes of an undetermined name or quantity. The `attributes()` method (note the s) is used exactly like the other two attribute routines. As shown next, this method accepts no parameter.

```
trace(xml.player.attributes());
```

Though the values returned in this example are exactly as shown in Figure 12-8, be advised that this example is only using one set of attributes. Unlike the previous two methods, which only returned attribute values associated with the attribute name, this method will return all attribute values associated with all child elements of the accessed XML element.

Bracket (array) notation

Having now thoroughly combed through the currently available XML data structure, it is about time we stop returning lists of data and started pinpointing individual values. To accomplish this ActionScript uses simple bracket notation ([0]). Bracket notation is used to access the values of a special type of data structure known as an **array**. Arrays are essentially variables that are used to store multiple values, or a list.

The following example demonstrates the building of an array (list):

```
var friends:Array = new Array("Tom","Dick","Harry");
trace(friends); //Tom,Dick,Harry
```

The values in this list can then be accessed individually through the use a set of brackets ([]) containing the index position of the value. If we wanted to trace Dick's name, we would use this notation as follows:

```
trace(players[1]); //Dick
```

We simply place the index value (position) of the item in our list inside brackets, directly after the name of the array. You're probably wondering why Dick's name was second in the list and accessed by a 1. Well, computers start counting with zeros. Therefore, the first index value of an array is always 0, so the first element in your list is going to be at the 0 position, not 1. So instead of thinking 1,2,3,4 . . . , start thinking 0,1,2,3 . . .

Virtually every example we have looked at over the last section has the ability to be augmented with array notation. When Flash parses XML data, the elements are stored as arrays (indexed lists), which allow us to use this same functionality.

Using the trace statements, you can see that the simple addition of bracket notation to each statement will allow you to no longer trace out entire lists associated with specific nodes but an individual value instead.

The first statement shown here will now only trace out the complete child for the first position of the list:

```
trace(xml.player[0]);

/*
<player name="Van der Sar">
  <pos>Keeper</pos>
  <number>1</number>
</player>
*/
```

You also have the ability to insert the array notation at several levels of the dot notation. The following example also targets the first player node, but it also uses the children() method to search for child elements. You can then use the array notation a second time to select only one specific child element and return the value. The following statement then traces 1, which is the value of the second child element of the first player:

```
trace(xml.player.children()[1]);  // 1
```

12

Finally, array notation can be used with the other XML methods in an abundance of combinations to achieve the desired result. The following code sample demonstrates possible outcomes when working with array notation and the previous examples:

```
trace(xml..pos.text()[0]);  //Keeper
trace(xml.player[2].@name); //Rooney
trace(xml.player.@name[2]); //Rooney

trace(xml.player.attribute("name")[4]);  //Vidic
trace(xml.player.attributes()[4]);  //Rinaldo
```

Filtering node values

One final aspect of accessing XML values that is definitely worth mentioning is the ability to filter various values using the filtering predicate operator (()). The **filtering predicate operator** allows values to be filtered based on a specific node or attribute value. By comparing the equality of a node and a value, we can pinpoint exact elements or groups of elements and various extra values.

The following uses the filtering predicate operator to determine which player elements have a pos value of Striker and returns the value of the number node:

```
trace(xml.player.(pos == "Striker").number); //10
```

In a similar fashion you can use this method to compare the values of attributes. The first example uses the filtering predicate in conjunction with an attribute identifier. This example returns the value of the name attribute that is associated with the player element whose pos value is equal to Striker. You are then given the output of Rooney.

```
trace(xml.player.(pos == "Striker").@name); //Rooney
```

In the second example you see that you can conveniently use the attribute identifier within the filtering predicate to achieve the almost reverse situation as the previous example. You are now looking for the pos value for the player element whose name attribute is equal to Rooney. The returned output is Striker.

```
trace(xml.player.(@name == "Rooney").pos); //Striker
```

Summary

The chapters in Part 3 have given you access to a tremendous amount of power with respect to ActionScript. As a Flash user, this is the material that is going to propel you into the realm of web application development. As a designer, you now possess the basic knowledge to begin communicating programmatically with web specialists authoring in an abundance of different programming languages.

In this chapter, we discussed the following important topics:

- Proper XML formatting and structure.
- The XML class, which is used for holding and manipulating an entire single XML object.
- The XMLList object, which is used to manipulate one or more elements or objects. You also have access to an additional level of functionality similar to the List class.

PART FOUR

ADDITIONAL USER INTERFACES

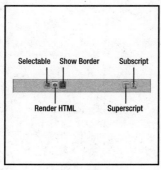

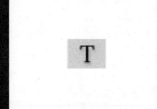

Text helped lift the popularity of Flash early on in its existence. Though it may not seem like much of a reason for anyone to consider Flash the conquistador of multimedia web development, using decorative text in the early days of web development was a luxury that was not easily achieved. Back then, developers were limited to standard system fonts for rendering textual data, and in some instances, this is still the case.

In order for a computer to display a certain font, the font must be installed on that computer. If a design required the use of an abstract font, the common solution would be to render special text as a bitmap graphic to be displayed as a picture on web sites. This solution was both time-consuming for the web developer and impractical when considering the loading differential between text and images.

Furthermore, if web developers used abstract or copywritten fonts, the likelihood of that font being installed on a visitor's computer was not very good. Therefore, web developers started using **web-safe fonts**, which are the fonts that are considered most likely to be installed on the majority of computers accessing the Internet. In the event the font does not exist, the browser would replace it with its own default font. You can see where this quickly became a point of degradation for web designers. There was simply no way to guarantee that the web site would render as designed by the web developer.

Flash, on the other hand, allowed designers to use text as they wanted. They had the ability to use whichever font they wanted, wherever they wanted. And because fonts are embedded in the Flash application, they would translate perfectly to any computer on any platform, through any browser. Designers were assured that users would see the text exactly as they designed it. And because Flash is using the actual font file and not an image generated from the font, this proved to be more efficient in terms of the end product's file size.

In this chapter we are going to explore the many subtleties of working with text in Flash. Conceptually, this chapter will be a bit less complex than the most recent ones. However, its content is no less relevant to the power of modern-day Flash design.

Let's first take a look at implementing text at author time.

Creating text with the Text tool

In Flash there are three primary types of text that can be used in any given Flash project. Each of these types of text is designed for a specific purpose, which means that they behave in different manners. These types are as follows:

- **Static text** is used primarily for text that does not change. This text makes it much simpler to work with complex fonts containing decorative aspects like cursive or handwriting. This type cannot be created or manipulated with ActionScript.

- **Dynamic text** is presentation text that is accessible using ActionScript. Its value can be manipulated and changed as required by the application. An excellent example of dynamic text is a player's score in a video game where text is constantly updated.

■ **Input text**, as its name indicates, is text that allows for user input. Though typically used in contact forms, input text is very useful in an application's communication with a user. This type of text is also able to be manipulated using ActionScript.

Having a good understanding of these types of text, and when best to use them, is extremely advantageous for any project. In the next several sections, we will be constructing a simple contact form that utilizes all of the previously mentioned text types.

Revisiting the Property inspector

As you have learned in several of the preceding chapters in this book, one of the best allies for manipulating elements at author time is the Property inspector. As it turns out, the Property inspector is the primary method for manipulating text fields that have been created with the Text tool. When a text field is selected on the stage, the Property inspector is populated with an abundant amount of editable information ranging from the text paragraph settings to how the text will be rendered at runtime. You can also change properties like color and size.

Starting a simple contact form

In this chapter we will build a simple contact form to help you get acclimated to the various aspects of working with the text options in Flash. Different variations of web forms are the primary methods to capture a user's information in Flash. To get started we will place a few text fields on the stage and manipulate those using the Property inspector. Once the interface for our form is complete, we will then manipulate these text fields further using ActionScript.

1. Open Flash and choose Flash File (ActionScript 3) to create a new Flash file. If the Property inspector is not yet open, open it by selecting Window ➤ Properties or by pressing Ctrl+F3 on your keyboard.

2. Change the document properties to better suit the contact form. We suggest setting the document size to 300 by 400 and the stage color to #FFFFCD.

3. Use the Text tool to add text to the stage in Flash. The unmistakable T icon, shown in Figure 13-1, represents the Text tool on the toolbar. You can also access this tool by pressing T on your keyboard.

Figure 13-1.
The Text tool is used to create text in Flash.

13

When you select the Text tool from the Tools panel, you should notice the Property inspector changes to immediately assist in the use of text. As shown in Figure 13-2, before text is even applied to the stage, you have the ability to edit its type as well as several other properties responsible for character and paragraph formatting.

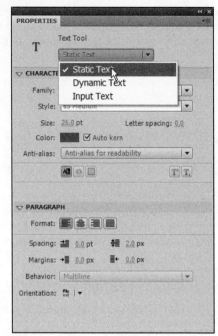

Figure 13-2.
The Text Type drop-drown box
allows a user to choose static,
dynamic, or input text.

For this example we will be creating text fields for collecting a user's information. Therefore, we will need several static text fields to use as labels and several input text fields to allow users to enter their information. We will be able to come back and format text fields later in the development cycle. For now, let's add a couple simple text fields.

4. With the Text tool selected, change the text type in the Property inspector to Static Text. You can then click the stage to place the text field.

5. Type the words First Name in the text field. Once the text is entered, you can exit the text field by clicking the stage. This text field will serve as our label for the area where the user will enter his or her first name.

> *Static text must contain characters. If you place a static text field on the stage and do not type anything in it, the field will disappear when it is deselected.*

6. Next, we need a place for the user to enter their information. The Text tool should still be selected from the previous entry. In the Property inspector, change the Text Type setting to Input Text.

7. Add the input text field to the stage by clicking the stage.

Unlike the static text field, runtime editable text, such as input and dynamic text, does not require the existence of any characters to remain on the stage during author time. When the field is deselected, you will still see the empty text field represented by a dotted line.

Ultimately, if any application uses an input text field, the information from that field is going to be used with ActionScript. You may have noticed that when you changed the text type from static to input that the <Instance Name> field appeared in the Property inspector above the Text Type drop-down menu. We are going to use this field to name our input and dynamic text fields so we can use them later in ActionScript.

8. Use the Selection tool (select the black arrow icon in the Tools panel or press V on your keyboard) to select the input field that you just created. In the <Instance Name> field in the Property inspector, enter a name that is descriptive of the information that will be in that field. For this example we used firstName as the instance name of our input field as shown in Figure 13-3.

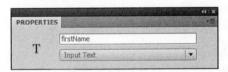

Figure 13-3.
The <Instance Name> field is used to give text fields descriptive names for use in ActionScript.

At this point, it will be a good idea to begin thinking about the layout of the form we are creating. Though it would be easy in this particular case to copy/paste (or Alt-drag on a PC, Option-drag on a Mac) and use the Align panel to quickly arrange multiple text fields on the stage, it is extremely important to begin seeing things the way ActionScript sees them.

When working with ActionScript, developers do not have the luxury of using a method such as myObject.align(center); because it simply does not exist. Objects in programming are typically placed on a stage using absolute coordinates like x and y. Even if the object is placed relatively in relation to another object, the programmer will ultimately need to know the absolute position of one of those objects. To use an analogy from football: if the football is 10 yards from the end zone, we still need to know exactly where the end zone is for this statement to make sense.

Positioning text fields

For this example, we will eventually be creating multiple text fields. Some of these text fields will be created using ActionScript. It is important that we have an understanding of where exactly our author time text fields are positioned so we know where our runtime text fields are supposed to go. To manage this, we will be using the Position and Size section of the Property inspector.

13

1. With the `firstName` input text field selected, click the small chain icon as shown in Figure 13-4. This icon is used to lock the aspect ratio of the height and width properties of the selected object. When this icon is showing as a broken chain, we can change the height and width properties independently of one another.

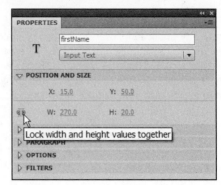

Figure 13-4.
The Lock feature is used to maintain the aspect ratio of height and width properties.

2. Now change the X, Y, W, and H properties of this section as shown in Figure 13-4. This helps us develop a framework for how the other items will be arranged on the stage.

3. Select the static text field you have created and adjust the font family, font color, size, and letter spacing. Experiment with several combinations until you find a look and feel that suits your design eye. For this exercise, it would be best to keep the font size under 20 pt, as you will be adding other text fields to the form.

There is a touch of method to this madness. Recall in Step 2 under "Starting a simple contact form" that we set the document width to 300 pixels (px). We then figured it would be a good idea for this form to have some kind of frame or margin, so we chose an arbitrary margin width of 15 px. Because the form will need a left and right margin, our total horizontal margin will be 30 px, which is 15 px on the left and 15 px on the right. If we subtract this value from the original 300 px width of the stage, we are left with 270 px. We can then use this value of 270 as the W, or width, property of the input text field. If we also set the X property to 15, the text field will be positioned 15 px from the left side of the stage. This will also leave 15 px on the right side of the stage. The result is a perfectly centered text field. The remaining two properties, Y and H, were then set to give an approximate starting point that also played into the layout aesthetically.

Once the input text field is set in its proper position, we are going to want to also do a bit of work on the static text that will serve as the label for this input area. To accomplish basic text styles, we can use the Character section of the Property inspector as demonstrated in Figure 13-5. Within this area are located the standard formatting properties that you would expect to find in a design-based IDE. From this area you can select the font to be used, style if the font contains additional styles like bold and italic, font size, font color, letter spacing, and auto-kerning.

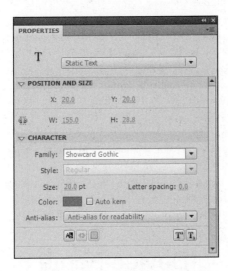

Figure 13-5.
Several basic properties can be applied to text using the Character section of the Property inspector.

*One common aspect of working with text in Flash that is often misconstrued is the use of letter spacing and kerning. **Letter spacing**, also known formally known as **tracking**, is the process of separating letters by adding the same amount of space between all letters in a word or phrase. **Kerning**, on the other hand, is a method that examines the area between every two characters to achieve a more accurate visual separation between characters. Flash will automatically set the kerning when the Auto kern check box is selected.*

Render modes and text field modifiers

In the Character section of the Property inspector we are also presented with a few special sets of attributes that can be modified for both text and text field rendering. Because Flash goes beyond the basics and offers several different kinds of text, it provides you with versatile enhancements. The first of these options is the ability to set the anti-aliasing properties, or render modes, of specific text fields. The anti-aliasing of text refers to how the text is rendered. When considering anti-aliasing, emphasis is typically placed on how the edges of text are rendered. Sharp or crisp edges tend to have a more jagged, less appealing appearance. Conversely, fully anti-aliased fonts have a smoother, more appealing look.

Flash offers the following options to consider when creating and rendering text. Figure 13-6 demonstrates the differences in these various types of rendering. Though the differences may seem subtle, they can have a dramatic effect on your application.

- Device fonts: Best used when the purpose of the text is utilitarian, or functional. The SWF file will look for standard texts that are stored on the machine on which the SWF is displayed. The primary benefit to this method is that file size is not increased because fonts are not embedded in the SWF. Quite simply, if the application does not require the use of special fonts, this is an excellent choice.

13

- **Bitmap text (no anti-alias):** Used to create sharper-looking text. This option applies no anti-aliasing to the font. As a result, text with this option applied will not scale well. This option also increases overall file size because font outlines are embedded.

- **Anti-alias for animation:** Best used when working with animation. It ignores information associated with kerning and alignment to generate a smoother effect. This is best used with fonts over 10 pt in size. This option will increase the overall file's size because font outlines are embedded.

- **Anti-alias for readability:** Can be used to improve the overall legibility of text. It should not be used on any text that is to be animated. This option will increase the overall file's size because font outlines are embedded.

- **Custom anti-alias:** Does exactly what it says it will do—allows you to determine your own custom anti-aliasing settings. This can be the most ideal setting, as it gives designers the maximum amount of control over font rendering.

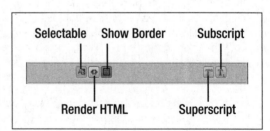

Figure 13-6.
Applying different rendering options to text can affect the text's look and size in the overall application.

The next set of text field modifiers offered in the Character portion of the Property inspector, shown in Figure 13-7, are several special behaviors that enhance the functionality of text fields.

Figure 13-7.
Text fields can be given special properties through the use of the text field modifiers.

These standard modifiers are as follows:

- Selectable gives you have the ability to toggle whether or not this text will be selectable at runtime. It is often necessary during the life cycle of an application for text to be either selectable or not. This feature makes that a simple task.

- Render HTML gives you the ability to have the text field render as HTML. This becomes an extremely useful tool when formatting large amounts of text that can be edited and reformatted externally without recompiling the SWF.

- Show Border is a feature that can be applied to input and dynamic text fields. The benefits of this feature are an increased degree of flexibility, as you will see when we use it later to enhance the form we created previously in the chapter. With the addition of this feature, designers now have the option of creating custom aesthetics for their input fields in Flash, Photoshop, or Illustrator and overlaying the transparent input field. Designers also have the ability to quickly apply a border to text fields by simply clicking the Show Border button.

- Subscript and Superscript are not exactly behaviors for text fields, but they are worthy of mention. Though these buttons made their debut with the release of Flash CS4, this functionality was present in Flash CS3 through the Text menu.

Embedding characters

When working with dynamic or input text in Flash, it is possible that you will want to display this text with a custom font that does not exist on the end user's machine. Perhaps you have created a game, and the score needs to be rendered in a space-age digital font. Or, maybe you have created a holiday e-greeting and the recipient's name is entered at runtime and displayed in a fancy cursive font. Often, there is no way to determine which characters will be used, but you must hold true to the design aspect of the application.

For situations such as this, Flash allows you to embed characters or sets of characters from custom font families that can be used at runtime. As discussed in the previous section, the Character section of the Property inspector has some added special functionality. You may notice when selecting either Dynamic Text or Input Text that another button, labeled Character Embedding, appears at the bottom of this section. When you click this button, the dialog shown in Figure 13-8 appears, allowing you to pick the characters or set of characters that will be embedded.

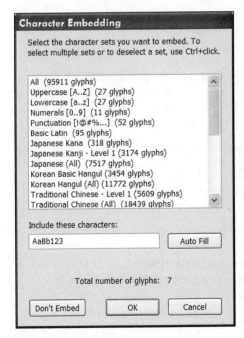

Figure 13-8.
Using the character embedding function lets you embed entire fonts or specific characters of a font.

13

Embedding characters with this feature is actually pretty easy. With a text field selected, type the characters in the fields just below Include these characters and click OK. You can also use the Auto Fill button to automatically embed all characters that currently exist in the selected text field. Finally, the Don't Embed button will clear all characters that have been previously embedded for the selected text field.

Formatting paragraphs

Like all good text editors in graphics programs should, Flash possesses additional functionality for dealing with paragraphs of text. Much like the Character section, the Paragraph section includes many of the usual suspects you would expect to find when working with paragraph data. Figure 13-9 displays the Paragraph section.

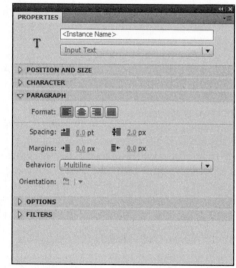

Figure 13-9.
The Paragraph section of the Property inspector is used to control paragraph settings for text fields.

Format allows you to adjust the alignment and justification of the paragraph. Spacing indents the first line of text as well as the spacing between lines. Margins adds extra space on the left and right of the paragraph. The two areas to take note of in this section are the Behavior and Orientation.

The Behavior field in the Paragraph section of the Property inspector adjusts how input and dynamic text fields will be used. These are the options:

- Single line displays runtime text in a single continuous string.
- Multiline allows runtime text to wrap to multiple lines within the text field.
- Multiline (no wrap) maintains multiple lines, but text will not wrap at the end of the text field.
- Password is a special case used with input text only. This behavior allows the text typed into an input field to appear as bullets rather than letters.

Finally, the Orientation button is used to adjust the orientation and direction of text. In a nutshell, you can use this option to have text display horizontally or vertically. Using the Rotate button, shown in Figure 13-10, allows you to change the relative orientation of the letters contained in the text field.

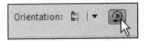

Figure 13-10.
The Rotate button is used to change the orientation of letters in text fields.

Using the Options section of the Property inspector

The Options section of the Property inspector is rather unique when working with textual data because it completely changes its parameters depending on the kind of text that is currently selected. Figure 13-11 outlines the options that are available for each type of text field.

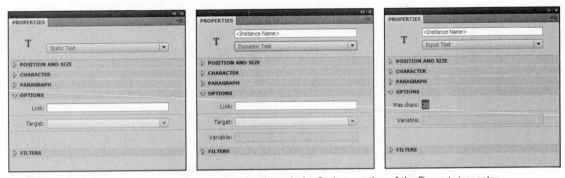

Figure 13-11. Text fields can be given special properties through the Options section of the Property inspector.

When Dynamic Text or Static Text is selected, designers have the ability to turn that text into a hyperlink, allowing this text to link your Flash movie to another web page.

When working with input text, the Max chars field in the Options section allows designers to restrict the number of characters a user can enter at runtime. This is especially helpful when dealing with passwords.

> When Input Text *is selected, the* Options *section of the* Property inspector *also displays a* Variable *field. This feature is considered deprecated in ActionScript 3.0. In order to utilize this feature, the Flash file will need to be of ActionScript 2.0 type. This field can then be bound to a specific variable reference in ActionScript.*

Filtering text elements

The final section that is active in the Property inspector when text is selected is the Filters section. Since filters were covered extensively in Chapter 5, we will not discuss them in further detail here. Just understand that text, like movie clip and button symbols, has the

13

ability to have filters applied to it for enhanced visual dynamics. Therefore, any filters like drop shadows and blurs can also be applied to text fields.

Continuing the contact form

Now that you have been fully introduced to the Property inspector as it relates to working with text, let's put the finishing touches on the front end of our contact form. To accomplish this you can use the file that you have been employing so far in this chapter or use ch13_01_02.fla from the working files.

To wrap this up we will need to add a few more text fields and a button to trigger the form's actions. You should already have a static text field and an input text field set up for the user's first name on the contact form. Now you will need to add a pair of fields for the following items:

- Last name
- Phone number
- Address
- Comments

The reason we are looking for a pair of fields for each item is that you need to create one static text field that serves as the label and one input field to allow users to supply information. This coincides with the two fields created for a user's first name from the example earlier in this chapter.

There are several different ways to accomplish the task of adding more text fields. You could create eight new text fields and format them. You could copy and paste (or Alt-drag on a PC, Option-drag on a Mac) the existing fields. For this exercise, we will go with the copy/paste method, because this method is easiest to conceptualize.

1. With ch13_01_02.fla or the aforementioned working file open, select the two existing text fields that reside on the stage by drawing a selection rectangle around them both using the Selection tool.

2. Press Ctrl+C (Cmd+C on a Mac) to copy the text fields.

3. Press Ctrl+Shift+V (Cmd+Shift+V on a Mac) to paste the fields in the exact location from which they were copied. This is referred to as **paste in place**.

Now, what you should have on your stage is two identical sets of text fields on top of each other. By using the paste-in-place command, we were able to maintain the integrity of the text fields' x positions. This simply means that the new text fields are in the exact position of the ones that we copied. All that remains is to adjust the y position to move our new text fields below the originals.

Because the approximate combined height of the two text fields is 50, we will use this value to offset our current value for y. Looking at the Y value in the Position and Size portion of the Property inspector, you can see that the current y value for these two sets of text fields is 20. If we then add the H, or height value, of 50 to the current y position, we get 70. We now have a pretty good y value for our newly pasted text fields.

4. With the pasted text fields still selected, set the Y value in the Position and Size section of the Property inspector to 70 and press Enter.

You should see that the text fields have changed position; the x position should be perfectly aligned and the y position of all four text fields should be adequately spaced. This is also demonstrated in Figure 13-12.

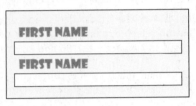

Figure 13-12.
Copy and paste allows you to quickly clone text fields.

Repeat step 4 until you have five sets of two text fields on the stage—that is, five static text fields and five input text fields. Remember to adjust in increments of 50.

Once all the text fields are in place, it will be necessary to do a little spring cleaning. Looking at the stage, you should have five text fields that all say First Name, similar to the image shown in Figure 13-13. What is not as obvious is the fact that you also have five input fields with the instance name of `firstName`. This is definitely not the most efficient contact form. What we need to do is change some of the naming used to make each field descriptive and unique.

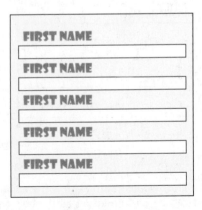

Figure 13-13.
All text fields have been properly added and spaced.

5. Go through each text field and rename them appropriately. For the static text fields, change the names starting with the second from the top to Last Name, Phone, Address, and Comments. For the input fields, again starting at the second from the top, change the instance name for each to `lastName`, `phone`, `address`, and `comments`.

Now, we only need to make two more tweaks, and the contact form interface will be completed.

13

6. With the Character section of the Property inspector open, select each input field and press the button for Show Border. This will ensure that your text fields are visible at runtime.

When you reach the input field for comments, you will need to make this field a bit bigger to allow users to input their comments.

7. Select the comment input field and change its H (height) property to 100 in the Position and Size section of the Property inspector. Then in the Paragraph section, change the Behavior setting to Multiline to allow users to enter lengthy comments.

8. Finally, open the Components panel (Window ➤ Components) and drag a button symbol onto the stage. With the button selected, change its X and Y properties in the Position and Size section of the Property inspector to 185 and 365, respectively.

When you are finished, save this file in a familiar place so you can access it later with ActionScript. Your final result should look similar to the image shown in Figure 13-14.

Figure 13-14.
The form is complete when the button is added.

Breaking apart and animating text

One of the more useful features for animators working with Flash is the ability to break apart text. The action of breaking apart can be performed on all symbols and bitmap assets that are used in a Flash movie. When you break apart an object, you are essentially separating it into its most basic parts. Static text, for example, can be broken into individual letters. Each letter of the original text is actually separated out into its own new text field. Designers then have the option to select this text again and break it apart further. In such cases, the letters would no longer be text fields. They would be basic vector shapes capable of being edited with Flash vector editing tools. As shown in Figure 13-15, a text field containing the phrase "Break Apart" is broken apart into its individual letters. The letters are then broken apart again to produce a series of basic vector shapes.

Figure 13-15. Text fields can be broken apart into letters and then vector shapes.

Animating text fields

Now you will see how quickly and easily you can break apart and animate text fields. In this example, because we are going to be animating our text, it will not be necessary for us to further break this text into its vector-based shapes. However, if you did want to convert this text into vectors, you would simply need to select the text fields again, right-click, and select Break Apart from the context menu.

1. Open ch13_02_start.fla, which is located in the source directory. You will notice the text field on the stage containing the phrase "Break Apart."

2. Right-click the text field and select Break Apart from the context menu. The text field should then be broken into individual text fields. Each new text field contains one letter from the original phrase as shown in Figure 13-15.

In order to animate these letters individually, they need to reside on their own independent layers. To achieve this quickly, we will use the Distribute to Layers command.

3. Using the Selection tool, draw a selection rectangle that contains all letters located on the stage. Using the selection rectangle will ensure that you have selected everything.

4. Right-click any one of the selected letters and select Distribute to Layers from the context menu.

Once the letters have been distributed, you should notice that each letter has been moved to a layer that has been conveniently labeled with respect to the letter that that layer contains. You should also take note that the Break Apart layer no longer contains any information or visual assets.

Now that the letters are in the proper location, it is possible to animate them individually.

5. With the timeline open, select frame 9 of the layer labeled B.

6. Holding down the Shift key, select frame 9 of the layer labeled t. You should notice that all the layers, with the exception of the Break Apart layer, are now selected.

7. Press F5 to add new frames to the selected layers. Your layer configuration should now resemble what is shown in Figure 13-16.

13

Figure 13-16.
Extra frames can be added to
the timeline by pressing F5.

Applying tweens to layers

The next steps to setting up the text "Break Apart" animation are going to be applying tweens to the appropriate layers. Similar to how we added additional frames to each layer, we will select all layers and apply motion tweens simultaneously.

1. Select frame 1 of the layer labeled B in the timeline.

2. Holding the Shift key, select frame 1 of the layer labeled t in the timeline.

3. With the layers still selected, right-click frame 1 of the layer labeled t and select Create Motion Tween from the context menu.

4. Save this file as ch13_02_a.fla.

When animating phrases, there are traditionally two ways in which your text could animate: explosion and implosion. **Explosion** simply means that the letters of the word start in their proper position and move away from each other, much like an explosion. **Implosion**, as you may have guessed, is exactly the opposite; letters typically come in from offstage and animate into position to reveal the word.

At this point, we will animate the letters in an exploding fashion. Because of Flash's new object-animation method, all you need to do is move the playhead of the timeline to frame 9, select the various letters, and move them to where you would like them to end up. When you test your movie, you should now see the letters of the words "Break Apart" explode off in many directions.

Imploding letters

To create the effect of implosion, as demonstrated in ch13_01_finish.fla, we will need to add a couple more steps to this exercise. Because the animated assets were derived from a text field that was broken apart, the inherited starting position for each letter is where that letter appears in the word. And because this starting point represents the first keyframe of the animation, we cannot update the position of each letter without affecting all subsequent frames on that layer.

In order to solve this situation, we will need to manually create a second keyframe to each layer. This will allow us to maintain the arrangement of the letters to form a word and change the position of the letters in the first keyframe to create an implosion.

1. Open ch13_02_a.fla.

2. With the timeline open, select frame 10 of the layer labeled B.

3. While holding down the Shift key, select frame 10 of the layer labeled t and press F6 to insert keyframes.

Once the new keyframes are added to the animation, you can successfully return the playhead of the timeline to frame 1 and begin changing the positions of the letters. Now when you test the movie, it will look like the letters are flying in from all over to form the words "Break Apart" as demonstrated in Figure 13-17.

Figure 13-17.
Broken-apart text can be animated to look like it is exploding or imploding.

Use the breaking apart and animating text techniques to experiment with different properties of each letter. You should be able to achieve some pretty cool effects. Try changing the size, alpha, and filtering of each letter and see what you can come up with.

Now that you have seen the robustness of Flash's text capabilities on the design side, let's jump into learning how to experiment with text and ActionScript.

Manipulating text with ActionScript

Creating text and text fields with ActionScript is something that you have already been introduced to on a basic level. In Chapter 8, we used a text field in the final example to display the text "Hello World!" In Chapter 10, when developing the Germaphobe game, the score was also displayed using a dynamically created text field. In this section we will take that exact same approach to create text fields dynamically using ActionScript. To further expand on this, we will now also be using ActionScript to add advanced formatting to dynamically created text.

We will also be using ActionScript to manipulate string data. As discussed in Chapter 8, String is one of the primitive data types. And though strings are basic, they are extremely powerful and fundamental to the development of any application.

Plucking some strings

A **string** by its most basic definition is nothing more than a character or a series of characters encapsulated within a set of quotation marks. In fact, it is possible to assign a string value simply by placing a set of quotation marks after the assignment operator in a declaration statement as shown here:

```
var aString:String = "";
```

The preceding example is considered an empty string, but you could have any number of characters contained within the quotation marks. Here's another example:

```
aString = "99 bottles of beer on the wall...0 bottles of beer wall";
```

The real power of strings comes with the ability to manipulate this information. Concatenation and deconstruction of strings give developers the ability to either create string data or extract certain elements from strings.

Table 13-1 lists some of the more useful string functions.

Table 13-1. A set of the more commonly used string methods

Function	Description
charAt	Locates and returns a character at a specific location
concat	Concatenates two strings
indexOf	Locates and returns a string from within a string
join	Converts the elements of an array to a string
slice	Extracts a substring from a string
split	Converts a string into an array
string	Converts another data type to String
substr	Returns a substring based on a given length
substring	Returns a substring based on a start and end point
toLowerCase	Converts a string to all lowercase letters
toUpperCase	Converts a string to all uppercase letters

Concatenation

Concatenation is a process in which various pieces of information are joined together to form a string. You have had a fair amount of exposure to concatenation throughout this book. Concatenation takes place when a string and any other type of information is joined together using the additive operator (+) as shown next. If the data type of one of the operands is not a string, it is converted to one when the join takes place.

```
var age:Number = 99;
var aString:String = "I am ";

aString = aString + age; // I am 99
```

Or, in short form:

```
aString += age; // I am 99
```

Don't be deceived by this; the 99 in the string has no numerical value whatsoever. When concatenation occurs, all values are converted to text strings. Therefore, the 99 in the previous example is no more valuable numerically than gg. This is important to understand because, as shown in the following code sample, adding a numeric to a string will always return a string:

```
var answer:* = 2 + "2"; // 22
```

In the previous code we created the variable answer and typed it miscellaneous using the untyped (*) data type. This will prevent a type mismatch, allowing our variable to accept both numeric and string data. When the values 2 and "2" are added together, the resulting data is the string value of "22". This reiterates the fact the numbers in strings have no numerical value at all.

Filtering and deconstructing strings

There are several methods available in ActionScript to extract various parts of strings based on character or location. This becomes extremely valuable when trying to extract information from a set of data that is retrieved in the form of a string. Often many web applications have a tendency to send information as encoded strings. In a situation like this, it is very important to be able to pull only the information that you need from this data. This process of filtering and extracting information from strings is also known as **deconstruction**. The three most commonly used methods for filtering strings are as follows:

- charAt
- substr
- substring

The charAt method is used to retrieve a character at a specific location. For example, when given the following code, if you wanted to retrieve the letters from the string, you could do so by using their location in the string. Starting with zero and including spaces, you would determine that the s was the ninth character in the string. The charAt function could then return the value of s based on that index or position.

```
var aSong:String = "99 bottles of beer on the wall";
aSong.charAt(9); //s
```

13

> We realize that logically speaking it doesn't do much good to have to count spaces and find a character. Compared to counting the letters in a sentence, it is actually easier to simply type the letter you need as its own variable. The preceding example is not the intended use of this function. The idea is that you would have a string of data in which you know where a specific piece of information is supposed to be but not what the value of that information is.

Similarly, the substr and substring methods return a group, or substring, of characters from a given string. These methods work in exactly the same manner with the exception of the second parameter each one accepts. Given the string "ABCDEFGHI", the following example demonstrates how these two methods operate.

The substr method accepts two parameters. The first of these is the starting index of the substring you would like to return. The second is the number of characters that are to be included with the return. Remember, the counting starts at zero.

```
var aString:String = "ABCDEFGHI";
aString.substr(3, 3); // DEF
```

The substring method also accepts two parameters. The first, like the substr method, is the starting point or index of the return value. The second, however, is the ending index. Therefore, this method simply means, "Get me the values between here and here."

```
var aString:String = "ABCDEFGHI";
aString.substring(4, 8); // EFGH
```

Formatting and creating text fields

The text field is the sole vessel for displaying textual data to the client in ActionScript. As mentioned earlier in this chapter, you have already had some exposure to working with text fields. Now we will take a closer look at how ActionScript allows us to apply various styles to text that is displayed within text fields as well as styling the text fields themselves.

TextFormat class

I (Paul) love the TextFormat class! When I think back to when I first began learning to work with text formats in ActionScript 2.0, I can remember thinking how much I hated them. A contradiction, I know. I could never understand why I couldn't simply apply formatting style directly to text fields. The interesting thing is that now that my mindset has changed, the TextFormat class makes it a lot easier to stay organized.

So what is the TextFormat class? Well, it is a special kind of object that contains all specific types of formats that can be applied to a text field. To create a TextFormat object, simply declare a variable and instantiate a new TextFormat class. Once the object is created, you can set the values of the various properties of the TextFormat object as shown here:

```
var tFormat:TextFormat = new TextFormat();
tFormat.font = "Tahoma";
tFormat.size = 24;
tFormat.color = 0xFF00FF;
tFormat.bold = true;
tFormat.align = "right";
```

Table 13-2 is a complete list of properties available through the TextFormat class.

Table 13-2. Properties for the TextFormat class

Property	Description
align	Aligns text
blockIndent	Indents all lines of a given paragraph
bold	Makes text bold
bullet	Converts text to a bulleted list
color	Sets the color of the font
font	Sets the font family to be used
indent	Indents the first letter of a paragraph
italic	Italicizes text
kerning	Sets special character spacing
leading	Sets the line spacing
leftMargin	Sets the left margin of text
letterSpacing	Adds space between characters
rightMargin	Sets the right margin of text
size	Sets the font size
tabStops	Sets the tab positions for text
target	Sets the target for text links
underline	Underlines text
url	Sets the URL of a text link

Assigning formats to text fields

Once the TextFormat object is created, it is very easy to assign the format to a text field. Flash offers two quick means for accomplishing this task. The first of these is to use the defaultTextFormat property, which is a property of the text field itself. As shown in the following code, you can simply set the value of defaultTextFormat as the TextFormat object itself:

```
var tField:TextFiled = new TextField();
tField.defaultTextFormat = tFormat;
```

13

The second way by which you can apply the formatting is to use the setTextFormat method. The setTextFormat method works in a similar manner to the defaultTextFormat property, the primary difference being that instead of assigning the TextFormat object as a value, you pass it as a parameter as shown here:

```
var tField:TextField = new TextField();
tField.setTextFormat(tFormat);
```

There are several other properties available when working with text fields that allow you to change the styling and format of that field directly. Table 13-3 lists a few of the more popular text field properties.

Table 13-3. Formatable properties associated with text fields

Property	Description
autoSize	Resizes text fields to fit text
background	Determines the existence of a background
backgroundColor	Sets the color of the background
border	Determines the existence of a border
borderColor	Sets the border color
defaultTextFormat	Applies a TextFormat object to the text field
multiline	Sets the multiline property
numLines	Sets the number of lines used with multiline text
restrict	Sets a character limit for a text field
selectable	Determines whether text is selectable
styleSheet	Applies a CSS style to a text file
text	Sets the textual value of a text field
textColor	Sets the text color
type	Sets the type of text field
wordWrap	Determines whether text wraps

Adding dynamic text fields to the contact form

The final stop we will make in this chapter will be to add some back-end functionality to our contact form. For this section you may elect to either construct your own back-end functionality or simply follow along with the working files that are associated with this chapter.

To finish the form we are going to need to create a document class that manages some of our additional functionality. The finished class can be found in the working files directory. You may also choose to use the ch13_01_finish.fla file or your saved version of the contact form from earlier in this chapter.

1. To get started, create a new ActionScript file. Save this file in your personal working directory as ContactForm.as.

2. Begin creating the class by adding the following package definition and import statements:

```
package
{
  import flash.display.Sprite;
  import flash.events.FocusEvent;
  import flash.events.MouseEvent;
  import flash.net.*;
  import fl.controls.Button;
  import flash.text.TextFormat;
```

For this class we will use the six imported classes just shown. Because our movie is only one frame, it is best to use Sprite as our display container. The next two import statements will be used to add the various event-based functionalities to the file. We then import the entire flash.net package to allow us to format and send information via URL. Finally, the Button and TextFormat classes are imported to govern our visual elements.

3. Next, enter the following code to define the class, properties, and constructor function:

```
public class ContactForm extends Sprite
{

  private var required:TextField;

  public function ContactForm()
  {
    this.addEventListener(FocusEvent.FOCUS_IN, focus_in);
    this.addEventListener(FocusEvent.FOCUS_OUT, focus_out);
    submit_btn.addEventListener(MouseEvent.CLICK, submit);

    clearFields();
  }
```

13

The class definition is standard. We are extending Sprite; again, this is the most efficient choice because we are only using one frame. At this time we define one private variable, required. This variable will be employed later to reference text fields used for required feedback.

In the constructor function, we define three event listeners. The first two are used to determine when a display object has the stage focus. In this case, we are particularly interested in knowing when the text fields have focus. These listeners are added to the main timeline using the this keyword. Recall that we can use a single set of event listeners to govern all display objects on the stage. The third listener is a simple CLICK event that handles the clicking of the Submit button.

Finally, we call the clearFields() method, which is responsible for clearing textual data from the text fields.

4. Enter the following code to create the handlers for the focus_in and focus_out events:

```
private function focus_in(e:FocusEvent)
{
  var t:TextField = TextField(e.target);
  t.borderColor = 0xFF0000; //Red

  removeChild(required);
}
```

The focus_in function is used to change the border color of any text field when a user focuses on it. In this function, we create the variable t, which is used to cast and reference the event's target as a TextField. The target in this case is any text field that has focus. We then set the border color of the text field to red using the borderColor property of the TextField.

```
private function focus_out(e:FocusEvent)
{
  var t:TextField = TextField(e.target);
  t.borderColor = 0x000000;
}
```

The focus_out function works in exactly the same manner as the focus_in function. We can then use this to change the border color of our text field back to black when a user leaves the text field.

5. Next, create the submit function that will be called by the Submit button's event listener. This method will serve a couple of different purposes.

First, the TextFormat object, errorFormat, is created. We will be creating required field error feedback to let users know that certain text information is required. In the format we set the font color to red and the font weight to bold.

```
private function submit(e:MouseEvent)
{
  var errorFormat:TextFormat = new TextFormat();
  errorFormat.color = 0xFF0000; //Red
  errorFormat.bold = true;
```

The next block of code in this function is used to create the text field itself. Once the field is created, we set its textual property to read Required Field. We then apply the errorCode format to the text field, which makes the text bold and red. Finally, we set the x position to 150 so we can have this text display next to the static fields we created in our form.

```
required = new TextField();
required.text = "Required Field";
required.setTextFormat(errorFormat);
required.x = 150;
```

We then check for required fields. This is a simple task that uses an if statement to determine whether or not our input fields contain text. If they do not contain any information, the subsequent code block executes. Within this code block we set the y value of the required text field to a position just to the right of the static text for that given input field. We then use addChild() to place the required field on the stage. The return keyword is used as a stop or break in this sequence. When the program comes across this, it will immediately stop executing the remaining code in this method.

In this example we are checking four of the five fields for valid information.

```
if(firstName.text == "")
{
  required.y = firstName.y - 21;
  addChild(required);
  return;
}

if(lastName.text == "")
{
  required.y = lastName.y - 21;
  addChild(required);
  return;
}

if(phone.text == "")
{
  required.y = phone.y - 21;
  addChild(required);
  return;
}
```

13

```
if(address.text == "")
{
    required.y = address.y - 21;
    addChild(required);
    return;
}
```

Finally, we call the two methods sendInfo() and clearFields(), which are both declared next. Because we used the return keyword throughout the function, these two methods are called only if all required information is completed.

```
sendInfo();
clearFields();

}
```

6. Create the clearfields() function as shown next. The clearFields function is used to reset the values of all the text fields.

```
private function clearFields()
{
    firstName.text = "";
    lastName.text = "";
    phone.text = "";
    address.text = "";
    comments.text = "";
}
```

7. The last method in this class is the sendInfo() function. And though it may seem a bit complicated at first, the following code is really nothing more than a simple URLRequest like those created in Chapter 11:

```
private function sendInfo()
{
    var url:String = "http://www.friendsofed.com/EssGuideFlashCS4/ur.php";
    var ur:URLRequest = new URLRequest(url);
        ur.method = URLRequestMethod.GET;

    var uv:URLVariables = new URLVariables();
        uv.fn = firstName.text;
        uv.ln = lastName.text;
        uv.ph = phone.text;
        uv.ad = address.text;
        uv.co = comments.text;

    ur.data = uv;

    navigateToURL(ur);
}
```

```
} // Close Class
} // Close Package
```

The first three lines in this method set up the URLRequest itself. The string variable url is used to reference the location of the web script where we will be receiving the information from our form. We declare the URLRequest (ur) and pass it the url variable. We then set the method property of the URLRequest object to URLRequestMethod.GET. Recall in Chapter 11 that we discussed the difference between sending information via GET or POST; the GET method will send information as part of the query string.

The next part of this function involves packaging the variable data for the URLRequest. We first create the URLVariables object (uv) and assign the current values of our text fields to properties of the uv object. Remember, these property names are completely arbitrary. Once the values are set, we can assign the uv object as the value of the ur.data property. This will effectively package the URLVariable with the URLRequest.

Finally, we use the navigateToURL() method to have our browsers navigate to the previously defined URL. We pass this function the URLRequest object as its parameter. This ensures that all information required for the request is packaged and included.

8. Once you have completed this function, save the AS file and test your FLA. Go ahead and fill out the form and click the Submit button. If you failed to provide the information correctly, you will get a notification as shown in Figure 13-18. If you did fill the form out correctly, you will be taken to a page that will display your information.

Figure 13-18.
Failing to properly fill in the form will prompt ActionScript to create an error message.

13

Summary

Though often overlooked, proper use of fonts is often just what an application needs to achieve that final look of professionalism. In mainstream development, it is not uncommon for developers to simply slap a few text fields on the stage and begin passing information to them. The reality is that text layout is as aesthetically important to a design as the most vibrant of colors.

In addition to good looks, it should not go without mention that a mastery of string data is essential to any great application developer's bag of tricks.

The following are the important topics covered in this chapter:

- Formatting, rendering, and modifying text fields
- Embedding characters
- Breaking apart text fields
- Concatenation, filtering, and deconstruction of strings
- Creating and formatting text fields with the TextField and TextFormat classes

CHAPTER 14

USING COMPONENTS

Components can be though of as premade, purpose-built mini-applications, or widgets of a sort. They come in all shapes and sizes. Some are made by Adobe and are included with Flash, others are made by the Flash community or other companies (third parties), and still others might possibly come from you after reading this chapter! In short, components give you, the Flash author, a quick way of including complex functionality in your applications quickly and consistently.

In this chapter we're going to talk about

- Compiled vs. FLA components
- Flash UI components
- Adding components to your applications
- Configuring components
- Listening to components

Understanding components

In the context of Flash, a component is a movie clip or compiled clip that the Flash developer can drag out of the Components panel into an FLA file or add to his or her application using ActionScript. Components expose parameters that can be set in the Parameters tab of the Property inspector or in the Component inspector. This lets nondeveloper types quickly and easily implement the component (whatever it may be) without having to know any ActionScript!

SWC-based components

SWC-based components are made of an FLA file and an ActionScript class file that have been compiled and exported together as a SWC. When you put a SWC-based component onto your stage, a compiled clip that cannot be edited is added to your library.

> *If you want to have a peek at the guts of a SWC-based component, just rename the file extension to .zip and open the file with your archive utility of choice.*

An advantage to using a SWC-based component is that it allows you to save some time and avoid recompiling symbols and code that will not change.

The downside, of course, is that the symbols and code can't change, so if you want to change anything that falls outside of the parameters available in the Component inspector, you're out of luck.

FLA-based components

FLA-based components are FLA files with built-in skins that you can access for editing by double-clicking such a component on the stage. When you put an FLA-based component onto your stage, all of the symbols that make up the component are added to your library and are available for you to edit.

The advantage to using FLA-based components is that you can easily manipulate the visual appearance of the component within the Flash environment. The downside might be that if you are using this type of component, all of your code and assets will be out there for everyone to see.

> The Adobe UI components are FLA components that include a SWC-based component to hold all of their ActionScript, allowing you to modify the visual elements without disrupting the code.

The component architecture reuses components by combining them with others to make more complex components. This includes not only visual assets, but also the ActionScript that the components use. This reuse results in a smaller file footprint when using many types of components in your application.

Tour de Components

Now that you have a little background info on components, let's have a look at the various groups of components included with Flash CS4. If you are targeting the Flash Player using AS 2, the components available to you will be different from those you would see if you are targeting the Flash Player using AS 3.

> You cannot mix ActionScript 2.0 components with ActionScript 3.0 components in an application.

Because this book is focused primarily on ActionScript 3.0, we will introduce you to each of the AS 3 components and what its main purpose is.

You will find the components in the aptly named Components panel, shown here in Figure 14-1. You can open the Components panel by selecting Window ➤ Components from the application menu or by pressing Ctrl+F7 (or Cmd+F7 on a Mac).

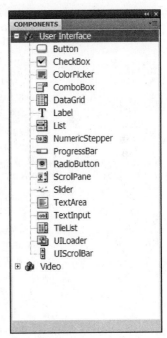

Figure 14-1. The User Interface group of components

14

User interface components

The user interface components shown in Figure 14-1 include the most common controls required when creating an application that deals with standard forms and data, such as text fields for entering data and buttons that can be used to let the user tell an application to submit or retrieve data.

There are many options for each component that can be configured using either the Components inspector or Property inspector, or through ActionScript. While we can't cover all these options in one chapter, we'll show you a few examples in the section of this chapter called "Configuring components in Flash."

The components that make up the User Interface group include the following:

- Button: Represents an element a user can press that initiates an action. While it can display a label or tooltip, it isn't used for presenting data.

- CheckBox: Represents a square that the user "checks" to indicate true. Components of this type can be grouped to provide an array of values.

- ColorPicker: Lets a user select a color from a grid of color boxes called a swatch list.

- ComboBox: Presents a list of options to the user for selection and can optionally include multiple selections.

- DataGrid: Presents data to the user in a table format, with each column having a heading that when clicked will raise an event that allows sorting on the column and cells that can display data or even other controls for input.

- Label: Presents text and can have properties to control font, size, color, and so forth.

- List: Presents a list of items. Usually this component contains text, but it can include images or other controls.

- NumericStepper: Provides an easy-to-use control for "stepping" up or down in numbers by a set number of "steps." For example, clicking the up arrow on a numeric stepper will change the input values by an increment set in the stepper for the step value.

- ProgressBar: Displays the progress of a background process that updates the component as it goes.

- RadioButton: Displays as filled when clicked, or true, and empty when false. This round component is typically grouped, with each option being unique to the group.

- ScrollPane: Represents an area on the screen that can display a larger image or movie/SWF file than is available by allowing scrolling.

- Slider: Allows the user to select from a range of values by sliding the control bar from one end to the other.

- TextArea: Allows entry of multiple lines of text, with optional scrollbars.

- TextInput: Allows entry of one line of text with input limits.

- TileList: Allows creation of a fixed or dynamic grid of other components such as a table of images in a "tiled" format.

- UILoader: Functions like a component without a visible part and allows you to load components and monitor the progress.

- UIScrollBar: Adds scrolling to other components or new components you may develop.

Video components

Components in the Video group of the Components panel include those that aid in the playback of video and provide captioning, as well as custom video controls like a volume slider or Play button. The components that make up the Video group, shown in Figure 14-2, include the following:

- FLVPlayback: Allows the Flash author to quickly and easily integrate video into his or her application. It combines a video player with play controls. For more information about using the FLVPlayback component, see Chapter 17.

- FLVPlaybackCaptioning: Allows you to synchronize specially formatted text documents with video playback. For more information about using the FLVPlaybackCaptioning component, see Chapter 17.

- **FLV custom UI components**: These components can be used to create custom controls for the FLVPlayback component:

  - BackButton: Seeks to the closest navigation cue point prior to the current playhead location. If your video is at 6:13 and there is a navigation cue point at 5:02 (and no other navigation cue points in between), clicking the BackButton will make the FLVPlayback component seek to 5:02 in the video.

  - BufferingBar: Represents an animated clip that is triggered when the FLVPlayback component enters the Buffering state.

  - CaptionButton: Toggles off and on closed captions provided by the FLVCaptionComponent.

  - ForwardButton: Causes the FLVPlayback component to seek to the next navigation cue point in a given video.

  - FullScreenButton: Causes the associated FLVPlayback component to enter full-screen mode.

  - MuteButton: Changes the volume of the audio for a video playing in the FLVPlayback component to 0.

  - PauseButton: Pauses playback of the associated FLVPlayback component.

  - PlayButton: Begins or resumes playback of the associated FLVPlayback component.

  - PlayPauseButton: Represents a toggle that combines both the PauseButton and PlayButton components.

  - SeekBar: Displays the progress of a video playing in the associated FLVPlayback component and can be made to allow the user to seek to other parts of the video by clicking it or dragging a handle.

14

- **StopButton:** Stops playback of the associate FLVPlayback component and returns its video to the beginning.

- **VolumeBar:** Allows the user to control the volume of the audio of the associated FLVPlayback component.

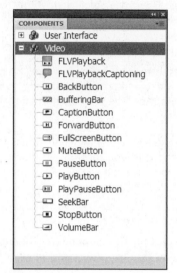

Figure 14-2.
The Video group of components

Using the video components is covered in depth in Chapter 17.

Third-party components

The list of third-party components is vast, and certainly we can't cover even a small number of the third-party components available. What we can do is tell you where to find them and what to expect when you install them.

The best place to find third-party components is on the Adobe Flash Exchange web site. Install third-party components at your own risk, and understand that not all third-party components are created equally. Some are tested more thoroughly than others, and there are varying degrees of reliability as well.

One way to distribute components is with an MXP file. While an in-depth discussion of MXP files is beyond the scope of this book, follow these brief instructions for installing and removing extensions.

The packaged Flash extension comes in the form of an MXP file. In order to use such files, you will need the Adobe Extension Manager, which comes with your installation of Flash CS4. The Adobe Extension Manager, shown here Figure 14-3, will allow you to install, remove, and otherwise keep track all of the extensions you have applied to Flash.

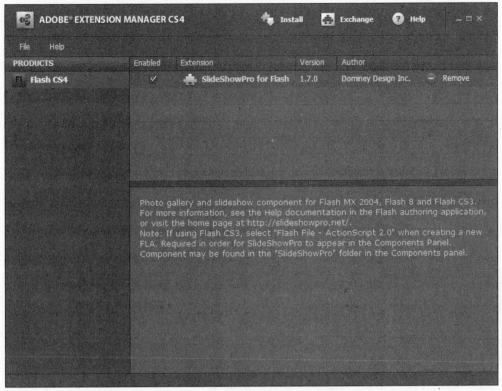

Figure 14-3. The Adobe Extension Manager allows you to manage extensions installed to all of your Adobe CS4 software. You can find this tool in your Start menu (Windows) or Applications folder (Mac).

To install a third-party extension, simply double-click the MXP file and follow the instructions given by the Adobe Extension Manager. To remove an extension, open the Adobe Extension Manager and select Remove on the row of the extension you wish to remove.

Now that you know more about the various types of components and their uses, let's look at how to add them to your application.

Adding components to your application

Generally speaking, there are two ways to get components into your applications; either by placing them on stage in Flash or through ActionScript. In this section we talk about how to do both.

14

Adding components to your application in Flash

To add a component to your application in the Flash authoring environment, either double-click the component in the Components panel or simply drag that component onto the stage. Double-clicking the component will add that component to the horizontal and vertical center of your visible document window. Figure 14-4 shows what happens when we double-click the Button component in the Components panel.

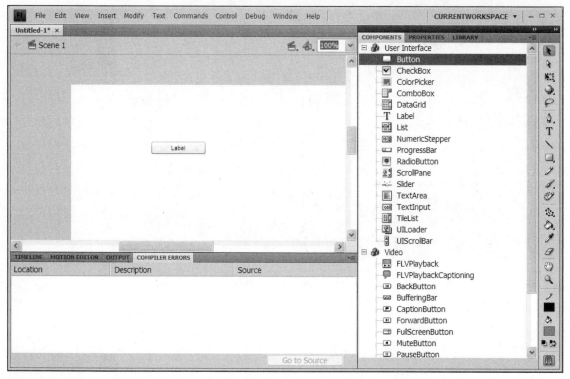

Figure 14-4. When you double-click a component in the Components panel, it will get placed smack in the center of your document window.

Adding components to your application using ActionScript

To add a component to your application using ActionScript is pretty straightforward. Whether you use a document class file (recommended as a best practice) or have your code in the FLA file itself, you *must* have a copy of the component you wish to add to your application in your library. In this example of a document class file, we add a ComboBox component and a Button component to the stage. Figure 14-5 shows the library of our file.

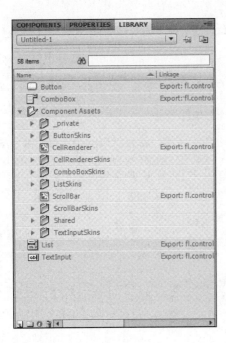

Figure 14-5.
Even though we only placed a ComboBox and Button component on stage, notice that the components used to make them, the List and TextInput components, appear in the Library panel as well.

```
package {

    import flash.display.MovieClip;
    import fl.controls.ComboBox;
    import fl.controls.Button;

    public class AddingComponents_AS extends MovieClip{

        public function AddingComponents_AS()     {
            var myCBox:fl.controls.ComboBox = new ComboBox();
            addChild(myCBox);

            var aButton:Button = new Button();
            this.addChild(aButton);
            aButton.label = "On/Off";
            aButton.toggle =true;
            aButton.move(50, 50);


        }
    }
}
```

Being able to add components to your application is nice; but what's nicer is being able to make them do stuff! So let's talk about controlling components.

14

Controlling components

When we talk about *controlling* components, we really mean two things: controlling what they do (configuring) and controlling what they look like (skinning).

Configuring components in Flash

By now you know that every component is different and built for a specific purpose. What they all have in common, however, is the Component inspector. When you select a component, the Component inspector changes to reflect the properties of that component that are configurable in Flash.

> *The* Bindings *and* Schema *tabs of the* Component inspector *serve no purpose when working on applications that use ActionScript 3.0.*

To configure a component in Flash, add it to the stage and open the Component inspector by pressing Shift+F7 or selecting Window ➤ Component Inspector. Select the component you wish to configure. Figure 14-6 shows the Component inspector for the ComboBox component.

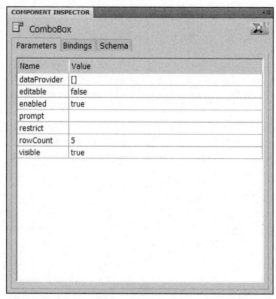

Figure 14-6. The Component inspector lets the Flash author configure a component without needing to use ActionScript.

Using the Component inspector

To configure a component, you'll need to understand the Component inspector. Since this book is focused primarily on ActionScript 3.0, we will limit our discussion to the Parameters tab of the Component inspector, as the Bindings and Schema tabs do not apply to ActionScript 3.0 projects.

The Parameters tab of the Component inspector is a panel divided into two columns, Name and Value. The Name column lists all of the parameters available for author-time configuration of the component. The Value column shows the default values for each of those parameters. Clicking into the Value column next to a parameter name will allow you to change the value assigned to that parameter.

> *Although we are talking about setting* parameter *values in the* Parameters *tab, what you are really doing in this panel is setting values of properties of the component's class.*

It's important to understand that the values you can assign to parameters are often limited. For instance, some can only have a value of True or False (Boolean), and others may only be allowed to be numbers. In any event, the Component inspector will provide you with an input method that best suits the type of value that can be entered—a drop-down menu for selecting between three possible alignment options, for instance.

Some parameters, like the source parameter of the Loader component, give you a free-form text box, while the source parameter of the FLVPlayback component will prompt you with a Content Path dialog. Let the Component inspector guide you.

When setting values for the dataProvider parameter, you will use yet another form of data entry called the Values dialog (which we discuss in the upcoming exercise).

Follow these steps to configure an instance of the ComboBox parameter with the options sometimes, always, and never:

1. Add a ComboBox component to an open FLA file by double-clicking the ComboBox component in the Components panel or by dragging it onto the stage.

2. Open the Component inspector. Make sure the ComboBox component you put on stage is selected.

3. Either double-click the value field of the dataProvider parameter or single click it, and then click the magnifying glass icon that appears next to it, as shown in Figure 14-7. You should now see the Values dialog, as shown in Figure 14-8.

Figure 14-7.
If you single-click the dataProvider parameter, use this magnifying glass icon to launch the Values dialog.

14

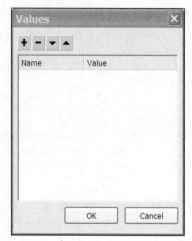

Figure 14-8.
An empty Values dialog
shows there is no data in the
dataProvider for this component.

4. Use the Add button (plus icon) to add a new label/data pair to your ComboBox component. The default name of the label/data pair you just added is label0. The name of the label/data pair merely reflects the value of its label property.

5. Click the Value column next to the label property and enter the text sometimes. Notice that the name of the label/data pair has changed to sometimes. You can collapse and expand the label/data pair by clicking the small triangle next to the label/data pair's name.

6. Click the Value column next to the data property and enter the number 1.

Repeat steps 4 through 6 until you have three label/data pairs with the labels sometimes, always, and never and values 1, 2, and 0, respectively, as shown in Figure 14-9.

Figure 14-9.
The Values dialog after some
data has been entered

7. Test your movie by selecting Control ➤ Test Movie or pressing Ctrl+Enter or Cmd+Enter on a Mac.

You should see a ComboBox component on stage that, when you click it, drops down a menu with the options sometimes, always, and never as we show in Figure 14-10.

Figure 14-10.
If you do not specify a value for the prompt parameter, the first item in the dataProvider will be the default selection.

Clearly there is much more to be done if we want this ComboBox to do anything worthwhile, and we will as we incorporate it into the activities that follow in the chapter.

Let's begin by making one small adjustment to it using the Component inspector before we move to ActionScript; we'll change the prompt—the default text that appears in the ComboBox as a nonselectable item. Having a prompt is considered good form when making your applications usable since it tells your users what the combo box is for.

To set the prompt of a ComboBox component, click the Value column of the prompt parameter in the Component inspector. Enter some meaningful text—in this case how often?—and test your movie again. You will notice that the ComboBox now appears with the text how often?, as you see in Figure 14-11.

Figure 14-11.
Use the prompt parameter to tell your users what type of data is in the drop-down menu before they have to open it.

Configuring components using ActionScript

In this section we're going to create a form using three TextInput components (and three Label components to label them) and a Button component. The form will be used to configure our ComboBox component from the previous section of this chapter. You might use this approach in the case where you have a multipage form for which data entered on one page might need to be reflected in the drop-down menu options on another.

The Flash UI components follow the usual convention of making properties, methods, and events available to the Flash developer through ActionScript, so if you want a little refresher, refer to Chapter 8 for the ActionScript primer and Chapter 9 for more on event-based ActionScript.

Creating an application using the document class

Throughout this book we have been encouraging you to go through the exercise of creating a document class for your FLA files and putting all of your ActionScript there, and this example is no exception.

14

To create an application using the document class, follow these steps:

1. Save your FLA (previously unnamed) from the previous section as menuForm.FLA and set the document class to MenuForm.

> *Set the document class in the document's* Property inspector, *as shown in Figure 14-12.*

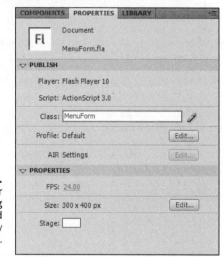

Figure 14-12.
Creating document classes for your Flash projects rather than putting ActionScript on the timeline is a good habit to get into. Use the Property inspector to define the document class.

2. Create a new AS file by selecting File ➤ New from the application menu (or by pressing Ctrl+N, or Cmd+N on a Mac) and then selecting New ActionScript file from the New Document window. Add the following ActionScript to the file and save it as MenuForm.AS:

```
package{
  import flash.display.MovieClip
  public class MenuForm extends MovieClip{
    public function MenuForm(){
      trace("menu form!"); //menu form!
    }
  }
}
```

3. Test your movie and make sure that menu form! appears in the Output window.

Creating the form

To simplify this example, we'll dispense with the code involved in laying out a form using ActionScript. We're going to add our form elements to the stage in Flash, and then configure them using ActionScript in our document class file.

To create the form, follow these steps:

1. Drag a TextInput component from the Components panel to the stage. Give it an instance name of item1input.

2. Drag a Label component from the Components panel to the stage.

3. Align the Label component with the TextInput component.

4. Select the Label component and open the Component inspector. In the Value column of the text parameter, enter the text item 1, as shown in Figure 14-13.

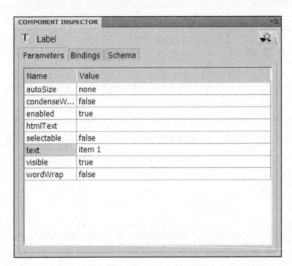

Figure 14-13.
The Component inspector for the Label component

Your stage should now look something like Figure 14-14.

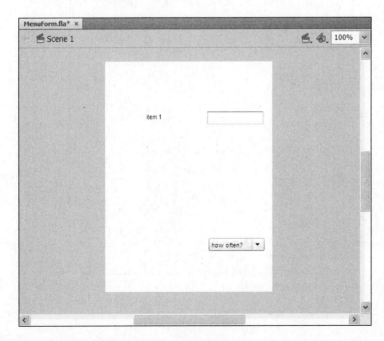

Figure 14-14.
Our initial layout

14

5. Select both the Label and the TextInput components and press Ctrl+C or Cmd+C on a Mac to copy them. Press Ctrl+Shift+V or Cmd+Shift+V to paste in place.

6. With the copies selected (they will be selected after you paste in place), press Shift+down arrow three times. (This will move them down 30 pixels, which should be enough to move them clear of the originals.)

7. With the copies still selected, repeat steps 5 and 6.

8. All of your labels will read item 1 at this point. Using the method from step 4, change the labels so they read item 1, item 2, and item 3 from top to bottom.

9. All of your TextInput component instances will be named item1input. Change their instance names so that they are item1input, item2input, and item3input from top to bottom.

10. Make sure your ComboBox has an instance name so you can address it in code—we named ours myCombo.

11. Finally, drag a Button component from the Component inspector to the stage, place it under your three text input fields, and give it an instance name of submitBtn.

12. Select the Button component. In the Value column of the label parameter on the Component inspector, change the text parameter to Submit.

Your stage should now look something like Figure 14-15.

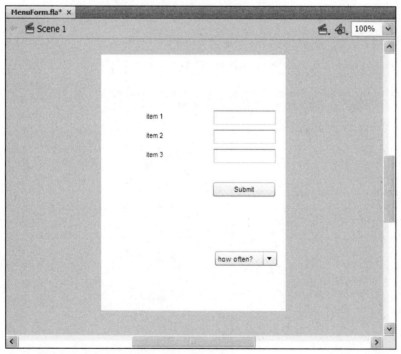

Figure 14-15. The finished layout of our simple form

Well now, isn't that lovely? Aside from setting a few parameters in the Component inspector, though, we haven't done anything spectacularly component-like, so let's make this form do something.

Making the form do something—listening to components

The goal here is to populate the ComboBox component with the values in the TextInput components when the Button component is clicked. The first step is getting our little application to listen for the button click. The following code shows how we import the flash. events.* package, add an event listener for the CLICK event, and create a handler function for the event:

```
package{
    import flash.display.MovieClip;

    // need to import these classes to listen for the event
    import flash.events.*;

    public class MenuForm extends MovieClip{

      public function MenuForm(){
        trace("menu form");
        // here we add a listener for the CLICK event
        addEventListener(MouseEvent.CLICK, handleClick);
      }

      // this function will execute when any object that broadcasts
      // the CLICK event is clicked.
      private function handleClick(e:MouseEvent){
          // this tells us who was clicked
        trace(e.target.name)
      }
    }
  }
```

Now that we can hear the clicking of the Submit button, what are we going do about it? With the following additions to the code (in bold), we're going to import the fl.controls. ComboBox class in order to configure the component in ActionScript, import the fl.Data. DataProvider class to create and manipulate the ComboBox's dataProvider, and lastly, quickly check to make sure that it's the Submit button being clicked before we go making any changes to our ComboBox:

```
package{
    import flash.display.MovieClip;
    import flash.events.*;

    // importing the necessary classes
    import fl.controls.ComboBox;
    import fl.data.DataProvider;
```

14

```
public class MenuForm extends MovieClip{

    // declare the data provder
    private var theDataProvider:DataProvider;

    public function MenuForm(){
      trace("menu form");
      // create the data provider
      theDataProvider = new DataProvider();
      addEventListener(MouseEvent.CLICK, handleClick);
    }
    private function handleClick(e:MouseEvent){

      // make sure it's the Submit button being clicked
      if(e.target.name == "submitBtn"){

        // clear any old data
        theDataProvider.removeAll();

        // adding new data for the ComboBox, these label/value pairs
        // are what you set in the Value dialog when changing the
        // dataProvider parameter in the Component inspector!
        theDataProvider.addItem({label:item1input.text, value:0});
        theDataProvider.addItem({label:item2input.text, value:1});
        theDataProvider.addItem({label:item3input.text, value:2});

        // finally set the dataProvider property of the
        // component the DataProvider instance we created
        // here - 'theDataProvider'
        myCombo.dataProvider = theDataProvider;
      }
    }
  }
}
```

When you test your movie, you should be able to enter text in the three TextInput components, click the Submit button, and see your new text in the drop-down of the ComboBox.

Now that you have your feet wet with making some components work, let's look at how to change their appearance using both the Flash CS4 authoring environment and ActionScript.

Skinning components in Flash

Skinning components should really be called *modifying the skins of components*. All of the assets that make up the visual appearance of all of the states of the components in your application are available to you in Flash as soon as you drag them onto the stage (or into your library).

As an example, open a new FLA file and add a UIScrollBar component to the stage. In the library, look in Component Assets ➤ ScrollBarSkins to see all of the symbols that make up all of the states for that component (or just look at Figure 14-16).

Figure 14-16. All of the skins that represent the various states of all of the parts of a scrollbar

Let's return to the FLA, menuForm.FLA, from the previous example to demonstrate how quickly you can modify a component's skin.

To quickly change the rollover color for the ComboBox component, follow these steps:

1. Open menuForm.FLA and save it as skinning_menuForm.FLA.

2. Double-click the ComboBox component on stage, and you will see the ComboBox skin palette screen shown in Figure 14-17.

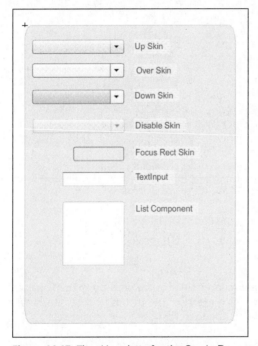

Figure 14-17. The skin palette for the ComboBox component. Notice that the List and TextInput components are included.

3. Double-click the symbol on stage labeled Over Skin.

4. Select the fill shape and change the color.

5. Test your movie.

You'll see that when you roll over the ComboBox on stage, the color now changes to the one you selected; but hold on, when you open the drop-down menu and roll over the menu items, the color has *not* changed. Why not?

14

The reason is because the drop-down menu of the ComboBox component is really a List component, and the List component uses the cell renderer skins to control the visual appearance of its items. Let's look at how to change that now.

To quickly change the rollover color for the items in the drop-down menu of a ComboBox component, follow these steps:

1. Open menuForm.FLA and save it as skinning_menuForm.FLA.
2. Double-click the ComboBox component on stage.
3. Double-click the symbol on stage labeled List Component.
4. Double-click the symbol on stage labeled Cell Renderer skins, and you will see the screen shown in Figure 14-18.

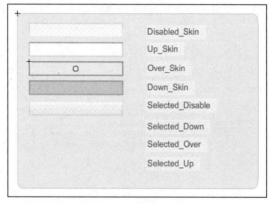

Figure 14-18. The cell renderer skins

5. Double-click the symbol on stage labeled Over_Skin.
6. Select the fill shape and change the color.
7. Test your movie.

Now you will see that the rollover color of the drop-down menu has changed to the color you selected in the preceding exercise. The trick is to be aware of what components are made of other components and therefore use their visual assets.

Skinning components using ActionScript

Because components are often made by reusing other components, they share the same visual assets—which is usually a good thing—unless of course you want the rollover color of your ComboBox component to be different from the rollover color of your List component. Or what if you wanted different instances of the same component to look different?

You saw in the previous section that the ComboBox uses the List component's cell renderer skins for its drop-down menus, so how can you change one without affecting the other? By using ActionScript, that's how.

Component style definitions

Style definitions dictate not only the size and placement of elements like text within a component, but also which skin assets to use for various states of a component.

The following code, which comes from the Flash documentation (http://help.adobe.com/en_US/AS3LCR/Flash_10.0/index.html), creates a style browser that lets you easily see what properties make up the style definition for many of the UI components. Paste this code into the Actions panel on the first frame of an FLA and make sure you have a ComboBox component and DataGrid component in your library. This collection of code will save you some time trying to track down what properties can be changed using the setStyle() method of the UI components. Figure 14-19 shows the style browser that the following code generates.

```
import fl.controls.*;
import fl.containers.*;
import fl.controls.listClasses.*;
import fl.controls.dataGridClasses.*;
import fl.controls.progressBarClasses.*;
import fl.core.UIComponent;
import fl.data.DataProvider;

var dp:DataProvider = new DataProvider();
dp.addItem( { label: "BaseScrollPane",   data:BaseScrollPane } );
dp.addItem( { label: "Button",            data:Button } );
dp.addItem( { label: "CellRenderer",     data:CellRenderer } );
dp.addItem( { label: "CheckBox",          data:CheckBox } );
dp.addItem( { label: "ColorPicker",      data:ColorPicker } );
dp.addItem( { label: "ComboBox",          data:ComboBox } );
dp.addItem( { label: "DataGrid",          data:DataGrid } );
dp.addItem( { label: "HeaderRenderer",    data:HeaderRenderer } );
dp.addItem( { label: "ImageCell",         data:ImageCell } );
dp.addItem( { label: "IndeterminateBar",data:IndeterminateBar } );
dp.addItem( { label: "Label",             data:Label } );
dp.addItem( { label: "List",              data:List } );
dp.addItem( { label: "NumericStepper",    data:NumericStepper } );
dp.addItem( { label: "ProgressBar",      data:ProgressBar } );
dp.addItem( { label: "RadioButton",      data:RadioButton } );
dp.addItem( { label: "ScrollPane",        data:ScrollPane } );
dp.addItem( { label: "Slider",            data:Slider } );
dp.addItem( { label: "TextArea",         data:TextArea } );
dp.addItem( { label: "TextInput",         data:TextInput } );
dp.addItem( { label: "TileList",         data:TileList } );
dp.addItem( { label: "UILoader",          data:UILoader } );
dp.addItem( { label: "UIComponent",       data:UIComponent } );

var cb:ComboBox = new ComboBox();
cb.move(10,10);
cb.setSize(300,25);
cb.prompt = "Select a component to view its styles";
```

14

```
cb.rowCount = 12;
cb.dataProvider = dp;
cb.addEventListener(Event.CHANGE, showStyleDefinition);
addChild(cb);

var dg:DataGrid = new DataGrid();
dg.setSize(425,300);
dg.move(10,50);
dg.columns = [ new DataGridColumn("StyleName"), new DataGridColumn➥
("DefaultValue") ];
addChild(dg);

function showStyleDefinition(e:Event):void {
  var componentClass:Class = e.target.selectedItem.data as Class;
  var styles:Object = componentClass["getStyleDefinition"].call(this);
  trace(styles.toString());
  var styleData:DataProvider = new DataProvider();
  for(var i:* in styles) {
    trace(i + " : " + styles[i]);
    styleData.addItem( { StyleName:i, DefaultValue:styles[i] } );
  }
  styleData.sortOn("StyleName");
  dg.dataProvider = styleData;
}
```

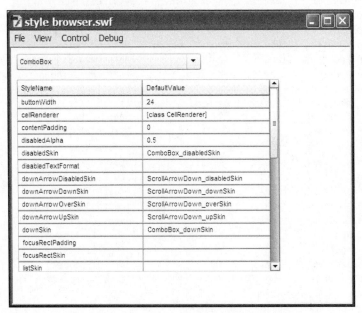

Figure 14-19. The style browser created with the code found at http://help. adobe.com/en_US/AS3LCR/Flash_10.0/index.html

Component styles work at three different levels. Using setStyle() or setComponentStyle(), you can

- Change the style of all Adobe UI components used in your application.
- Change the style of all of one type of component in your application—all of your Button instances, for example.
- Change the style of an instance of a component in your application.

To change the style of all components used in your application, use the following convention:

```
StyleManager.setStyle("textFormat", myTextFmt);
```

What you do not see in this example is that you need to import the StyleManager class in your code (which we show how to do in the next exercise) and that a TextFormat object named myTextFmt has been created.

To change the style of all of one type of component in your application, use the following convention:

```
StyleManager.setComponentStyle(Button, "textFormat", myTextFmt);
```

What you do not see in this example is that you need to have the class for the component you're trying to change imported in your code and that a TextFormat object named myTextFmt has been created. You also need to have the StyleManager class imported (which, again, we will show how to do in the next exercise).

To change the style of an instance of a component in your application, use the following convention:

```
instanceName.setStyle("styleName", value);
```

Let's look at one last example to demonstrate the flexibility we have with skinning components. We're going to build on the simple form we made earlier in the chapter and change the text formatting of our TextInput components (component-wide style change). Then we'll change the focus rectangle color of each TextInput component to be different from the others (instance-level style change).

To make component-wide style changes as well as instance-level style changes, follow these steps:

1. Open menuForm.FLA and save it as styles_menuForm.FLA. Change its document class to StylesMenuForm.

2. Open MenuForm.AS and save it as StylesMenuForm.AS. Change the class name and constructor function to match as shown here in bold:

```
public class StylesMenuForm extends MovieClip{
    private var theDataProvider:DataProvider;
    public function StylesMenuForm(){
```

14

3. In StylesMenuForm.AS import the StyleManager class, TextInput class, and the TextFormat class using the following code:

```
import fl.controls.TextInput;
import fl.managers.StyleManager;
import flash.text.TextFormat;
```

4. Add the following code to the constructor function of StylesMenuForm.AS to apply a component-wide change to the text formatting of the TextInput component:

```
var myTxtFmt:TextFormat = new TextFormat();
myTxtFmt.color = 0x1234FF; //Blue!
myTxtFmt.font = "Arial";

StyleManager.setComponentStyle(TextInput, "textFormat", myTxtFmt);
```

5. Add the following code to the constructor function to change the skin clip that's used for each TextInput component's instance in the focus state. The parameters customFocus1, customFocus2, and customFocus3, shown in bold, refer to clips in the library of styles_MenuForm.FLA, which we have not created yet. What we're doing here is telling each instance of the TextInput component individually what skin clip (e.g., customFocus1 for item1input) to use when it enters the focus state.

```
item1input.setStyle("focusRectSkin", customFocus1);
item2input.setStyle("focusRectSkin", customFocus2);
item3input.setStyle("focusRectSkin", customFocus3);
```

Now let's create the custom focus clips in styles_MenuForm.FLA.

6. Open styles_menuForm.FLA, in the library browse to Component Assets ➤ Shared, and find the focusRectSkin movie clip.

7. Right-click (or Ctrl-click on a Mac) the focusRectSkin movie clip and select Duplicate from the menu. Name the new clip customFocus1.

8. In the Linkage section of the Duplicate Symbol dialog, select the Export for ActionScript option. The class should auto-populate with the name of the symbol.

9. Repeat steps 7 and 8 to create customFocus2 and customFocus3.

10. Edit each of the new symbols so that the color of the border shape shown in Figure 14-20 is different for each symbol.

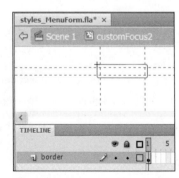

Figure 14-20.
Changing the color of
the border graphic for
the customFocus2 skin

11. Test your movie.

Click into each TextInput component and notice that the focus rectangle for each is a different color. You might also notice that the text of the ComboBox is now blue instead of black. Why do you think that is? If you guessed that it's blue because the ComboBox component uses the TextInput component for the prompt, you would be correct!

If you wanted the TextInput components to have a different text style from that of the ComboBox prompt text, you'd need to set the TextFormat style at the *instance* level for each TextInput component.

Summary

Many components are available for Flash, and there are many, many things you can do with them. It is our hope that you are now comfortable enough with components to use them effectively in your work.

In this chapter we talked about

- The types of component architectures
- The array of UI and video components available in Flash CS4
- How to add components to your application using Flash or ActionScript
- How to control the configuration, behavior, and appearance of the components you use through the Flash authoring environment and through ActionScript

14

PART FIVE

ENHANCED MEDIA DEVELOPMENT

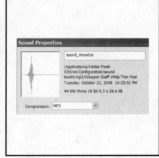

The new Adobe Media Encoder CS4 combines the most useful functions of the Flash Video Encoder, the Flash CS3 Video Import Wizard, and the Adobe Media Encoder found in Adobe Premiere CS3 into one stand-alone tool.

It will output files compatible with devices such as an iPod PSP and many others and has a handy list of presets to help get you started. You no longer have the option of using Flash to convert video using the Flash CS4 Video Import Wizard. If you try to import video that is not in a format that the Flash Player can play back, Flash will let you know that the player cannot play back media in that format and direct you to try using the Media Encoder to convert the video to a format the Flash Player can play and/or add cue points to the video file.

In this chapter we'll tour the interface of the Adobe Media Encoder and show you how to encode your video using presets as well as using some custom settings. We'll also talk briefly about what the advanced settings mean and show you how to add cue points and metadata directly to the video. Let's begin with the interface.

Introduction to the interface

The Media Encoder interface is deceptively simple when you open it (see Figure 15-1). It looks a lot like the Flash CS3 Video Encoder—but there's plenty more under the hood.

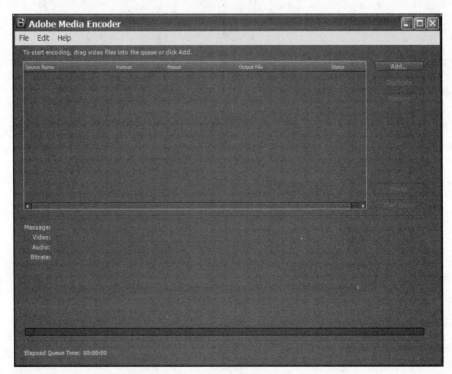

Figure 15-1. The Queue window of the Adobe Media Encoder

The top half is the **queue**—it's a list of all the media you have waiting to be encoded. It shows you the source file path, the video format you've chosen to encode to, the preset (or custom settings) being used, the output file path, and the status of that file.

To the right of the queue are the five following buttons, which manage the items in the queue and whether the queue is running or not:

- Add
- Duplicate
- Remove
- Pause
- Start Queue

We'll use these buttons later in this chapter.

Figure 15-2 displays the bottom half of this screen of the interface, which shows you information about what is being encoded at any given moment. Below that section is a sliver of the interface reserved for showing you how long the queue has been running in total.

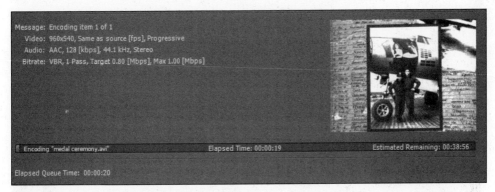

Figure 15-2. Basic information about the status of the queue

So with that very brief description of the interface, let's encode some video! (Hey, it's a crash course, right?)

Encoding your first video using presets

Most of us will just need to pull out the old encoder to convert a video or two for a project. Nothing fancy, just turning that professionally polished AVI (or MOV) file into something for that Flash microsite you may have just finished to play back. Doing this is as easy as dragging your source file into the queue and clicking the Start Queue button to the bottom right of the queue. You could also use the Add button to the right of the queue and browse to your file. Figure 15-3 shows the queue with one item waiting to be encoded. It's true—that's all you have to do—although many of us might want just a *tad* more control.

15

For instance, you may need to resize the video, add cue points for navigation, or perhaps tweak the bitrate settings to meet your particular needs.

Figure 15-3. The queue shown with a single file to be encoded. The preset and output file names are links to the Save As and Export Settings windows.

Choosing a preset

After dropping your source file into the queue, you'll notice that under the Preset column a default preset has been selected for you. You will also notice a small arrow button to the left of that (still under the Preset column). Click this arrow to see a drop-down of available presets, as shown in Figure 15-4. The Media Encoder will default to the last-used preset, but you can choose from any preset listed. You can also select Edit Export Settings from the bottom of the list, which will open the Export Settings window. You'll learn about the options in this window later in the chapter.

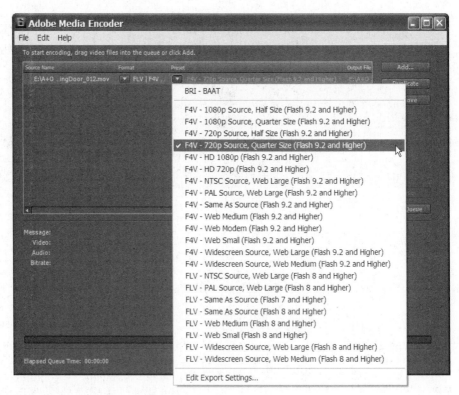

Figure 15-4. The Presets drop-down menu in the queue

The names of the presets are fairly descriptive and include (in parentheses) the version number of the oldest Flash Player that will support playback of video made with that preset. Refer to the section "Advanced mode encoding features" later in this chapter and Chapter 17 for a more in-depth explanation of video compression options.

Now that you've selected a preset for encoding your video, let's make sure that the file is named the way you need it and that it gets saved to a location of your choosing.

Choosing your output file name and location

To change the file name and location of the output file, click the text under the output file column of the queue. This will open the Save As dialog (see Figure 15-5). Proceed through this dialog as you would with any other type of file.

Figure 15-5. Choosing a file name and location should be a familiar task.

After selecting the file name and location for your output file, click the Start Queue button. You will see a small version of your video as it is being encoded along with information about its progress as shown previously in Figure 15-2. Once the encoding is complete, browse to your file and play it back to see the result.

Adobe Bridge CS4, which comes with Flash CS4, will play back Flash video files as will the Adobe Media Player, which comes as an installation option with Flash CS4.

Congratulations! Now that you've successfully encoded your file, let's look at how to encode many files at once.

Encoding multiple files

It's as easy to encode multiple files as it is to encode a single file. Simply select multiple files and drop them into the queue or browse to them individually using the Add button. Once you have adjusted the encoding and output settings for each file, press the Start Queue button, and all of the files in the queue will be encoded in turn.

In the cases where you need to encode the same file for different audiences (broadband, dial-up, DVD-ROM, etc.), the Duplicate button is an easy way to add another encoding job to the queue. Since you would be using the same source file, this button saves you the trouble of browsing for it or dragging it into the queue again.

Adobe Media Encoder will auto-increment the output file name by default. For instance, if your first item in the queue is set to output a file named myVideo_1.flv, pressing the Duplicate button will duplicate all of the settings but change the output file name to myVideo_2.flv. You can change this behavior in the Preferences dialog by unselecting Increment output file name if file with same name exists (see Figure 15-6). So by using the Presets drop-down menu (shown earlier in Figure 15-4) and the Duplicate button, you can very quickly and easily encode video for multiple audiences.

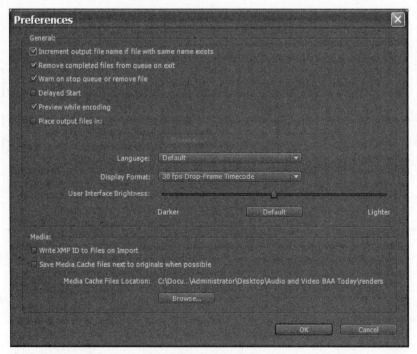

Figure 15-6. The Preferences dialog of the Adobe Media Encoder. The first option allows the Media Encoder to auto-increment file names for you.

Now that you can add multiple files to the queue, you might also need to remove an item from the queue. To do this, simply select the item in the queue and click Remove. The Media Encoder will pop up a confirmation dialog to make sure you really want to remove this item from the queue. In the event that you need to stop encoding temporarily, you can do so by clicking the Pause button.

Next we'll take a closer look at the Export Settings window.

Taking a close look at the Export Settings window

There's more to the interface than the Queue and Progress windows. You can choose to customize your encoding by selecting Edit Export Settings from the bottom of the Presets drop-down menu or clicking the name of the preset as it appears in the queue. Doing so will open the Export Settings window shown in Figure 15-7.

Figure 15-7. The Export Settings window shown here with the Video tab in advanced mode

The Export Settings window is divided into two main sections and has two main view options: Simple Mode and Advanced Mode. To switch between these modes, click the round arrow toggle button shown in Figure 15-8.

15

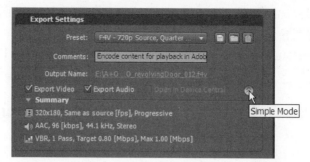

Figure 15-8. The button shown here toggles between simple and advanced mode.

On the left side in simple mode you can see the video as it is before encoding and a preview of the video as it will appear after encoding. You can select the portion of the original video clip you want encoded, set cropping of the original video, select the pixel mode of your video, and adjust the size of the video playback window.

Switching to advanced mode allows you to add cue points to the output file.

On the right side of the interface in simple mode you can select a preset (this is useful for getting to a starting point quickly for custom encode settings), manage custom presets, and choose to include or exclude audio or video from the encoding process.

Switching to advanced mode adds the ability to apply filters to the video, choose a video format, select a video codec, change the output size of the video, modify bitrate settings, modify the audio format, modify audio bitrate and quality settings, configure FTP settings for uploading the queue, as well as modify and include/exclude XMP data.

Simple mode encoding features

Simple mode offers quite a bit of control over your output but generally speaking leaves out the more technical decisions where video, audio, and ActionScript are concerned. Simple mode provides the following features:

- Cropping video
- Setting in and out points
- Managing custom presets

Cropping your video

The user experience in cropping video is *much* improved over the Flash CS3 Video Encoder. If you're one of those who have used the disassociated slider method of cropping video in previous versions of the Flash Video Import Wizard and Flash CS3 Video Encoder, you will appreciate being able to drag the cropping bounds to size and then move the crop area around on the video preview window. In order to crop your videos, you must first enable cropping by clicking the Crop button in the upper-left corner of the interface, as shown in Figure 15-9.

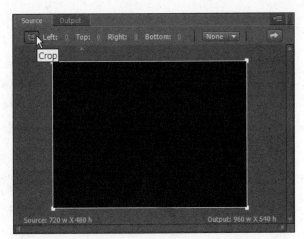

Figure 15-9. The source preview of the Export Settings window with cropping enabled

After cropping is enabled you'll notice that the text above the video preview is now active. You can modify the cropping values using the hot text for each value, which is handy when you know the exact cropping you need. The values you can change here are as follows:

- Left: How many pixels from the left edge of the video to cut off
- Right: How many pixels from the right edge of the video to cut off
- Top: How many pixels from the left top of the video to cut off
- Bottom: How many pixels from the bottom edge of the video to cut off

Figure 15-10 shows 140 pixels from the left edge of the video will be cropped out of the video during encoding.

Figure 15-10. The numeric controls for cropping video

To the right of these values is a drop-down menu of fixed-aspect ratios. Selecting one of these aspect ratios from the drop-down will resize your current crop settings to satisfy the ratio and also make sure that the aspect ratio of the cropping bounds is maintained through further adjustments.

> The cropping proportions drop-down is populated with standard aspect ratios used in traditional video production as well as some aimed at portable devices.

You can also resize the cropping bounds (the white box that now appears over the video preview) by clicking and dragging any of the corner handles to change the height and width at the same time or by grabbing and dragging any of the sides of the cropping

15

bounds shown here in Figure 15-11. You can then go back to the numeric entry and fine-tune if needed. You can also move the cropping bounds around on the video by clicking and dragging anywhere inside the cropping bounds.

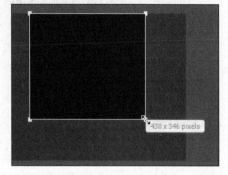

Figure 15-11.
The cropping bounds can be
resized using the handles.

Now that you have a crop area, you need to tell the Media Encoder how you want your cropping to impact the final video dimensions. You have three options, listed here:

- Scale to Fit: The Media Encoder will scale your crop area until it matches the height or width of your output size, whichever comes first.

- Black Borders: The Media Encoder will simply replace any video falling outside of your crop area with black but maintain the original output dimensions of your video.

- Resize Video: The Media Encoder will change the output dimensions of your video to match that of your crop area. It's important to note that after selecting Resize Video, selecting one of the other two crop settings *will not resize the video*. You'll need to uncheck the Resize Video option to return your output to its original dimensions.

Setting in and out points

Setting an in point and an out point for your video allows you to encode and output smaller portions of a larger source file without having to edit it first. Let's suppose you have been handed a video file of a professional conference that includes four different speakers. You might consider the following workflow to output a separate video file for each of them:

1. Open the Adobe Media Encoder.

2. Locate the source video file and drag it into the queue.

3. With your video selected in the queue, open the Export Settings window.

4. Drag the playhead until you locate the point in the larger video where you'd like your shorter video to begin.

5. Click the Set In Point button above the playhead (see Figure 15-12).

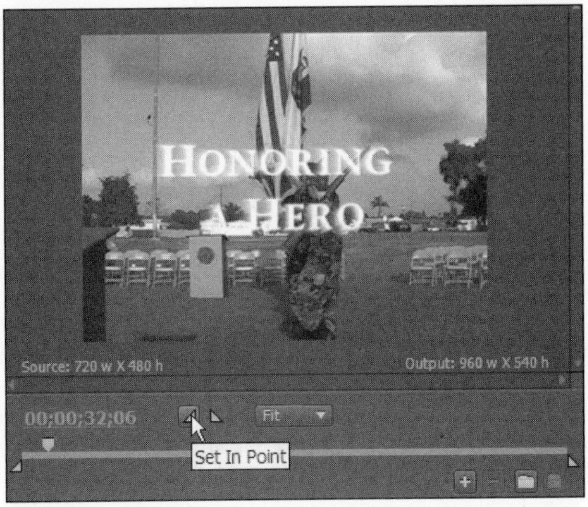

Figure 15-12.
The Set In Point button

6. Drag the playhead until you locate the point in the larger video where you'd like your shorter video to end.

7. Click the Set Out Point button above the playhead (see Figure 15-13).

Figure 15-13.
The Set Out Point button

8. Use the output name link to open the Save As dialog and choose a file name and location for the output file.

9. Click the OK button at the bottom-right corner of the window.

10. With the video you just modified active in the queue, click Duplicate on the side of the queue. Doing this will create a new item in the queue with identical settings, with the file name automatically incremented for you. (You may select any file name and location you wish at any time until the file has been exported.)

15

11. Repeat steps 3 through 10 until you have set up four items in the queue with the in and out points marked. You'll notice that duplicating a queue item also duplicates the in and out point settings.

12. Click the Start Queue button and let the Media Encoder do its thing.

You should wind up with four separate files trimmed to show only the portions of the larger video that you want.

Managing custom presets

Finally, in simple mode you can manage your presets in the Export Settings area of the Export Settings window. We highly recommend using one of the many presets as a starting point for creating your own presets. The dimensions, codecs, and bitrates in the presets are based on commonly used settings and will save you time and effort. After selecting a preset, making any change to the settings will change the preset selection to Custom. Figure 15-14 shows the three following preset management buttons:

- Save: Select this button (disk icon) to save the current settings as a preset.
- Load: Select this button (folder icon) to load an existing preset.
- Delete: Select this button (trash can icon) to delete a preset.

Figure 15-14.
The buttons used for managing
your custom presets

When you are done making your adjustments, simply click the disk icon next to the Presets drop-down. You will be presented with a dialog where you name and save your preset. The next time you use the Presets drop-down menu, your custom preset will appear at the top of the list under Custom.

To delete a custom preset, select it from the Presets menu, and then click the trash can icon. Read the confirmation dialog and click OK to delete or Cancel to cancel.

Advanced mode encoding features

The advanced mode gives you an opportunity to make technical decisions about your settings at a deeper level. These settings are geared toward the user who deals with encoding and distributing media on a regular basis. That being said, it is not outside the realm of possibility that your customers will have you reaching for the advanced mode as you try to balance the priorities between quality, bitrate, and file size. Nothing tells you more about what these settings do than trying out a lot of things in a systematic fashion and paying close attention to the result. Hint: test small portions of video to avoid the long wait between comparisons.

Advanced mode encoding features consist of the following:

- Cue points
- Advanced encoding options

- Filters tab
- Format tab
- Video tab
- Audio tab
- Others tab

Let's start with a discussion of cue points.

Cue points

In short, a **cue point** is a special event triggered at a specified point in time during video playback. Although you can add cue points using ActionScript, you can also embed them into the video stream itself during the encoding process, which is what we'll cover in this section.

> To learn more about using these cue points in your Flash application, read Chapter 17.

Adding cue points   Generally speaking, you add a cue point to video because you want something to happen in your Flash application when the video reaches a particular moment during playback or you want to leave a marker in the video that can be used as a navigation point. Here's how to add a cue point to your video:

1. Make sure you are in advanced mode.

2. Drag the playhead to the desired point in your video.

3. Click the plus icon.

Voilà! You have added a cue point to your video—well, technically it will be added during the encoding, but you get the idea. Figure 15-15 shows the cue point listing with one cue point added to it.

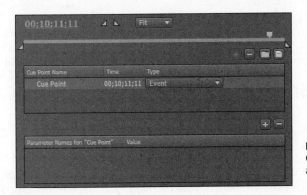

Figure 15-15.
One cue point has been added to the video.

15

Two types of cue points can be added as metadata to your video stream, event and navigation. Another type, an ActionScript cue point, can be added via ActionScript. (Bet you didn't see that coming.) To select either the event or the navigation type, use the drop-down menu under the Type column of the cue points table below the video preview.

Adding parameters to cue points Parameters are passed to the event handler for a cue point as an object comprised of name-value pairs. To add parameters to your cue points, first select a cue point. This will make the Parameters section below it active. If you selected Cue Point from the list of cue points, you should now see Parameter names for: "Cue Point" as the parameter names column header of the parameters grid, indicating that this is the cue point you will be adding parameters to.

Add a parameter by clicking the plus button. By default the first parameter is named Name_0 and the value for it is Value_0, as shown here in Figure 15-16. To change these to something more useful, click a name or value and tailor the parameter to your own needs.

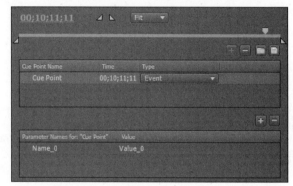

Figure 15-16.
A parameter has been added to the cue point. Shown here are the default names for both.

Remember, the parameters are passed to the event handler for a cue point as an object, so the names will be properties of that object, and the values will be the values of those properties. For this reason, parameter names must be unique within each cue point.

See the "Understanding Cue Points" section in Chapter 17 for more details.

Saving cue points Click the Save Cue Points button (disk icon) shown in Figure 15-16 to save your cue points as an XML file. This can come in handy if you need to pass the cue points from, say, a producer's workstation where cue points are entered, to a developer who adds parameters to cue points, or perhaps to a compression workstation where the files are actually compressed.

Saving a preset does not save cue point data!

Importing cue points The other half of saving cue points is being able to import them. If you're the developer or the person running the compression, and you receive a cue point file from the producer via e-mail, you can import this file by clicking the Import Cue Points button (folder icon) shown in Figure 15-17. Importing cue points might also come in handy in a situation where you have created a custom tool that creates cue points dynamically.

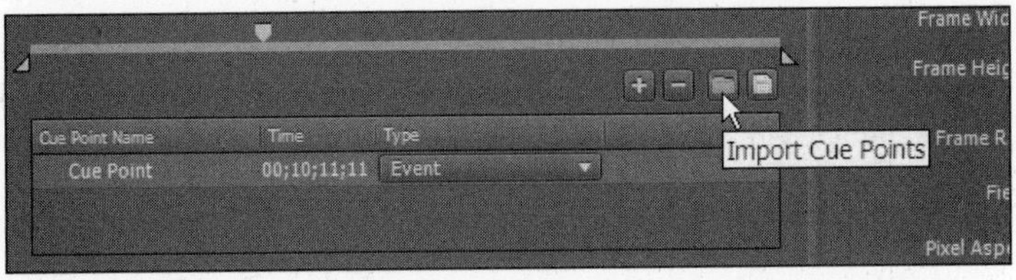

Figure 15-17. The buttons used for managing your cue point parameters

Removing cue points and parameters Of course, nothing is ever set in stone, so you have the ability to manage your cue points. Figure 15-17 shows the following cue point management buttons, from left to right:

- Add Cue Point
- Delete Cue Point
- Import Cue Points
- Save Cue Points

To delete a cue point, just select it and then click the Delete Cue Point button (minus icon) above the cue point grid. Confirm and that's it. It works the same way for removing parameters.

Advanced encoding options

If you're not already using advanced mode, you can switch to it by clicking the advanced/simple mode toggle show previously in Figure 15-8. In advanced mode you will see the following row of tabs under the Export Settings area of the Export Settings window, further expanding your options:

- Filters
- Format
- Video
- Audio
- Others

Read on for the skinny, starting with the Filters tab.

Filters tab

At the moment you have one choice for applying filters to your output and that is Gaussian Blur. To apply this filter, first select the Filters tab. You have three parameters:

- On/Off: You can include/exclude the filter (handy for quick comparisons using the preview window) using this check box option.
- Blurriness: You can enter the size of the blur using the Blurriness control. A value between 0 and 50 is valid.
- Blur Dimension: This control lets you determine which direction the blur is applied—horizontally, vertically, or both.

15

Format tab

The Format tab lets you select the file format of your output. Your decision here will be based on your audience and what player versions and computer systems you assume them to have. You can choose from FLV or F4V. Depending on which file format you choose, your options under the Video and Audio tabs will change.

The FLV format   The FLV format (which stands for Flash Video) uses either the Sorenson Spark codec or the On2 VP6 codec. While the On2 VP6 codec produces higher-quality video at lower bitrates, keep in mind that it is more computationally expensive—so for audiences with older, slower processors, you will want to consider using the Sorenson Spark codec.

It's important to know that the amount of math a computer needs to execute (computational expense) in order to make sense of your video file (decompress it) will impact the computer's processor and is not related to the connection speed your user has to the Internet (and therefore your video file).

The F4V format   The F4V format, which uses the MainConcept H.264 video codec, provides an even better quality-to-bitrate value but it is *even more* computationally expensive than the On2 VP6 codec.

> *Notice that choosing a format in the* Export Settings *window of the Media Encoder will not let you choose H.264 for the MP4 format. To choose H.264 for the MP4 format, you'll need to select it from the* Format *column of the* Queue *window, as shown in Figure 15-18.*

Figure 15-18. Selecting the H.264 codec for the MP4 file format has to be done from the queue.

Video tab and bitrate settings

The video tab is where you make all of your decisions around how the video is handled. Prior to this most of your selections have been around what the video will be—not how it will be transformed. Figure 15-19 shows the three following areas of the Video tab in advance mode:

- Basic Video Settings
- Bitrate Settings
- Advanced Settings

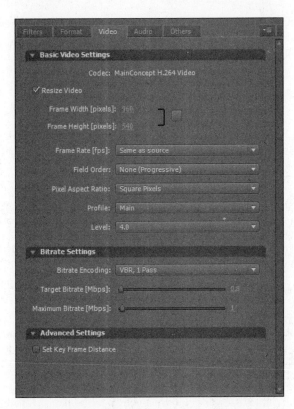

Figure 15-19.
Advanced encoding options
with the Video tab selected

Basic video settings If you chose to export to the FLV format under the Format tab, your first choice will be whether to use the Sorenson Spark or On2 VP6 codec for compression as discussed in the previous section. Additionally, choosing the On2 VP6 format adds the ability to take advantage of any alpha channel in the source video as well as using variable bitrate (VBR) encoding and multipass encoding (explained in the "Passes" section). If you chose to export to the F4V format, you can only use the MainConcept H.264 codec for compression.

Bitrate settings "Bitrate" here is the amount of data (usually kilobits) per amount of time (usually seconds) needed to "feed" the playback software so that the video plays back smoothly. And to be clear, it's the video stream itself that dictates how much data per second is needed in order to play back, and *that need* is what we're talking about setting here.

So you have some real flexibility when it comes to bitrate. Even though there are only a few choices to make, the number of combinations and range of quality you can achieve here (or not) is vast. In order to get the most out of the bitrate settings, you should understand what bitrate means and how it impacts the transmission of video online.

Imagine that you are a waiter or waitress at a famous beverage shop. You can serve one gallon of liquid (data) every second, and you have a tap that happens to spit out one gallon of water every second. You can get every drop of that water to your customer, and you

15

can keep on serving for as long as the water comes out of the tap without ever keeping your customer waiting for water (assuming that your customer will drink no more than one gallon of water per second).

Now let's imagine that you have another tap that spits out only a half gallon of water per second. Again, you will have no problems serving that half gallon of water to your customer every second.

Finally, let's bring out the big tap. This thing spits out a whopping two gallons of water every second. NO WAY can you serve it all *at the same speed it comes out of the tap*. You'd have to store enough at the table (where the customer can get to it) before you start serving so you could let the customer drink while you try to keep up.

This is what buffering is all about. **Buffering** essentially means collecting and "setting aside" enough video before playback so that the video does not get interrupted during playback. Since you don't want your viewer to experience hiccups in the video, you just let it collect until you're sure that you can keep up with "two gallons per second" until the "water" runs out. Of course, this only works when you know how much video there is to serve.

In the transmission of video (or audio), you *have* to deliver it at the minimum amount per second in order for the viewer to see the video without stuttering or buffering.

Bitrate encoding It would be nice if video were as simple as water, but it's not. Some frames of video are a lot more complicated than others, whereas one sip of water is pretty much the same as the next. They're pictures after all, and if you consider the simplicity of a picture of a box versus the complexity of a picture of a tree, you sort of get the idea.

You can select CBR, or constant bitrate encoding, and treat your video so that the picture of the tree takes as much bandwidth to deliver as the picture of the box, but you don't have to. The good news is that the very smart people who created these codecs understand that video is not the same on every frame, and they actually let you use this to your advantage by giving you something called VBR, or variable bitrate encoding. They basically rob from the data used for the picture of the box and give it to the picture of the tree.

Passes Since this is a pretty complicated bit of data juggling, the software can do it only so well if it gets one chance. So, there's an additional option for the number of passes the encoder takes over the video—one or two. The benefit is that you have a ton of flexibility in how the encoder distributes the data in that you can set constraints on how high (Maximum Bitrate setting) and how low (Minimum Bitrate setting) as a percentage the bitrate will go as well as control the overall variability of the target bitrate, as shown here in Figure 15-20.

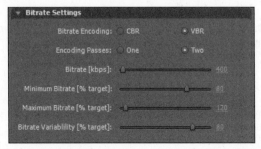

Figure 15-20.
The multipass VBR options for F4V

Experiment with these settings to get a feel for what produces the quality bandwidth compromise you can live with. Can you live with a slightly blocky video in order to maintain the feeling of fluid motion and still keep the video within your required bandwidth? Or is it more important to have a crystal-clear image with a lower frame rate? The answer will differ from one situation to the next.

Depending on the nature of the video you are encoding—a talking head vs. a roller derby, for example—different compression settings will be required for each to produce an acceptable result.

The drawback to multipass encoding is that it takes longer than one-pass encoding, which can be a small price to pay for the quality. One thing that you do want to consider is that the multipass VBR encoded video is a lot more complicated than a CBR encoded video and requires more processing power on your end user's computer in order to decode and watch.

Bitrate   Finally! The bitrate settings should now be fairly meaningful and straightforward for you. Using what you know about your target audience and the connection speed you assume them to have to your video, select a bitrate.

Remember that the lower your bitrate is, the less data per second can be given to your video—and with that sacrifice in "amount of data" per second comes a sacrifice in the quality of the images that can be created.

Advanced settings   The advanced settings vary depending on what video format is selected for output, but in general include the following:

- Keyframe Distance: The term "keyframes" in video compression refers to frames where a complete set of the image data is stored in the video stream.
- Encoding Profile: Setting this to Simple eliminates the ability for the resulting video to use frames that come after it for encoding, resulting in a less-compressed file.
- Compression Quality: Setting this higher will result in better image quality but requires more time to encode. A lower setting will encode faster but sacrifice some quality.

The advanced video settings give you tremendous control over how your video is compressed and enter into topics about video compression that fall outside the scope of this book. Refer to http://en.wikipedia.org/wiki/H.264/MPEG-4_AVC#Profiles for a technical introduction to the various profiles and levels included in the H.264 specification.

Audio tab

The video format you choose has an impact on how audio is handled during compression. Audio that accompanies video of the FLV format is MP3. Audio that accompanies the video of the F4V format is AAC.

The preceding discussion of bitrate applies to audio as it does to video—the main difference being that you can get a lot more bang for your buck from a few Kbps more of audio than you can for video. Little changes make more perceivable differences in audio than they do with video. Furthermore, changing your audio setting has a very small impact on

15

your overall output file size. To illustrate this point, we want to point out the Estimated File Size indicator at the bottom of the encoder screen.

Change all of the audio settings to the lowest quality for its format. Figure 15-21 shows the Audio tab of the Export Settings window. Make it mono if it is an option, set the frequency as low as it will go, and do the same for the bitrate all the while keeping your eye on that estimated file size. You can run the gamut from worst possible audio quality to best possible quality and see little to no change whatsoever in the overall file size. Add this to the fact that you get big gains in perceived quality for little increases in file size, and you see that cheating a few Kbps from audio for the benefit of the video stream is a bad bet. Play with these settings and pay close attention to your results.

Figure 15-21. The audio options. You get a lot of bang for your buck with audio. Using a little more bandwidth for audio will make the user experience much more enjoyable.

Audio that isn't being given enough bandwidth can sound crackly, watery, or fuzzy depending on the nature of the source audio. Speech will generally require less bandwidth than music to produce acceptable results; however, if that speech audio content contains a lot of reflective secondary audio (reverb), you may find that you have to bump the audio bitrate in order to achieve an intelligible result.

The Others tab

One very exciting addition to the Media Encoder is the Others tab, which at this time allows you to set up an FTP destination for your output file (see Figure 15-22). How sweet is that?! It gets a little better in that you can have different settings for each file. The downside is that you can't save FTP locations (although the Media Encoder remembers the last settings used), nor do the settings get saved with a custom profile.

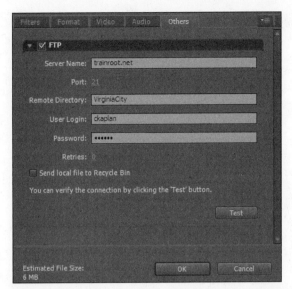

Figure 15-22. The Others tab lets you designate an FTP account to upload your files to after encoding is complete.

XMP metadata

XMP, which stands for Extensible Metadata Platform, is an open standards–based labeling technology that allows you to embed data about a file into the file itself. You can choose to include or exclude XMP metadata by clicking the menu icon of the Advanced Settings area (shown in Figure 15-23) and selecting or deselecting Include Source XMP Metadata.

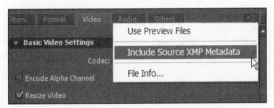

Figure 15-23. Launching the XMP info inspector

To modify the XMP metadata in your video or audio file, select File Info. This will open the XMP window shown in Figure 15-24. As you can see, the categories of information are extensive, but because XMP is open and therefore allows for the possibility of being extended rather than replaced, it can be made to include more information as more people adopt it without making older metadata obsolete.

15

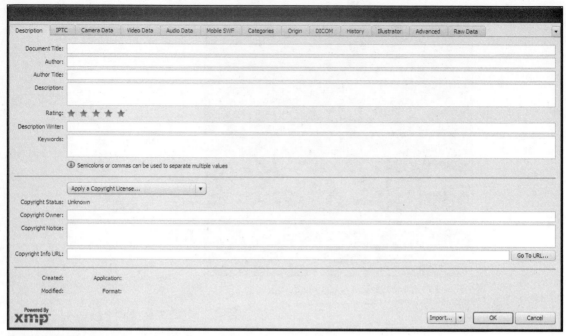

Figure 15-24. The XMP info inspector

To find out more about XMP, visit www.adobe.com/products/xmp/.

Summary

Like most topics covered in this book, the discussion of video compression could be a book in and of itself, as could the operation of the Adobe Media Encoder, but we hope that with what we covered here, you have enough background to produce quality work while you are getting to know this evolving tool. In this chapter, we talked about

- The basic operation of the Adobe Media Encoder including how to encode one or more files and the various file formats the Media Encoder can output
- Using the Adobe Media Encoder for common tasks like cropping, resizing, and trimming the beginning and end of your video
- Bitrate and the basics of video transmission over the Internet
- Audio compression and its impact on video
- The advanced video settings for compression and format, as well as embedding cue points and parameters in your video

- Things to consider when preparing video for your audience such as connection speed and computer performance and how to adjust encoding settings to match the needs of your audience
- Using the Adobe Media Encoder to automatically post your encoded video to an FTP site

CHAPTER 16
WORKING WITH AUDIO IN FLASH

When I (Chris) was thanking my first video customer for hiring me to add sound and music to his video, he said, "No, thank *you*. Without audio, video is just surveillance." Ironically, good audio is almost never heard—or maybe we should say never *noticed*. In order to effectively add audio to your Flash projects, you'll need to have an understanding of the various ways audio can be included in those projects as well as all of the things you can do with it once it's in there.

In this chapter we'll talk about

- Thinking about audio
- Importing audio into the Flash authoring environment
- Using audio in the authoring environment
- Using library audio assets at runtime
- The Sound API
- Loading audio at runtime
- Manipulating audio at runtime

Let's begin this chapter by thinking about how you might approach using audio for your project. Is your audio going to be design or content? Roll-over sounds for buttons or full-length songs for playback? Perhaps both? Once you know what your sound is going to be used for, you can create a plan for successful integration.

Thinking about audio

If a tree falls in the woods and no one is there to hear it, does it make a sound? If you're a sound designer, your response would likely be "What kind of tree was it, soft wood or hard wood? They sound different."

In sound design you paint pictures with sound. You give weight to objects, add speed to animation, add comedy to animated characters, and a whole lot more. Your job is to use sounds that are the *result of something happening*. Within the world of Flash, that could be most anything: a button click, a moving panel, a morphing shape, a change in the state of an application, a color transformation. The bottom line is that there is a wealth of opportunity for sound design in Flash.

As it happens, Flash is also a tremendous platform for presenting linear media, which could be anything that plays from beginning to end without opportunity for the user to interact with it, like cartoons or movies or songs or audio books.

Flash is a great choice for a custom media player with the usual capabilities: select a track, play, stop, select another track. Not only can you use Flash to load and play back audio files at the implicit request of the user, you can also programmatically respond to the audio itself, offering you the opportunity to create a responsive interface.

Understanding audio in the Flash authoring environment

Even though a vast majority of the control you have over audio comes through ActionScript, you may never have a need to use ActionScript for audio if you use the timeline for sound design. Even if you do, you may choose to import your audio resources into your FLA or perhaps create a SWF made entirely of sounds to be used as a library for shared use among many other SWFs. In short, there are many reasons you may need to import audio into the Flash authoring environment.

To import audio into the Flash authoring environment, do the following:

1. Choose Import or Import to library from the file menu.

2. Browse to your file or files.

3. Click Import.

This will add audio assets to your library bearing the file name of the source files. Once you've imported some audio into the authoring environment, you can put audio on your timeline by selecting a keyframe and then either dragging the audio file from your library onto the stage or using the Sound panel, explained next. While audio can span many frames, it must begin on a keyframe.

Using the Sound panel

The Sound panel, shown here in Figure 16-1, is your primary tool for dealing with audio in the interface. This panel is an extension of the frame Property inspector so the changes you make here deal with instances of audio files that are actually on the timeline.

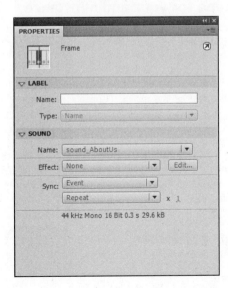

Figure 16-1.
The Property inspector when a keyframe with audio has been selected. Here you can select which library asset to apply to the keyframe, effect, sync type, and repeat settings.

Applying audio to a keyframe

Use the Name drop-down menu in the Sound panel section of the Property inspector (see Figure 16-1) to select an audio file to put on the currently selected keyframe. You can also select a number of keyframes to add sound to all of those keyframes at once.

Quickly applying effects

The Effect drop-down menu lets you quickly add fades and pans and other effects to your audio. You have the following options for volume presets:

- Left Channel plays only the left channel of audio by turning the volume of the right channel all the way down.

- Right Channel plays only the right channel of audio by turning the volume of the left channel all the way down.

- Fade to Right is actually fade from left to right: it turns the volume of the left channel from all the way up to all the way down while at the same time turning the volume of the right channel from all the way down to all the way up over the duration of the audio.

- Fade to Left works in the opposite manner as Fade to Right.

- Fade In does just what it sounds like. At the beginning of the audio, on both channels it will change the volume from all the way down to all the way up over time.

- Fade Out also does just what it sounds like. On both channels it will change the volume from all the way up to all the way down so that the volume is off at the end of the audio.

- Custom will open the Envelope Editor discussed later in this chapter in the section "Fine-tuning audio with the Envelope Editor."

Selecting a synchronization type for your audio instance

Audio can be treated in two ways when working on the timeline: it can be event audio or streamed audio. Both have their pros and cons and behave differently both at author time and runtime.

Event audio just happens. When the playhead reaches a frame with event audio on it, the audio plays with complete disregard for the rest of the movie. "Complete disregard" may sound like a negative; however, it could be just what you need. Consider a sound effect that needs to continue, even if the visual event it's associated with stops or gets interrupted.

It is important to know that event audio must be completely downloaded to the end user's player before it will play at all, so if you plan to use event audio, be sure to preload your sound library. Also, you cannot trigger playback of the audio at author time by dragging the playhead over it; you must play the timeline.

> Event audio has the benefit of needing to be downloaded only once, regardless of how many times it's used in your file as event audio.

Audio designated as **streaming** behaves much differently. When the playhead reaches a frame with streaming audio on it, the Flash Player will only play back the portion of audio on that frame. Using streaming audio will ensure that the playhead keeps up with the audio at runtime; however, it's important to know that it accomplishes this by dropping frames of animation if the host computer cannot keep up. It's also important to note that each instance of streaming audio needs to be downloaded, so using the same sound repeatedly would add significantly to file size.

Streaming audio instances are commonly used if you are working on animation tasks like lip syncing where keeping the visual contents of each frame synchronized with the audio is crucial. If you drag the playhead on a timeline that has an audio instance set to stream-ing, the audio will **scrub**, or play back, at the speed at which you drag the playhead, for-ward and backward. You can use this feature to find the approximate frame where an event in the sound happens (a loud crash or a big empty space, for instance) so you can synchronize your visuals to it or even use it as a reference for editing using the Envelope Editor (explained in detail later in this chapter in the section "Fine-tuning audio with the Envelope Editor").

> *Streaming also refers to cases where sound is being loaded from external sources (a web server for instance) but begins playback while downloading is still in progress. Don't be confused!*

To understand the difference between these sync types, set up a file as shown in Figure 16-2. In this example, both audio files are much longer than the timeline of the movie. The sound on the event layer is set to sync type event and the sound on the stream layer is set to stream. If you position the playhead on frame 1 and play the timeline, you'll notice that when the playhead reaches the end (assuming Control ➤ Loop playback is unselected), the event audio continues to play, while the audio on the stream layer stops when the play-head does.

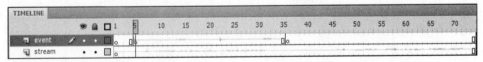

Figure 16-2. The top sound set to event will continue to play even after the playhead reaches the end of the timeline.

Also in the Sync section of the Sound panel is where you can set how many times to repeat an instance of a sound, if at all, or to designate it as a loop, which will repeat it indefinitely.

Info

The bottommost section of the Sound panel is the Info section. This unlabeled area shows you abbreviated information about the source audio file being referenced by Flash during author time including the sample rate, channels, bit depth, duration, and file size. For more complete information about the source file, double-click the sound icon in the library next to the sound you want to find out about. This will open the Sound Properties dialog.

Export settings in the Sound Properties dialog

The Sound Properties dialog, shown in Figure 16-3, is where you manage an individual sound asset's properties and export settings, including its library name, compression type, bitrate, and quality. You can also use this dialog to test output settings and update or import over sound assets (just as you can with bitmaps).

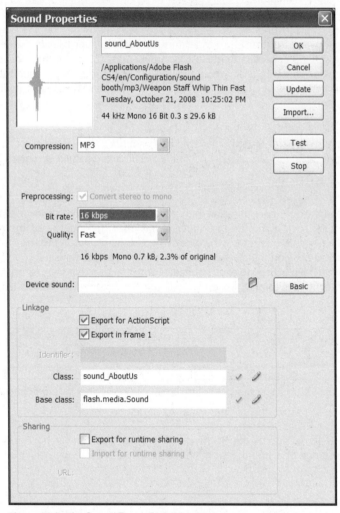

Figure 16-3. The Sound Properties dialog is where you manage a sound asset's properties, including its library name and compression settings. You can also use this dialog to test output settings and update or import over sound assets.

Basic operation of the panel is as follows:

- To save any changes made in the Sound panel, click the OK button.
- To close the panel without making any changes, click the Cancel button.
- To update your audio file with a newer version, click the Update button.
- To replace your audio file with a different one, click the Import button, browse to the new file, and click open.
- To hear what your audio will sound like after compression, click the Test button.
- To stop hearing what your audio will sound like while testing, click the Stop button.

To change the compression type of your audio, use the Compression drop-down to select from the following options:

- Default, which will use the compression settings of the document
- ADPCM (Adaptive Pulse Code Modulation)
- MP3 (MPEG-1 Audio Layer 3)
- RAW, which will not compress the audio at all
- Speech, which applies an aggressive compression tailored for the spoken word

> *To find out more about compression and bandwidth considerations, see Chapter 15.*

You'll notice as you change your selection from one codec to the next that your compression options change as well, including the availability of preprocessing (converting a stereo file into a mono file) and the range of options in the Bit rate and Quality drop-down menus. As a general rule, the larger the bitrate, the better the audio will sound—but the larger the resulting file. Make adjustments to your settings and then use the Test button to listen until you have a quality-to-file-size compromise that suits you. Use the information just beneath the Quality drop-down menu to determine the final file size of the audio you are compressing.

To replace audio with files intended for mobile devices, use the Device sound text input field. Using this will replace the file used during authoring with a file that is meant for use on a mobile device and cannot be played back within the Flash authoring environment.

To make a sound file available for use in ActionScript or assign a custom class to a sound, make sure the Export for ActionScript check box in the Linkage area is selected.

To make a sound available for runtime sharing, select the Export for runtime sharing check box in the Sharing area and then enter the URL where your SWF will be posted. The author of other SWF files can then use the sound object by referencing that URL or by dragging the library symbol of that sound into his or her FLA.

Fine-tuning audio with the Envelope Editor

You can use the Envelope Editor to fine-tune the volume and duration of your instances of audio assets. Fine-tuning in the editor will only affect the instance of the audio that is on the keyframe selected when the editor is opened.

Open the editor by clicking the Edit button (the button with a pencil icon) next to the Effect drop-down box or by selecting Custom from that same drop-down box. Refer to Figure 16-4 as you read through the following sections.

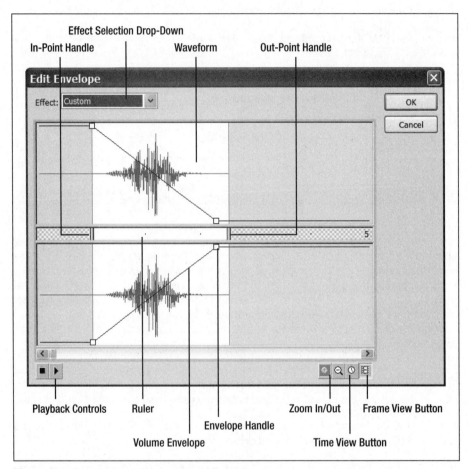

Figure 16-4. The Envelope Editor consists of these elements.

Trimming your audio

To change the point in your audio where this instance of audio will begin playback, use the in-point handle. Simply drag it to the point of the waveform that you want to be the beginning of that instance.

Setting the point in the audio source where you want your instance to end is almost identical except that instead of moving the in-point handle, you will drag the out-point handle back to the point in the audio source where you want your instance to end. If your source audio file is long, you may need to zoom out so you can see more of the waveform in the editor or scroll to the end.

> *Using a combination of zooming and scrolling should help you place the in and out points with a reasonable degree of accuracy.*

Custom effects

A custom effect is any volume envelope that does not conform to the preset effects discussed earlier in this section.

The Envelope Editor is by no means a fully featured audio editor, but it will let you add up to seven handles in the amplitude (volume) envelope, allowing you to adjust the volume. Click anywhere on the amplitude envelope to add a handle. When you add a handle on one channel, a handle is added on the other channel as well. These handles are locked together, and the pair only count as one of the seven permitted.

Certainly there are more comprehensive tools geared toward audio work, but it's quite likely that you will receive audio from a customer that needs some minor tweaking even if you are working without the benefit of these tools—and for this purpose the Envelope Editor will serve you well.

We've also seen it used quite effectively for breaking up longer files of dialog into separate instances for each character so that different animators can use the same finished source audio to work with during lip syncing.

Changing the view

As you work through trimming and adding custom effects to your audio, you might find it helpful to be able to manipulate the view of your audio. The Envelope Editor offers you a few different ways of looking at your source waveform.

The most fundamental is zooming (mentioned before). You can use the Zoom In/Zoom Out buttons (Figure 16-4) to zoom in to the waveform to help make trimming more accurate or to show more of the waveform to help you quickly move from point to point in longer audio.

You can also choose to change the ruler from time increments to frame numbers in the event that you either know the time or frame number of an event in your audio by clicking the Frame View or Time View buttons.

Adding audio to a button

Now that you know how to bring audio into the workspace and understand the basics of how sound is handled, let's look at a practical application of audio in the timeline as it is added to the over state of a button.

Buttons can help set the tone of your interface with audio on them. Let's see how it's done when you want your audio embedded in the movie.

To add audio to a button in the timeline, follow these steps:

1. Import the audio.
2. Add the audio to the Over state frame of your button as shown in Figure 16-5.

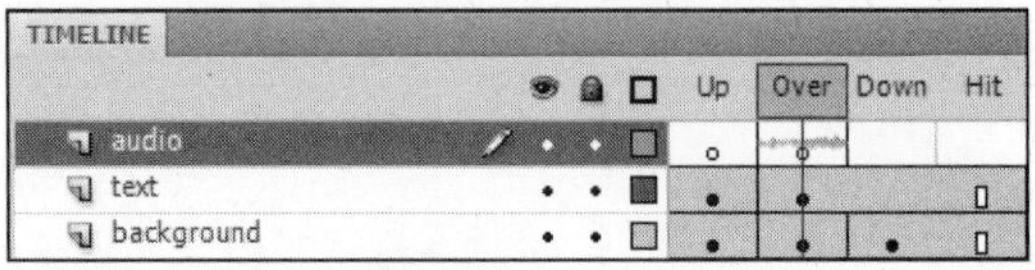

Figure 16-5.
The timeline of a button with audio in the over state. Whenever this button is rolled over, the audio will play.

3. Trim the audio if needed.
4. Adjust the volume if needed.
5. Address export settings.
6. Test your movie.

So that was a very straightforward process, but what if you want to choose from different sounds depending on what was going on in your Flash movie at the moment? For instance, what if you want the roll-over sound of your navigation to be different for each area of your site? You *could* create a set of buttons for each area of your site, but maintenance could get out of hand in a hurry! A more dynamic approach might be to create a button that, on roll-over, asks the application what area the user is currently viewing and then plays the appropriate sound. If you're interested in using Flash to control audio in the way we just described, then read on!

Using library audio assets at runtime

We're now going to walk through our earlier scenario in which the button asks the application where our user is and changes sounds accordingly. Rather than create a full-on application with navigation, we're going to scale it back a wee bit, but leave in enough to show you what you need to know.

This is a long example, so for clarity here are the major steps we're going to cover:

1. Create the application and document class files.
2. Establish application state.
3. Create the user interface and add code to handle user input to change application state.
4. Add sounds to the library and make them available to ActionScript.
5. Create the sound objects and change sounds at runtime.

We'll cover the following Flash concepts and skills in this example on using audio assets at runtime:

- Using the document class (which we covered in detail in Chapter 8)
- Using variables (also covered previously in Chapter 8)
- Making library assets available to ActionScript (this chapter)
- Using the Sound class (this chapter)
- Handling events (this chapter)

You can see that they are not all sound related, but they are covered elsewhere in this book. The purpose of this section is to provide examples that are relevant in the real world.

First things first—let's create our application

It's a good idea to get into the practice of setting up applications in Flash that use the document class. Even though this example could be done with code in the FLA, it's more and more likely that you will need to know how to do it from an external ActionScript class file.

To create the dynamic button audio application, start with these steps:

1. Create a new FLA and save it as DynamicButtonAudioApp.fla.

2. In the Class field of the document's Property inspector type DyanmicButtonAudioApp. Now you must make a class with that name for your FLA to use when it compiles the SWF, or it will create its own. Since you don't want that, move on to step 3.

3. Create a new AS file named DynamicButtonAudioApp.as and save it in the same directory as DynamicButtonAudioApp.fla.

4. Add the code shown here to DynamicButtonAudioApp.as:

```
package {

  import flash.display.MovieClip;

  public class DynamicButtonAudioApp extends MovieClip {

    public function DynamicButtonAudioApp() {

      trace("You have a working document class!)
    }
  }
}
```

5. Test your FLA by pressing Ctrl+Enter (PC) or Cmd+Enter (Mac).

You should be rewarded with the text You have a working document class! in your Output window.

Application states made simple

In order for your application to have an answer when your button asks what state it's in, you'll need to establish and keep track of its state. And what's good for storing information? Variables, that's what!

> See Chapter 8 for more on variables.

Let's create a property in the application class that represents the state of the application. Add the following code in bold to DynamicButtonAudioApp.as:

```
package {

    import flash.display.MovieClip;

    public class DynamicButtonAudioApp extends MovieClip {

        private var myState:String;

        public function DynamicButtonAudioApp() {

            this.myState="Home";
            trace("You have a working document class!);
            trace("My app state is: "+ this.myState);
        }
    }
}
```

When you test the movie, you should be rewarded with the text You have a working document class! My app state is: Home in the Output window.

Buttons please—changing states

In this section you'll add to your interface a text field that will help you observe the state of your application as well as two buttons.

To add two buttons and a dynamic text field to the stage for changing and displaying the application state, follow these steps:

1. Add a dynamic text field to your stage and name it state_txt.
2. Add two Button components to the stage as well. Give one an instance name of home_btn and the other aboutUs_btn.
3. Label the two buttons Home and About Us, respectively.

4. Add the following bold lines of code to DynamicButtonAudioApp.as:

```
package {

  import flash.display.MovieClip;

  // we need to import the flash.events package in order to add event
  // listeners to the buttons and handlers to handle events.

  import flash.events.*;

  public class DynamicButtonAudioApp extends MovieClip {

    private var myState:String;

    public function DynamicButtonAudioApp() {

      this.myState="Home";
      this.state_txt.text=myState;

      // adding event listeners to the buttons here and designating the
      // 'navClick' function as the handler

      home_btn.addEventListener(MouseEvent.CLICK, navClick);
      aboutUs_btn.addEventListener(MouseEvent.CLICK, navClick);

    }

    // The navClick function handles the mouse events generated by the
    // mouse clicks on the buttons.  We use the label text of the
    // clicked button to set the state of the app.

    private function navClick(e:MouseEvent) {
      this.myState=e.currentTarget.label;
      this.state_txt.text=myState;
    }
  }
}
```

We have had you add quite a bit there, so check out the comments for brief explanations of the code. In a nutshell what you want to happen is when you click either button, the application state will be changed and displayed in the text field.

> If you have any questions about the preceding code or steps, refer to Chapter 8 and Chapter 9.

Making library audio assets available to ActionScript

For this example you're going to need two different sounds: one for the roll-over sound in the Home state and the other for the roll-over sound in the About Us state. After you have these assets in your document, you'll need to make them available to ActionScript at runtime.

If you don't happen to have any sounds handy, fear not. With Flash CS4 comes a new common library with just audio in it. From the Window menu select Common libraries ➤ Sound. This will open the SOUNDS.FLA library.

Since this is an exercise in Flash and not in sound design, pick any two short but distinctly different sounds from the SOUNDS.FLA library. We chose Weapon Knife Sharpen On Metal 01.mp3 for the Home state and Weapon Staff Whip Thin Fast 02.mp3 for the About Us state. To add them to our FLA, just drag them from the common library onto the document library. We renamed them in the document library to sound_Home and sound_aboutUs, respectively.

To make a sound available to ActionScript at runtime, right-click (or Ctrl-click on Mac) the sound in the library and select Properties to open the Sound Properties window shown earlier in Figure 16-3. Make sure the advanced options are visible and select Export for ActionScript. The Class field will auto-populate with the name of the library symbol and the Base Class field with flash.media.Sound.

Creating sound objects and changing sounds at runtime

Now that the audio symbols are available to you via ActionScript, you need to import the classes that let you work with sounds. You'll also create a sound object for each of your sounds and rollOver events to the buttons by adding the following code in bold to DynamicButtonAudioApp.as:

```
package {

    import flash.display.MovieClip;
    import flash.events.*;

    // we need to import the flash.media package in order
    // to create and use Sound objects in our code

    import flash.media.*;

    public class DynamicButtonAudioApp extends MovieClip {

        private var myState:String;
        private var soundHome:Sound;
        private var soundAboutUs:Sound;
```

```
public function DynamicButtonAudioApp() {

    this.myState="Home";
    this.state_txt.text=myState;

    home_btn.addEventListener(MouseEvent.CLICK, navClick);
    aboutUs_btn.addEventListener(MouseEvent.CLICK, navClick);

    // here we add an event listener for the rollOver event and
    // designate the navRoll function as the handler

    home_btn.addEventListener(MouseEvent.ROLL_OVER, navRoll);
    aboutUs_btn.addEventListener(MouseEvent.ROLL_OVER, navRoll);

    //  here we instantiate our two Sound objects.
    soundHome = new sound_Home();
    soundAboutUs = new sound_AboutUs();
}

private function navClick(e:MouseEvent) {
    this.myState=e.currentTarget.label;
    this.state_txt.text=myState;
}

private function navRoll(e:MouseEvent){

    // all we do here is check the value of myState
    // and play a different sound accordingly
    switch (myState)
    {
      case "Home":
        soundHome.play();
        break;
      case "About Us":
        soundAboutUs.play();
        break;
      default:
        trace("play no sound");
    }
  }
 }
}
```

You should now have a good idea how to use sounds in your library at runtime using ActionScript; however, there may be times when you won't want to or be able to store all of your audio assets in the source file library to reference. In these cases you'll need to load them in at runtime.

Loading audio at runtime

There are a lot of things to consider when loading audio into your application at runtime. You want to consider giving your sounds time to load, what happens if the sound file can't be found, and what will be the impact on your UI if a sound fails to load prior to the UI being used.

The first step in learning to load audio at runtime is understanding the audio-related classes in the flash.media package.

Understanding the Flash.media package

Before you start creating a media player that loads audio at runtime, let's discuss some of the basic elements of the Flash.media package as it pertains to audio in Flash, namely these three classes:

- Sound
- SoundChannel
- SoundTransform

The Sound class lets you create objects that can load an external file into them and then access data about that file such as the number of bytes in the file and ID3 metadata like artist and album information, which we talk about later in this chapter.

Once you have that Sound object, you'll want some control over it. This is performed through the SoundChannel and SoundTransform classes. As the sound comes into a real audio mixer channel, you can adjust the volume, EQ (equalization), and PAN position (left-to-right balance) of the sound on that channel strip. You can think of the SoundChannel class as the channel strip on an audio mixer and the SoundTransform class properties as all of the things (like volume, EQ, and PAN) you can adjust that change the sound as it is sent to the speakers.

While it's possible you may need to load sounds at runtime for sound design, it's much more likely to be the case when making a media player application (or adding narrations to a slide show); so we'll use that example as a basis for the next section of this chapter.

You're going to create a very simple media player that allows the user to cycle through a set of songs that you define using XML. To do this you'll need to

1. Create a playlist (in an XML file).
2. Write ActionScript that loads the playlist into Flash.
3. Create buttons the user can click to load the audio files referenced in the playlist for playback.

Creating a playlist with XML

Let's begin by creating a list of audio for the user to choose from by using this very basic XML as the basis for your playlist and saving it as playlist.xml:

```
<?xml version="1.0" encoding="UTF-8"?>
<PLAYLIST>
  <PLAYLIST_ITEM file="Fish Bonz.mp3" />
  <PLAYLIST_ITEM file="Mailbox Pony.mp3" />
</PLAYLIST>
```

Loading the playlist into the media player application

Next you need an application to load the playlist into—call your authoring document jukebox.fla and the document class file Jukebox.as. Save them in the same location as playlist.xml.

> See Chapter 8 or the previous section in this chapter for how to create an application in Flash.

In Jukebox.as start with the code shown here:

```
package {


  import flash.display.MovieClip;
  import flash.errors.*;
  import flash.events.*;

  import flash.net.URLLoader;
  import flash.net.URLRequest;

  public class Jukebox extends MovieClip
  {
    private var theData:XML;
    private var tracks:XMLList;

    public function Jukebox(){
      loadData();
    }

    public function loadData(){

      // here's where we load the playlist file
      var request:URLRequest = new URLRequest("playlist.xml");
```

```
var dataLoader:URLLoader = new URLLoader();
// designate the 'handleData' function to
// execute when the COMPLETE event is broadcast.
dataLoader.addEventListener(Event.COMPLETE, handleData);

// catching errors will help you deal gracefuly with failures in
// loading data
try{
  dataLoader.load(request);
}catch (error:ArgumentError){
  trace("An ArgumentError has occurred.");
}catch (error:SecurityError){
    trace("A SecurityError has occurred.");
}
}

public function handleData(e:Event):void{
  // the loaded XML
  var theXML = XML(e.target.data);

  // this line makes an XMLList out of every PLAYLIST_ITEM node in
  // 'theXML' - our playlist.
  tracks = theXML.PLAYLIST_ITEM;

  // we subtract 1 from the number of our tracks
  // because the index of the last track in the
  // XMLList is one less than the number of
  // tracks we have - XMLList is zero based.
  trackCount = tracks.length()-1;
 }
 }
}
```

Creating the user interface

So now that you have some data in your application and a general understanding of the basic ActionScript classes involved with sound, you'll create a very simple interface that will allow a user to click through all of the tracks in your playlist. (Later you'll add some text feedback that shows the volume, artist, song name, and album information.)

> *Even though this example will only consist of a* Next *and* Previous *button, keep in mind that the process for loading the audio file and creating the Sound and SoundChannel objects would be the same if you were selecting tracks from a track listing or some other UI control.*

For convenience, use flat blue back and flat blue forward from the Buttons common library. (Window ➤ Common Libraries ➤ Buttons) Open jukebox.fla, drag an instance of each onto the stage, and name them next_btn and prev_btn.

Next, open Jukebox.as and add the bold code shown in the next example. As you go through the code in the following sections, keep in mind the following things that need to happen (the STEP numbers correspond to comments in the code in this and the next section):

STEP #1 Import related classes and instantiate a SoundChannel object.

STEP #2 Determine which track to load.

STEP #3 Request the audio file on UI click.

STEP #4 Instantiate a Sound object to load your audio data into.

STEP #5 Load the file into the Sound object.

STEP #6 Assign the sound to the SoundChannel object.

```
package {

    import flash.display.*;
    import flash.errors.*;
    import flash.events.*;

    // STEP #1
    // we also need the URLLoader and URLRequest classes to request and
    // handle the loading the audio files
    import flash.net.URLLoader;
    import flash.net.URLRequest;

    // STEP #1
    // the three classes discussed previously need to be imported
    import flash.media.Sound;
    import flash.media.SoundChannel;
    import flash.media.SoundTransform;


    public class Jukebox extends MovieClip
    {
        private var theData:XML;
        private var trackNow:Number = 0;
        private var tracks:XMLList;
        private var trackCount:Number;

        // STEP #1
        // instantiate a soundChannel object as we declare it
        private var channel:SoundChannel = new SoundChannel();
        private var mySound:Sound;
        private var mySoundTransform:SoundTransform;

        // rest of class remains unchanged
        .
          .
            .
    }
}
```

Wiring the UI and making it play

Believe it or not, it's time to wire up your (two-button) user interface and make this thing play. (Remember—you'll need to have audio files with the names indicated in your playlist.xml in order for this to work.) This next stretch of code covers steps 2 through 6, which continue from the previous example.

```
package {
  .
  .
  .
  public class Jukebox extends MovieClip
  {
    .
    .
    .
    public function Jukebox()   {

      loadData();

      // STEP #2 - determining which track to load
      // here we add event listeners to the prev_btn
      // and next_btn buttons for the CLICK event.
      prev_btn.addEventListener(MouseEvent.CLICK, navClick);
      next_btn.addEventListener(MouseEvent.CLICK, navClick);
    }
    .
    .
    .
    // STEP #2 (also)
    // this function is called when either of our
    // two buttons is clicked
    private function navClick(e:MouseEvent)
    {
      // e.currentTarget.name tells us the instance
      // name of what dispatched the CLICK event.
      if(e.currentTarget.name == "next_btn"){
        // check to see we're not at the end of our
        // playlist then either increment our track
        // number or reset to 0.
        if(trackNow < trackCount){
          trackNow++;
        }else{
          trackNow = 0;
        }
      }else if(e.currentTarget.name == "prev_btn"){
        // check to see we're not at the beginning of
        // our playlist then either decrement our track
        // number or set to the last track.
```

```
        if(trackNow == 0)      {
         trackNow = trackCount;
        }else{
          trackNow--;
        }
      }

      // now that we have our track number figured out, play the track
      playTrack();

    }

    private function playTrack(){

      // this function will get called every time we want to
      // change songs, so the first thing to do is stop any
      // and all sounds playing in the SoundChannel named
      // 'channel'

      channel.stop();

      var fileLoader:URLLoader = new URLLoader();

      // STEP #3
      // tracks[trackNow].@file  resolves to a file name -
      // remember that tracks is an XMLList and you access
      // its items the way you would items in an Array.
      // 'trackNow' represents the index of tracks that
      // we're interested in.  Finally we use the handy @
      // method of E4X to give us the vaule of the attribute
      // 'file' - the file we want to load.
      var soundRequest:URLRequest = new URLRequest➡
(tracks[trackNow].@file);

      // STEP #4
      // here we create the sound object that our URLRequest
      // (audio file) gets loaded into.
      mySound = new Sound();

      // STEP #5
      // now we tell the sound to go ahead and load the file
      mySound.load(soundRequest);

      // STEP #6
      // this may be the single most confusing line of code
      // here, but all we're doing is assigning 'mySound'
      // to the soundChannel 'channel' and telling the sound
      // to play.
      channel = mySound.play();

    }
  }
}
```

Manipulating audio at runtime

At this point you should have a working, albeit limited, little media player application; and it's the "limited" part of it that brings about the need for this section. In order to impart control to your user, you need to know the basics of manipulating audio at runtime.

In practice, most of the control you exercise over audio at runtime is at the request of the user—change the volume, pause, stop, play, etc.; but other times you may want to do these things to audio as a result of your own intention—slowly fading a background track as a user visits a section of your site, and then bringing it back up again as that user navigates to another, for instance.

Of the many things you will no doubt be asked to do when integrating audio into a Flash project, allowing the user to control the volume will top the list. In this example you're going to accomplish this by using a **volume strip**, which is essentially a volume bar without the slider; the mouse's position over the bar will dictate the volume.

The first thing you're going to do is create a dynamic text box named vol_txt and a rectangular movie clip named volumeStrip to the user interface. vol_txt will show us what the volume is and volumeStrip will act as our control. Add the following code in bold to Jukebox.as:

```
package {
    .
    .
    .
    // in order to adjust volume we need to have the SoundTransform class
    // available
    import flash.media.SoundTransform;

    public class Jukebox extends MovieClip
    {
        .
        .
        .
        // new var 'mod' (short for modifier) for volume calculation
        private var mod:Number;

        public function Jukebox()    {

            loadData();
            // since we don't always know how wide our volume bar
            // will be we'll divide 1 (our range of volume is 0 to 1) into
            // equal parts of the total width of our bar
            mod = 1/volumeStrip.width;

            // now add an event listener so that when the
            // mouse moves and is over the volumeStrip clip, it calls the
            // 'doVolume' function.
            volumeStrip.addEventListener(MouseEvent.MOUSE_MOVE, doVolume);
```

```
        // rest of function remains the same
    }
    .
    .
    .
    private function playTrack(){

        channel.stop();
        var fileLoader:URLLoader = new URLLoader();
        var soundRequest:URLRequest = ➡
new URLRequest(tracks[trackNow].@file);
        mySound = new Sound();
        mySound.load(soundRequest);
        channel = mySound.play();

        // we need to instantiate our SoundTransform object.  The .7 is
        // starting volume and the 0 is for center panning.
        // Panning can be anything from -1 (all the way left)
        // to 1 (all the way right) with 0 being in the center.
        mySoundTransform = new SoundTransform(.7, 0);
    }


    // this function gets called when the mouse moves and is over the
    // volumeStrip clip
    private function doVolume(e:MouseEvent){

        // as the mouse moves, we take the localX position of the mouse
        // and multiply it by the modifier we calculated earlier - then
        // cast it as a String so we can display it as text in 'vol_txt'.
        vol_txt.text = "Volume: "+String(mod*e.localX);

        // tell our SoundChannel, named 'channel', that the
        // sound transform object it should use is 'mySoundTransform'.
        channel.soundTransform = mySoundTransform;

        // finally we set the value of the volume property of
        // 'mySoundTransform' to correlate to the x position of the mouse
        mySoundTransform.volume = mod*e.localX;
    }
    .
    .
    .
    // rest of class remains unchanged
    }
}
```

Now that you have given the user a little bit more control over the sound, let's have a look at how the sound can in turn influence the user interface.

When the music stops—handling audio events

Your little playback application is starting to take shape, but it's still missing the feedback that your users need in order to connect with the content. In this section you'll add some text to the UI that shows users some information about what they are hearing by listening for the id3 event of the Sound class.

ID3 is arguably the most popular audio file data tagging format in use. ID3 is a data container within an MP3 file that usually carries information about the MP3 file such as artist, album, etc.

The id3 event is broadcast when ID3 data from a Sound object becomes available. You listen for it in ActionScript by adding an event listener to your Sound object. To include this functionality in your player, put a dynamic text field on the stage called id3_txt and add the following bold code to Jukebox.as:

```
package {
    .
    .

    // in order to read the ID3 info we need to have the ID3Info class
    // available
    import flash.media.ID3Info;

    public class Jukebox extends MovieClip
    {
        .
        .
        .

        private function playTrack(){

            channel.stop();
            var fileLoader:URLLoader = new URLLoader();
            var soundRequest:URLRequest = ➥
    new URLRequest(tracks[trackNow].@file);
            mySound = new Sound();

            // Here's where we add any event listeners to our sound object.
            // Events for the Sound class have to do with DATA;
            // IO errors, Loading progress, load completion, etc.
            // AUDIO-related events like when a song is done playing
            // belong to the SoundChannel class.
            mySound.addEventListener(Event.ID3, id3Handler);

            mySound.load(soundRequest);
            channel = mySound.play();
            mySoundTransform = new SoundTransform(.7, 0);
        }
```

```
    private function id3Handler(event:Event):void {

        // id3 is now a property of 'mySound', and that property is
        // an object with properties of its own, like artist,
        // songName, and album.
        var myId3:ID3Info = mySound.id3;

        // clear the text from the previous track if any.
        id3_txt.text = "";

        //add the text for this track
        id3_txt.appendText("\n" + "Artist: " + myId3.artist + "\n");
        id3_txt.appendText("Song name: " + myId3.songName + "\n");
        id3_txt.appendText("Album: " + myId3.album + "\n\n");
    }
    .
    .
    .
    // rest of class remains unchanged
  }
}
```

It's important to note the difference between the complete event of the Sound class, which lets you know when the sound data has finished loading, and the complete event of the SoundChannel, which lets you know when a Sound object has finished playing.

Summary

In this chapter we talked about some different approaches to audio and the impact they have on how you might bring audio into Flash and work with it. No doubt the flash.media package holds much more than we can cover in one chapter, but this foundation should serve you well as you work with audio in your Flash projects. We talked about

- Importing audio in the Flash authoring environment
- Using the Sound panel
- Choosing export settings for audio
- Using the Envelope Editor
- Changing sounds dynamically
- Choosing and loading sounds dynamically
- Modifying audio at runtime
- Handling audio events

CHAPTER 17

WORKING WITH VIDEO IN FLASH

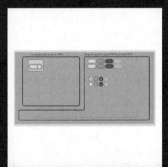

This chapter aims to provide you with the skills needed to handle common requests related to using video in Flash. We'll discuss

- Using the Video Import Wizard
- Understanding the FLVPlayback component
- Skinning the FLVPlayback component
- How to create an interface that can play back user-selected video clips from a menu or list of videos
- Customizing the playback controls of the FLVPlayback component to match the rest of a custom design
- Using cue points to synchronize text and other media, like images and animations, with video

When two of the largest viewer-supplied video web sites got together, our lives as Flash developers changed forever. Everyone suddenly knew for sure that Flash could do video on a large scale, and since Google was doing it, then maybe it was good enough for them too. As a result, skill in integrating video with Flash is now a table stake of the Flash designer and developer resume.

While popularity and high adoption rates for the Flash Player are good reasons to use Flash for video, there are some other reasons.

Flash offers a unique environment for video in that the Flash Player can respond to and interact with video content in ways that other technologies cannot. Bidirectional communication between the Flash Player and the Flash Media Servers offers even more possibilities in connecting many users around video content in meaningful ways.

Consider a training simulation where participants in geographically disparate locations all contribute to the outcome. Each of their decisions, or perhaps all of the decisions, made during the simulation can contribute to what pieces of video are shown and in what order during the simulation; and because it's Flash, everything will happen within a single interface.

Before you can run, though, you have to walk, so let's put one foot in front of the other and get some video playing in Flash using the Video Import Wizard.

Using the Video Import Wizard

Using Flash for the delivery of video has become so popular that you will at least want to know the very basics of putting video into your Flash applications. Fortunately, Flash comes with a wizard to help you quickly and easily integrate video with Flash. In order to use the Video Import Wizard, you will need to use video files that can be played back via Flash such as FLV or F4V files. To open this wizard, select File ➤ import ➤ Import Video. The Video Import Wizard is shown in Figure 17-1.

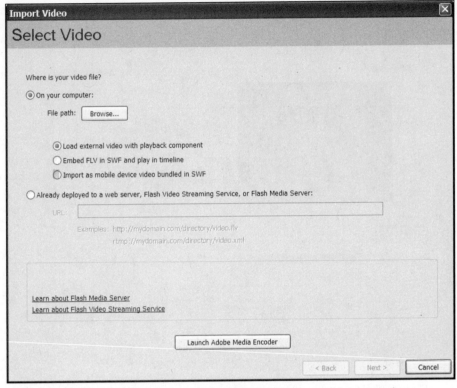

Figure 17-1. Select the location of your video and how you want to use it in your movie.

First, you will need to tell the wizard where your file is located. It is either on your computer (or local network) or it has been deployed to a web server, Flash Video Streaming Service (FVSS), or Flash Media Server (FMS) of your own. The wizard provides handy links to learn more about FVSSs and the family of Flash Media Servers shown at the bottom of Figure 17-1.

If the file resides on your computer or local network, you have two options. The first option is to have the wizard create an FLA file that uses the FLVPlayback component to play back your video. The second option is to import the video into your FLA for use on the timeline. If the file resides with an FVSS or on an FMS, you will need to provide the wizard with a URL for the video.

Click Next (or Continue on a Mac) to proceed.

If you elected to have the wizard use an instance of the FLVPlayback component or if the video resides on a server, you will be given an opportunity to select a skin for your FLVPlayback component on the Skinning screen shown in Figure 17-2. The skin is an external SWF file that, as stated in the dialog, "determines the appearance and position of the play controls."

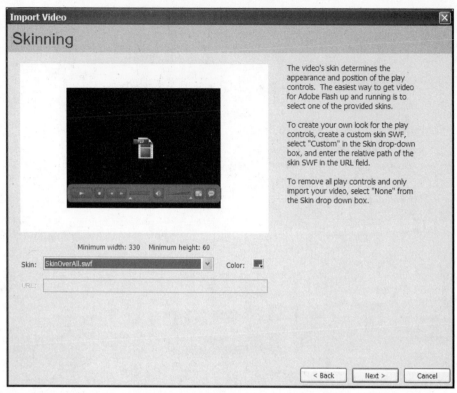

Figure 17-2. Select a skin from the drop-down menu. Then choose your skin color with the color chip. Flash will copy the required skin file to your project directory automatically.

> See "Customizing the FLVPlayback component skin" later in this chapter for details on skins.

If you elected to embed the FLV file into the timeline, you'll get the Embedding screen displayed in Figure 17-3. On this screen you select the type of symbol—embedded video, movie clip, or graphic—your video is put into. Other options include whether or not you want an instance of that symbol placed on stage automatically, and if so, whether you would like the timeline to expand to the duration of your video. You can also choose to exclude the audio content of the video at this time.

The next screen is the Finish Video Import screen, as shown in Figure 17-4. This screen gives you detailed instructions for what to do next and what you can expect to see depending on the selections you made during import. If you try to import video that cannot be played back by Flash, you will be prompted to open the Adobe Media Encoder and convert your video.

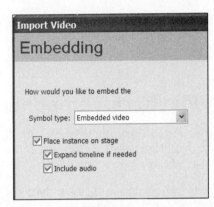

Figure 17-3.
Options for embedding a Flash
video file within your FLA

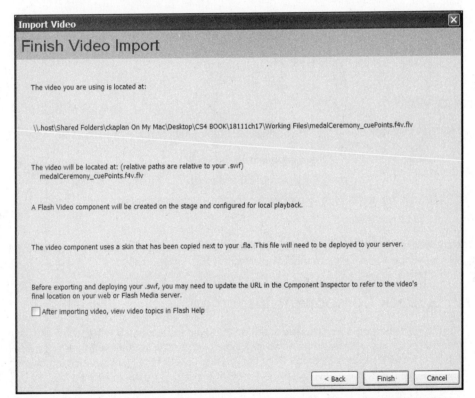

Figure 17-4. The finish screen when importing a local video file where Flash will create an instance
of the FLVPlayback component on the stage. This screen gives you information about what you will
see next and where to find your assets.

See Chapter 15 for a discussion of the Adobe Media Encoder.

The Video Import Wizard provides a step-by-step guided method for including video in Flash. If you need more control over how your video is implemented in your project, read on to explore the FLVPlayback component.

Understanding the FLVPlayback component

The FLVPlayback component is designed to let you easily add video to Flash. It enables video playback and includes play controls that provide the user with all of the standard capabilities found on a media player, such as play, pause, seek, and volume controls.

The FLVPlayback component can be added to your movie by using the Video Import Wizard or dragging an instance of the component onto the stage of your movie, or through ActionScript.

Using the component in the Flash authoring environment provides you with an easy-to-use component inspector for controlling, among other things, what file to play and what the playback controls should look like.

Hello World

The "Hello World" example of the FLVPlayback component involves the following steps:

1. Drag an instance of the component to the stage.

2. Open the Component inspector (discussed next).

3. Enter name and path to a video file for the source parameter.

4. Test the movie.

Many quickly find themselves needing to know how to say more than just "Hello," so next let's learn how to say "Nice to meet you. Where is the bathroom?"

FLVPlayback Component inspector

The FLVPlayback component consists of the video player and its play controls, which you can manipulate through the Component inspector. After you drag an instance onto the stage, you can launch the Component inspector from the Property panel of the FLVPlayback component. The Parameters tab of the FLVPlayback Component inspector is shown in Figure 17-5.

The Component inspector shows a subset of parameters of the component that can help with some general behaviors such as how the player adjusts its size to accommodate different-sized video (scaleMode), whether or not the player plays its video as soon as the source is set (autoPlay), and the playback skin along with some of the skin's properties. We'll discuss the following parameters:

- scaleMode
- skin
- source

17

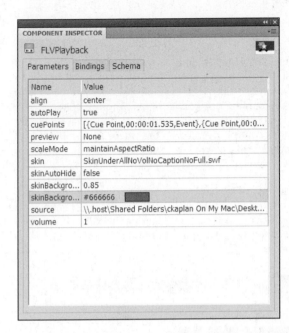

Figure 17-5.
The FLVPlayback Component inspector shows the basic parameters of the component, but even these few parameters offer you ample control. Further control over the component can be achieved through ActionScript.

Understanding and setting the scaleMode parameter

The scaleMode property determines how the video will resize after loading. This property can be confusing, and it might not behave the way you first expect. For instance you might assume that the noScale property set to true would prevent the video from changing dimensions. Instead, what it does is force the FLVPlayback component to take on the size of the source file. So if your component on stage is 320 × 240 but your source video is 640 × 480, the component will resize to 640 × 480 when the noScale property is set to true.

You have the following three options for the scaleMode parameter:

- maintainAspectRatio: Adjusts the video aspect ratio and dimensions to fit within the rectangle defined by the size and location of your FLVPlayback instance on stage or its registrationX, registrationY, registrationWidth, and registrationHeight properties.

- noScale: Causes the video to size automatically to the dimensions of the source FLV file. This parameter refers to the control of the video—not the playback component instance.

- exactFit: Causes the dimensions of the source FLV file to be ignored, and the video is stretched to fit the rectangle defined by the size and location of your FLVPlayback instance on stage or the registrationX, registrationY, registrationWidth, and registrationHeight properties. If this is set after an FLV file has been loaded, an automatic layout will start immediately.

To set the scaleMode parameter in the Component inspector, click in the Value column next to the scaleMode parameter. Use the drop-down menu to select one of the three options.

Setting the skin parameters

Another key parameter is the skin parameter. What you are doing when you select a skin here is telling Flash to load an external SWF file at runtime that handles the layout and configurations of the play controls. There are essentially 34 configurations of the same skin to choose from. For instance, you might choose to have only a play button and a full screen button on your controls. That would be one configuration. Another configuration might include the play button, the stop button, and the caption button. That would be another. Further, you might want those controls overlaid on the video. That would be yet another configuration. Add the multiple arrangements of controls to the color variations and alpha control, and most of us will have all the variety we need.

To select a skin, click in the Value column next to the skin parameter and then select a configuration from the drop-down menu shown in Figure 17-6 that meets your needs. You can also select the background color for your skin at this time using the color chip next to the drop-down menu. You can select and reselect as many times as you need before leaving the Select Skin dialog.

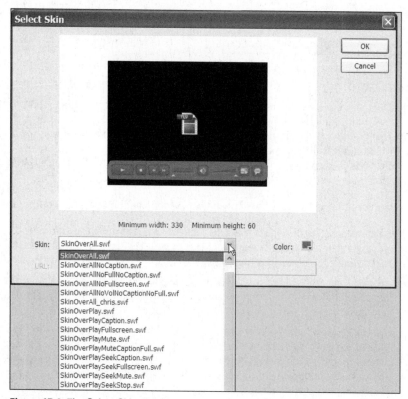

Figure 17-6. The Select Skin dialog

When you return to the Component inspector, you can choose to adjust the color further without having to reopen the Select Skin dialog by clicking in the Value column next to skinBackgroundColor. You can also adjust the skin's transparency by clicking in the Value column next to skinBackgroundAlpha and entering a value between 0 (for transparent) and 1 (for solid).

Setting the source parameter

Flash Player can play FLV and F4V formats, but with Flash Player 9 update 3, Adobe added the ability to play back MPEG 4 formats that use H.264 encoding. These formats include MP4, M4A, MOV, MP4V, 3GP, and 3G2.

To set the source parameter for your instance, click in the Value column next to the source parameter of the Component inspector. Then browse to the file you wish to play back and select it or enter the URL to your video. When setting the source parameter in this way, Flash will read the metadata of the file you have selected and can therefore give you the option of sizing your playback component to match. If you weren't involved in production of the video and weren't told the dimensions of the video, this can eliminate some guesswork for you.

Menu-driven video playback

As mentioned at the beginning of this chapter, creating an interface that can play back user-selected video clips from a menu tops our list of requests when it comes to using video in Flash.

Following are the steps for creating a menu-driven video playback application. This example shows how to load and playback video from a combo box component.

1. Create an FLA and make its document class VideoPlayer_understanding.as.
2. Drag an instance of the FLVPlayback component from the Components panel to the stage of the FLA. Name it myVideoPlayer.
3. Drag an instance of the ComboBox component from the Component panel to the stage and name it selector_cb. Load your combo box with titles and file names of videos you have encoded for playback in Flash using the Component inspector. Please refer to Chapter 14 for more information about the ComboBox component.
4. Create a dynamic text field on stage and call it feedback_txt.
5. Create the file VideoPlayer_understanding.as and insert into it the following code:

```
package{

    import flash.display.MovieClip;
    import flash.events.*;
    import flash.text.*;

    import fl.video.FLVPlayback;
    import fl.video.VideoEvent;

    public class VideoPlayer_understanding extends MovieClip{

        public function VideoPlayer_understanding(){
            // this one will show us selecting from multiple videos and➥
    multiple sizes
```

```
        selector_cb.addEventListener(Event.CHANGE, handleChange);
        myVideoPlayer.addEventListener(VideoEvent.READY, playerReady);
    }

    private function handleChange(e:Event){
        // do the video selection
        trace(selector_cb.selectedItem.data);
        feedback_txt.text = "You have selected:➥
    "+selector_cb.selectedItem.data;

        myVideoPlayer.load(selector_cb.selectedItem.data);
        myVideoPlayer.play();

    }
    private function playerReady(e:VideoEvent)  {
        myVideoPlayer.x = 0;
        myVideoPlayer.y = 0;
    }
  }
}
```

Here's what this code does (please read through the comments for specific details):

1. Import the necessary classes.

2. Add event listeners for the combo box CHANGE event and the FLVPlayback READY event.

3. Load the selected video file into the player and update the feedback text.

4. When the player broadcasts the READY event, you reposition the player. If the loaded video's size is different from the player's size, its position will change depending on the scaleMode setting. After the auto layout process, you can safely reposition the video display.

> See "Synchronizing video, text, and other media using events" later in this chapter for more information about events.

As you can see, creating this functionality can be very straightforward. So now that you are able to select and play back video from a menu, let's move on to making the component look the way we want it to by creating a custom skin.

Customizing the FLVPlayback component skin

One very common request you might get is to make the video player controls match the carefully crafted design elements that surround it. Another might be to apply design elements provided to you by the designer to the playback controls. In this section we're going to take a closer look at the FLVPlayback component's skin and how you can use the prebuilt skins as a starting point to create your own custom skins. We're also going to show you how to use ActionScript with your own custom assets to control the FLVPlayback component.

As mentioned before, you can make some color and alpha (and control configuration) selections using the Component inspector; however, what we're talking about here is a complete departure from the skins that are included with Flash CS4.

Understanding the FLVPlayback component skin

In order to customize the FLVPlayback component skin, you need to understand how it's put together. You can find the source files where Flash was installed on your computer.

> *On a Mac, you can find the source FLA files for skins here: file:/// MacintoshHD:Applications:AdobeFlashCS4:Common:Configuration: FLVPlayback Skins:FLA:ActionScript 3.0.*
>
> *On a Windows XP PC, you can find the source FLA files for skins here: C:\Program Files\Adobe\Adobe Flash CS4\Common\Configuration\ FLVPlayback Skins\FLA\ActionScript 3.0.*

When you first open the FLA for an FLVPlayback skin, the first thing you should do is save it with a new name. This will prevent you from overwriting any of the original files from the installation of Flash.

In the FLA you will see two distinct areas labeled Layout Layer (Exported to SWF) and Sample Controls Layers (NOT Exported to SWF) on stage as shown in Figure 17-7. In the Layout Layer area you see the skin as it will appear applied to your FLVPlayback component. In the Sample Controls Layers area you can see all of the states (normal, over, down, and disabled) for each of the skin elements.

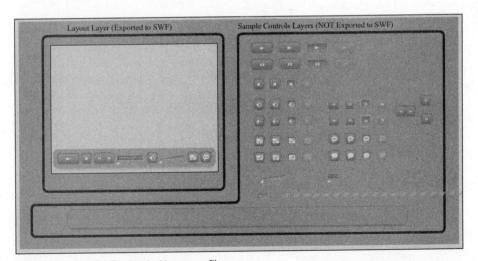

Figure 17-7. The FLVPlayback skin source file

If you look at the Timeline panel, you'll see that the symbols on stage are arranged nicely into two folders of layers, and each element resides on its own layer within that folder. The layers in the Sample Controls Layers folder are set as guide layers and will not export with the layout layers.

> *Guide layers can be used to guide a symbol's path during a classic tween, but it is common practice to use them to put elements on stage that should not be published. An image provided by a designer to be used as a guide for layout is one example.*

There is a third (topmost) layer in the timeline called All Scripts. Have a look if you like, but it's not necessary to make any changes in the ActionScript in order to modify the skin.

Since you've saved this FLA as a new file with a new name, you can go ahead and play around in the library. As you can see here in Figure 17-8, the library is organized into folders that contain the unique parts of each respective control.

Figure 17-8.
The library of the FLVPlayback skin source file is organized into a useful folder hierarchy.

You want to drill into each folder until you see a folder called Assets (see Figure 17-9). It's the elements in these Assets folders that you should modify to make visual changes to individual controls.

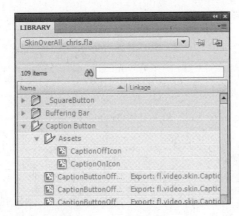

Figure 17-9.
Exploring the structure of the library to reveal the Assets folder of the Caption Button control

So now that you have your bearings, let's make a custom skin by replacing some of the graphic elements. The goal is to quickly convert the square buttons in this skin into round buttons with different colors for each button state.

1. Open SkinOverPlayMute.FLA and then save the source FLA as SkinOverPlayMuteRound.FLA.

2. With the source FLA open, browse to the _SquareButton folder in the library. You should see three MovieClip symbols in this folder, SquareBgDown, SquareBgNormal, and SquareBgOver, as shown in Figure 17-10.

3. Double-click SquareBgDown to open it in edit mode. Add a layer to the timeline and move it to the topmost layer. Draw a circle on this layer that covers the existing artwork. Your screen should look similar to Figure 17-11. You can delete the other layers if you wish.

Figure 17-10. The three movie clips used for the down, normal, and over state backgrounds

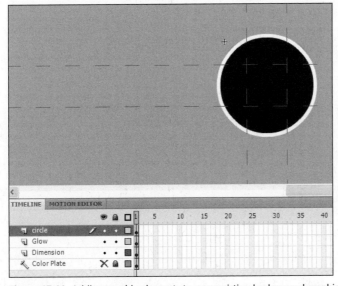

Figure 17-11. Adding graphic elements to a preexisting background graphic

441

4. Select and copy the circle you drew to your clipboard by pressing Ctrl+C or Cmd+C.

5. Repeat step 3 with SquareBgNormal and SquareBgDown, in turn changing the color of the circle in each clip. (Paste the circle from your clipboard to the new layer in each symbol using paste-in-place by pressing Ctrl+Shift+V or Cmd+Shift+V on a Mac to ensure consistent placement from clip to clip.)

6. Return to the main timeline. Your stage should look similar to Figure 17-12.

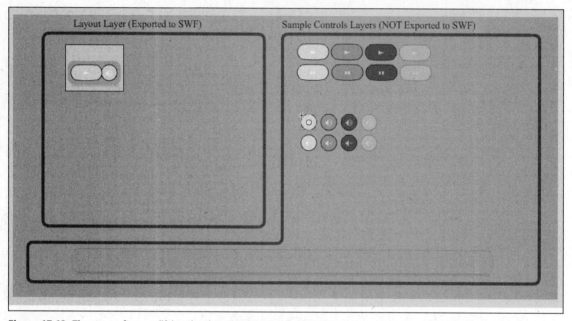

Figure 17-12. The stage after modifying the three button state movie clips

7. Export the skin, and then move the resulting SWF to the FLVPlayback Skins/ ActionScript 3.0 directory.

> *On a Windows XP PC, you can find the skins here: C:\Program Files\ Adobe\Adobe Flash CS4\Common\Configuration\FLVPlayback Skins\ ActionScript 3.0.*
>
> *On a Mac OS X system, you can find the skins here: file:///Macintosh HD:Applications:Adobe Flash CS4:Common:Configuration:FLVPlayback Skins:ActionScript 3.0.*

8. Create a new FLA and drag an instance of the FLVPlayback component to the stage. Open the FLVPlayback Component inspector and skin the component with your custom skin. (See "Setting the skin parameters" earlier in this chapter to see how.)

9. Set the source parameter in the Component inspector and then test your movie so you can see your custom skin in action! Your SWF might look something like the one in Figure 17-13.

Figure 17-13. The custom skin on the FLVPlayback component

The easiest way to modify a given button is to drill into it from the stage, keeping track of what symbol you're in and making the changes you want.

You should not replace a clip that is set to export for ActionScript. If you want to change the way one of these clips looks, then put your new design elements *in* that clip—*do not replace it*. The reason for this is that the skin uses those classes to control how the skin lays out, how it controls its video player, and how it responds to user input (like rollover or click events). If you want to replace the whole thing altogether, simply give it the same class name when you set it to export for ActionScript.

Figure 17-14 shows the symbol properties of the down state of the caption button when captions are turned off. Notice in the Linkage section that Export for ActionScript is selected and the class is CaptionButtonOffDown, the fully qualified class name being fl.video. skin.CaptionButtonOffDown. To open the Symbol Properties dialog, right-click (or Ctrl+click on a Mac) any symbol and select Properties from the context menu.

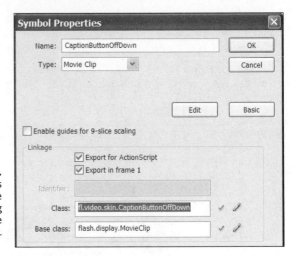

Figure 17-14.
It is critical that the class remains the same while modifying or replacing elements of the FLVPlayback skin.

One benefit of customizing the FLVPlayback component this way is that you don't need to write any code to make it work. You can also easily distribute the new skin SWF to other members of your team or the Flash developer community. Also, if your custom skin SWF is placed in the skins directory, it will appear in the list of available skins while setting the skin property in the Component inspector, allowing you to use it right away like the one we just made, SkinOverPlayMuteRound.swf, show in Figure 17-15.

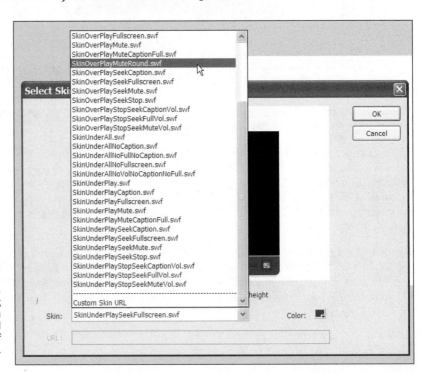

Figure 17-15.
The Select Skin dialog shows the custom skin SWF after it is published to the directory with all of the built-in skin SWF files.

On the downside, using the prebuilt skins as a starting point restricts you to using one of the predetermined configurations of controls and its layout. Fortunately, the controls come as separate components, and you can customize and use these individual components to configure your own custom play controls and layouts.

Creating custom play controls

In order to successfully customize and use the play control components (see Figure 17-16), you'll need an understanding of how they are put together so you know which pieces to replace and which ones to keep intact. We'll use the PlayButton as an example; you can find it in the Components panel.

Figure 17-16.
The play control components available in the Components panel

Understanding play control components

When you assign a movie clip to be the play button (or any other control) for an instance of the FLVPlayback component, that clip needs to define the class for each of its button states. If you look at the ActionScript in frame 1 of the script layer of an instance of the PlayButton component, you'll find the code that does just that:

```
stop();
this.upLinkageID = "customPlayNormal";
this.overLinkageID = "customPlayOver";
this.downLinkageID = "customPlayDown";
this.disabledLinkageID = "customPlayDisabled";
```

The values defined for each state's linkage ID corresponds to the class name (or linkage ID) of the movie clips found on frame 2 of the PlayButton component. Your linkage IDs can change, but not the property they are being assigned to. For instance, the following code will work just fine as long as you have a clip in your library with a linkage ID or class name of myUserDefinedUpLinkageID:

```
this.upLinkageID = "myUserDefinedUpLinkageID ";
```

More to the point, the following code will *not* work because there is no reference to userDefinedPropertyLinkageID in the FLVPlayback component:

```
this.userDefinedPropertyLinkageID = "myUserDefinedUpLinkageID ";
```

17

445

So when you customize or replace the visual elements of these components, it is critical that you maintain the script in frame 1 of your new control.

Keep in mind that some of the buttons are toggles and are made up of two sets of buttons. If you drag an instance of the PlayButton to your stage and double-click it to enter edit mode, you'll see that it is comprised of two layers and two frames. The top layer is for ActionScript; the second layer, named contents, contains the visual contents of the component. The first frame of the contents layer represents the normal state of the component. The second frame has an instance of all four states of the button, which are as follows:

- Normal
- Over
- Down
- Disabled

Notice that none of these clips have instance names; however, if you find them in the library, you'll see that their class names (or linkage IDs) are, respectively, as follows:

- PlayButtonNormal
- PlayButtonOver
- PlayButtonDown
- PlayButtonDisabled

It is *within* these MovieClip symbols where you will put custom graphics, animations, sound, and so forth because it is the class name that links the clip to the control component. Figure 17-17 shows these clips in the library.

Figure 17-17.
The PlayButton components that
are used for the four button states

Assigning custom play controls to an FLVPlayback component

Whether or not you replace the visual elements of a play control component, you will need to associate the component with an instance of the FLVPlayback component. Doing this is incredibly straightforward. Assuming you have an instance of the FLVPlayback component named myVideoPlayback and an instance of the PlayButton control named customPlay_btn on stage (or instantiated through code), you can assign a play button to myVideoPlayback with the following line of code:

```
myVideoPlayback.playButton = customPlay_btn;
```

> There are a number of controls you can assign to the FLVPlayback component. Refer to the FLVPlayback definition in the documentation (http://help.adobe.com/en_US/AS3LCR/Flash_10.0/fl/video/FLVPlayback.html) to see a list of public properties that can be set via ActionScript.

At this point you should be familiar with the FLVPlayback skins, their source files, and how to customize them. You should also understand how the play control components work as stand-alone components in Flash and how to assign them to an instance of the FLVPlayback component.

Now that we have explored how to customize the FLVPlayback component using skins and play control components, let's look at how to get your interface and related media to respond to the video.

Synchronizing video, text, and other media using events

In order to understand how to synchronize text and other media like images and animation to video playback, you need to understand how to handle events and, more specifically, how to handle the CUE_POINT event.

Responding to events allows you to do things like apply cue points to video dynamically and react to changes in the player's state. You saw in the previous example of menu-driven video playback that we waited until the playback component was ready before we attempted to reposition it by listening for the ready event. If we had tried to change its position prior to the player going through its layout process, it would not have worked. Either the properties needed to position the player would not have been available to us or the component would have overwritten them as part of another process.

You can also use cue points to load and display text, images, animations, or other media at specific points during a video's playback. If you know how to use cue points and events, you can sync anything to your video—except maybe the kitchen sink.

> If you're unfamiliar with handling events in ActionScript, refer to Chapter 9.

Beyond the Ready event—other key video events

The FLVPlayback component inherits a long list of events but also adds its own. Here's a brief introduction to a few events we've found to be key when integrating video with Flash using the FLVPlayback component:

- bufferingStateEntered: This event is dispatched when the FLVPlayback instance enters the buffering state. This event comes in handy for assessing the quality of your user's experience. You can also use it to have your interface respond while video buffers.

- Complete: This event is dispatched when playing completes because the player reached the end of the FLV file. The most obvious use of this event is to auto-advance to another video in a playlist, but you could just as easily switch to another view state or send a message to a server-side application; whatever you need to do when the video reaches the end, do it with this event.

- cuePoint: This event is dispatched when a cue point is reached. For us, this is the mother of all video events. It's the key to synchronizing associated content with your video, and we cover it detail in the next section.

- Layout: This event is dispatched when the video player is resized or laid out.

- metadataReceived: This event is dispatched the first time the FLV file's metadata is reached. If you need to display information about the video or use it for layout purposes, you won't be able to access it until this event is dispatched.

- playheadUpdate: This event is dispatched while the FLV file is playing or when rewinding starts. This event is essential for repetitive actions tied to playback such as runtime indicators.

- Ready: This event is dispatched when an FLV file is loaded and ready to display. This is one of our favorite events. There's little you can't do to the FLVPlayback component or its video source after this event is dispatched.

- stateChange: This event is dispatched when the playback state changes—which is indispensable for troubleshooting.

Regardless of how you choose to use these events, implementing listeners for them is the same. Consider this excerpt from our preceding example:

```
// here we add a listener to the FLVPlayback instance 'myVideoPlayer'
// and designate the 'playerReady' function as the event handler - both
// player instance and handler function are named by the programmer
myVideoPlayer.addEventListener(VideoEvent.READY, playerReady);
```

```
// this is the handler function for the READY event
private function playerReady(e:VideoEvent) {
     myVideoPlayer.x = 0;
     myVideoPlayer.y = 0;
}
```

> *Be sure to include the necessary packages in your code. The preceding excerpt will not work on its own. See the full example for working code.*

Mastering the handling of events and understanding when and in what order these events occur will open new possibilities for working with video. The most obvious event for creating synchronized content is the CUE_POINT event.

Understanding cue points

In this section we'll talk about the general categories of cue points, what specific types of cue points fall into each category, and how you create them.

Generally speaking, there are two ways to create cue points. The method you use determines what type of cue point you can make as well as how that cue point can be referenced via ActionScript. The two categories of cue points are embedded and ActionScript.

- **Embedded**: Of the three types of cue points available, two can be created during encoding: event and navigation. These can be referred to as *embedded*.
- **ActionScript**: The third type of cue point is the actionscript cue point. It can be added only through ActionScript.

> *To create embedded cue points during encoding, refer to Chapter 15 where we cover adding and editing embedded cue points and parameters.*

The secret to understanding cue points is that they are not just events dispatched by the FLVPlayback component. They are also a special type of object, and furthermore not all cue points are the same.

All of the cue points are similar in that each has a name, a time, and a parameters object. Name and time values are required when creating a cue point. Event cue points can be thought of as baked-in ActionScript cue points. Both are intended to trigger the CUE_POINT event during playback and can carry additional information via the parameters property of the event, which we cover later in this chapter. Navigation cue points come with the built-in ability to allow your user to skip from cue point to cue point using the forward and back buttons of the FLVPlayback skin.

As you can imagine, each category comes with its own pros and cons. While embedded cue points are more accurate, they can only be enabled or disabled at runtime and cannot be changed unless the file is reencoded—sometimes a lengthy process. ActionScript cue points, on the other hand, can be created at runtime but lack the accuracy of embedded cue points.

Creating ActionScript cue points

To create ActionScript cue points you can use the Cue Points inspector in Flash shown in Figure 17-18, or use ActionScript as explained in the next section. To open the Cue Points inspector, double-click the cuePoints property in the FLVPlayback Component inspector. Using the Cue Points inspector has the advantage of simplicity and speed when you are only concerned with the playback of a single video.

It is important to know that while you can see and disable embedded cue points (those added during encoding), you cannot edit them.

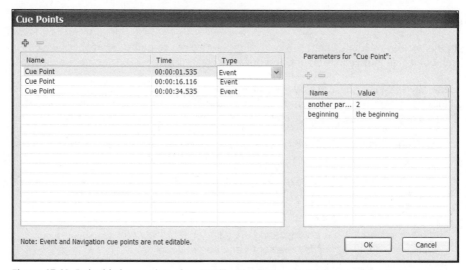

Figure 17-18. Embedded cue points of an FLV file. The first cue point (selected) has two parameters.

To add a cue point to your video, click the plus icon at the top of the dialog and name it myCuePoint. Note that you cannot change the cue point's type. Creating it here precludes it from being an event or navigation cue point—it will be an ActionScript cue point.

To add parameters to the cue point, select the cue point and then use the plus icon under Parameters for "myCuePoint": as shown here in Figure 17-19. Each parameter must have a unique name.

Use ActionScript if you want to apply your cue points at runtime; doing so will give you great flexibility. You can change your mind about just when an event occurs, and what happens as a result of it, based on other data in your application.

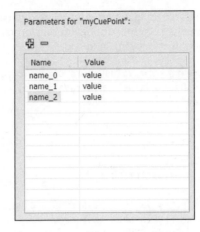

Parameters for "myCuePoint":

Name	Value
name_0	value
name_1	value
name_2	value

Figure 17-19.
Cue point parameters
must have unique names
for any given cue point.

To apply a cue point at runtime, call the addASCuePoint method of the FLVPlayback component shown here:

```
addASCuePoint(timeOrCuePoint:*, name:String = null, ➥
parameters:Object=null):Object
```

The addASCuePoint method can be a little confusing at first. How can it be expecting a cue point as the first parameter if we are now *making* the cue point?! Don't worry. What it means is that there are two ways to call this method. The following examples show both ways:

```
// the first method involves creating an object with time and name
// properties. Both are required in order to successfully create the
// cue point.

Var tmpGenericObject:Object;
tmpGenericObject.time = 2; // in seconds
tmpGenericObject.name = "slideCue";

// the object ('tmpGenericObject') is then passed as a single parameter
// to add the cue point to the FLVPlayback instance.
// myVideoPlayer is the name of our FLVPlayback instance

myVideoPlayer.addASCuePoint(tmpGenericObject);

// OR you could call the addASCuePoint method and pass the required
// parameters.
myVideoPlayer.addASCuePoint(2, "slideCue");
```

So that covers the minimum requirements for using ActionScript to create a cue point, but don't forget about parameters. They are the secret to storing information related to that point in time for use at runtime. Consider the following bold code:

```
// Here we create an object with name value pairs of our choosing.
var parametersObj:Object = {pOne:"aValue", pTwo:aVariable, pThree: ➥
"you should always have three"};

var tmpGenericObject:Object;
tmpGenericObject.time = 2;  // in seconds
tmpGenericObject.name = "slideCue";
tmpGenericObject.parameters = parametersObj;

// the object ('tmpGenericObject') is then passed as a single parameter
// to add the cue point to the FLVPlayback instance.
// myVideoPlayer is the name of our FLVPlayback instance

myVideoPlayer.addASCuePoint(tmpGenericObject);

// OR you could call the addASCuePoint method and pass the required
// info separately.
myVideoPlayer.addASCuePoint(2, "slideCue", parametersObject);
```

So now not only can you direct an event to be dispatched at a given time in video, you're also able to store information related to that event as well. Next we'll look at handling those events and accessing the related information.

Handling the CUE_POINT event and reading cue point parameters

So now you know how to create cue points, but how do you use them exactly? In this section we look at how to listen for the CUE_POINT event and access the parameters object.

Listening for CUE_POINT events is similar to listening for video events, but keep in mind that the CUE_POINT event is a MetadataEvent, so in order to listen for such events, you need to import the MetadataEvent into your class, like this:

```
import fl.video.MetadatEvent;
```

and add an event listener like so:

```
// whenever a cue point is reached, the doCue function is called.
myVideoPlayer.addEventListener(MetadataEvent.CUE_POINT, doCue);

// this is the handler function we created for the CUE_POINT event
private function doCue(e: MetadataEvent)  {
  // your code goes here
}
```

With this code, every time a cue point is reached during the playback of the video, the doCue function will be called, passing with it an event object.

When an event of any type is broadcast in Flash, the event handler receives an event object as a parameter. In the case of the CUE_POINT event, we are interested in the info property of that event object. Here's an example of info:

```
private function doCue(e: MetadataEvent) {
    // e is user defined - you can name it whatever you like - but it
    // represents the eventObject being passed to this function.

    // We look at the properties of e using dot notation.
    trace("1: "+e.info); // 1: [object Object]
}
```

The info property of the event object is where you find the cue point's name, time, parameters, and type properties.

```
private function doCue(e: MetadataEvent) {
    // your code goes here
    trace("1: "+e.info); // 1: [object Object]
    trace("2: "+e.info.name); // 2: slideCue
    trace("3: "+e.info.parameters); // 3: [object Object]
    trace("4: "+e.info.type); // 4: actionscript
}

// recall that our parameters object looked like this:
var parametersObj:Object = {pOne:"aValue", pTwo:aVariable, pThree: "you ➡
should always have three"};
```

The parameters property of the info object is where you access the parameter values of your parametersObj, as shown here:

```
// this is the handler function for the CUE_POINT event
private function doCue(e: MetadataEvent) {
    // your code goes here
    trace("1: "+e.info); // 1: [object Object]
    trace("2: "+e.info.name); // 2: slideCue
    trace("3: "+e.info.parameters); // 3: [object Object]
    trace("4: "+e.info.parameters.pThree); // 4: you should always ➡
have three
}
```

> *The important thing to keep in mind is the object hierarchy:*
> *eventObject.infoObject.parametersObject.parameterName*
> *= parameterValue.*

With the ability to respond to events of the FLVPlayback component and an understanding of the CuePoint class, you could create a whole range of interactivity tied to the playback of video—including a framework for closed captioning; on the other hand, you could use the built-in FLVPlaybackCaptioning component, which we introduce next.

Adding captions to the FLVPlayback component

More and more, captioning video is becoming a requirement in the development of video for the Web. Fortunately, the requirement to caption video is not a secret, and now Flash comes with a component to do just that: the FLVPlaybackCaptioning component.

Use of the FLVPlaybackCaptioning component itself is fairly straightforward and is covered shortly; however, preparing the caption file itself is a nontrivial task at best. Adobe Premiere and Adobe Soundbooth both have speech-to-text transcription services that come with the software and allow you to export the transcripts to XML, but do not use the XML Schema the FLVPlaybackCaptioning component requires.

We'll look at how to apply the FLVPlaybackCaptioning component to an FLVPlayback component and explore the Timed Text XML Schema that the FLVPlaybackCaptioning component uses. We'll also show you how to use the FLVPlaybackCaptioning component.

> *Adobe provides two files to help you learn the* FLVPlaybackCaptioning *component quickly: caption_video.flv (an* FLVPlayback *sample) and caption_video.xml (a captioning sample). Access these files at www.helpexamples.com/flash/video/caption_video.flv and www.helpexamples.com/flash/video/caption_video.xml.*

Timed Text XML Schema for the FLVPlaybackCaptioning component

The FLVPlaybackCaptioning component needs XML source files that use the W3C Timed Text (TT) Authoring Format 1.0—Distribution Format Exchange Profile (DFXP) for the source file for captioning. This standard provides a robust set of options for styling your captions but goes far beyond the scope of this chapter and this book. We will create a sample file as part of showing you how to use the FLVPlaybackCaptioning component, however.

> *The W3C Timed Text (TT) Authoring Format 1.0—Distribution Format Exchange Profile (DFXP) can be found at www.w3.org/TR/2006/CR-ttaf1-dfxp-20061116/. (Warning—it's long and detailed but chock-full of standards goodness!)*

The root node of the Timed Text XML Schema used by the FLVPlayback captioning is the <tt> element, with two required child nodes, the <head> and <body> elements, like so:

```
<?xml version="1.0" encoding="UTF-8"?>
<tt xml:lang="en" xmlns="http://www.w3.org/2006/04/ttaf1"  ➥
xmlns:tts="http://www.w3.org/2006/04/ttaf1#styling">
  <head>
    <!-- there will be more here shortly -->
  </head>
  <body>
    <!-- there will be more here shortly -->
  </body>
</tt>
```

Within the head element you can add the <styling> element for setting CSS 2 styles using <style> elements as shown here in bold:

```
<?xml version="1.0" encoding="UTF-8"?><tt xml:lang="en"  ➥
xmlns=http://www.w3.org/2006/04/ttaf1  ➥
xmlns:tts="http://www.w3.org/2006/04/ttaf1#styling">
  <head>
    <styling>
      <style id="1" tts:textAlign="right"/>
      <style id="2" tts:color="transparent"/>
      <!--notice here that the id attribute from the previous node is➥
used to help define this node's style -->
      <style id="3" style="2" tts:backgroundColor="white"/>
      <style id="4" style="2 3" tts:fontSize="20"/>
    </styling>
  </head>
  <body>
    <!-- there will be more here shortly -->
  </body>
</tt>
```

This is all well and good, but let's get into the timed part of "timed text," shall we? Consider the following XML added into the body elements of our XML:

```
<?xml version="1.0" encoding="UTF-8"?><tt xml:lang="en"  ➥
xmlns="http://www.w3.org/2006/04/ttaf1"  ➥
xmlns:tts="http://www.w3.org/2006/04/ttaf1#styling">
  <head>
    <styling>
      <style id="1" tts:textAlign="right"/>
      <style id="2" tts:color="transparent"/>
      <style id="3" style="2" tts:backgroundColor="white"/>
      <style id="4" style="2 3" tts:fontSize="20"/>
    </styling>
  </head>
```

17

```
<body>
  <div xml:lang="en">
    <p begin="00:00:00.00" dur="00:00:04.07">This is some text</p>
    <p begin="00:00:04.07" dur="00:00:03.85">for captioning.</p>
    <p begin="00:00:07.92" dur="00:00:03.08">It will be displayed</p>
    <p begin="00:00:11.00" dur="00:00:01.44">on the video.</p>
  </div>
</body>
</tt>
```

Within the body we added a <div> element. This is considered a logical collection of content by the Timed Text standard. Within the <div> element are the <p> elements; these contain text information used as the actual caption but also use the begin and dur attributes, which ultimately tell Flash when to show text and how long to leave it on screen.

As you might imagine, creating an XML file for captioning video of any length would be quite a task, so if this is your bread and butter, we highly recommend building yourself a tool that lets you record the start time and duration of captions and that then writes the XML for you.

Now that you have a basic understanding of the XML required to power the FLVPlaybackCaptioning component, you'll next put it together with the component. Save the preceding code as myCaptionSource.xml. In the same location, save a new FLA called Video Player_understanding.fla.

Understanding the FLVPlaybackCaptioning component

The FLVPlaybackCaptioning component allows you to apply the external Timed Text XML Schema file as captions on an instance of the FLVPlayback component. In order to use the FLVPlaybackCaptioning component, you have to tell it which FLVPlayback component it belongs to. If you don't tell it which playback component to apply captions to, the FLVPlaybackCaptioning component will look in its own display object to find one. If it finds more than one FLVPlayback component, it will assume it belongs to the first one it finds. You also need to tell it where to find the captioning information—the file we created in the previous section.

To add the FLVPlaybackCaptioning component to an FLVPlayback component, open Video Player_understanding.fla and follow these steps:

1. Open Video Player_understanding.fla (created earlier in this chapter) and drag an instance of the FLVPlayback component to the stage. Name the instance myVideoPlayer.

2. Create a new layer (optional) named caption component (or name of your choosing) and drag an instance of the FLVPlaybackCaptioning component from the Components panel to the new layer. The FLVPlaybackCaptioning component will look as it does in Figure 17-20 when you drop it on stage; this component has no physical appearance when the movie is published, so it doesn't matter where you drop it.

3. Name your FLVPlaybackCaptioning instance. What you name it is up to you—we used myCaption for this example.

4. With your FLVPlaybackCaptioning component selected, open the Component inspector and set the source property to myCaptionSource.xml.

5. With myVideoPlayer (the instance of our FLVPlayback component) selected, set the source property in the Component inspector.

6. Test the movie and enjoy the captioned goodness.

Figure 17-20.
What the placeholder FLVPlaybackCaptioning component looks like on stage. Once the FLA is published, the component is not visible at all.

The FLVPlaybackCaption component class comes with a healthy API for use at runtime for more control over your application. As with everything, we encourage you to explore it further.

Summary

Even though we covered a lot of ground in this chapter, we assure you that this was just the tip of the iceberg that is video in Flash. Our goal in this chapter was to teach you the core concepts integral to the day-to-day integration of video into Flash. We talked about

- Using the Video Import Wizard
- Understanding the FLVPlayback component
- Understanding and customizing the FLVPlayback component skins
- Customizing the play control components
- The core concepts behind synchronizing text and other media with your video playback
- The types of cue points in Flash and how to handle them when they occur
- Adding captions to the FLVPlayback component using the FLVPlaybackCaptioning component

PART SIX

PREPARING YOUR PROJECT FOR DEPLOYMENT

CHAPTER 18

PUBLISHING, EXPORTING, AND DEBUGGING YOUR FLASH PROJECT

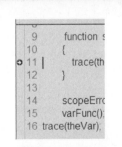

This chapter is all about the things you need to do with your project before you present it to the world. While debugging happens throughout the various stages of development, exporting and publishing usually happen at or near completion. In this chapter we'll talk about the following:

- Publishing your project
- Exporting your content to various file formats
- Identifying types of errors
- Using the debugger

Let's begin with the various ways you can prepare your work for the world with the Publish Settings window.

Understanding the Publish Settings window

Publishing your work means turning it into file formats that can be consumed by your users. Whether they are watching through a web browser or a stand-alone projector or mobile device, your source files must be compiled into something the playback environment understands.

Flash has to know as much about the environment your users will be viewing your work in as possible in order to create a compatible file or set of files for them. To do this you will need to understand the publish settings of Flash. The Publish Settings window's Formats tab, shown in Figure 18-1, is where you decide what types of files Flash needs to create when you publish. You can also adjust format-specific options that impact the file's quality and behavior as well as its name and where it will be created on your computer.

There are three main functions of the Publish Settings window:

- Create and manage publish profiles using the profile management area.
- Select output file formats to be created during publishing.
- Choose settings for each format.

At the top of the Publish Settings window is the profile management area. It contains a drop-down menu for selecting profiles and a series of buttons for managing them. Please see Chapter 2 and later in this chapter for further discussion of publish profiles.

Below the profile management area is a row of tabs that will change to reflect the file types you have selected for publishing. The order of these tabs is determined by the order in which you select the file type to be published.

Beneath that is the Type area where you will find check boxes to select or deselect formats to be created during publishing. The File area lets you select the location and file name for your published files.

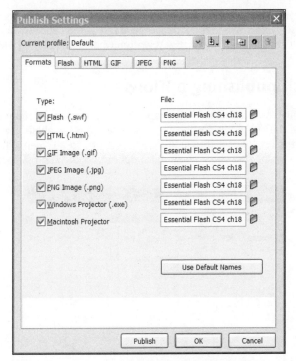

Figure 18-1. The Publish Settings window's Formats tab

To select the file name and location of a published file, either enter the path and file name into the text input box directly or click the folder icon to the right of the text input field and browse to the location where you would like your published file to be written on your computer. Enter a file name of your choosing and click OK. If things change (and they always do) and you need to reset all of the file names and paths, click the Use Default Names button under the format selection list.

To leave the Publish Settings dialog without saving any changes, click the Cancel button. To begin publishing with the current settings, click the Publish button.

Selecting publish formats

While the primary output file format of Flash is SWF, Flash will let you output your work in a variety of additional formats including

- HTML
- GIF
- JPEG
- PNG
- Projectors for Mac (APP) and PC (EXE)

Most of these formats stand alone. However, it important to know that the HTML and SWF formats are closely intertwined during publishing because the choices you make about the options for SWF impact the HTML that gets written when you add the HTML format.

Setting Flash publishing options

Each format comes with a laundry list of options. To change the options for a given file type, make sure the check box for the file type is selected for publishing, and then click the tab above the list for that format. This will take you to a screen with the file type's publish options. Figure 18-2 shows the publish options for the Flash format.

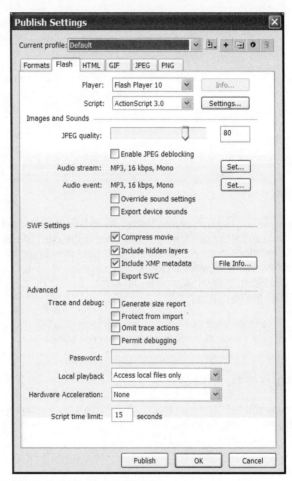

Figure 18-2. The Flash settings tab

The Flash output settings window is broken into four main sections:

- An area showing the player version and ActionScript version
- Images and Sounds
- SWF Settings
- Advanced

There's a lot here so let's just work our way down from top to bottom.

Targeting player version and ActionScript version

This is where you decide which version of the Flash Player and ActionScript to target. If you are building an application for a customer that is slower to adopt new versions of technology, you may not be able to develop and publish for the latest version player. Making changes here has an impact on which ActionScript settings options are available to you.

Targeting player versions   On the Flash tab, use the Player drop-down menu to target Flash Player versions 1 through 10—you can only target one player version, so choose the version that supports all of the code and other features you plan to use in your project. You also use the Player drop-down to target the Adobe Integrated Runtime (AIR) version 1.1 as well as Flash Lite players 1 through 3.

If you target AIR 1.1 using the Player drop-down, the Settings button to the right of the drop-down will become active. Clicking the Settings button will open the AIR—Application & Installer Settings window.

If you target any of the Flash Lite players using the Player drop-down, the Info button will become active, and clicking it will open an information dialog that tells you the subset of ActionScript that the selected Flash Lite player supports.

> *The* Player *and* Script *settings are chosen for you when you use the* Welcome Screen *profiles to create new FLA files. See Chapter 2 for more about choosing profiles from the* Welcome Screen. *For more about publishing for AIR, see Chapter 19.*

Targeting ActionScript versions   Use the Script drop-down menu to select a version of ActionScript to target. The script versions available for selection are dictated by the player version selection. Table 18-1 shows ActionScript support for player versions.

Table 18-1. ActionScript support for player versions

Player version	ActionScript support
1–5	ActionScript 1.0
6–8	ActionScript 1.0–2.0
9–10	ActionScript 1.0–3.0

Images and Sounds area

As the name suggests, the Images and Sounds area is where you control output settings of images and sounds in the SWF. While you can also control the compression and quality settings of image and audio assets in the library individually, the settings here give you the option to override those settings with a global setting.

To adjust the amount of image compression used when publishing Flash files, use the JPEG quality slider in the Images and Sounds section of the Flash Publish Settings window. This setting dictates compression of bitmap assets in the library for use in the finished file and has a range of 1 to 100, with 1 being the lowest quality and 100 being the best quality; 80 is the default. Checking Enable JPEG deblocking will reduce compression artifacts on images using low-quality settings.

While authoring, you can direct audio assets in the timeline to be either event audio or stream audio. When publishing your SWF, you can apply different compression settings to each. This allows you the flexibility of exporting your shorter sounds—usually set as event sounds—at a higher quality and exporting your longer sounds—generally set as stream sounds—at a lower quality to reduce bandwidth requirements.

Click the Set button next to Audio stream to choose compression settings for audio in your FLA that is set to sync type Stream. Figure 18-3 shows the Sound Settings dialog. Click the Set button next to Audio event to choose compression settings for audio in your FLA that is set to sync type Event.

Figure 18-3. The Sound Settings dialog lets you set audio compression settings globally.

To override any export settings made to individual audio assets in the library, check the Override sound settings check box.

> See Chapter 16 for information on audio compression settings, sync types, and device sounds.

SWF Settings area

The SWF Settings area shown in Figure 18-2 allows you to decide whether or not to compress your movie, include hidden layers, and include XMP metadata about your movie as well as indicate whether or not to publish your file as a SWC.

While hiding layers in the workspace can be useful when authoring, you need to be aware of whether the Include hidden layers *option is enabled, as it may cause headaches when trying to figure out why some of your content didn't make it into the movie!*

Whether you have selected Include XMP metadata in your SWF publish settings or not, the File Info button will be active so that you may add information about your file such as when the file was created, who created it, or what content may be found within it. See Chapter 15 for more information about XMP metadata.

Advanced area

The Advanced settings section comes last and includes a variety of options. The Trace and debug options allow you to do the following:

- **Generate a size report for your movie**: Choose the Generate size report option for a text file that lists the size of each frame, shape, text, sound, video, and ActionScript script by frame. This will let you see how the total file size is distributed over frames of your movie.

- **Protect your movie from being imported into Flash**: Choose the Protect from import option to require a password when importing your SWF into Flash. This will help prevent other folks from reusing your SWF files within their own FLAs. When you check this option, the Password field below will become active. Enter the password you will require for importing your SWF into Flash.

- **Omit trace actions**: Choose the Omit trace actions option to have the compiler skip over any trace actions in your application. This can reduce the amount of work the Flash Player has to do while running your program.

- **Permit debugging**: Choose the Permit debugging option if you wish to publish a SWF that can be debugged remotely.

The next setting in the Advanced area, Local playback, is an either/or proposition. By default, SWF files can access local files and networks but cannot communicate with or send files or information to remote networks. Choose Access network only to reverse this and give the SWF file the ability to communicate and send files but *not* the ability to access local files or the local network.

The Hardware Acceleration menu dictates whether or not the published SWF takes advantage of any graphics processing power of the computer it is being played on. You can choose from these three options:

- None: Select this option if you do not wish for your published SWF to take advantage of the host computer's graphics hardware.

- Level 1 Direct: Select this option if you want the Flash Player to use the most direct method available on the host machine to render—bypassing the browser's rendering for instance.

- Level 2 GPU: Take special care when selecting this option, as there are specific hardware requirements involved, and if your user's computer has an incompatible graphics card, you may run into performance issues. Content should be designed specifically to take advantage of GPU acceleration such as full-screen refreshes.

18

The final publish setting in the Flash options page is the Script time limit option. Enter a value in this input box to set a time limit on how long your published SWF is permitted to run a script before a timeout alert is shown to the user.

Setting HTML publishing options

The options on the HTML tab are used to determine what HTML and JavaScript need to be written to the published HTML document in order to display your SWF and support the functionality you need. Refer to Figure 18-4 as you read through the settings presented in this section.

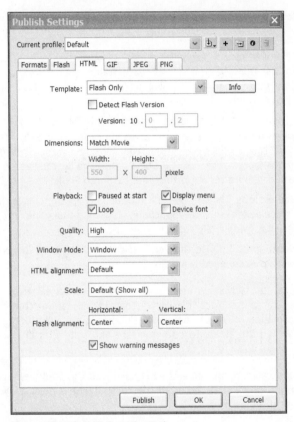

Figure 18-4. The HTML settings tab

Choosing a template

HTML templates are used to quickly generate HTML that properly supports Flash for various purposes, each specific to a particular template as outlined in the template's description, like adding support for AICC tracking or for use with HTTPS. To read a template's description, select the template from the Template drop-down menu, and then click the Info button that appears to the right of it. The Flash Only template, for instance, creates HTML that supplies only the necessary elements to include SWF content on an HTML document.

To create code in your published HTML that compares the version of the Flash plug-in version of your user's system against a version of your choosing, check the Detect Flash Version check box.

Once the Detect Flash Version check box is checked, you may enter major revision and minor revision numbers in the available text input boxes, but you cannot change the player version. The player version is set on the Flash tab of the Publish Settings window.

> *The Flash Player has been released in 10 versions. These versions of the player represent major changes in how the player operates, and they usually, but not always, coincide with new releases of the Flash authoring software. Sometimes Adobe will make significant changes to the player, such as adding support for new additions to ActionScript, that do not warrant a new release. These releases are called **major revisions**. Between major revisions may come some small tweaks to the player that include things like security patches; these releases are called **minor revisions**.*

Setting dimensions

The Dimensions setting changes the dimensions of your SWF as it is embedded in the HTML document. It does not change the stage dimensions of your FLA or your published SWF. Change the dimensions of the stage of your document itself by using the Document Properties dialog. To do so, select Modify ➤ Document.

Using the Dimensions setting is akin to setting dimensions of an image in HTML. Your options are as follows:

- Match Movie uses the document dimensions to dictate the size reflected in the HTML as shown in Figure 18-4.

- Pixels lets you manually enter the dimensions you want your published SWF to have in the HTML as shown in Figure 18-4.

- Percent makes the dimensions of your Flash movie a percentage of the available area in the HTML document.

> *The Dimensions setting works together with the Scale setting discussed later in this section.*

Changing Playback options

Use the Playback options to determine how your SWF will behave once it is downloaded into the browser. Your options are as follows:

- Paused at start will stop the main timeline of your SWF on the first frame. This is unchecked by default.

- Display menu will allow the user to right-click (Ctrl+click on a Mac) anywhere over the embedded Flash movie to see the extended shortcut menu. This menu gives the user the ability to zoom in and out as well as control playback of the timeline.

18

- Loop will cause the SWF to repeat. This is checked by default.
- Device font allows the Flash Player to replace any fonts used in the SWF that are not installed on the user's computer with a font that is on the user's system. This option applies only to the Windows version of the Flash Player.

Changing quality

Use the Quality drop-down menu to determine how the Flash Player prioritizes the rendering quality of its visual assets. The default value is High, but your options are as follows:

- Low turns off all anti-aliasing, making it easier for slower computers to render the SWF but at a much lower quality.
- Auto Low starts with low-quality rendering but will switch to higher quality if the user's system is powerful enough to maintain playback using high-quality processing.
- Auto High starts with high-quality rendering but will switch to low quality if the user's system cannot keep up with the high-quality processing requirements.
- Medium uses anti-aliasing when rendering vector graphics but at a lower resolution than the High quality setting.
- High uses a higher-resolution anti-aliasing when rendering vector graphics than the Medium quality setting. If the SWF contains animation, bitmaps are not smoothed. Otherwise, bitmaps are smoothed.
- Best is the same as High with the exception that bitmap graphics are smoothed whether there is animation or not.

Changing window mode

The Window Mode setting determines how the SWF interacts visually with its container in the HTML document. You have the following options:

- In Window mode, which is the default, the HTML cannot render on top (in front) of or under (behind) the SWF, and the SWF will use the HTML background color.
- In Opaque Windowless mode, the background of the SWF will be opaque (hiding anything behind it on the page) but will allow HTML to render on top of it.
- In Transparent Windowless mode, the background of the SWF will be transparent. This is the mode for those "appear anywhere" ads that move around on your browser.

> *Turning on* Hardware Acceleration *in the* Flash *tab of the* Publish Settings *window will cause the* Window Mode *setting to be ignored when deployed. In this case, the* Window *setting will be used instead.*

Changing HTML alignment

The HTML alignment setting positions the SWF file window in the browser window. You have the following options:

- Default will center the SWF in the browser window. This will crop the edges if the browser window is smaller than the SWF dimensions.
- Left, Right, Top, or Bottom options will align the SWF file along the selected edge of the browser window. This will crop the other sides of the SWF as needed.

Changing scale behavior

The Scale setting places the SWF within certain boundaries if you've changed the SWF's original width and height. Your options here are as follows:

- Default (Show all) will show the entire SWF in the HTML with the original aspect ratio of the SWF.
- No Border will scale the SWF to the specified area while maintaining the SWF file's original aspect ratio.
- Exact Fit resizes the SWF; however, if it needs to stretch or compress the SWF horizontally and vertically in order to fill the available area, it may cause distortion.
- No Scale prevents the SWF from scaling when the Flash Player window is resized.

Changing Flash alignment

The Flash alignment setting works with the Dimensions and Scale settings. If cropping occurs due to the other settings, the Flash alignment setting determines how the Flash content will be cropped. You can control the vertical and horizontal options for this setting independently according to the following options:

- Horizontal
  - Left aligns Flash content left in the player, cropping the right side.
  - Center horizontally centers Flash content in the player, cropping the left and right sides.
  - Right aligns Flash content right in the player, cropping the left side.
- Vertical
  - Top top-aligns Flash content in the player, cropping the bottom.
  - Center vertically centers Flash content in the player, cropping the top and bottom.
  - Bottom bottom-aligns Flash content in the player, cropping the top.

Setting GIF publishing options

Flash offers you the full range of settings for outputting the GIF file format as part of publishing your movie. Use Figure 18-5 as reference as we go over these options. Usually this image would be used in place of your SWF in an HTML document if the user does not have the Flash Player.

18

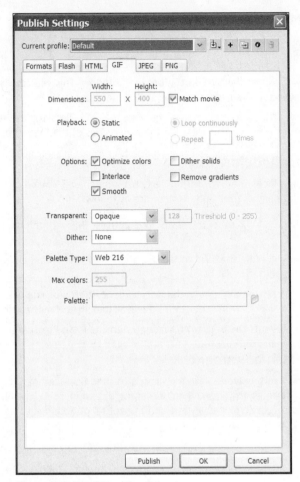

Figure 18-5. The GIF settings tab

Setting image dimensions

Use the Dimensions options to determine the dimensions of the GIF file. The Match movie check box is selected by default and will create a GIF that has the same dimensions as your FLA document. To change the dimensions, uncheck the Match movie check box and manually enter the dimensions you want.

Changing playback behavior

Flash can generate a static or animated GIF. A static GIF is a single image created from the first frame of your FLA. If you wish to publish an animated GIF, click the Animated radio button. This will enable the Loop continuously and Repeat options. Leaving Loop continuously (the default) selected will obviously create an animated GIF that loops over and over without end. Alternatively, you could select the Repeat radio button and enter the number of times you wish the animation to loop.

Other options

The Options settings control a variety of appearance settings for the published GIF. You have the following choices:

- Optimize colors will remove any unused colors from a GIF file's color table.
- Dither solids will apply dithering (the process of using pixels of two or more different colors to approximate an in-between color) to solid colors of the published GIF.
- Interlace shows the published GIF incrementally as it downloads.
- Remove gradients will convert all gradient fills in the published SWF to solid colors using the first color in the gradient. This option is disabled by default.
- Smooth will apply anti-aliasing to a published GIF. This will produce a higher-quality image and may improve the readability of text. Beware of artifacts around the edge of your image.

Changing transparency

The Transparent settings determine if and how transparency will be applied to your published GIF. These are your options:

- Opaque will create a GIF with a solid background.
- Transparent will make the background of the Flash document transparent.
- Alpha will make everything in your Flash document whose alpha value is below the threshold in the Threshold setting completely transparent. For instance, if your Threshold is set to 128, anything in your Flash document with an alpha of 50 percent or lower will be 100 percent transparent in the published GIF. This is the only transparency option to which the threshold can be applied.

Changing dither

The Dither option determines how pixels in the GIF's color table are combined to simulate colors that are not in the color table. Your options for dithering are as follows:

- None turns off dithering and replaces colors not in the basic color table with the solid color from the table closest to it.
- Ordered is good-quality dithering with little increase in file size.
- Diffusion will give you the highest-quality results. This option only works if the Web 216 color palette (discussed next) is selected.

> *Dithering increases file size and processing time.*

Changing palette type and other color settings

The Palette Type setting determines the GIF file's color palette. You can choose from one of the following palette types:

- Web 216 will use the standard 216-color, web-safe palette to create the GIF image.
- Adaptive will have Flash analyze the colors in the image and create a color table based on the content in your movie. This creates the best palette for your image but increases file size.
- Web Snap Adaptive will also have Flash analyze your image but will replace colors that are not in the Web 216 color palette with similar colors of the Web 216 color palette.
- Custom lets you determine the palette for your image. To select a custom palette, click the folder icon next to the Palette text field at the bottom of the GIF tab, and then select a palette file.

If you selected the Adaptive or Web Snap Adaptive palette options, you can enter a value for Max colors to set the number of colors actually used in the GIF image. Reducing the number of colors can produce a smaller file but, of course, may cost you in quality.

Setting PNG publishing options

The PNG file format is another image format available for publishing from your Flash file.

Many of the settings for PNG (shown in Figure 18-6) behave in a similar fashion to the settings for the GIF file format, which we just discussed. Please refer to the publishing options for the GIF file format for explanations of the following settings:

- Dimensions
- Options
- Dither
- Palette Type

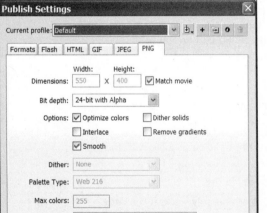

Figure 18-6. The PNG settings tab

Bit depth

PNG files can be published at two different bit depths from Flash, 8 bit and 24 bit. There is a third option, 24 bit with alpha, which is technically 32 bits per channel (bpc). Use the Bit depth drop-down menu to set the number of bits per pixel and colors to use while publishing the PNG. (The higher the bit depth, the larger the file.) These are your options:

- 8-bit will create a 256-color image.
- 24-bit will create an image with thousands of colors.
- 24-bit with Alpha will create an image with thousands of colors and transparency (32 bpc).

Filter options

The Filter options settings for publishing a PNG file determine what type of algorithm and/ or processing is applied to your image. Select from the following options:

- None turns off filtering. Files with this setting might be larger than they need to be.

- Sub uses information from comparing one pixel to the previous pixel (horizontally).

- Up uses information from comparing one pixel to the pixel that is immediately above it.

- Average uses information from comparing one pixel to two neighboring pixels (left and above).

- Path uses information from the three neighboring pixels (left, above, upper left) to help predict a pixel's color.

- Adaptive analyzes all of the colors in an image and creates a unique color table. This will create the most accurate result but generate the largest file size.

Setting JPEG publishing options

Another option for publishing a bitmap from your movie is the JPEG file format. The JPEG settings tab is shown in Figure 18-7.

Dimensions

Use the Dimensions options to determine the dimensions of the JPEG file. The Match movie check box is selected by default and will create a JPEG that has the same dimensions as your FLA document. To change the dimensions, uncheck the Match movie check box and manually enter the dimensions you want.

Quality

To adjust the amount of compression applied to the published JPEG, drag the slider or enter a value. Select the Progressive check box to publish a JPEG that shows incrementally in a web browser. This can make your image appear faster when loading with a slow network connection (but at a lower quality at first). This option has a similar effect to that of interlacing in GIF and PNG images.

Managing publish profiles

Flash will let you save a selection of output formats and their settings as a single profile. Publish profiles are a great way to repeatedly and consistently generate files for specific situations or clients.

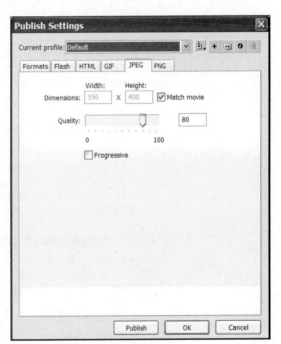

Figure 18-7. The JPEG settings tab

The five controls across the top of the Publish Settings window help you manage publish profiles. These controls are shown in Figure 18-8.

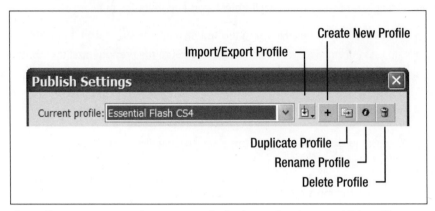

Figure 18-8. You can save and manage sets of selections and settings as publish profiles.

Importing and exporting profiles

Importing and exporting profiles can be useful when trying to maintain standards while working on a team. Taking advantage of this capability allows a standard to be created and exported to a file, which can then be imported by other members of the team.

To import your current selections and settings as a publish profile, click the Import/Export Profile button and select Import. Browse to the publish profile file and click OK. To export your current selections and settings as a publish profile, click the Import/Export Profile button and select Export. Browse to the location where you wish to save your publish profile, name the file, and save.

Creating publish profiles

After carefully selecting all the right settings for all of your output formats, you'll want to create a publish profile for yourself that you can use quickly and easily. To add a publish profile to your drop-down list of available profiles, click the Create New Profile button shown in Figure 18-8. Name your profile and click OK. The current set of selections and settings will be immediately available as a profile in the Current profile drop-down menu.

Duplicating publish profiles

Duplicating publish profiles might be a handy feature if you decide you need to create slight variations on a profile. Simply select a profile from the Current profile drop-down menu and click the Duplicate Profile button (shown in Figure 18-8).

Use the Rename Profile button shown in Figure 18-8 to quickly rename the currently selected profile.

Deleting publish profiles

Of course, you don't want to have a bunch of old stale profiles stinking up the joint, so to delete a publish profile, select a profile from the Current profile drop-down menu and click the Delete Profile button (shown in Figure 18-8).

While the Publish Settings window offers many options for preparing your content for the world to see, there may be times when you need less control and more convenience or perhaps a format or two not supported under the Publish Settings window. For this we have the ability to quickly export various files from Flash, which we'll cover next.

Exporting file formats

To export a single file format from Flash without having to publish it, you can use the Export menu from the File menu (File ➤ Export). You can choose to either export an image file or a movie file and image sequence. Although the movie file and image sequence options are listed together, exporting your FLA as a movie file creates a single video or SWF file, while exporting your FLA as an image sequence will create many image files.

Exporting an image

To export an image from your Flash file, select File ➤ Export ➤ Export Image. This will open the Export Image dialog, shown in Figure 18-9. This dialog works just like a standard Save As dialog, with a Save as type drop-down menu from which to select a file format to export to. Use this dialog to choose a file name and location. Then from the Save as type drop-down menu, select what image format you want to create.

Figure 18-9. Exporting an image begins with a Save as type dialog

Exporting your FLA as a movie or image sequence

To export your FLA as a movie or image sequence, select File ➤ Export ➤ Export Movie. This will open the Export Movie dialog shown in Figure 18-10. Again, this dialog works just like a standard Save As dialog, with a Save as type drop-down menu from which to select a file format to export to. Use this dialog to choose a file name and location. Then from the Save as type drop-down menu, select a movie format or image sequence format.

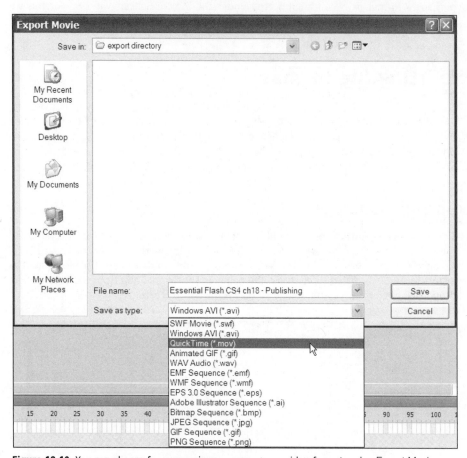

Figure 18-10. You can choose from many image sequence or video formats using Export Movie.

QuickTime

Selecting QuickTime (*.mov) from the Save as type drop-down menu will open the QuickTime Export Settings dialog shown in Figure 18-11. This dialog has some options for controlling the disk process of exporting such as the following:

- Stop exporting allows you to choose to stop exporting at the last frame of the FLA or at a specified time.

■ **Store temp data** allows you to choose between storing temporary data to memory or to a specified place on your system's hard disk.

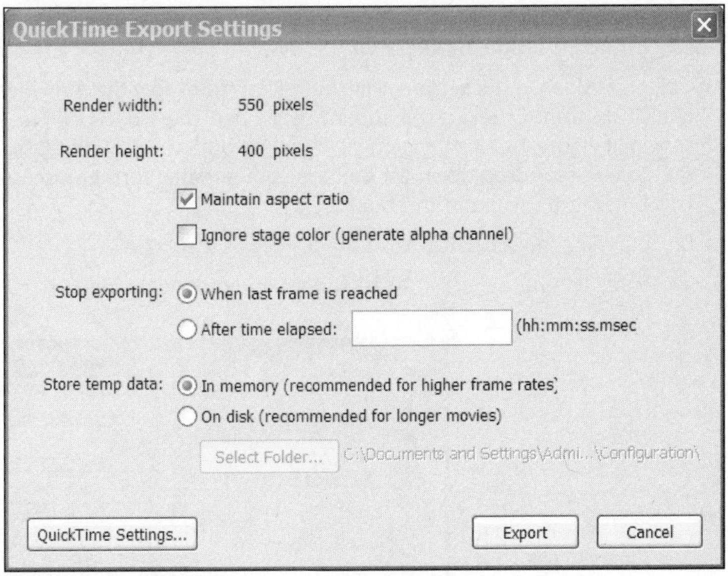

Figure 18-11. The QuickTime Export Settings dialog

At the bottom of the QuickTime Export Settings dialog is a button labeled QuickTime Settings. Click this button for extended control over the QuickTime video settings used to export your FLA as a video. The options and dialogs brought up by QuickTime Settings fall outside the scope of this book. We recommend you refer to the documentation provided with Apple QuickTime Pro for detailed information.

Windows AVI

If you are on a Windows system, you will have the additional capability of selecting Windows AVI (*.avi) from the Save as type drop-down menu. If you select this format, clicking Save will open the Export Windows AVI dialog box, which you see in Figure 18-12.

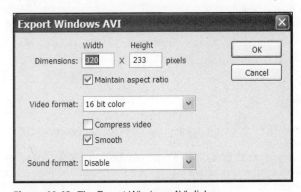

Figure 18-12. The Export Windows AVI dialog

Your options are as follows:

- **Dimensions** changes the dimensions of the video file. Uncheck the Maintain aspect ratio check box to control the height and width values independently.
- Video format controls the bit depth of the AVI.
  - Compress video, if unchecked, will cause Flash to export the AVI when you click the OK button. Checking this option will open the Video Compression dialog shown in Figure 18-13 when you click the OK button. Some of CODECs listed in the Compressor drop-down list box are configurable; further discussion of this falls outside the scope of this book.
  - Smooth will apply anti-aliasing to the frames of the video.
- Sound format lets you select a format for the audio of your video.

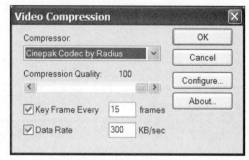

Figure 18-13.
If you choose to compress your AVI, you can choose what compressor to use.

Long before you are ready to publish or export your work for the world, you will no doubt encounter some issues in getting your project to work as intended. To help exterminate the errors in your application, continue on for some strategies for debugging in Flash.

Debugging in Flash

Whether you are just writing your first few lines of code or wrapping up a project, there are usually some things that don't work in the way that you expect them to. Technically speaking, that's what a **bug** is. In order to find the bugs, you need to be able to determine what kinds of errors are happening. We're concerned with the three following types of errors:

- Compile-time errors
- Runtime errors
- Syntax errors

Compile-time errors occur as the code in your application is compiled.

Technically speaking, **syntax errors** are a type of compiler error. Syntax errors result when the text that makes up the code in your project does not follow the rules of the programming language—just as if we were to leave the period off of the end of this sentence.

Syntax errors are usually the easiest type of bug to find and fix—and not that hard to make either! **Runtime errors** are errors that happen as your application is running.

Here is one example of a syntax error since the variable declaration is missing:

```
example:String = "this won't work";
```

The code should be as follows:

```
var example:String = "this will work";
```

You can check the syntax of your code in the Actions panel as you work by pressing Ctrl+T (or Cmd+T on the Mac) at any time. If there are syntax errors in your code, you will see the alert window shown in Figure 18-14.

Figure 18-14. You'll see this alert if you check the syntax of a script and have errors.

Finding other types of compiler errors is almost as easy as finding syntax errors, the difference being that you will need to test your movie to expose them. To do so, press Ctrl+Enter (or Cmd+Enter on a Mac). If there are compiler errors, you will not necessarily receive an alert. You will need to check the Compiler Errors panel to see if there were any errors. Let's take a closer look at that panel right now.

Using the Compiler Errors panel

It's important to understand that although Flash tries really hard to tell you what errors are occurring, you will need to understand ActionScript in order to properly interpret the errors. Consider the following code:

```
package {
  import flash.display.MovieClip;
  public class ErrorExample extends MovieClip{
    private var bigBoy:String = "The Big Boy is a steam locomotive";
    public function ErrorExample()
    {
      trace("sometimes errors need interpretation")
    }
  }
}
```

Type the preceding code in the Actions panel and then press Ctrl+T (Cmd+T on the Mac) to check the syntax. Click OK to close the alert and look at the Compiler Errors panel, which should appear similar to what you see in Figure 18-15.

18

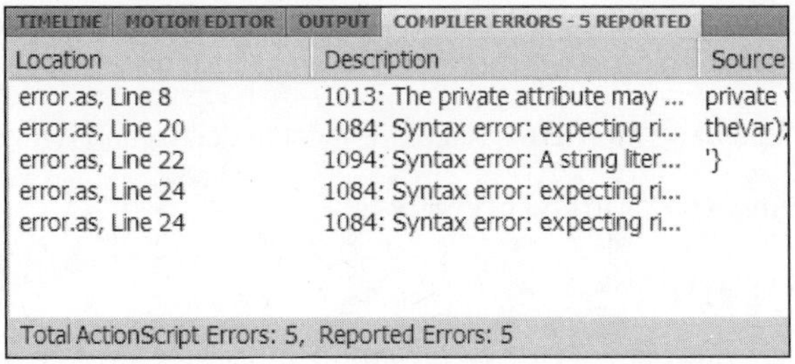

TIMELINE	MOTION EDITOR	OUTPUT	COMPILER ERRORS - 5 REPORTED	
Location		Description		Source
error.as, Line 8		1013: The private attribute may ...		private
error.as, Line 20		1084: Syntax error: expecting ri...		theVar);
error.as, Line 22		1094: Syntax error: A string liter...		'}
error.as, Line 24		1084: Syntax error: expecting ri...		
error.as, Line 24		1084: Syntax error: expecting ri...		

Total ActionScript Errors: 5, Reported Errors: 5

Figure 18-15. Most of your debugging happens in the Compiler errors panel (shown) and the Output panel (tabbed).

The columns in the Compiler Errors panel show the following information:

- Location will indicate what file, layer (if in an FLA), and line of code the error is on.
- Description will show you the error code and a prescribed text description of your error.
- Source shows the actual source code where the error is occurring.

The only one thing missing from the script is a right brace (}) to close the class definition code block. However, there are five errors, because those errors are created with that one thing missing.

If you look at the bold line of code in the preceding example, you'll see that there's nothing wrong with it by itself; however, it violates the rule stated in error 1013, part of which is shown in Figure 18-15. The entire rule is as follows:

```
1013: The private attribute may be used only on class property
definitions
```

The error is generated because of how that line of code (in bold) appears within the rest of the code. Therefore, since the line by itself is good, you would have to interpret the error description to mean that the code you have written does not properly define a class.

Adding the right brace (}) as shown next completes the class definition and eliminates all of the errors.

```
package {
  import flash.display.MovieClip;
  public class ErrorExample extends MovieClip{
    public function ErrorExample()
    {
      trace("sometimes errors need interpretation");
      var bigBoy:String = "The Big Boy is a steam locomotive";
    }
  }
}
```

You can navigate directly to the source code that is indicated in an error by clicking the Go to Source button on the bottom-right corner of the panel.

It's possible for your Flash application to run—or appear to run—while it has compile-time errors. So be sure to check the Compiler Errors *panel if things don't seem to be working properly.*

Using the Output window—strategies for tracing

In our experience, 90 percent of bugs in ActionScript come from programming the following kinds of errors:

- Scope errors
- Typos
- Timing errors

Because Flash can only tell you the errors that result from your code and not necessarily how to fix them, you may need to get creative in looking for what's causing the problem.

Hunting scope errors

As we defined in Chapter 8, the term **scope** refers to what parts of a program's code have the ability to reference a variable. To find an error in scope using the trace statement, simply try to trace the variable in question where you are trying reference it, and then look in the Output window to see if it has the value you expect it to have—or any value at all. If it has an unexpected value, you can move on to finding out why; if it has no value, most likely you are attempting to use a variable that does not exist within the scope of the code block where it is being referenced.

Running the following code will result in an error:

```
function varFunc(){
   var theVar:String = "this string will only be available in this ➡
function because it was declared here using the var keyword";
}

function scopeErrorFunction(){
   trace(theVar);
}
varFunc();
scopeErrorFunction();
```

The error description 1120: Access of undefined property theVar simply means that the compiler does not know about an object (variable) called theVar within the context of the function that's trying to use it. To correct the error, you would need to declare the variable in a place where the varFunc function would have access to it as shown in the following code:

```
var theVar:String;

function varFunc(){
  theVar = "this string will now be available elsewhere ➥
because it was declared elsewhere";
}

function scopeErrorFunction(){
  trace(theVar);
}
varFunc();
scopeErrorFunction();
```

Finding typos

Typos are usually exposed when checking syntax but can sometimes result in a scope error or the code not compiling at all. The following code will result in an error because theBar (shown in bold) does not exist. These are easy mistakes to make but can cause a significant amount of hair loss.

```
var theVar:String;

function varFunc(){
  theVar = "this string will now be available elsewhere ➥
because it was declared elsewhere";
}

function scopeErrorFunction(){
  trace(theBar);
}
varFunc();
scopeErrorFunction();
```

Tracking timing errors

Timing errors occur when trying to reference objects or values that don't exist yet. If we continue with our previous example (correcting our typo) and switch the last two lines of code as shown next, we will see null in our Output window because the value of the variable has not been set yet.

```
var theVar:String;

function varFunc(){
  theVar = "this string will only be available in this ➥
function because it was declared here using the var keyword";
}

function scopeErrorFunction(){
  trace(theVar); //null
```

```
    }
    scopeErrorFunction();
    varFunc();
```

This is an extremely simplified example, as you can plainly see the functions being called in the wrong order. Most timing errors occur because Flash executes your code in a way that you may not expect. In these cases, tracing to the Output window may not give you enough information to track down exactly where or when the error is occurring. To track down this type of issue, you will want to use the Flash debugger. You might want to pay particular attention to the discussion of the call stack in the section "Understanding the call stack" later in this chapter.

Using the debugger

It may not seem like it on the surface, but as you use ActionScript to create your applications, you are actually taking advantage of a lot of ActionScript written as part of the language itself. Because of this, you may not always be aware of how Flash is executing your part of the code in turn with its own internal processes.

Additionally, you may find yourself on a project where you lack the benefit of having written the application code yourself and therefore may not know exactly where to start when attempting to fix bugs. Flash debugger helps give you this insight.

To use the Flash debugger, select Debug ➤ Debug Movie from the application menu. This will compile your application for debugging and change your workspace to the Debug workspace shown in Figure 18-16. You can also enter the Debug workspace by using the workspace menu explained in Chapter 2.

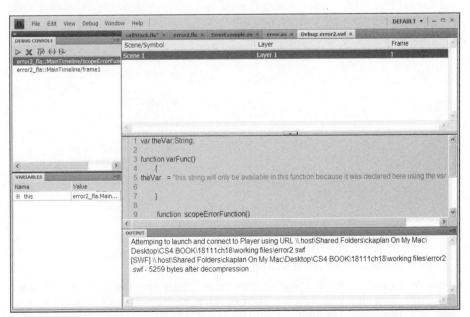

Figure 18-16. The Flash Debug workspace includes the Debug Console panel, Variables panel, script pane, and Output panel.

485

Setting and removing breakpoints

A **breakpoint** is a point you set during authoring where the debugger will stop executing code normally and wait for you to advance the program. To set a breakpoint, click in the margin of the Actions panel to the left of the line numbers. If the line numbers are not visible, click to the left of the hairline to add a breakpoint. Figure 18-17 shows a breakpoint that has been set at line 7.

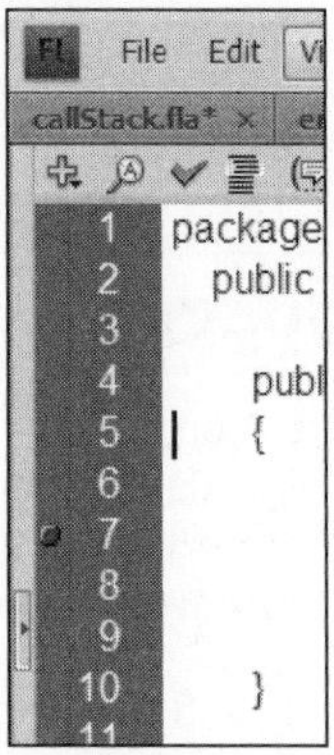

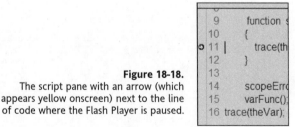

Figure 18-17.
The dot (which appears red onscreen) to the left of the code line numbers is a breakpoint. The debugger will stop here during a debug session.

> To turn line numbers off and on in an ActionScript document, click View ➤ Line Numbers. If you're using the Actions panel of an FLA, click Line Numbers in the panel menu.

To remove all of the breakpoints in a given script at once, click Debug ➤ Remove Breakpoints in This File in an ActionScript document or select Debug ➤ Remove All Breakpoints when working in the Actions panel of an FLA. Now when you debug your movie, you'll notice that the execution of code has been stopped at your breakpoint. Figure 18-18 shows the script pane with an arrow next to the line of code where the Flash Player is paused.

Figure 18-18.
The script pane with an arrow (which appears yellow onscreen) next to the line of code where the Flash Player is paused.

Understanding the call stack

While the player has stopped executing code temporarily is when you can look around and see what's going on in your program. The **call stack** is a list, or "stack," of all the function calls that have been made but not yet completed. This list is key in identifying timing errors, as in the example in "Tracking timing errors" earlier in this chapter, and shows what functions are being called and in what order.

You'll find the call stack in the Debug Console panel, which is shown in Figure 18-19. The topmost item in the stack is the function executed most recently.

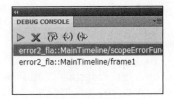

Figure 18-19.
The call stack during a debug session

Now, consider the following code:

```
function one(){
  trace("function one");
  three();
}

function two(){
  trace("function two will be called first");
}

function three(){
  trace("this is called as function one executes");
}

two();
one();
```

Figure 18-19 shows the call stack as function three in the preceding code (highlighted in the call stack) is executed. Notice that after it begins execution, function one takes a second spot on the call stack while it waits for function three to complete.

This example is much easier to understand as you step through the code. So do just that. What we have are three function declarations followed by two function calls. The functions are executed in the order in which they are called. Use the call stack and breakpoints to observe the execution order.

Navigating code while debugging

At this point you want to carefully go through the execution of code one line at a time. To execute one line of code at a time, click the Step In button at the top of the Debug Console panel shown in Figure 18-20. As you step through the code, the arrow that you saw in Figure 18-18 will point to the line of code that will execute when you click the Step In button.

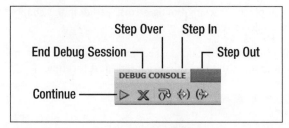

Figure 18-20. The Debug Console panel controls

As you go through the code, you may wish to skip a line altogether. To do this click the Step Over button at the top of the Debug Console panel. You can also choose to step out of the current function by clicking the Step Out button. This will take you to the line of code that would have executed after that function.

Resuming normal code execution

When you want the application to run normally until the next breakpoint is reached, click the Continue button (see Figure 18-20). And of course when you are done debugging, click the End Debug Session button (also shown in Figure 18-20).

Using the Variables panel

Understanding the call stack and knowing how to step in and out of code will only get you so far unless you can inspect the value of the variables in your code. For this we have the Variables panel. Figure 18-21 shows the Variables panel during debugging.

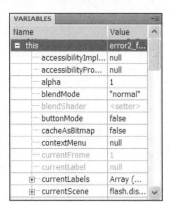

Figure 18-21.
The Variables panel shown with main timeline (this) variables expanded. These are really the properties of the display container that is the main timeline.

To change the value of a variable during debugging, simply click the Value column next to the variable you wish to change, type in the new value, and press Enter. Changing the value of a variable as the application is running is a good way to test theories about what might be broken or to deliberately make some code function by changing the outcome of a conditional evaluation (if...then). To see the values of variables in a given function, select the function in the call stack and look in the Variables panel.

A nice feature of the AS3 debugger is that you can change the value of a variable as you debug.

Summary

There's a lot to do before you can set your creations free on the Web, CD, DVD, or mobile device; and with so many possibilities come many, many options to consider and bugs to look out for. In this chapter we talked about the following:

- Choosing options in the Publish Settings window
- Managing publish profiles as well as importing and exporting profiles
- Exporting images, image sequences, and video from Flash
- Finding different types of errors in our code
- Using the Compiler Errors panel, Output panel, and debugger to track down and correct errors

18

CHAPTER 19

BUILDING AIR APPLICATIONS WITH FLASH CS4

The Adobe Integrated Runtime (AIR) is to the desktop what the Flash Player is to the browser. You could say that Adobe AIR is a like a plug-in for your operating system, but what it really does is give you the benefits of being connected to the Internet while at the same time being a first-class citizen on the host computer, breaking the constraints of living within the web browser!

So what does the runtime integrate exactly? At the heart of AIR are three big pillars:

- The WebKit Hypertext Markup Language (HTML) rendering engine
- The Flash Player
- SQLite as a database engine

Because of these three core parts, you can build desktop applications with web technologies like JavaScript, HTML, and Flash or Flex. Unlike in Silverlight (which is limited to the web browser and more akin to the Flash Player plug-in), building applications in AIR gives you the ability to add real desktop functionality like file system access and drag-and-drop while using the web technologies you may already be familiar with.

In this chapter we're going to talk about

- Using AIR application programming interfaces (APIs)
  - The Windowing API
  - The Menu API
  - The Network Detection API
  - The File System API
- Configuring the application using the AIR – Application & Installer Settings dialog
- Deploying and packaging the application for distribution

Later in this chapter, we'll show you how to build a working AIR application, but before we do that, it is important that you learn about some of the AIR APIs.

> If you want to learn more about AIR, go to www.adobe.com/go/air, or check out the title The Essential Guide to Flash CS4 AIR Development by Marco Casario (friends of ED, 2008).

Using AIR APIs

In order to create applications that behave like first-class citizens, AIR provides extra APIs for you to call and use. Before you start building your first application, it may be a good idea to learn about these APIs as you will need them in most of your applications. In this section, we'll cover the Windowing API, Menu API, Network Detection API, and File System API. These are the APIs you'll use in the sample application.

Windowing API

Your first application window is created automatically, but in some cases one window is not enough. In a chat application, for instance, you may want to open up the conversation in a different window or pop up a small window when one of your friends signs on. The AIR Windowing API allows you to do just that.

The normal window

The normal window, as shown in Figure 19-1, looks and behaves just like a typical application window on your operating system. It has all the standard features like Close, Minimize, and Maximize buttons, a title bar, and a status bar. The status bar is shown by default. You can remove the status bar by setting the showStatusBar property to false. The title bar in the main application window will display the application name if no other title is specified. You can specify a different title by setting the title property for your window.

Figure 19-1.
A normal window

The utility window

The utility window, as shown in Figure 19-2, almost looks the same as the normal window with the exception of a smaller title bar and no status bar. This type of window is typically used to display notifications—for example, when a friend logs on to an instant messaging server or when you received a new e-mail.

Figure 19-2.
The utility window

For both these windows, the resize gripper is optional. When you set the window's resizable property to false, the resize gripper will not appear. Alternatively, you can set the showGripper property to false, which results in the default resize gripper not being shown. This can be used to create your own resize icon.

The lightweight window

The last option is the lightweight window, as shown in Figure 19-3. This option does not have any system chrome and is perfect for creating your own custom chrome. Because no chrome is available, you must create the standard window functionality, such as closing and resizing, yourself. When creating a new window, you can also set the chrome options that are shown in Figure 19-4.

Figure 19-3.
A lightweight window
does not have any
system chrome.

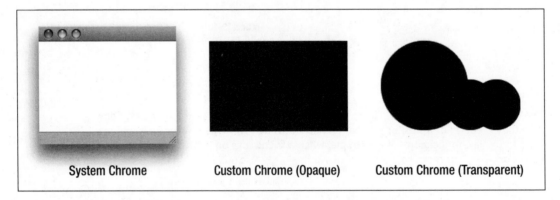

Figure 19-4. Chrome options available in the AIR Windowing API

> *The* System Chrome *option will add the system chrome to your window regardless of the operating system your application runs on. So if you run this application on Windows, your application's windows will look like any other application's windows. The same goes for OS X and Linux operating systems.*

If you want to create custom chrome, you have two options available to you—Custom Chrome (opaque) and Custom Chrome (transparent). With Custom Chrome (transparent), your window chrome can be a free-form shape. If you want your custom chrome to have an irregular shape (as is the chrome on the far right in Figure 19-4), this option allows you to do that. A click anywhere in the black area shown in Figure 19-4 will register in the application. A click anywhere outside this black area will register on the desktop or the application behind your application.

Creating windows with the NativeWindow class

The NativeWindow class allows you to create new windows with ActionScript. The options for this window are declared in an instance of the NativeWindowInitOptions class, as shown here:

```
// create an instance of the NativeWindowInitOptions
// and set all the options for your window
var myWindowOptions:NativeWindowInitOptions =➡
 new NativeWindowInitOptions();
myWindowOptions.transparent = false;
myWindowOptions.systemChrome = NativeWindowSystemChrome.STANDARD;
myWindowOptions.type = NativeWindowType.UTILITY;

// create the actual window
var myWindow:NativeWindow = new NativeWindow(myWindowOptions);
myWindow.title = "My Utility Window";
myWindow.width = 200;
myWindow.height = 100;

// activate and show the new window
myWindow.activate();
```

In this case we created a utility window that has standard system chrome, is 200 by 100 pixels big, and has the title set to My Utility Window, as shown in Figure 19-5.

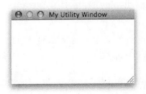

Figure 19-5.
The result from the
NativeWindowInitOptions
class code example

Windowing API methods

Since you are working with windows, you obviously also need a number of methods to interact with those windows. Here are a few examples of methods that you might find useful:

- NativeWindow.activate() and NativeWindow.close(): Opens and closes the newly created window
- NativeWindow.maximize() and NativeWindow.minimize(): Maximizes and minimizes your window

- NativeWindow.orderInBackOf(NativeWindow) and NativeWindow.orderInFrontOf (NativeWindow): Sends the window directly in the back or the front of the specified window
- NativeWindow.orderToBack() and NativeWindow.orderToFront(): Sends your window behind or in front of any other visible windows

Windowing API events

When your users interact with your application windows, you also need to be able to listen to specific events. These are the event listeners available in the flash.events.Event class:

- Event.activate: Dispatches after the window has been activated
- Event.deactivate: Dispatches when the window has been deactivated
- Event.closing: Dispatches immediately before the window is about to be closed (for instance, when your user clicks the Close button of your window
- Event.close: Dispatches after the window has been closed

The following event listeners are available in the flash.events.NativeBoundsEvent class:

- NativeBoundsEvent.moving: Dispatches immediately before the window is about to be moved
- NativeBoundsEvent.move: Dispatches after the window has been moved
- NativeBoundsEvent.resizing: Dispatches immediately before the window is about to be resized
- NativeBoundsEvent.resize: Dispatches after the window has been resized

Finally, here are the event listeners in the flash.events.NativeWindowDisplayStateEvent class:

- NativeWindowDisplayStateEvent.display_state_changing: Dispatches immediately before the window changes its display state (for instance, from regular view to full-screen mode)
- NativeWindowDisplayStateEvent.display_state_change: Dispatches after the window's displayState property is changed

Using these events is as simple as adding an event listener to your window. For instance:

```
myWindow.addEventListener(NativeBoundsEvent.moving, WinMoving);
function WinMoving(evt:Event)
{
    trace("MyWindow is moving");
}
```

Menu API

Various operating systems have very different menu options. For this reason, you need to add some OS-specific code to make sure that your menus work across all the operating systems supported by AIR. This section will discuss the following types of menus:

- Window menu
- Application menu
- System tray menu
- Dock menu

Window menu

The window menu, shown in Figure 19-6, is always associated with a single window and is always displayed below the title bar. Different windows can also have different menus. The window menu is only available on Windows operating systems, not on OS X systems. You create a window menu by using the following code:

```
var myMenu:NativeMenu = new NativeMenu();
myWindow.menu = myMenu;
```

Figure 19-6.
Example of a window menu

Application menu

An application menu (see Figure 19-7) applies to the whole application. Application menus are supported on OS X but not on Windows systems. On OS X, the application is always in the global menu bar. To create an application menu, use this code:

```
var myMenu:NativeMenu = new NativeMenu();
NativeApplication.NativeApplication.menu = myMenu;
```

Figure 19-7.
Example of an application menu

In most cases your application will have only one global menu. Since your AIR application can run on a variety of Windows, OS X, or Linux operating systems, you need to perform a quick check to see whether window menus or application menus are supported on the system the user is running your application on. The following code should be all you need to do this:

```
if (NativeApplication.supportsMenu)
{
  // for OSX
  NativeApplication.nativeApplication.menu.addItem(myMenuItem);
}
else if (NativeWindow.supportsMenu)
{
  // for Windows
  var myWindowMenu:NativeMenu = new NativeMenu();
  this.stage.nativeWindow.menu = myWindowMenu;
  myWindowMenu.addItem(myMenuItem);
}
```

This code snippet will check whether the operating system supports application menus (NativeApplication.supportsMenu) or window menus (NativeWindow.supportMenu) and set up your menu accordingly.

System tray menu

An AIR application can run in the background. On a Windows machine, you can opt to show an icon in the system tray to let the user know that this application is still running. When the user right-clicks a system tray icon, a menu can appear, as shown in Figure 19-8. To add a system tray menu, you use this code:

Figure 19-8. Example of a system tray menu

```
SystemTrayIcon(NativeApplication.nativeApplication.icon).menu = myMenu;
```

Dock menu

OS X doesn't have a system tray but does have a dock. The Mac operating system allows you to add menus to dock icons. They appear when the user right-clicks the dock icon (see Figure 19-9). To add a menu to the dock icon, use this code:

```
DockIcon(NativeApplication.nativeApplication.icon).menu = myMenu;
```

Handling menu events

Figure 19-9. Example of a dock menu

Handling menu events is as easy as listening for a specific event. The select event will be dispatched every time the user clicks one of your menu items. All you have to do is add an event listener to your menu that fires off the correct function as shown in this code:

```
myWindowMenu.addEventListener(Event.SELECT, menuSelection);

function menuSelection(event:Event):void
```

```
{
  var menuItem:NativeMenuItem = event.target as NativeMenuItem;
  trace(menuItem.label + " has been selected");
}
```

Network Detection API

As AIR applications can run both on- or offline, it may be a good idea to check whether or not a network connection is available. You may also check to see whether a certain service is available or not, such as the Flash Media Server your application uses. When your application does not have access to the network or service, your application can display a message to the user and/or behave differently. Your application can, for instance, have a limited feature set when it is not connected to the network.

There are two ways of detecting whether or not a network and service is available: you can use either a URLMonitor or a SocketMonitor.

URLMonitor

The URLMonitor allows you to check whether or not a specific URL is available. In this code snippet, we set up a URLMonitor that checks for the URL www.adobe.com:

```
var myMonitor:URLMonitor;
myMonitor = new URLMonitor(new URLRequest('http://www.adobe.com'));
```

The URLMonitor triggers events that will tell you the availability of the specified URL. Just add an event listener to listen to the StatusEvent.STATUS event. In the following code, we added the event listener that will trigger the statusChange function. After we added the event listener, we also start the monitor by calling myMonitor.start().

```
myMonitor.addEventListener(StatusEvent.STATUS, statusChange);
myMonitor.start();
function statusChange(e:StatusEvent):void
{
  trace("URLMonitor status change. Current status: " ➡
  + myMonitor.available);
}
```

SocketMonitor

The SocketMonitor is almost identical to the URLMonitor. The only difference is that instead of specifying a URL to check, you check for a specific server (either by URL or IP address) and a specific network port. The following code will check whether port 1935 on IP address 127.0.0.1 is accepting connections:

```
var myMonitor:SocketMonitor;
myMonitor = new SocketMonitor('127.0.0.1', 1935);
```

The SocketMonitor also triggers events in exactly the same way as the URLMonitor. So listening to these events and firing off the correct function is exactly the same as for the URLMonitor:

```
myMonitor.addEventListener(StatusEvent.STATUS, statusChange);
myMonitor.start();
function statusChange(e:StatusEvent):void
{
  trace("URLMonitor status change. Current status: " ➥
  + myMonitor.available);
}
```

File System API

Your AIR application behaves just like any other desktop application and therefore also has access to the file system to read files from and write files to.

Common file paths

File paths are very different across platforms. On Mac OS X, the path for my document folder is /Users/Serge/Documents, while on Windows XP the paths are C:\Documents and Settings\Serge\My Documents and C:\Users\Serge\Documents. This is exactly why these common file paths can be called using a method of the File class in AIR so you don't have to worry about this. The following file paths exist on all the platforms that AIR supports—Mac, Windows, and Linux. These methods are available to point to the associated directories:

- File.applicationDirectory: The folder containing the application's installed files
- File.applicationStorageDirectory: The private storage available to this application
- File.desktopDirectory: The user's desktop directory
- File.documentsDirectory: The user's document folder
- File.userDirectory: The user's personal directory

Reading and writing files

Reading files from and writing files to the file system is actually pretty straightforward. First, you create a File object, which represents the path to a file or a directory. The File class has all the properties and methods for interacting with the File object. The FileStream class can be used to read and write files. Before you can use these classes, you'll need to import them to your project by adding the following import statement:

```
import flash.filesystem.*
```

Before you can read or write a file, you need to create a reference to its file path. You do this by creating a new File object. In this case, you create a File object that points to a particular file, named test.txt in this example:

```
var myFile:File = File.desktopDirectory.resolvePath("test.txt");
```

Now, to read the content of this file, you create a new `FileStream` object and open up the file you just specified in the `File` object:

```
var myFileStream:FileStream = new FileStream();
myFileStream.open(myFile, FileMode.READ);
```

Next, you read the content of that file. Since this is a simple text file, you know that whatever comes back is going to be a string. The following code reads the content of the text file and assigns it to a string variable:

```
var myString:String = myFileStream.readMultiByte(myFile.size, ➥
File.systemCharset);
trace(myString);
fileStream.close();
```

Writing files is almost identical. Instead of using `FileMode.READ`, you use `FileMode.WRITE`, and instead of reading bytes, you are writing them. In this example, we will be writing a text file in the documents directory.

```
var myFile:File = File.documentsDirectory.resolvePath("test.txt");
```

The only difference with reading a file is that the file specified here does not exist. The file will be automatically created once we write to it. You do this in mostly the same way as when you're reading files.

```
var myFileStream:FileStream = new FileStream();
myFileStream.open( myFile, FileMode.WRITE );
myFileStream.writeUTF( "Hello World!" );
myFileStream.close();
```

The result from this code is a text file in the documents directory with the file name test. txt. The contents of the file is the text "Hello World!"

The Windowing, Menu, Network Detection, and File System APIs are the most commonly used APIs in AIR applications. If you want to find out more about all available APIs, a lot of information is available in Flash's documentation. Alternatively, you should check out *The Essential Guide to Flash CS4 AIR Development* (friends of ED, 2008), which provides more details on the APIs and how to use them.

Now that you've learned about these common APIs, it's time to build your first application.

Building your first AIR application with Flash CS4

When you launch Flash CS4, you will see that the splash screen now allows you to create a new Flash file with the Adobe AIR profile (see Figure 19-10). As soon as you select this option, Flash CS4 will open up a new document and automatically make sure that all the settings are correct.

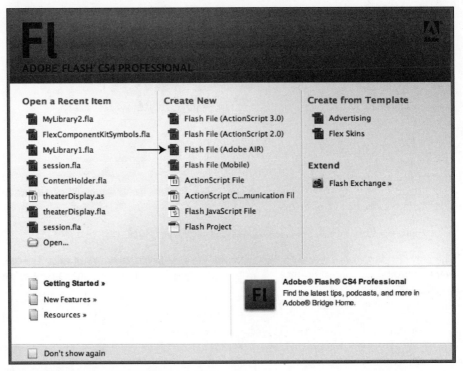

Figure 19-10. The Flash CS4 Professional splash screen

In previous versions of Flash, you had to download a separate extension for Flash in order to build applications targeted at AIR. When you install Adobe Flash CS4 Professional, everything you need is installed and ready to go. The first time you launch Flash CS4 Professional, you'll immediately notice that Flash File (Adobe AIR) *is now an option on the splash screen, as shown in Figure 19-10.*

When you create a new Flash file using the Adobe AIR profile, the targeted player in the document's Property inspector (see Figure 19-11) is set to Adobe AIR 1.5 and the script is set to ActionScript 3.0. Since all AIR APIs are written in ActionScript 3.0, this is the only option if you want to use these APIs.

Because the targeted player is now the Adobe AIR runtime, the AIR Debug Launcher (ADL) will automatically be used when you test your project. ADL is exactly the same as AIR, but it is only used to test and debug your applications without having to install them. So instead of launching your application in the browser, it will open it in ADL.

Figure 19-11.
The Property inspector

19

Creating your AIR application

Right, now that you have the basics down, go ahead and create your AIR application. We'll quickly write a simple program to show you all the fundamentals of creating AIR applications in Flash CS4.

1. Set up your document so that it's 200 pixels wide and 200 pixels tall.

2. Draw what is going to be your main application window. You can choose the Rectangle Primitive **tool to draw this background shape that uses the total available application size (see Figure 19-12).**

Figure 19-12.
The shape of the application window

3. Set the stroke to 2 pixels.

4. Set the fill color to 80% black.

5. Convert this shape into a movie clip and name it windowbackground.

6. Test your application by clicking the Test Movie **option in the** Control **menu. The application will launch in the ADL.**

Note that your AIR application now runs as a separate application. Your application now has its own icon in your OS X dock or Windows taskbar. You should also see that your application is now surrounded by system chrome. It looks exactly like any other application window (see Figure 19-13).

Figure 19-13.
Your application
running in ADL

7. Select the transparent window chrome by clicking the Edit button next to AIR Settings in the Property inspector. This pops up the AIR – Application & Installer Settings dialog, as shown in Figure 19-14.

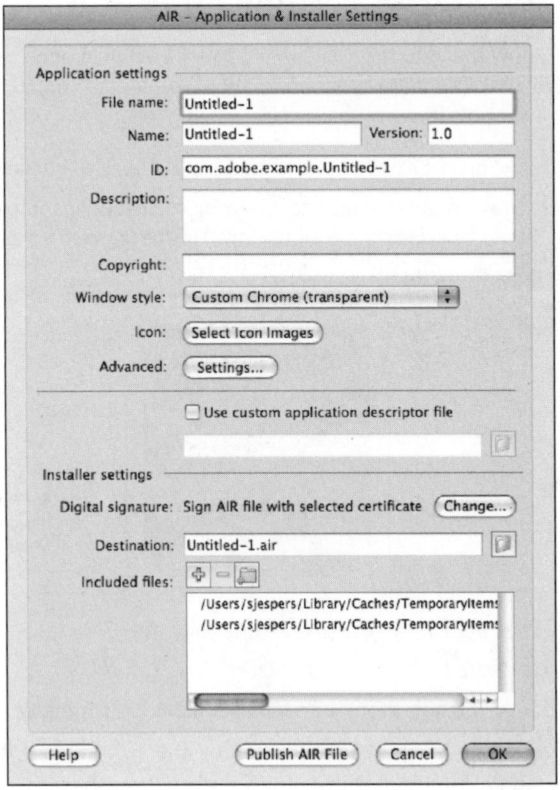

Figure 19-14.
AIR – Application &
Installer Settings dialog

The AIR – Application & Installer Settings dialog

The AIR – Application & Installer Settings dialog is where you specify items like the name of your application, what is displayed in the installer window, the application icon, and also the chrome settings for your application window. The settings are as follows:

- File name: This is the name of the AIR file you are going to create once your application is ready.

- Name: This is the name that will be shown in the installer and in the title bar of your initial window.

- Version: This setting is used to determine which version of your application you have installed on your system.

- ID: The value for this setting needs to be unique. It is used to detect whether or not the application is already installed and then launch it from the browser or another AIR application.

- Description: The text specified here will be used to give a more detailed description of the application in the installer window.

- Copyright: This text is used to add an application's copyright information in the installer window.

- Window style: Here you set the window type of your application.

- Icon: This option allows you to specify your application icon. Note that the icon does not show up in ADL. You have to install the application to see the application icon.

- Advanced: This pops up an additional dialog (see Figure 19-15) that allows you to set even more options for your application and your initial window.

- Use custom application descriptor file: Instead of filling out this dialog box, you could also write an XML file with all these settings. This is where you specify the application descriptor file you want to use.

- Digital signature: All AIR applications must be signed with a code signing certificate. Here you can specify the location of your certificate.

- Destination: This is the destination where you want to save your AIR file once you publish it.

- Included files: Here you can specify additional files that will be included in your AIR package. These files will be installed in the application directory. You can use this to add any files your application depends on.

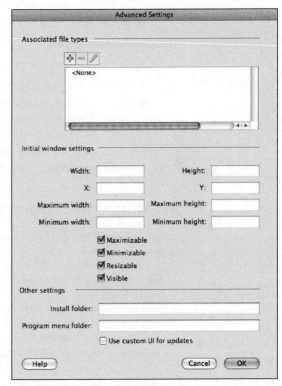

Figure 19-15. Advanced settings

505

The Advanced Settings dialog

When you click the Settings button next to Advanced in the AIR – Application & Installer Settings dialog, the Advanced Settings dialog pops up. This dialog box allows you to associate a file type with your application and set the position, width, and height for your initial window. You can also define whether or not your initial window is maximizable, minimizable, resizable, and visible. You can even define in which folder you want to install your application and specify a name for the program menu folder. The settings are as follows:

- Associated file types: Your AIR application can be associated with a specific file type. For instance, if you want your application to accept SERGE files, this is where you specify that file type.

- Width and Height: This is where you specify the width and height of your initial window. These will override the document's width and height. If these are not specified, the application will use the document's width and height.

- X and Y: These fields allow you to specify the x and y coordinates of your initial window.

- Maximum width and Maximum height: If your application is resizable, this is where you specify the maximum width and height.

- Minimum width and Minimum height: If your application is resizable, this is where you set the minimum values for width and height.

- Maximizable: If selected, your initial application window is maximizable.

- Minimizable: If selected, your initial application window is minimizable.

- Resizable: If selected, your initial application window is resizable.

- Visible: if selected, your initial application window is visible.

- Install folder: Here you specify the folder where you would like to install the application on the user's machine. Note that the user can still select a different folder to install your application to.

- Program menu folder: If this is specified, the AIR Application Installer will create a folder in Windows' Program menu.

Creating applications with custom chrome

Now, for our demo application, setting the window type to Custom Chrome (transparent) in the AIR – Application & Installer Settings dialog (as shown earlier in Figure 19-14) is all you have to do. Then click OK and test your application again. You should now see the same application without the system chrome, as shown in Figure 19-16.

You'll immediately notice that because you didn't add any window functionality, you can't close, resize, or move the window. When you create applications with custom chrome, you need to add that functionality yourself. When you've verified that your application looks like Figure 19-16, you can close the application by pressing Alt+F4 or Cmd+Q on a Mac.

Figure 19-16.
Your application is no longer surrounded by system chrome.

Enabling dragging

The first thing you want to add is a little bit of code that will enable you to drag your window around the screen. In your Actions panel, add the following code:

```
stage.addEventListener(MouseEvent.MOUSE_DOWN, startMove )

function startMove(event:MouseEvent):void
{
    stage.nativeWindow.startMove();
}
```

This will listen for the MOUSE_DOWN event and call the startMove() method of the main window, allowing you to move the window around your screen. You can also draw a title bar and add the event listener to that instead of adding it to the entire stage.

Adding Close and Minimize buttons

Next we want to add the Close and Minimize buttons shown in Figure 19-17. Just create two simple buttons like the ones in the figure and give them instance names of btn_close for the red one and btn_minimize for the yellow one.

Figure 19-17.
Creating Close and Minimize buttons

In your Actions panel, add the following lines to the code that is already there. This bit of code will listen for the CLICK event on both your Minimize and Close buttons and will fire off the associated code.

```
btn_minimize.addEventListener(MouseEvent.CLICK, minimize_CLICK);
function minimize_CLICK(e:MouseEvent):void
{
    stage.nativeWindow.minimize();
}
```

```
btn_close.addEventListener(MouseEvent.CLICK,closeButton_CLICK);
function closeButton_CLICK(e:MouseEvent):void
{
    NativeApplication.nativeApplication.exit();
}
```

Go ahead and test your application. Try dragging the application around your screen. Then press the Minimize button, and try the Close button last.

Adding functionality

Now that we created the application chrome, it's time to add some functionality. We want this application to periodically check whether a certain server is available or not and alert us when it's not.

Creating a three-state icon

We'll need some sort of easy-to-understand icon to tell the user when there's something wrong or when everything is fine. We'll create a very simple three-state icon with a gray, red, and green oval. We'll use the gray icon when the application is launching, the red icon when the specified server is not available, and the green icon when the server is available.

First, create a new symbol and draw a gray oval on the first keyframe. Now create a new keyframe on the second and third frame and draw a red and green oval on each of those (see Figure 19-18).

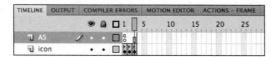

Figure 19-18. Timeline for our icon

Next, give each keyframe a different name. Name the keyframe with the gray icon default, the keyframe with the red icon error, and the keyframe with the green icon ok. Put a stop() action on the first frame so the icon stays in the first frame (the gray icon) when it launches.

Checking server and service availability

In order to check whether or not a server is available, we're going to use the service monitoring API we discussed earlier.

Before you can use the service monitoring API, you need to add the servicemonitor.swc file to your library. Follow these steps to do so:

1. In the Property inspector, click the Edit button in the Profile area.

2. Click the Settings button for ActionScript 3.0 and select the Library Path tab.

3. Click the Browse to SWC button and browse to your Flash CS4 [install directory] /AIK1.5/frameworks/libs/air/servicemonitor.swc (see Figure 19-19).

4. Click the OK button.

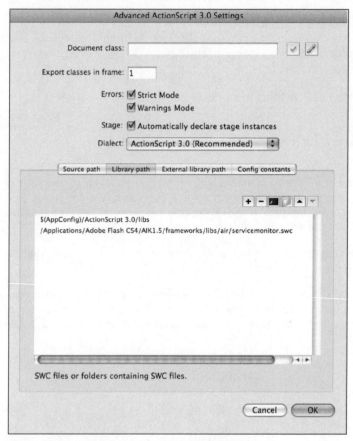

Figure 19-19. Adding the servicemonitor.swc file

Now go back to your Actions panel and add the following import statements to your code. You need to import these to actually use the classes in your project.

```
import air.net.URLMonitor;
import flash.net.URLRequest;
import flash.events.StatusEvent;
```

Using the URLMonitor class

For this example, we will be using the URLMonitor class to check whether an HTTP request can be made to the specified address, which is also why the URLRequest class needs to be added. Whenever the URLMonitor's status changes, it's going to fire off a StatusEvent, which is why we also need to import that class.

See Chapter 11 for a discussion of the URLRequest class.

Add the URLMonitor by including the following code in your Actions panel:

```
var myMonitor:URLMonitor;
myMonitor = new URLMonitor(new URLRequest('http://www.adobe.com'));
myMonitor.addEventListener(StatusEvent.STATUS, statusChange);
myMonitor.start();

function statusChange(e:StatusEvent):void
{
  trace("URLMonitor status change. Current status: "➥
  + myMonitor.available);
}
```

After making a new instance of the URLMonitor, we specify which address it should check. In this case, we're going to check whether www.adobe.com is available or not. By adding an event listener to the instance of the URLMonitor, we can check when the network status has changed and call a function to warn the user of this change.

If you test this application, your Output panel should show the message, "URLMonitor status change. Current status: true."

When myMonitor.available returns true, we want to display the green icon. When it returns false, we should display the red icon. In order to display the correct icon, you'll need to change the statusChange function by adding this simple if...else statement:

```
function statusChange(e:StatusEvent):void
{
    if (myMonitor.available)
    {
      mc_statusIcon.gotoAndStop("ok");
    } else {
      mc_statusIcon.gotoAndStop("error");
    }
}
```

Now, whenever the network status changes, it will display the correct icon. Go ahead and test your application again. It should now show the green icon when you launch it. It may take a few seconds to get the response back from the server. To test the red icon, you can simply disable or unplug your network.

Saving the last server

While this is already pretty cool, we actually want to be able to save the last server we checked. If we add that functionality, the application will read the last saved address when we launch the application.

Let's change the code a little bit so it starts the URLMonitor on demand. We'll just wrap that code in a new function called startMonitoring and pass the address to check as a variable for this function:

```
var myMonitor:URLMonitor;
function startMonitoring(myAddress:String):void
{
  myMonitor = new URLMonitor(new URLRequest(myAddress));
  myMonitor.addEventListener(StatusEvent.STATUS, statusChange);
  myMonitor.start();
}
```

It's important to keep the myMonitor declaration outside of this function. The URLMonitor will be out of scope if you add it to this function.

On a new layer, add a TextInput and a Button component from your component library to the stage (see Figure 19-20). This will enable the user of this application to simply enter an address and start the monitor when he or she wants to. Remember to set the instance names for these components—inp_address for the TextInput component and btn_go for the Button component. Also add http:// as the default text for the TextInput component to easily show the user that a URL is expected here. You can specify that in the Component inspector.

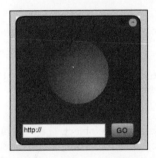

Figure 19-20.
Adding a TextInput and
a Button component

Whenever the user clicks the GO button, the URLMonitor should start checking the specified address. Add the following code to the code you already have to enable this functionality:

```
btn_go.addEventListener(MouseEvent.CLICK, saveAndStart);

function saveAndStart(event:MouseEvent):void
{
  mc_statusIcon.gotoAndStop("default");
  startMonitoring(inp_address.text);
}
```

Whenever the user clicks the GO button now, it's going to trigger the saveAndStart function. When that function is called, the status icon is reset, and then the startMonitoring function we created earlier is called. The URLMonitor will now check the URL we entered in the TextInput component.

The user may want to use this little application to check whether his or her web server is still running or not. To increase the user experience, we're going to save the last address the user entered. Whenever the user launches the application, we're going to automatically show the last entered address.

The first thing we need to add is a function to write the last entered address to a text file.

Writing and reading files

Because the user doesn't really need to open the saved file in another application, we're going to save the last entered address in a text file located in the applicationStorageDirectory. The applicationStorageDirectory is a private storage directory for your application.

Like we discussed in the section "Using AIR APIs," you first need to import the file system classes to your project before you can start using them. So the first thing you need to add is this import statement:

```
import flash.filesystem.*
```

To save the last entered address to a text file in the applicationStorageDirectory, add the following code to the saveAndStart function we created earlier:

```
var myFile:File = ➡
File.applicationStorageDirectory.resolvePath("last.txt");

var myFileStream:FileStream = new FileStream();
myFileStream.open(myFile, FileMode.WRITE);
myFileStream.writeUTF( inp_address.text );
myFileStream.close();
```

Like we discussed before, you first create a new File object. The File object points to the path of a file or a directory. The File object can also be a file or directory that doesn't exist yet. In this case we are writing the file and thus we use FileMode.WRITE. Next we save the address the user entered in the TextInput component in Unicode Transform Format (UTF), after which we close the FileStream. We then write the address typed into the TextInput field in UTF and close off the FileStream after that. To make it easier to test your application, you could temporarily change the file path to File.desktopDirectory.resolvePath("last.txt"). By saving the file on your desktop, it's very easy to quickly check whether your function is working.

When we launch the application, we'll also need to read the value we saved in the text file. To do that, we are going to add an init() function that will be launched when we start the application.

```
var mySavedAddress:String;
function init():void
{
  var myFile:File = ➡
File.applicationStorageDirectory.resolvePath("last.txt");
  if (myFile.exists)
```

```
      {
        var myFileStream:FileStream = new FileStream();
        myFileStream.open(myFile, FileMode.READ);
        mySavedAddress = myFileStream.readUTF();
        inp_address.text = mySavedAddress;
        startMonitoring(inp_address.text);
        myFileStream.close();
      }
    }
    init();
```

First of all, we declare the mySavedAddress variable outside the function to make it a public variable. In the init() function, we create a file object that points to the location we
saved our text file to. If the file exists, it is going to read it by creating a new FileStream
object. That allows us to open the file (in this case with FileMode.READ) and read the text
in this file. We then set the text of our input field and call the startMonitoring() function, passing the address we just read from our text file. You shouldn't forget to also call
the init() function somewhere. If you forget to call the init() function, the last saved
value will not be read and thus will not be shown in your application.

This is what the completed code should look like:

```
      import air.net.URLMonitor;
      import flash.net.URLRequest;
      import flash.events.StatusEvent;
      import flash.filesystem.*;

      var myMonitor:URLMonitor;
      var mySavedAddress:String;

      stage.addEventListener(MouseEvent.MOUSE_DOWN, startMove);
      btn_go.addEventListener(MouseEvent.CLICK, saveAndStart);
      btn_minimize.addEventListener(MouseEvent.CLICK, minimize_CLICK);
      btn_close.addEventListener(MouseEvent.CLICK, closeButton_CLICK);

      function init():void
      {
        var file:File = ➥
      File. applicationStorageDirectory.resolvePath("last.txt");

        if (file.exists)
        {
          var fileStream:FileStream = new FileStream();
          fileStream.open(file, FileMode.READ);
          mySavedAddress = fileStream.readUTF();
          inp_address.text = mySavedAddress;
          startMonitoring(inp_address.text);
          fileStream.close();
        }
      }
```

19

```
function saveAndStart(event:MouseEvent):void
{
  mc_statusIcon.gotoAndStop("default");
  startMonitoring(inp_address.text);
  var myFile:File = ➡
File. applicationStorageDirectory.resolvePath("last.txt");
  var myFileStream:FileStream = new FileStream();
  myFileStream.open(myFile, FileMode.WRITE);
  myFileStream.writeUTF(inp_address.text);
  myFileStream.close();
}

function startMonitoring(myAddress:String):void
{
  myMonitor = new URLMonitor(new URLRequest(myAddress));
  myMonitor.addEventListener(StatusEvent.STATUS, statusChange);
  myMonitor.start();
}

function statusChange(e:StatusEvent):void
{
  if (myMonitor.available)
  {
    mc_statusIcon.gotoAndStop("ok");
  } else {
    mc_statusIcon.gotoAndStop("error");
  }
}

function startMove(event:MouseEvent):void
{
  stage.nativeWindow.startMove();
}

function minimize_CLICK(e:MouseEvent):void
{
  stage.nativeWindow.minimize();
}

function closeButton_CLICK(e:MouseEvent):void
{
  NativeApplication.nativeApplication.exit();
}

init();
```

Your application is now ready. When you've thoroughly tested and verified the application, the next thing to do is build an AIR package to distribute to your users.

Creating your AIR package

Before you can create your AIR package, you need to sign the application with a digital certificate. AIR applications can be signed either by linking a certificate from an external certificate authority (CA) such as Thawte or Chosen Security or by creating your own certificate. It is important to note that self-signed certificates do not provide any assurance to the end user that the named publisher has genuinely created the application, and as such self-signed applications represent a security risk. The AIR installer will also tell the user that the publisher's identity is unknown (see Figure 19-21).

Figure 19-21. Self-signed AIR applications will alert the user that the publisher's identity is unknown.

> *While developing and testing your application, it is no problem to use a self-signed certificate. However, you should plan on using a certificate from an external certificate authority when you publicly release your application so your users can be certain this application and its source can be trusted.*

When you want to use a self-signed certificate during testing and development, you only need to create it once. Follow these steps to do so:

1. Click the Edit button next to AIR Settings in your Property inspector. This will open up the AIR – Application & Installer Settings dialog we discussed earlier.

2. Click the Change button to create a new self-signed certificate or select an existing certificate (see Figure 19-22).

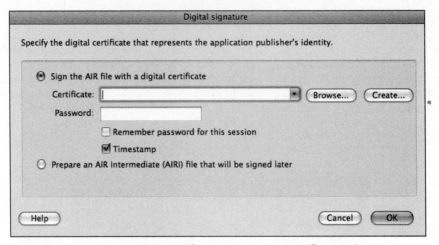

Figure 19-22. Browse to an existing certificate or create a new certificate to sign your application.

3. Click the Create button.

4. Enter information for the publisher name, organization unit, and organization name.

5. Select your country and then enter a password of your choice.

6. Select a location on your system to save the certificate.

7. Click OK to create the self-signed digital certificate (see Figure 19-23).

Figure 19-23. Creating a new self-signed certificate. Note that all fields are required!

8. Save the certificate to the specified location.

9. Enter the password you selected and press OK.

10. Finally, specify the location where you want to save your AIR file and click the Publish AIR File button.

Now that we created our AIR file, we'll also need to distribute it. In the next section, you'll see how to this.

Deploying your AIR application

The easiest thing to do with your application at this point would be to upload the AIR file to your server and put a link to it on your web site. But this is not very user friendly for whomever is going to download and install your application. In some cases, when your server isn't configured to handle AIR files, it may even fail altogether. That's why Adobe created the concept of install badges. **Install badges** are basically a small Flash application that handles download and installation in such a way that it becomes very easy for the end user to install your application.

The install badge (see Figure 19-24) is part of the AIR SDK. You can download the AIR SDK from the Adobe web site at www.adobe.com/products/air/tools/sdk/. If you download and extract that ZIP file, there's a folder called samples that includes a ready-to-go example. Just change the parameters in the source of the HTML, upload the files and your AIR file to your server, and you're done.

Figure 19-24.
An install badge

This install badge also has a bunch of extra features that need a bit of extra coding. For one, the install badge can determine whether the application is already installed and then prompt the user to launch the application right from within the browser. It also detects whether the user has the correct version of the runtime installed; if not, it will offer to download it. This badge also allows you to add a little bit of support information when the user clicks the question mark icon.

The second option would be to build your own install badge. Don't worry . . . you don't have to start from scratch. The source files for the install badge are available in the SDK downloads so you can use these as the basis for your own. You could literally just change the graphics and publish it. It's as simple as that. The great thing is that this can be anything you want to it to be and can have all the features you want it to have because, well, you are building it. If you want to ping your server whenever someone starts the install of your application, for instance, that is absolutely possible.

Summary

AIR is not just another runtime; it combines the rich interactive capabilities of Flash with the power of the desktop and freedom from the web browser to allow us to create rich, connected, desktop applications using the web-centric languages we already know like ActionScript, HTML, and JavaScript.

Building applications for AIR can be very fulfilling and rewarding, and if you build a useful application, you might even see some financial appreciation for your efforts! To see what other people are building with AIR, have a look at the AIR marketplace (www.adobe.com/go/marketplace) where you will find a broad variety of AIR applications.

You've now been introduced to all of the basics needed to start building your own AIR applications. In this chapter we talked about the following:

- Understanding what makes AIR different from the Flash Player and Silverlight runtimes
- Understanding the most common APIs and how to use them
- Customizing and configuring the installer for an AIR application
- Reading files from, and writing files to, the host system with an AIR application
- Publishing and deploying your AIR application

INDEX

Numbers and Symbols

A

XYZ